# 2004

# WORLD DRUG REPORT

## Volume 2: Statistics

The Office for Drug Control and Crime Prevention (UNODCCP) became the Office on Drugs and Crime (UNODC) on 1 October 2002. The Office on Drugs and Crime includes the United Nations International Drug Control Programme (UNDCP).

United Nations Publication
Sales No. E.04.XI.16
ISBN 92-1-148186-4
Volume 2

# 2004

# WORLD DRUG REPORT

## Volume 2: Statistics

# Contents

## Volume I. Analysis

# Volume II. Statistics

# 3. PRODUCTION

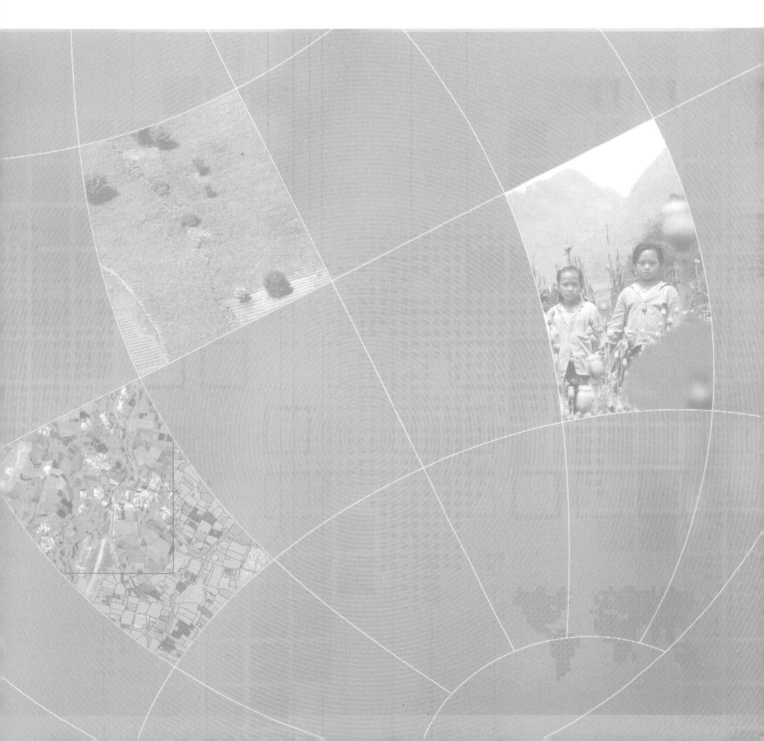

# 3.1 Opium/heroin

## OPIUM

### GLOBAL ILLICIT CULTIVATION OF OPIUM POPPY AND PRODUCTION OF OPIUM, 1990-2003

| | 1990 | 1991 | 1992 | 1993 | 1994 | 1995 | 1996 | 1997 | 1998 | 1999 | 2000 | 2001 | 2002 | 2003 |
|---|---|---|---|---|---|---|---|---|---|---|---|---|---|---|
| **CULTIVATION[1] IN HECTARES** | | | | | | | | | | | | | | |
| **SOUTH-WEST ASIA** | | | | | | | | | | | | | | |
| Afghanistan | 41,300 | 50,800 | 49,300 | 58,300 | 71,470 | 53,759 | 56,824 | 58,416 | 63,674 | 90,583 | 82,171 | 7,606 | 74,100 | 80,000 |
| Pakistan | 7,488 | 7,962 | 9,493 | 7,329 | 5,759 | 5,091 | 873 | 874 | 950 | 284 | 260 | 213 | 622 | 2,500 |
| Subtotal | 48,788 | 58,762 | 58,793 | 65,629 | 77,229 | 58,850 | 57,697 | 59,290 | 64,624 | 90,867 | 82,431 | 7,819 | 74,722 | 82,500 |
| **SOUTH-EAST ASIA** | | | | | | | | | | | | | | |
| Lao PDR | 30,580 | 29,625 | 19,190 | 26,040 | 18,520 | 19,650 | 21,601 | 24,082 | 26,837 | 22,543 | 19,052 | 17,255 | 14,000 | 12,000 |
| Myanmar | 150,100 | 160,000 | 153,700 | 165,800 | 146,600 | 154,070 | 163,000 | 155,150 | 130,300 | 89,500 | 108,700 | 105,000 | 81,400 | 62,200 |
| Thailand [2] | 1,782 | 3,727 | 3,016 | 998 | 478 | 168 | 368 | 352 | 716 | 702 | 890 | 820 | 750 | |
| Viet Nam [2] | 18,000 | 17,000 | 12,199 | 4,268 | 3,066 | 1,880 | 1,743 | 340 | 442 | 442 | | | | |
| Subtotal | 200,462 | 210,352 | 188,105 | 197,106 | 168,664 | 175,768 | 186,712 | 179,924 | 158,295 | 113,187 | 128,642 | 123,075 | 96,150 | 74,200 |
| **LATIN AMERICA** | | | | | | | | | | | | | | |
| Colombia [3] | | 1,160 | 6,578 | 5,008 | 15,091 | 5,226 | 4,916 | 6,584 | 7,350 | 6,500 | 6,500 | 4,300 | 4,100 | 4,100 |
| Mexico [4] | 5,450 | 3,765 | 3,310 | 3,960 | 5,795 | 5,050 | 5,100 | 4,000 | 5,500 | 3,600 | 1,900 | 4,400 | 2,700 | 4,800 |
| Subtotal | 5,450 | 4,925 | 9,888 | 8,968 | 20,886 | 10,276 | 10,016 | 10,584 | 12,850 | 10,100 | 8,400 | 8,700 | 6,800 | 8,900 |
| **OTHER** | | | | | | | | | | | | | | |
| Combined [5] | 8,054 | 7,521 | 2,900 | 5,704 | 5,700 | 5,025 | 3,190 | 2,050 | 2,050 | 2,050 | 2,479 | 2,500 | 2,500 | 3,000 |
| **GRAND TOTAL** | 262,754 | 281,560 | 259,686 | 277,407 | 272,479 | 249,919 | 257,615 | 251,848 | 237,819 | 216,204 | 221,952 | 142,094 | 180,172 | 168,600 |

| | 1990 | 1991 | 1992 | 1993 | 1994 | 1995 | 1996 | 1997 | 1998 | 1999 | 2000 | 2001 | 2002 | 2003 |
|---|---|---|---|---|---|---|---|---|---|---|---|---|---|---|
| **POTENTIAL PRODUCTION IN METRIC TONS** **OPIUM** | | | | | | | | | | | | | | |
| **SOUTH-WEST ASIA** | | | | | | | | | | | | | | |
| Afghanistan | 1,570 | 1,980 | 1,970 | 2,330 | 3,416 | 2,335 | 2,248 | 2,804 | 2,693 | 4,565 | 3,276 | 185 | 3,400 | 3,600 |
| Pakistan | 150 | 160 | 181 | 161 | 128 | 112 | 24 | 24 | 26 | 9 | 8 | 5 | 5 | 52 |
| Subtotal | 1,720 | 2,140 | 2,151 | 2,491 | 3,544 | 2,447 | 2,272 | 2,828 | 2,719 | 4,574 | 3,284 | 190 | 3,405 | 3,652 |
| **SOUTH-EAST ASIA** | | | | | | | | | | | | | | |
| Lao PDR | 202 | 196 | 127 | 169 | 120 | 128 | 140 | 147 | 124 | 124 | 167 | 134 | 112 | 120 |
| Myanmar | 1,621 | 1,728 | 1,660 | 1,791 | 1,583 | 1,664 | 1,760 | 1,676 | 1,303 | 895 | 1,087 | 1,097 | 828 | 810 |
| Thailand [2] | 20 | 23 | 14 | 17 | 3 | 2 | 5 | 4 | 8 | 8 | 6 | 6 | 9 | |
| Viet Nam [2] | 90 | 85 | 61 | 21 | 15 | 9 | 9 | 2 | 2 | 2 | | | | |
| Subtotal | 1,933 | 2,032 | 1,862 | 1,998 | 1,721 | 1,803 | 1,914 | 1,829 | 1,437 | 1,029 | 1,260 | 1,237 | 949 | 930 |
| **LATIN AMERICA** | | | | | | | | | | | | | | |
| Colombia [3] | | 16 | 90 | 68 | 205 | 71 | 67 | 90 | 100 | 88 | 88 | 58 | 50 | 50 |
| Mexico | 62 | 41 | 40 | 49 | 60 | 53 | 54 | 46 | 60 | 43 | 21 | 71 | 47 | 84 |
| Subtotal | 62 | 57 | 130 | 117 | 265 | 124 | 121 | 136 | 160 | 131 | 109 | 129 | 97 | 134 |
| **OTHER** | | | | | | | | | | | | | | |
| Combined [5] | 45 | 45 | - | 4 | 90 | 78 | 48 | 30 | 30 | 30 | 38 | 40 | 40 | 50 |
| **GRAND TOTAL** | 3,760 | 4,274 | 4,143 | 4,610 | 5,620 | 4,452 | 4,355 | 4,823 | 4,346 | 5,764 | 4,691 | 1,596 | 4,491 | 4,765 |
| **HEROIN** | | | | | | | | | | | | | | |
| Potential HEROIN | 376 | 427 | 414 | 461 | 562 | 445 | 436 | 482 | 435 | 576 | 469 | 160 | 449 | 477 |

(1) Potentially harvestable, after eradication.
(2) Due to low levels of production, cultivation and production for Viet Nam as of 2000 and for Thailand as of 2003 were included in the category "Other countries".
(3) According to the Government of Colombia, cultivation covered 7,350 ha and 6,500 ha and production amounted to 73 mt and 65 mt in 1998 and 1999 respectively.
(4) Sources: As its survey system is under development, the Govt of Mexico indicates it can neither provide cultivation estimates nor endorse those published by UNODC which are derived from US Government surveys.
(5) Includes countries such as Russia, Ukraine, Central Asia, Caucasus region, Egypt, Peru, Viet Nam (as of 2000) and Thailand (as of 2003)

## 3.1.1. Afghanistan

During the 1990s, Afghanistan firmly established itself as the largest source of illicit opium and its derivative, heroin. In 2003, opium production in Afghanistan still accounted for more than three quarters of the world's illicit opium production. In October 2003, UNODC and the Afghan government conducted a farmers' intentions survey that revealed that almost 70% of the farmers interviewed in the opium growing regions of Afghanistan intended to increase poppy cultivation in 2004, while only 4% considered reducing it.

**Results of the 2003 UNODC Afghanistan Annual Opium Survey**

*(1)*      *Opium poppy cultivation (hectares) is spreading*

In 2003 the total area under opium poppy cultivation in Afghanistan increased by 8%, from 74,000 hectares in 2002 to 80,000 hectares in 2003. The current level ranks third in the country's recent history.

*(2)*      *Geographical spread has reached 28 provinces (out of 32)*

There has been a clear and accelerating extension of opium cultivation to previously unaffected, or marginally affected areas. The number of provinces where opium poppy cultivation was reported has steadily increased: from 18 provinces in 1999, to 23 in 2000, up to 24 in 2002 and to a staggering 28 provinces in 2003 (out of a total of 32).

*(3)*      *Opium production (metric tons) is also increasing*

Potential opium production amounted to 3,600 tons in 2003, an increase of 6% compared to last year's 3,400 tons. The 2003 harvest is the second highest recorded so far in Afghanistan.

*(4)*      *Opium prices are declining, though still high*

Although about ten times higher than during the 1990s, when it was around US$ 30 per kg, the average price of fresh opium recorded in 2003 of US$ 283 per kg, represents a 19% decrease over last year's price of US$ 350. The decline of 2003 opium prices in Afghanistan resulted in a 15% reduction in the related income to farmers compared to last year. As of February 2004, the price continued to decrease to an average US$176/kg for dry opium.

*(5)*      *264,000 families now grow opium poppy*

The number of opium farmers was estimated at about 264,000 families, cultivating an average of 0.3 hectare of opium poppy per family. Considering that the average family consists of 6-7 people, it can be estimated that opium poppy cultivation plays a direct role in the livelihood of about 1.7 million rural people, or about 7% of the total population of Afghanistan.

*(6)*      *Country's opium income is down 15%*

Despite the higher output, the aggregate value of this year's Afghan opium harvest (at farm-gate prices) declined to US$ 1.02 billion, compared to US$ 1.2 billion in 2002 (-15%). Almost 80% of farmers income was generated in the traditional opium producing areas of the Eastern and Southern regions.

*(7)*      *Per capita income from opium is several times GDP per capita*

The 2003 harvest represents, on average, a potential income of about US$ 3,900 per opium-growing family. The potential opium income per capita for the 1.7 million people averaged US$ 594. In comparison, on the basis of a population estimated at 24 million and a GDP estimated at US$ 4.4 billion, Afghanistan had a GDP per capita of about US$ 184 in 2002.

*(8)*      *Eradication*

Eradication activities were conducted by the Afghan authorities in some provinces. In total, 21,430 ha were eradicated in this campaign. The Afghanistan opium survey did not assessed the effectiveness of the eradication campaign. The timing of the survey and the methodology employed ensured that the results were post-eradication and reflected the net amount of opium poppy which was harvestable.

**Fact Sheet : Afghanistan 2003**

Source: UNODC/CND survey report, available at www.unodc.org/unodc/en/crop_monitoring

| | |
|---|---|
| Opium poppy cultivation: | 80,000 ha against 74,000 ha in 2002 (8% increase) |
| 2002-2003 trends in some provinces: | Hilmand:      - 49%<br>Kandahar:    - 23%<br>Nangarhar:   - 4%<br>Badakhshan:  + 55% |
| Potential opium production: | 3,600 metric tons against 3,400 metric tons in 2002 (6% increase) |
| Number of farmers cultivating opium: | 264,000 farmers |
| Population of farmers cultivating opium: millions) | 1,700,000 rural people (7% of total population of 24 |
| Opium poppy cultivation in % of the total Arable land: | 1% of total arable land |
| Opium poppy cultivation in % of irrigated Land: | 3% of irrigated land |
| Average poppy farmers land devoted to opium opium poppy cultivation: 0.3 ha | |
| Average fresh opium price at harvest: | US$283/kg |
| Total farmers' income from opium: | US$1 billion |
| In % of 2002 Afghan GDP: | 23% (with a GDP of US$ 4.4 billion) |
| Average annual farmer income from opium: | US$ 3,900 |
| Average opium income per capita: | US$594 (2002 GDP per capita: US$184) |
| Reported eradication: | 21,430 ha |
| As of October 2003, % of farmers who intended to increase opium poppy cultivation in 2004: | 70% |

*Graphs, tables, maps: Afghanistan*

**Afghanistan, Opium Poppy Cultivation, in thousands of ha, 1990 to 2003**

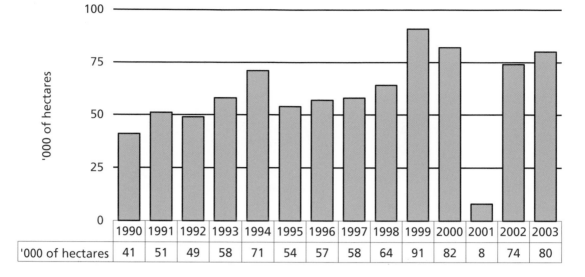

| | 1990 | 1991 | 1992 | 1993 | 1994 | 1995 | 1996 | 1997 | 1998 | 1999 | 2000 | 2001 | 2002 | 2003 |
|---|---|---|---|---|---|---|---|---|---|---|---|---|---|---|
| '000 of hectares | 41 | 51 | 49 | 58 | 71 | 54 | 57 | 58 | 64 | 91 | 82 | 8 | 74 | 80 |

**Afghanistan, largest opium poppy cultivating provinces in 2003 (ha)**

| Provinces | 2002 | 2003 | one year change | % of total in 2003 | Cumulative % in 2003 |
|---|---|---|---|---|---|
| Nangarhar | 19,780 | 18,904 | -4% | 23% | 23% |
| Hilmand | 29,950 | 15,371 | -49% | 19% | 43% |
| Badakhshan | 8,250 | 12,756 | 55% | 16% | 58% |
| Uruzgan | 5,100 | 7,143 | 40% | 9% | 67% |
| Ghor | 2,200 | 3,782 | 72% | 5% | 72% |
| Kandahar | 3,970 | 3,055 | -23% | 4% | 76% |
| Rest of the country | 4,850 | 19,471 | 301% | 24% | 100% |
| Rounded Total | 74,000 | 80,000 | 8% | | |

**Afghanistan, potential opium production by region and at national level in 2003**

| Region | Yield irrigated (kg/ha) | Yield rainfed (kg/ha) | Cult. irrigated (ha) | Cult. rainfed (ha) | Prod. irrigated (tons) | Prod. rainfed (tons) | Prod. total (tons) |
|---|---|---|---|---|---|---|---|
| Center (Bamyan, Ghor, Kabul, Kapisa, Wardak) | 46 | 28 | 7,605 | 85 | 350 | 2 | 352 |
| North East (Badakhshan, Baghlan, Kunduz, Takhar) | 41 | 24 | 12,559 | 1,224 | 515 | 29 | 544 |
| North West (Baghis, Balkh, Faryab, Jawzjan, Samangan, Sari Pul) | 43 | 34 | 3,618 | 842 | 156 | 29 | 184 |
| South East (Khost, Kunar, Laghman, Nangarhar, Nuristan, Paktya) | 51 | 32 | 24,103 | 478 | 1,229 | 15 | 1,245 |
| South West (Farah, Hilmand, Hirat, Kandahar, Nimroz, Uruzgan, Zabul) | 43 | 18 | 29,815 | 156 | 1,282 | 3 | 1,285 |
| Rounded total | | | 77,700 | 2,780 | 3,530 | 80 | 3,600 |
| Average Weighted Yield | 45 | 29 | | | | | 45 |

**Afghanistan, Opium production,1990 to 2003**

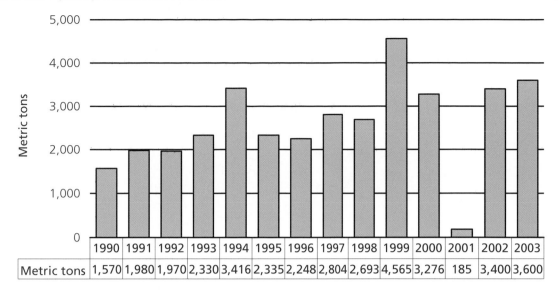

| | 1990 | 1991 | 1992 | 1993 | 1994 | 1995 | 1996 | 1997 | 1998 | 1999 | 2000 | 2001 | 2002 | 2003 |
|---|---|---|---|---|---|---|---|---|---|---|---|---|---|---|
| Metric tons | 1,570 | 1,980 | 1,970 | 2,330 | 3,416 | 2,335 | 2,248 | 2,804 | 2,693 | 4,565 | 3,276 | 185 | 3,400 | 3,600 |

**Afghanistan, largest opium producing provinces in 2003**

| Provinces | Opium production in tons | % of total |
|---|---|---|
| Nangarhar | 964 | 27% |
| Hilmand | 676 | 19% |
| Badakhshan | 508 | 14% |
| Uruzgan | 314 | 9% |
| Ghor | 174 | 5% |
| Kandahar | 134 | 4% |
| Others | 849 | 23% |
| **Rounded Total** | **3,600** | 100% |

**Afghanistan, largest opium producing provinces in 2003**

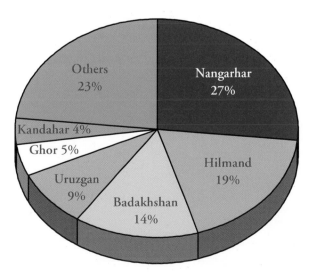

## Afghanistan, opium poppy cultivation 2003

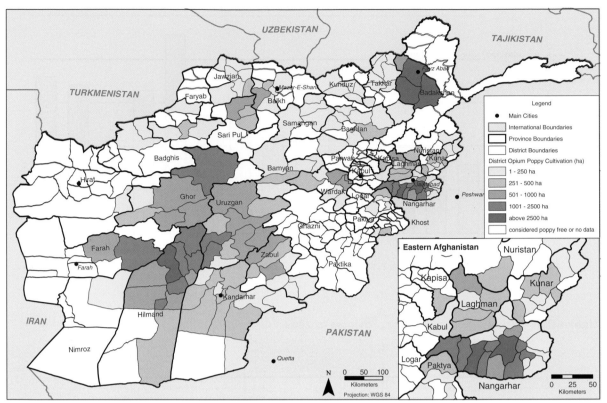

Source: CND - UNODC *Afghanistan Opium Survey 2003*

## Afghanistan, opium poppy cultivation changes 2002 - 2003

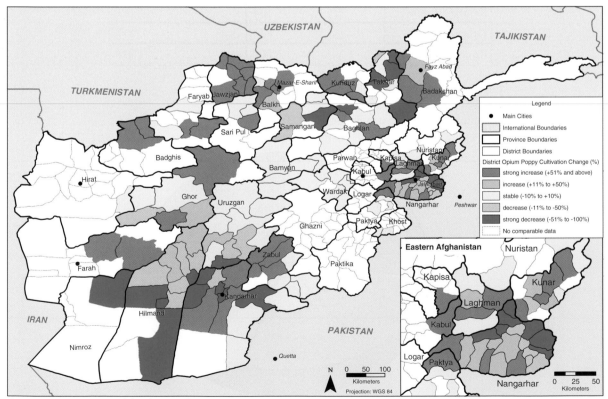

Source: CND - UNODC *Afghanistan Opium Survey 2003*

**Afghanistan, farmgate prices for opium, US$/kg (all observations Nov. 2002 - Mid. Oct 2003)**

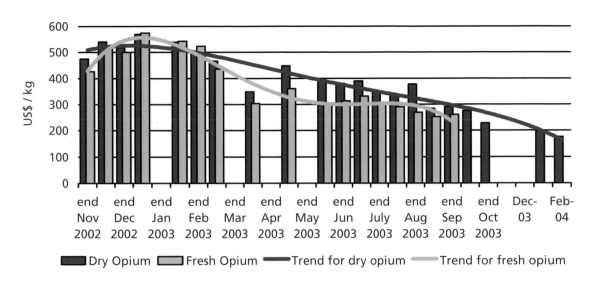

Dry Opium ▇ Fresh Opium ▇ Trend for dry opium ━ Trend for fresh opium

Source: UNODC (ICMP-AFG/F98 Monitoring of opium production in Afghanistan)

**Afghanistan, opium farmgate prices in 2003 ($US/kg)**

| Period | Dry opium | n | Fresh opium | n |
|---|---|---|---|---|
| End Nov 2002 | 475 | 28 | 426 | 51 |
| Mid Dec 2002 | 540 | 47 | 521 | 47 |
| End Dec 2002 | 519 | 40 | 500 | 46 |
| Mid Jan 2003 | 570 | 47 | 575 | 29 |
| End Jan 2003 | | | | |
| Mid Feb 2003 | 540 | 48 | 543 | 31 |
| End Feb 2003 | 498 | 47 | 524 | 29 |
| Mid Mar 2003 | 466 | 44 | 436 | 33 |
| End Mar 2003 | | | | |
| Mid Apr 2003 | 348 | 42 | 304 | 31 |
| End Apr 2003 | | | | |
| Mid May 2003 | 448 | 40 | 361 | 41 |
| End May 2003 | | | | |
| Mid Jun 2003 | 393 | 32 | 297 | 32 |
| End Jun 2003 | 380 | 37 | 313 | 39 |
| Mid July 2003 | 390 | 37 | 332 | 39 |
| End July 2003 | 351 | 35 | 308 | 37 |
| Mid Aug 2003 | 334 | 37 | 290 | 39 |
| End Aug 2003 | 378 | 37 | 270 | 39 |
| Mid Sep 2003 | 285 | 35 | 253 | 37 |
| End Sep 2003 | 291 | 35 | 261 | 37 |
| Mid Oct 2003 | 276 | 33 | | |
| End Oct 2003 | 228 | 33 | | |
| Nov 2003 | | | | |
| Dec 2003 | | | | |
| Jan 2004 | 197 | 26 | | |
| Feb 2004 | 176 | 20 | | |

Notes: n = number of observations, empty cells = no data collection during the period considered.  All transactions in the three provinces are reported by surveyors to be made in Pakistani Rupees. The prices were converted in US$, using the exchange rate prevailing on the day each observation was made.

**Afghanistan: Prices of dry opium obtained from traders in Nangarhar and Kandahar in US-$ per kg**

### 1997

| Date | Nangarhar | Kandahar | Simple Average |
|---|---|---|---|
| Jan-97 |  |  |  |
| Feb-97 |  |  |  |
| Mar-97 | 93 |  | 63 |
| Apr-97 | 102 |  | 68 |
| May-97 | 108 |  | 71 |
| Jun-97 | 114 |  | 74 |
| Jul-97 | 91 |  | 62 |
| Aug-97 | 97 | 34 | 65 |
| Sep-97 | 97 | 33 | 65 |
| Oct-97 | 86 | 33 | 60 |
| Nov-97 | 83 | 30 | 57 |
| Dec-97 | 66 | 34 | 50 |

### 1998

| Date | Nangarhar | Kandahar | Simple Average |
|---|---|---|---|
| Jan-98 | 67 | 46 | 57 |
| Feb-98 | 76 | 53 | 65 |
| Mar-98 | 95 | 41 | 68 |
| Apr-98 | 70 | 38 | 54 |
| May-98 | 65 | 38 | 52 |
| Jun-98 | 83 | 44 | 64 |
| Jul-98 | 54 | 49 | 51 |
| Aug-98 | 55 | 67 | 61 |
| Sep-98 | 63 | 54 | 59 |
| Oct-98 | 78 | 59 | 69 |
| Nov-98 | 96 | 54 | 75 |
| Dec-98 | 101 | 56 | 79 |

### 1999

| Date | Nangarhar | Kandahar | Simple Average |
|---|---|---|---|
| Jan-99 | 116 | 59 | 87 |
| Feb-99 | 100 | 60 | 80 |
| Mar-99 | 100 | 50 | 75 |
| Apr-99 | 80 | 45 | 62 |
| May-99 | 91 | 43 | 67 |
| Jun-99 | 86 | 41 | 63 |
| Jul-99 | 82 | 37 | 59 |
| Aug-99 | 62 | 39 | 51 |
| Sep-99 | 61 | 36 | 49 |
| Oct-99 | 40 | 33 | 37 |
| Nov-99 | 38 | 31 | 34 |
| Dec-99 | 39 | 32 | 35 |

### 2000

| Date | Nangarhar | Kandarhar | Simple Average |
|---|---|---|---|
| Jan-00 | 41 | 31 | 36 |
| Feb-00 | 43 | 30 | 37 |
| Mar-00 | 46 | 29 | 38 |
| Apr-00 | 44 | 30 | 37 |
| May-00 | 42 | 30 | 36 |
| Jun-00 | 38 | 31 | 35 |
| Jul-00 | 44 | 35 | 39 |
| Aug-00 | 87 | 78 | 82 |
| Sep-00 | 76 | 43 | 60 |
| Oct-00 | 124 | 70 | 97 |
| Nov-00 | 107 | 61 | 84 |
| Dec-00 | 159 | 101 | 130 |

### 2001

| Date | Nangarhar | Kandahar | Simple Average |
|---|---|---|---|
| Jan-01 | 173 | 128 | 150 |
| Feb-01 | 214 | 162 | 188 |
| Mar-01 | 367 | 205 | 286 |
| Apr-01 | 383 | 260 | 322 |
| May-01 | 398 | 270 | 334 |
| Jun-01 | 368 | 250 | 309 |
| Jul-01 | 424 | 288 | 356 |
| Aug-01 | 657 | 446 | 551 |
| 10-Sep-01 | 700 | 650 | 675 |
| 15-Sep-01 | 194 | 180 | 187 |
| 24-Sep-01 | 95 | 90 | 93 |
| 10-Oct-01 | 134 | 150 | 142 |
| 15-Oct-01 | 190 | 327 |  |
| 28-Oct-01 | 210 | 270 |  |
| 01-Nov-01 | 327 | 340 |  |
| 05-Nov-01 | 330 | 350 |  |
| 19-Nov-01 | 343 | 364 |  |
| 15-Dec-01 | 316 | 275 |  |

### 2002

| Date | Nangarhar | Kandarhar | Simple Average |
|---|---|---|---|
| 15-Jan-02 | 423 | 407 | 415 |
| 15-Feb-02 | 409 | 395 | 402 |
| 15-Mar-02 | 416 | 343 | 379 |
| 14-Apr-02 | 583 | 450 | 517 |
| 25-Apr-02 | 361 | 385 | 373 |
| 07-May-02 | 381 | 304 | 343 |
| 15-May-02 | 444 | 376 | 410 |
| 20-May-02 | 444 | 380 | 412 |
| 09-Jun-02 | 514 | 480 | 497 |
| 15-Jun-02 | 514 | 436 | 475 |
| 15-Jul-02 | 380 | 422 | 401 |
| 15-Aug-02 | 398 | 350 | 374 |
| 09-Sep-02 | 418 | 370 | 394 |
| 23-Sep-02 | 434 | 414 | 424 |
| 01-Oct-02 | 450 | 430 | 440 |
| end Nov-02 | 481 | 538 | 510 |
| mid Dec-02 | 506 | 602 | 554 |
| end Dec-02 | 524 | 556 | 540 |

### 2003

| Date | Nangarhar | Kandarhar | Simple Average |
|---|---|---|---|
| Mid Jan-03 | 512 | 640 | 576 |
| End Jan-03 | 499 | 609 | 554 |
| Mid Feb-03 | 529 | 577 | 553 |
| End Feb-03 | 447 | 577 | 512 |
| Mid Mar-03 | 445 | 509 | 477 |
| End Mar-03 | 381 | 444 | 412 |
| Mid Apr-03 | 299 | 386 | 343 |
| End Apr-03 | 355 | 426 | 390 |
| Mid May-03 | 430 | 469 | 449 |
| End May-03 | 416 | 452 | 434 |
| Mid Jun-03 | 353 | 436 | 394 |
| End Jun-03 | 339 | 415 | 377 |
| Mid Jul-03 | 353 | 423 | 388 |
| End Jul-03 | 327 | 379 | 353 |
| Mid Aug-03 | 272 | 375 | 323 |
| End Aug-03 | 286 | 432 | 359 |
| Mid Sep-03 | 261 | 312 | 286 |
| End Sep-03 | 247 | 321 | 284 |
| Mid Oct-03 | 221 | 303 | 262 |
| End Oct-03 | 197 | 249 | 223 |
| Nov-03 | 219 | 225 | 222 |
| Dec-03 | 229 | 203 | 216 |

### 2004

| Date | Nangarhar | Kandarhar | Simple Average |
|---|---|---|---|
| Jan-04 | 211 | 184 | 197 |
| Feb 04 | 184 | 177 | 180 |

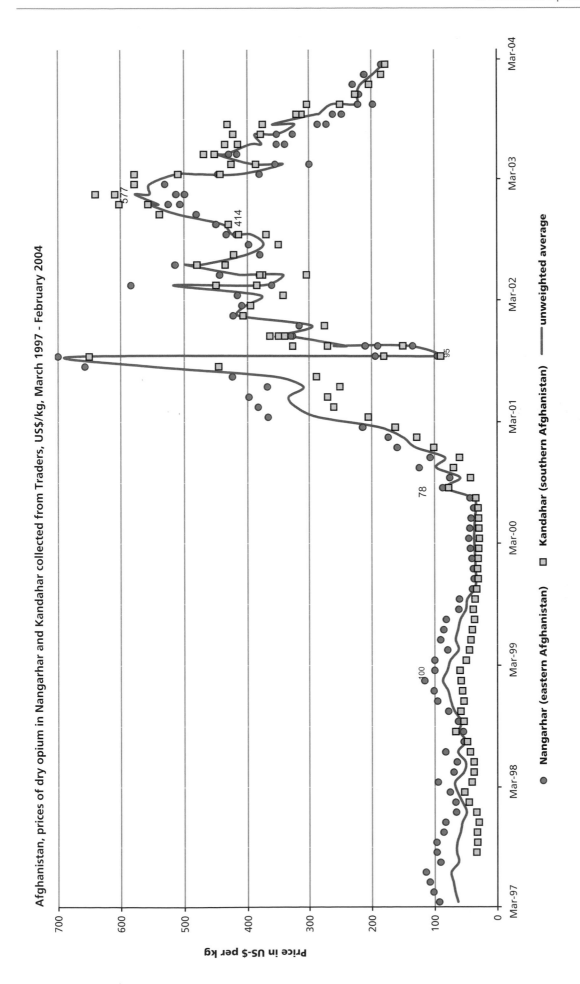

Afghanistan, prices of dry opium in Nangarhar and Kandahar collected from Traders, US$/kg, March 1997 - February 2004

Price in US-$ per kg

● Nangarhar (eastern Afghanistan)     □ Kandahar (southern Afghanistan)     —— unweighted average

**Afghanistan, eradication report from CND, in ha, 2003**

| Provincial Report | Hectares |
|---|---|
| Nangarhar | 7,376 |
| Kabul | 43 |
| Parwan | 80 |
| Helmand | 8,500 |
| Kandahar | 2,719 |
| Uruzgan | 1,510 |
| Zabul | 1 |
| Wardak (Maind Shaher) | 9 |
| Heart | 932 |
| Nimroz | 260 |
| Badghis | - |
| Ghor | - |
| Farah | - |
| **Country Total** | **21,430** |

## 3.1.2. Myanmar

In Myanmar, the problem of opium and heroin has deep historical roots that reach back to the 19th century. The second source of illicit opium and heroin in the world after Afghanistan during the last decade, the country has recorded an encouraging decline of illicit opium cultivation since the mid-1990s.

**Results of the 2003 UNODC Myanmar Annual Opium Survey**

*(1) Opium poppy cultivation*

The total opium poppy cultivation in Myanmar in 2003 was estimated at 62,200 ha. Compared to the previous year, this represented a decrease of 24% in opium poppy cultivation at the national level.

*(2) Opium production*

At the country level, the potential opium production was estimated at 810 metric tons. This represented a decrease of 4 % compared to last year. This year favourable weather conditions for opium poppy cultivation accounted for the higher potential yield of about 13 kg/ha.

*(3) Opium Prices and Cash Income*

Combining the opium production estimates and the anticipated 2003 opium prices at the time of the survey (130 US$/kg), the total farm gate value of opium in Myanmar in 2003 ranged from US$70 to US$ 140 million, with a mean value of US$105 million.

*(4) Addiction*

The data collected in 2003 showed that 0.65% of the population surveyed, age 15 and above, was smoking opium on a daily basis. The data also indicated that opium addiction is still far more widespread than heroin and ATS addiction in the Shan State. Less than 2% of village headmen reported cases of heroin addiction in their villages and less than 1% reported cases of ATS addiction.

*(5) Eradication*

The Government of the Union of Myanmar reported eradicating 638 ha of opium poppy fields in 2003. The opium survey was not designed to monitor or validate the results of opium poppy eradication campaign. The methodology employed ensured that the results were post-eradication and reflected the net amount of opium poppy which was harvestable.

**Fact Sheet : Myanmar 2003**

Source: UNODC survey report, available at www.unodc.org/unodc/en/crop_monitoring

| | |
|---|---|
| Opium poppy cultivation: | 62,200 ha against 81,400 ha in 2002 (24% decrease) |

2002-2003 trends in some areas:

Northern Shan State:    - 45%
Eastern Shan State:    - 26%
South Shan State:    - 19%
Wa Special Region 2:    + 21%
*(of which Wa Alternative Dvpt project:-19%)*

Potential opium yield:    13 kg/ha against 10 kg/ha in 2002

Potential opium production:    810 metric tons against 828 metric tons in 2002 (2% decrease)

Number of households cultivating opium:    350,000 households

Approximate fresh opium price at harvest:    US$130/kg

Total farm gate value of opium:    US$105 million

Average household cash income from opium:    between US$160 and US$190

Average opium income per capita:    US$594 (2002 GDP per capita: US$184)

Opium smoking prevalence rate in the population interviewed:    0.6% of the population aged 15 and above

Reported eradication    637 ha

*Graphs, tables, maps: Myanmar*

**Myanmar, opium poppy cultivation 1990 – 2003 (in thousand of ha)**

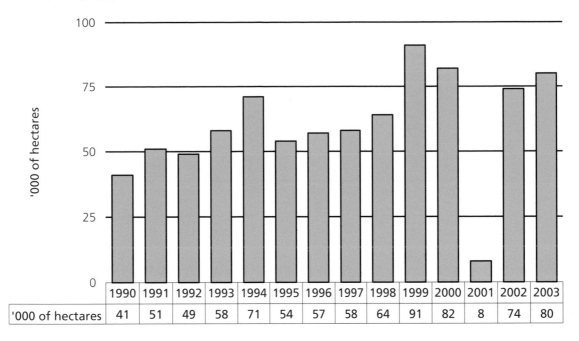

| '000 of hectares | 1990 | 1991 | 1992 | 1993 | 1994 | 1995 | 1996 | 1997 | 1998 | 1999 | 2000 | 2001 | 2002 | 2003 |
|---|---|---|---|---|---|---|---|---|---|---|---|---|---|---|
| | 41 | 51 | 49 | 58 | 71 | 54 | 57 | 58 | 64 | 91 | 82 | 8 | 74 | 80 |

**Myanmar, opium poppy cultivation in 2002 and 2003**

| Regions | 2002 (rounded ha) | 2003 (rounded ha) | % of change 2002-2003 |
|---|---|---|---|
| Northern Shan State | 37,500 | 20,700 | -45% |
| Eastern Shan State | 7,800 | 5,800 | -26% |
| Southern Shan State | 11,600 | 9,400 | -19% |
| Wa Special Region Number 2 | 17,600 | 21,300 | 21% |
| (of which Wa Alt Dvpt Project) | 962 | 775 | -19% |
| Shan State | 74,600 | 57,200 | -23% |
| Outside Shan State | 6,800 | 5,000 | -26% |
| **National total** | **81,400** | **62,200** | **-24%** |

**Myanmar, average regional yields (kg/ha)**

| Regions | Number of observations | Average opium yield (kg/ha) |
|---|---|---|
| Northern Shan State | 0 | 11* |
| Wa Special Region 2 | 268 | 16 |
| WADP (Mongyang Township) | 230 | 11 |
| Central Shan State | 60 | 11 |
| Southeastern Shan State | 56 | 8 |
| Southwestern Shan State | 58 | 14 |
| **Shan Sate** | **672** | **13** |

\* Average opium yield of neighbouring Central Shan State used as best estimate

217

## Myanmar opium production 1990 – 2003 (in metric tons)

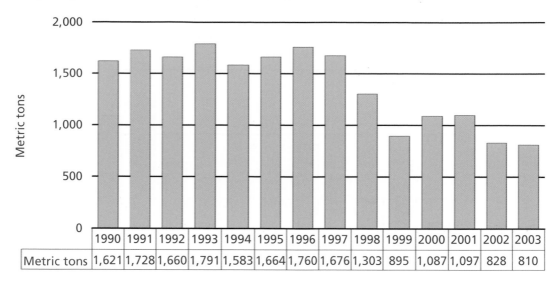

| | 1990 | 1991 | 1992 | 1993 | 1994 | 1995 | 1996 | 1997 | 1998 | 1999 | 2000 | 2001 | 2002 | 2003 |
|---|---|---|---|---|---|---|---|---|---|---|---|---|---|---|
| Metric tons | 1,621 | 1,728 | 1,660 | 1,791 | 1,583 | 1,664 | 1,760 | 1,676 | 1,303 | 895 | 1,087 | 1,097 | 828 | 810 |

## Myanmar, opium farmgate prices in Mong Pawk market, US$/kg (Wa Special Region 2)

| Year | Jan | Feb | Mar | Apr | May | Jun | Jul | Aug | Sep | Oct | Nov | Dec |
|---|---|---|---|---|---|---|---|---|---|---|---|---|
| 1999 | 172 | 97 | 110 | 125 | 136 | 123 | 133 | 152 | 119 | 173 | 144 | 163 |
| 2000 | 195 | 193 | 203 | 172 | 236 | 226 | 202 | 230 | 210 | 210 | 203 | 218 |
| 2001 | 218 | 208 | 188 | 201 | 195 | 182 | 182 | 195 | 195 | 188 | 162 | 150 |
| 2002 | 151 | 158 | 136 | 124 | 119 | 108 | 107 | 124 | 132 | 127 | 127 | 144 |
| 2003 | 158 | 165 | 127 | 117 | 128 | 132 | 138 | 147 | 139 | 137 | 146 | 152 |
| 2004 | 155 | 151 | 216 | | | | | | | | | |

## Myanmar, opium farmgate prices in Mong Pawk market, US$/kg (Wa Special Region 2)

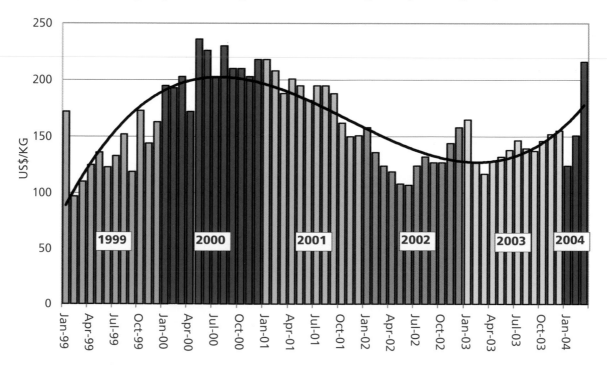

3. Production: Opium/heroin

**Myanmar, Shan State, 2002 opium prices by sale periods**

| Period | Equivalent months range | Answers | Average weight of opium sold (kg) | Kyat/kg | USD/kg | Exchange rate (Kyat/US$) |
|---|---|---|---|---|---|---|
| Before harvest | Before Jan. 02 | 160 | 0.64 | 102,000 | 135 | 753 |
| During harvest | Jan-Mar 2002 | 729 | 0.88 | 108,000 | 143 | 753 |
| Just after harvest | Apr-May 2002 | 1,478 | 1.29 | 106,000 | 107 | 855 |
| Rainy Season | Jun-Sep 2002 | 353 | 0.96 | 104,000 | 106 | 985 |
| Dry Season | Oct-Dec 2002 | 272 | 1.04 | 120,000 | 110 | 1,090 |
| **For 2002** | | **2,992** | | **107,00** | **115** | **931** |

*Average weighted by number of answers and average weight of opium sold for each period.

**Myanmar, Shan State annual source of cash income for opium farmers in 2002**

| Source of Cash Income | Annual cash income (in Kyat) | % of total income | Number of answers | Annual income ( US$) |
|---|---|---|---|---|
| Opium | 148,000 | 69% | 2,010 | 159 |
| Cattle | 22,000 | 10% | 669 | 23 |
| Other | 13,000 | 6% | 341 | 15 |
| Upland | 11,000 | 5% | 388 | 12 |
| Paddy | 7,000 | 3% | 247 | 8 |
| Labour | 7,000 | 3% | 388 | 8 |
| Vegetable | 3,000 | 1% | 265 | 3 |
| Maize | 3,000 | 1% | 162 | 3 |
| Total | 216,000 | | | 232 |

Sample size: 2,426 interviews of opium farmers

**Myanmar, Shan State opium addiction in the Shan State by regions in 2003**

| Regions | Number of villages sampled | Total population above 15 years old | Number of addicts | % of opium addicts in population age 15 and above |
|---|---|---|---|---|
| Northern Shan | 373 | 73,041 | 263 | 0.4% |
| Wa Special Region 2 | 269 | 50,863 | 385 | 0.8% |
| Southwestern Shan | 248 | 35,257 | 216 | 0.6% |
| Central Shan | 361 | 53,753 | 94 | 0.2% |
| Southeastern Shan | 310 | 33,124 | 593 | 1.8% |
| **Shan State** | **1,561** | **246,038** | **1,551** | **0.6%** |

**Myanmar, Shan State, demographic distribution of opium addicts by gender and age in 2003**

| Age class | Man | Woman | Total | % of Total |
|---|---|---|---|---|
| <10 | 2 | 2 | 4 | 0.3% |
| 10-20 | 4 | 3 | 7 | 0.5% |
| 20-30 | 93 | 15 | 108 | 7.0% |
| 30-40 | 231 | 24 | 255 | 16.5% |
| 40-50 | 293 | 24 | 317 | 20.5% |
| 50-60 | 325 | 23 | 348 | 22.5% |
| 60-70 | 291 | 30 | 321 | 20.8% |
| 70-80 | 129 | 14 | 143 | 9.3% |
| 80-90 | 26 | 7 | 33 | 2.2% |
| 90-100 | 7 | 2 | 9 | 0.6% |
| Total | 1,401 | 144 | 1,545 | |

**Myanmar, Shan State, demographic distribution of opium addicts by age in 2003**

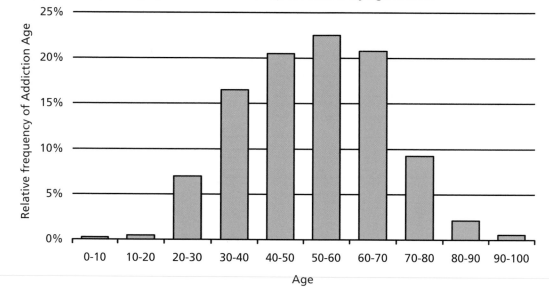

**Myanmar, reported eradication by region and state in 2003**

| State | Eradication (ha) |
|---|---|
| Northern Shan State | 235 |
| Southern Shan State | 182 |
| Eastern Shan State | 91 |
| WADP | 55 |
| Kachin State | 56 |
| Chin State | 2 |
| Kayah State | 9 |
| Mandalay Division | 8 |
| Total | 638 |

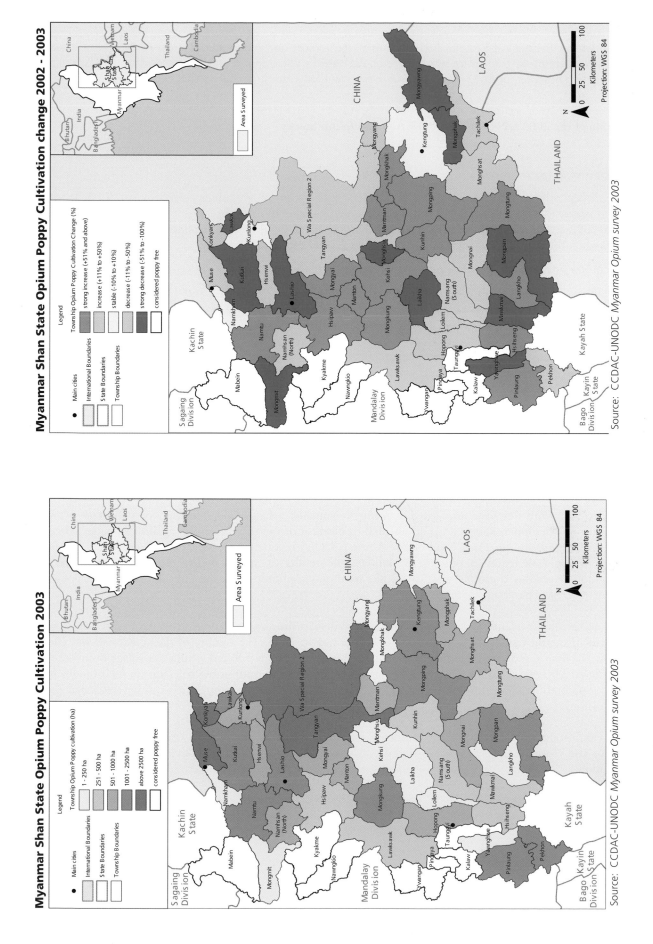

**Myanmar Shan State Opium Poppy Cultivation change 2002 - 2003**

Source: CCDAC-UNODC *Myanmar Opium survey 2003*

**Myanmar Shan State Opium Poppy Cultivation 2003**

Source: CCDAC-UNODC *Myanmar Opium survey 2003*

## 3.1.3. Lao PDR

Although far behind Afghanistan and Myanmar, the remote and mountainous areas of Northern Laos have consistently come in third place as a source of the world's illicit opium and heroin during the last ten years. Since 1998, however, opium poppy cultivation has recorded a steady decline in that country.

**Results of the 2003 UNODC Lao PDR Annual Opium Survey**

*(1) Opium poppy cultivation*

The survey estimated that there were 12,000 hectares of opium poppy under cultivation in 2003. It was the lowest national estimate since 1989 and represented a reduction of 2,100 hectares (or 15%) compared with the 2001-2002 season (14,100 ha). It confirmed the downward trend of opium poppy cultivation in Laos since 1998 when the cultivation of opium poppy reached 26,800 hectares.

*(2) Opium production*

In 2003, the average potential opium yield was estimated to range between 6 and 14 kg/ha, with a mean value of 10 kg/ha. In 2002, the potential yield was estimated at 8 kg/ha. This potential yield may differ from the actual harvest, and does not include possible post-harvest losses.

Based on the estimated 12,000 ha of opium poppy cultivation and an average yield of 6 to 14 kg/ha, the potential production of opium in Laos would range between 72 and 168 metric tons, with a mean value of 120 metric tons. In terms of potential opium production, this represented an increase of 7% compared to last year.

*(3) Number of farmers involved in opium poppy cultivation*

Based on an average of 0.29 ha of opium poppy cultivation by household (results of the sample ground survey), there would be between 35,000 and 45,000 households cultivating opium poppy in Laos in 2003 (mean of 40,000).

*(4) Voluntary eradication*

For the first time this year, the Lao Government launched a large-scale campaign of voluntary or agreed eradication. The opium survey was not designed to monitor or validate the results of this campaign. However, the Lao Commission on Drug Control and Abuse (LCDC) reported the eradication of 4,134 ha. The opium survey was not designed to monitor or validate the results of opium poppy eradication campaign. The methodology employed ensured that the results were post-eradication and reflected the net amount of opium poppy which was harvestable.

Prior to the opium planting time, the provincial and district drug control committees made agreements with a number of opium farmers to stop growing opium poppy in 2003. The validity of the agreement was checked during the opium growing season. When opium poppy cultivation was found within the village boundaries and considered a breech of the agreement, the farmers were asked by the authorities to eradicate their opium poppy fields (voluntary eradication), or the farmers to give permission for the opium fields to be eradicated (agreed eradication).

The eradication teams were made of students and staff from the district mass organisations like the Youth Union, the Women Union or other district departments. The military and the police were not involved in these operations.

If the farmers refused the eradication, the assistance of the village headman was requested to convince the farmers to respect the agreement and not to plant opium poppy in the future. The data on eradication, as reported by the Lao Government, is presented in annex.

**Fact Sheet : Lao PDR 2003**

Source: UNODC survey report, available at www.unodc.org/unodc/en/crop_monitoring

| | |
|---|---|
| Opium poppy cultivation: | 12,000 ha against 14,100 ha in 2002 (15% decrease) |
| Potential opium yield: | 10 kg/ha against 8 kg/ha in 2002 |
| Potential opium production: | 120 metric tons against 112 metric tons in 2002 (7% increase) |
| Number of households cultivating opium: | 40,000 households |
| Most recent opium prices available (average for 2002): | US$160 |
| Average household cash income from opium In 2002: | US$92 |
| Number of addicts reported by the authorities: | 30,000 persons (5,600 women or 18%, and 9,700 over 60 years old or 32%) |
| Average annual domestic consumption of opium : | between 1.3 and 1.5 kg/year |
| Estimated annual domestic consumption of opium: | 42 metric tons |
| Reported eradication | 4,134 ha. |

*Graphs, tables, maps: Lao PDR*

**Lao PDR, opium poppy cultivation 1990-2003 (in ha)**

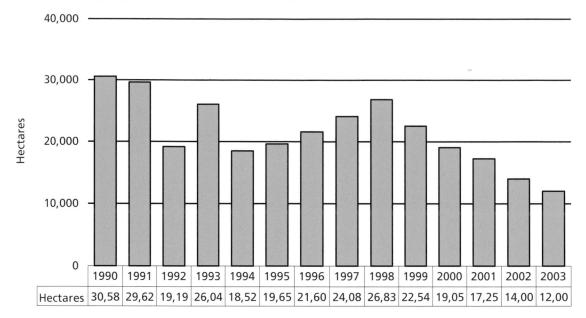

| | 1990 | 1991 | 1992 | 1993 | 1994 | 1995 | 1996 | 1997 | 1998 | 1999 | 2000 | 2001 | 2002 | 2003 |
|---|---|---|---|---|---|---|---|---|---|---|---|---|---|---|
| Hectares | 30,58 | 29,62 | 19,19 | 26,04 | 18,52 | 19,65 | 21,60 | 24,08 | 26,83 | 22,54 | 19,05 | 17,25 | 14,00 | 12,00 |

**Lao PDR, evolution of the area under opium poppy cultivation by province, 1992-2003**

| | 1992 | 1996 | 1998 | 2000 | 2001 | 2002 | 2003 |
|---|---|---|---|---|---|---|---|
| Luang Prabang | 3,510 | 3,550 | 2,786 | 3,036 | 2,950 | 3,400 | 2,576 |
| Huapanh | 3,770 | 3,817 | 3,450 | 3,921 | 2,903 | 2,934 | 2,530 |
| Phongsaly | 2,840 | 3,558 | 5,778 | 3,872 | 3,278 | 1,703 | 1,602 |
| UdomXay | 1,860 | 2,416 | 5,597 | 4,061 | 3,112 | 1,901 | 1,579 |
| Luang Namtha | 1,730 | 2,197 | 3,593 | 1,514 | 1,687 | 1,355 | 1197 |
| Xieng Khuang | 2,880 | 2,916 | 2,902 | 1,376 | 1,426 | 1,078 | 979 |
| Bokeo | 620 | 785 | 428 | 448 | 427 | 332 | 480 |
| Xayabouri | 400 | 754 | 1,014 | 508 | 729 | 857 | 472 |
| Xaisombun | N/a | n/a | n/a | 224 | 521** | 240 | 354 |
| Vientiane | 880* | 900* | 672* | 19 | 117** | 210 | 130 |
| Bolikhamsay | 700 | 708 | 617 | 73 | 105 | 42 | 74 |
| Total | 19,190 | 21,601 | 26,837 | 19,052 | 17,255 | 14,052 | 11,973 |
| **Rounded Total** | **19,200** | **21,600** | **26,800** | **19,100** | **17,300** | **14,100** | **12,000** |

*Includes Xaisombun
**Previously within Xaisombun, the districts of Hom and Longxan are part of Vientiane Province since 2001.

## Lao PDR, potential opium production since 1992 (in metric tons)

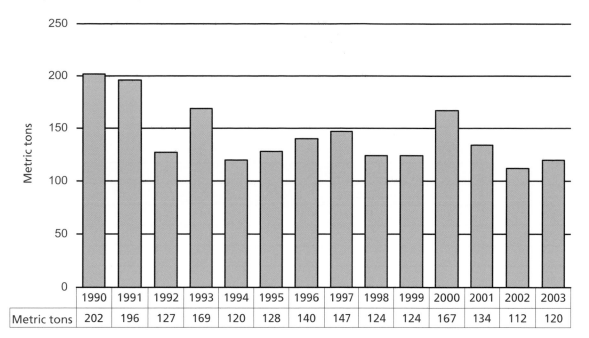

| Metric tons | 1990 | 1991 | 1992 | 1993 | 1994 | 1995 | 1996 | 1997 | 1998 | 1999 | 2000 | 2001 | 2002 | 2003 |
|---|---|---|---|---|---|---|---|---|---|---|---|---|---|---|
| | 202 | 196 | 127 | 169 | 120 | 128 | 140 | 147 | 124 | 124 | 167 | 134 | 112 | 120 |

## Lao PRD, 2002 opium prices by sale periods

| Period | Equivalent months range | Answers | Average weight of opium sold (kg) | KIP/kg | US$/kg |
|---|---|---|---|---|---|
| During harvest | Jan-Mar 2002 | 46 | 0.64 | 1,781,855 | 186 |
| Just after harvest | Apr-May 2002 | 310 | 0.98 | 1,568,448 | 163 |
| Rainy Season | Jun-Sep 2002 | 97 | 1.50 | 1,660,996 | 160 |
| Dry Season | Oct-Dec 2002 | 85 | 1.22 | 1,583,858 | 146 |
| **For 2002** | | 538 | | 1,600,000* | 160 |

*Average weighted by number of answers and average weight of opium sold for each period.

## Lao PDR, 2002 annual source of cash income for opium farmers

| Source of Cash Income | Annual cash income (Kip) | % of total income | Number of answers | Annual income (US$) |
|---|---|---|---|---|
| Paddy | 36,130 | 1.7% | 37 | 4 |
| Upland | 121,721 | 5.8% | 180 | 12 |
| Animal | 716,480 | 34.2% | 633 | 70 |
| Vegetable | 74,614 | 3.6% | 374 | 7 |
| Opium | 889,885 | 42.4% | 535 | 88 |
| Labor | 75,300 | 3.6% | 209 | 7 |
| Trade | 22,111 | 1.1% | 39 | 2 |
| Wood | 101,284 | 4.8% | 292 | 10 |
| Non Timber Forest Products | 32,546 | 1.6% | 99 | 3 |
| Other | 26,477 | 1.3% | 75 | 3 |
| **Total** | **2,096,548** | **100%** | | **206** |

Sample size: 1,142 interviews of opium farmers

**Lao PDR, Number of opium addicts 2000-2003**

| Year | Addicts |
|------|---------|
| 2000 | 63,000 |
| 2001 | 58,000 |
| 2002 | 53,000 |
| 2003 | 30,000 |

**Lao PDR, Demographic Distribution of Opium Addicts by Gender and Age in 2003**

| Age | 2003 | | | | 2002 | 2001 |
|-----|------|--------|-------|------------|------------|------------|
| | Male | Female | Total | % of Total | % of Total | % of Total |
| 10-20 | 1 | 0 | 1 | 0.1% | 1.14% | 1.20% |
| 20-30 | 22 | 6 | 28 | 4.1% | 9.23% | 10.85% |
| 30-40 | 56 | 12 | 68 | 10.0% | 22.13% | 21.90% |
| 40-50 | 93 | 23 | 116 | 17.1% | 22.85% | 23.27% |
| 50-60 | 146 | 41 | 187 | 27.6% | 21.46% | 22.53% |
| 60-70 | 149 | 38 | 187 | 27.6% | 16.71% | 14.52% |
| 70-80 | 44 | 15 | 59 | 8.7% | 5.17% | 4.57% |
| 80-90 | 13 | 13 | 26 | 3.9% | 1.05% | 0.90% |
| 90-100 | 4 | 2 | 6 | 0.9% | 0.22% | 0.27% |
| Total | 528 | 150 | 678 | | | |
| % | 78% | 22% | 100% | 100% | 100% | 100% |

**Laos PDR, demographic distribution of opium addiction by age in 2003**

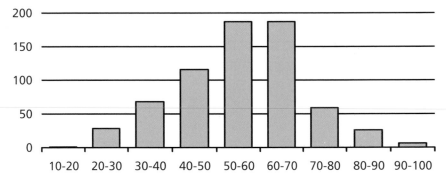

**Lao PDR, reported voluntary eradication in 2003**

| Province | Hectares |
|----------|----------|
| Phongsaly | 416 |
| Luang Namtha | 1,005 |
| UdomXay | 428 |
| Bokeo | 58 |
| Luang Prabang | 1,315 |
| Huapanh | 549 |
| Xayabouri | 305 |
| Xieng Khuang | 18 |
| Bolikhamsay | 40 |
| Total | 4,133 |

**Northern Laos Opium Poppy Cultivation change 2002 - 2003**

**Northern Laos Opium Poppy Cultivation 2003**

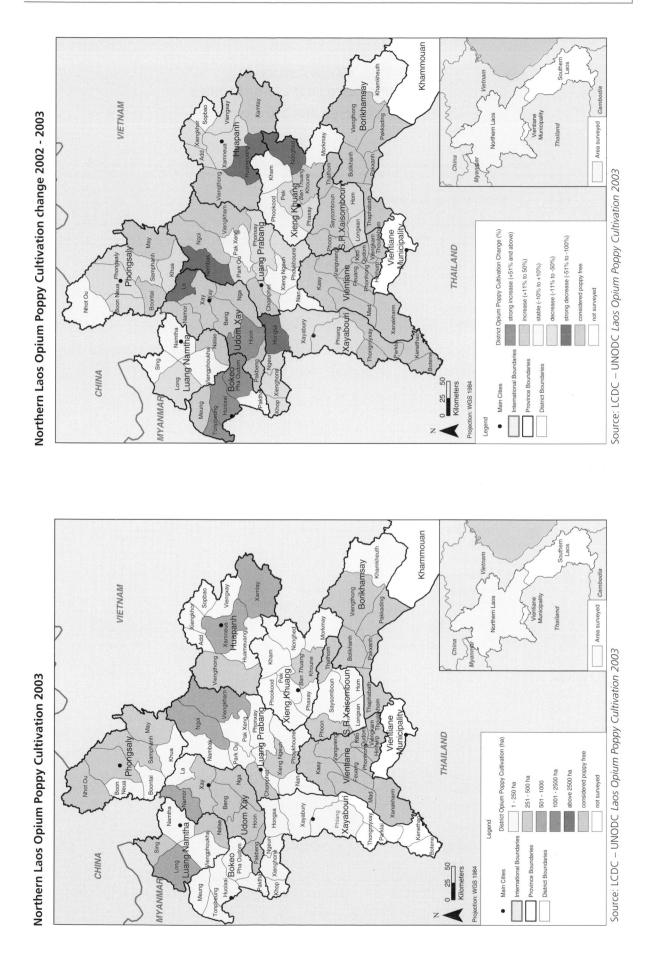

Source: LCDC – UNODC *Laos Opium Poppy Cultivation 2003*

Source: LCDC – UNODC *Laos Opium Poppy Cultivation 2003*

## 3.1.4. Seizure of Illicit Laboratories

### MANUFACTURE
### SEIZURES OF ILLICIT LABORATORIES
### REPORTED FOR 2001 - 2002

Remark: For convenience, an attempt was made to group the reported estimates by drug categories. however, due to inconsistencies and gaps in the reporting, no overall analysis of the data set was performed. Numbers are presented as reported to UNODC and should be interpreted with caution.

Source: Annual Report Questionnaire if not otherwise indicated

| Country or Territory | Year | Name of drug seized | Number of laboratories (and quantity of drug) | Source |
|---|---|---|---|---|
| **OPIATE GROUP** | | | | |
| **Americas** | | | | |
| North America | | | | |
| Mexico | 2001 | Heroin | 1 Lab. | |
| | 2002 | Heroin | 1 Lab. | |
| Subtotal North America | | | 2 Lab. | |
| South America | | | | |
| Colombia | 2001 | Heroin | 6 Lab.(1.400 kg) | |
| | 2002 | Heroin | 3 Lab. | |
| Subtotal South America | | | 9 Lab.(1.400 kg) | |
| Total Americas | | | 11 Lab.(1.400 kg) | |
| **Asia** | | | | |
| East and South-East Asia | | | | |
| *Hong Kong SAR, China* | 2001 | Heroin | 12 Lab. | |
| | 2002 | Heroin | 6 Lab. | |
| Myanmar | 2001 | Heroin | 16 Lab. | |
| | 2002 | Heroin | 9 Lab. | |
| Subtotal East and South-East Asia | | | 43 Lab. | |
| South Asia | | | | |
| India | 2001 | Morphine | 1 Lab. | |
| | 2001 | Heroin | 6 Lab. | |
| | 2002 | Heroin | 7 Lab.(28.000 kg) | |
| | 2002 | Morphine | 1 Lab.(5.000 kg) | |
| Subtotal South Asia | | | 15 Lab.(33.000 kg) | |
| Total Asia | | | 58 Lab.(33.000 kg) | |
| **Europe** | | | | |
| Eastern Europe | | | | |
| Poland | 2001 | Polish heroin | 408 Lab.(280.000 lt.) | |
| | 2002 | Polish heroin | 14 Lab. | |
| Republic of Moldova | 2001 | Opium | 11 Lab. | |
| Russian Federation | 2001 | Opium | 232 Lab.(24.114 kg) | |
| | 2002 | Opium | 91 Lab. | |
| Ukraine | 2001 | Poppy | 30 Lab. | |
| Subtotal Eastern Europe | | | 786 Lab.(24.114 kg)(280.000 lt.) | |
| Turkey | 2002 | Heroin | 10 Lab. | |
| Total Europe | | | 796 Lab.(24.114 kg)(280.000 lt.) | |
| Opiate group | | | 865 Lab.(58.514 kg)(280.000 lt.) | |

## 3.2. Coca/ Cocaine

### GLOBAL ILLICIT CULTIVATION OF COCA BUSH AND PRODUCTION OF COCA LEAF AND COCAINE, 1990-2003

| | 1990 | 1991 | 1992 | 1993 | 1994 | 1995 | 1996 | 1997 | 1998 | 1999 | 2000 | 2001 | 2002 | 2003 |
|---|---|---|---|---|---|---|---|---|---|---|---|---|---|---|
| **CULTIVATION[1] OF COCA BUSH IN HECTARES** | | | | | | | | | | | | | | |
| Bolivia [2] | 50,300 | 47,900 | 45,300 | 47,200 | 48,100 | 48,600 | 48,100 | 45,800 | 38,000 | 21,800 | 14,600 | 19,900 | 24,400 | 23,600 |
| Colombia [3] | 40,100 | 37,500 | 37,100 | 39,700 | 44,700 | 50,900 | 67,200 | 79,400 | 101,800 | 160,100 | 163,300 | 144,800 | 102,000 | 86,000 |
| Peru [4] | 121,300 | 120,800 | 129,100 | 108,800 | 108,600 | 115,300 | 94,400 | 68,800 | 51,000 | 38,700 | 43,400 | 46,200 | 46,700 | 44,200 |
| Total | 211,700 | 206,200 | 211,500 | 195,700 | 201,400 | 214,800 | 209,700 | 194,000 | 190,800 | 220,600 | 221,300 | 210,900 | 173,100 | 153,800 |
| **POTENTIAL PRODUCTION OF DRY COCA LEAF IN METRIC TONS** | | | | | | | | | | | | | | |
| Bolivia | 77,000 | 78,000 | 80,300 | 84,400 | 89,800 | 85,000 | 75,100 | 70,100 | 52,900 | 22,800 | 13,400 | 20,200 | 19,800 | 17,100 |
| Colombia | 45,300 | 45,000 | 44,900 | 45,300 | 67,500 | 80,900 | 108,900 | 129,500 | 165,900 | 261,000 | 266,200 | 236,000 | 222,100 | 168,000 |
| Peru | 196,900 | 222,700 | 223,900 | 155,500 | 165,300 | 183,600 | 174,700 | 130,600 | 95,600 | 69,200 | 46,200 | 49,300 | 52,500 | 50,790 |
| Total | 319,200 | 345,700 | 349,100 | 285,200 | 322,600 | 349,500 | 358,700 | 330,200 | 314,400 | 353,000 | 325,800 | 305,500 | 294,400 | 235,890 |
| **POTENTIAL[5] MANUFACTURE OF COCAINE IN METRIC TONS** | | | | | | | | | | | | | | |
| Bolivia | 189 | 220 | 225 | 240 | 255 | 240 | 215 | 200 | 150 | 70 | 43 | 60 | 60 | 60 |
| Colombia | 92 | 88 | 91 | 119 | 201 | 230 | 300 | 350 | 435 | 680 | 695 | 617 | 580 | 440 |
| Peru | 492 | 525 | 550 | 410 | 435 | 460 | 435 | 325 | 240 | 175 | 141 | 150 | 160 | 155 |
| Total | 774 | 833 | 866 | 769 | 891 | 930 | 950 | 875 | 825 | 925 | 879 | 827 | 800 | 655 |

(1) Potentially harvestable, after eradication.
(2) Source: CICAD and US Department of State, International narcotics Control Strategy Report.
(3) Estimates for 1999 and subsequent years come from the national monitoring system established by the Colombian government with the support of UNODC. Due to the change of methodology, figures for 1999 and after cannot be directly compared with data from previous years.
(4) Since 2000 the results are those of the illicit crop monitoring system established with the support of UNODC
(5) Potential manufacture of cocaine is the amount of cocaine that can be made from coca leaf produced in the country concerned. It does not take into account importation of coca base from other countries.

## 3.2.1. Colombia

Colombia remains the largest producer of coca leaf and its derivative, cocaine. In 2003, 67% of the world's cocaine supply was produced in Colombia. However, Colombia has recorded its third straight year of decline: after declining 38% between 2000 and 2002, coca cultivation declined a further 16% in 2003.

**Results of the 2003 UNODC Colombia Annual Survey**

### (1) Coca Cultivation

According to the findings of the Colombia Coca Survey for 2003, conducted by the Government of Colombia with the support of UNODC, 86,000 hectares of coca were cultivated last year. This represented a decrease of about 16,000 ha (or 16%) since December 2002, when coca cultivation stood at 102,000 ha. As in the previous year, the decline is partially attributed to an intensification of eradication efforts, in particular the aerial spraying campaign which peaked at 133,000 ha. Including the decrease in 2003, coca cultivation has decreased a total of 47% since 2000.

### (2) Geographical Distribution

In 2003, important year on year variations and shifts took place in coca cultivation at the department level. Significant reductions in coca cultivation between 2002 and 2003 were found in the departments of Guaviare (-11,218 ha or 41% decrease), Putumayo (-61,666 ha or 45% decrease) and Norte de Santander (-4,471 ha or 44% decrease), while coca cultivation increased in two departments: Nariño (17,628 ha or 17% compared to 2002) and Meta (12,695 ha or 38% compared to 2002). This change in the composition of departments under cultivation is thought to be a result of an increase in eradication. In 2003, the major coca growing departments were Nariño, Guaviare and Meta, which together accounted for 54% of coca cultivation in the country. The same three departments accounted for 61% of the aerial eradication efforts.

### (3) Coca Production

UNODC has not yet conducted a scientific and comprehensive study on coca leave and cocaine productivity in Colombia. UNODC relies on information available from other sources, in particular the US Government. For the purposes of the 2003 survey report, UNODC used a conversion rate of 4.7 Kg of cocaine per hectare under cultivation. Using this rate, the potential cocaine production in 2003 was 440 metric tons. (This does not include the cocaine which could have been produced in Colombia from imported Peruvian coca base.)

### (4) Coca prices

In 2003, the average price for one kg of coca base amounted COP 2,251,000. Coca base prices in local currency remained largely stabled compared to 2002, but fell in terms of US$ by 6%, from US$ 847/kg to US$ 793.

### (5) Opium cultivation and production

As of November 2003, the DIRAN's estimates based on reconnaissance flights and spray operations, identified 4,026 hectares of opium poppy under cultivation, compared to 4,253 hectares in 2002. The total potential heroin production in Colombia would amount to about 5 metric tons of heroin in 2003.

The price of opium latex for 2003 averaged US$156/kg. With an estimated potential latex production of 121 metric tons, the potential value of the 2003 farm gate production of opium latex would amount to about US$ 19 millions.

The average price for one kg of heroin, as collected by the National Alternative Development Programme, was estimated in US$ 5,660/kg.

### (6) Eradication

Colombia's eradication campaign was sustained in 2003. A total of 136,828 ha were eradicated. DIRAN reported the aerial spraying of 133,000 ha (or +2% from 2002) of coca bush and 3,000 ha (-12% from 2002) of opium poppy cultivation.

The UNODC survey was not designed to monitor or validate the results of the eradication campaign. The results for coca cultivation are considered post-eradication and reflected the net amount harvestable.

**Fact Sheet: Colombia**

**Source:** UNODC survey report, available at www.unodc.org/unodc/en/crop_monitoring

| | |
|---|---|
| Coca cultivation: | 86,000 ha against 102,000 ha in 2002 (or a 16% decrease) |

| 2002-2003 trends in some areas: | | |
|---|---|---|
| | Nariño: | +17% |
| | Guaviare: | - 41% |
| | Meta | +39% |
| | Putumayo: | - 45% |
| | Caqueta: | -14% |
| | Norte de Santander: | - 44% |

| | |
|---|---|
| Potential cocaine production 2003: | 440 metric tons against 580 metric tons in 2002 |
| Average annual coca base price in 2003: | US$793/kg |
| Total potential farmgate value of coca base in 2003: | US$350 million |
| Opium poppy cultivation in 2003: | 4,026 ha (DIRAN estimates) against 4,253 ha (DIRAN estimates) in 2002 |
| Potential opium latex production in 2003: | 121 metric tons |
| Price of opium latex as of December 2002: | US$194/kg |
| Total potential farmgate value of opium latex in 2002: | US$25 million |
| Potential heroin production in 2003: | 5 metric tons |

Reported eradication (DIRAN):

| | |
|---|---|
| in 2002 | Coca bush: 133,116 ha (+ 39% from 2001) Opium poppy: 3,728 ha (-20% from 2001) |
| in 2003 | Coca bush: 136,828ha (+ 3% from 2002) Opium poppy: 3,547 ha (-2% from 2002) |

*Graphs, tables and maps: Colombia*

**Colombia, coca cultivation, in ha, 1990 – 2003**

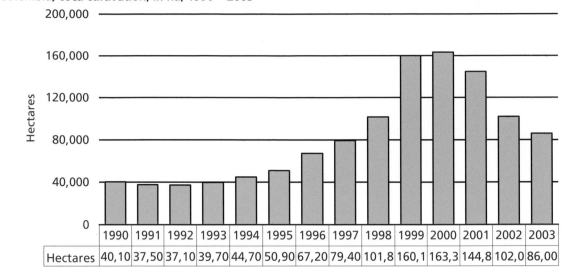

| | 1990 | 1991 | 1992 | 1993 | 1994 | 1995 | 1996 | 1997 | 1998 | 1999 | 2000 | 2001 | 2002 | 2003 |
|---|---|---|---|---|---|---|---|---|---|---|---|---|---|---|
| Hectares | 40,10 | 37,50 | 37,10 | 39,70 | 44,70 | 50,90 | 67,20 | 79,40 | 101,8 | 160,1 | 163,3 | 144,8 | 102,0 | 86,00 |

**Colombia, main departments of coca cultivation, in ha, 2001 – 2002**

| Departments | 2002 | 2003 | % annual change | % of 2003 country total |
|---|---|---|---|---|
| Nariño | 15,131 | 17,628 | 17% | 20% |
| Guaviare | 27,381 | 16,163 | -41% | 19% |
| Meta | 9,222 | 12,814 | 39% | 15% |
| Putumayo | 13,725 | 7,559 | -45% | 9% |
| Caquetá | 8,412 | 7,230 | -14% | 8% |
| Norte de Santander | 8,041 | 4,471 | -44% | 5% |
| Rest of the country | 20,088 | 20,135 | 0% | 23% |
| **Rounded Total** | **102,000** | **86,000** | -16% | 100% |

**Colombia, coca cultivation trends by regions, in ha, 1999 – 2003**

| Region | 1999 | 2000 | 2001 | 2002 | 2003 |
|---|---|---|---|---|---|
| Putumayo-Caqueta | 82,015 | 92,625 | 61,636 | 22,137 | 14,789 |
| Meta - Guavare - Vaupes | 40,833 | 30,235 | 38,896 | 38,088 | 30,134 |
| Bolivar - Antioqua - Cordoba | 11,461 | 8,624 | 8,647 | 6,150 | 7,885 |
| Cauca - Nariño | 10,250 | 13,919 | 10,633 | 17,251 | 19,071 |
| Others | 15,560 | 17,107 | 24,995 | 18,445 | 14,121 |
| **Grand Total** | **160,119** | **162,510** | **144,807** | **102,071** | **86,000** |

**Colombia: Cultivation change 2002-2003 (%)**

**Colombia: Coca cultivation by muncipality in 2003**

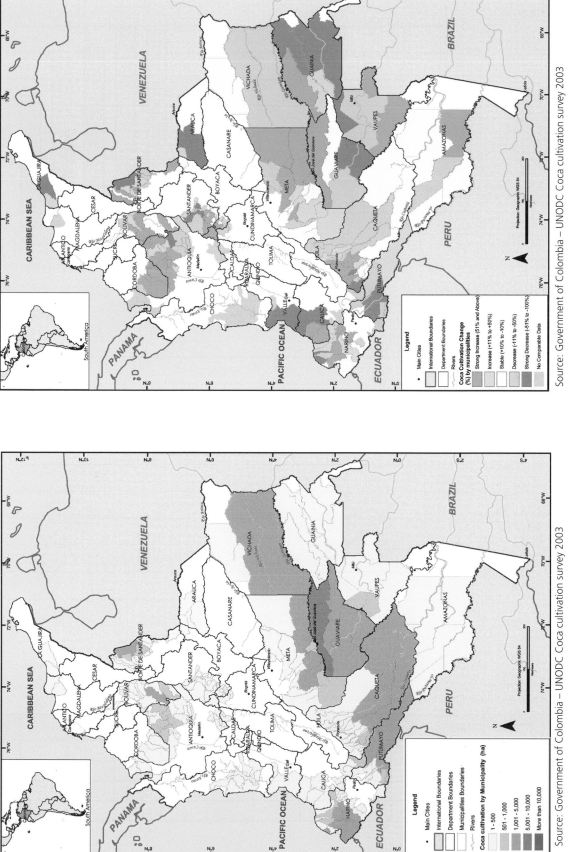

Source: Government of Colombia – UNODC Coca cultivation survey 2003

Source: Government of Colombia – UNODC Coca cultivation survey 2003

## Colombia, potential cocaine production, 1990 - 2003

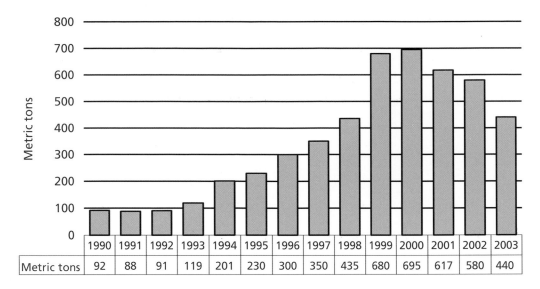

| | 1990 | 1991 | 1992 | 1993 | 1994 | 1995 | 1996 | 1997 | 1998 | 1999 | 2000 | 2001 | 2002 | 2003 |
|---|---|---|---|---|---|---|---|---|---|---|---|---|---|---|
| Metric tons | 92 | 88 | 91 | 119 | 201 | 230 | 300 | 350 | 435 | 680 | 695 | 617 | 580 | 440 |

## Colombia, average coca base price, 2000 – 2003 (thousand of pesos /kg)

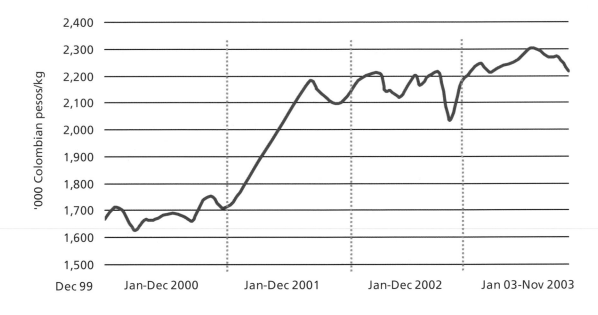

## Colombia, average coca base price 2000 – 2003 (thousand of pesos /kg)

| | Jan | Feb | Mar | Apr | May | Jun | Jul | Aug | Sept | Oct | Nov | Dec |
|---|---|---|---|---|---|---|---|---|---|---|---|---|
| **2000** | 1,714 | 1,690 | 1,628 | 1,666 | 1,666 | 1,682 | 1,691 | 1,680 | 1,665 | 1,740 | 1,750 | 1,710 |
| **2001** | 1,730 | | | | | | | 2,179 | 2,150 | | 2,096 | |
| **2002** | 2,192 | 2,208 | 2,146 | 2,146 | 2,124 | 2,204 | 2,165 | 2,203 | 2,208 | 2,034 | 2,162 | |
| **2003** | 2,213 | 2,247 | 2,215 | 2,231 | 2,242 | 2,263 | 2,300 | 2,295 | 2,269 | 2,270 | 2,217 | |

Colombia, average opium latex price, August 2001-November 2003, per kg.

| Month/Year | Nariño | Cauca | Tolima | Huila | All regions (Colombian Pesos/kg) | All regions (US$/kg) |
|---|---|---|---|---|---|---|
| Aug-01 | 800,000 | 700,000 | 600,000 | 700,000 | 700,000 | 306 |
| Sep-01 | - | - | - | - | 637,500 | 270 |
| Oct-01 | 648,652 | 648,652 | 648,652 | 648,652 | 648,652 | 273 |
| Nov-01 | 660,000 | 660,000 | 660,000 | 660,000 | 660,000 | 276 |
| Dec-01 | - | - | - | - | 632,554 | 271 |
| Jan-02 | 606,250 | 606,250 | 606,250 | 606,250 | 606,250 | 266 |
| Feb-02 | - | - | - | - | 606,250 | 266 |
| Mar-02 | 606,250 | 606,250 | 606,250 | 606,250 | 606,250 | 266 |
| Apr-02 | 500,000 | 546,000 | 600,000 | 544,000 | 547,500 | 242 |
| May-02 | 700,000 | 543,000 | 550,000 | 537,000 | 582,500 | 252 |
| Jun-02 | 440,000 | 544,000 | 450,000 | 536,000 | 492,500 | 209 |
| Jul-02 | 502,143 | 544,000 | 500,000 | 520,000 | 516,536 | 206 |
| Aug-02 | 300,000 | 559,080 | 433,333 | - | 430,804 | 163 |
| Sep-02 | 300,000 | 393,000 | 325,000 | - | 339,333 | 123 |
| Oct-02 | 300,000 | 393,000 | - | - | 346,500 | 122 |
| Nov-02 | 500,000 | 413,000 | - | - | 456,500 | 167 |
| Dec-02 | 600,000 | 293,636 | - | - | 446,818 | 159 |
| Jan-03 | - | - | - | - | 288,182 | 100 |
| Feb-03 | - | - | - | - | 440,000 | 153 |
| Mar-03 | - | - | - | - | 392,727 | 137 |
| Apr-03 | - | - | - | - | 424,444 | 148 |
| May-03 | - | - | - | - | 518,500 | 180 |
| Jun-03 | - | - | - | - | 476,429 | 166 |
| Jul-03 | - | - | - | - | 480,000 | 167 |
| Aug-03 | - | - | - | - | 531,111 | 185 |
| Sep-03 | - | - | - | - | 534,000 | 186 |
| Oct-03 | - | - | - | - | 468,750 | 163 |
| Nov-03 | - | - | - | - | 388,751 | 135 |

## Colombia, average opium latex price, August 2001-November 2003, US$/kg

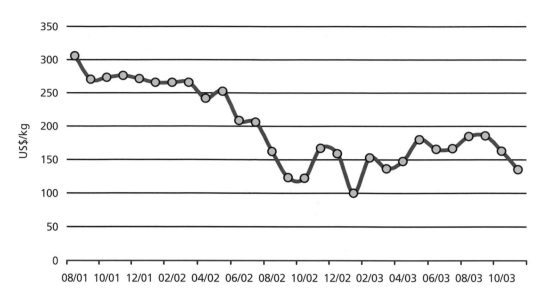

## Colombia, cumulative aerial spraying of coca bushes by department (in ha), 1994- 2003

| Sources: | Environmental Audit of the National Narcotics Bureau | | | | | | Antinarcotics Police Department | | | |
|---|---|---|---|---|---|---|---|---|---|---|
| Department | 1994 | 1995 | 1996 | 1997 | 1998 | 1999 | 2000 | 2001 | 2002 | 2003 |
| Guaviare | 3,142 | 21,394 | 14,425 | 30,192 | 37,081 | 17,376 | 8,241 | 7,477 | 7,207 | 37,493 |
| Meta | 729 | 2,471 | 2,524 | 6,725 | 5,920 | 2,296 | 1,345 | 3,251 | 1,496 | 6,973 |
| Caqueta | - | - | 537 | 4,370 | 18,433 | 15,656 | 9,172 | 17,252 | 18,567 | 1.059 |
| Putumayo | - | - | - | 574 | 3,949 | 4,980 | 13,508 | 32,506 | 71,891 | 8,342 |
| Vichada | - | 50 | 85 | - | 297 | 91 | - | 2,820 | - | - |
| Antioquia | - | - | 684 | - | - | - | 6,259 | - | 3,321 | 9,835 |
| Cordoba | - | - | 264 | - | - | - | - | - | 734 | 550 |
| Vaupes | - | - | - | - | 349 | | | - | - | - |
| Cauca | - | - | - | - | - | 2,713 | 2,950 | 741 | - | 1,308 |
| Norsantander | - | - | - | - | - | - | 9,584 | 10,308 | 9,186 | 13,822 |
| Nariño | - | - | - | - | - | - | 6,442 | 8,216 | 17,962 | 36,910 |
| Santander | - | - | - | - | - | - | 470 | - | - | 5 |
| Boyaca | - | - | - | - | - | - | 102 | - | - | - |
| Bolivar | - | - | - | - | - | - | - | 11,581 | - | 4,783 |
| Arauca | - | - | - | - | - | - | - | - | - | 11,734 |
| Sub-total | 3,871 | 23,915 | 18,519 | 41,861 | 66,029 | 43,111 | 58,073 | 94,153 | 130,364 | 132,817 |
| Manual eradication | - | - | - | - | - | - | - | 1,745 | 2,752 | 4,011 |
| Total | 3,871 | 23,915 | 18,519 | 41,861 | 66,029 | 43,111 | 58,073 | 95,898 | 133,116 | 136,828 |

**Colombia, cumulative aerial spraying of opium poppy, by department (in ha), 1994- 2003**

| Sources: | Environmental Audit of the National Narcotics Bureau | | | | | | Antinarcotics Police Department | | | |
|---|---|---|---|---|---|---|---|---|---|---|
| Department | 1994 | 1995 | 1996 | 1997 | 1998 | 1999 | 2000 | 2001 | 2002 | 2003 |
| Antioquia | - | - | 120 | - | - | - | - | - | - | 0 |
| Caldas | - | - | - | - | - | - | - | - | - | 0 |
| Caqueta | - | - | - | 383 | - | - | - | - | 401 | 0 |
| Cauca | 102 | 53 | 123 | 50 | - | 828 | 1,601 | 387 | 236 | 550 |
| Cesar | 128 | 305 | 713 | 91 | 650 | 125 | 423 | 426 | 548 | 1.004 |
| Guajira | 81 | 177 | 371 | | 50 | | | | | 75 |
| Huila | 2,057 | 1,383 | 715 | 2,175 | 749 | 1,426 | 2,421 | 429 | 545 | 391 |
| Meta | | | | | | | | | | 0 |
| Nariño | | | | | | 313 | 1,090 | 630 | 788 | 725 |
| Tolima | 1,169 | 1,549 | 4,843 | 4,290 | 1,452 | 5,557 | 3,720 | 194 | 854 | 250 |
| Sub-total | 3,537 | 3,466 | 6,885 | 6,988 | 2,901 | 8,249 | 9,254 | 2,066 | 3,371 | 2,995 |
| Manual eradication | | | | | | | | 2,586 | 205 | 257 |
| Total | 3,537 | 3,466 | 6,885 | 6,988 | 2,901 | 8,249 | 9,254 | 4,652 | 3,577 | 3,252 |

**Colombia, comparison of net coca cultivation and reported cumulated sprayed area¹, in ha, 1990-2003**

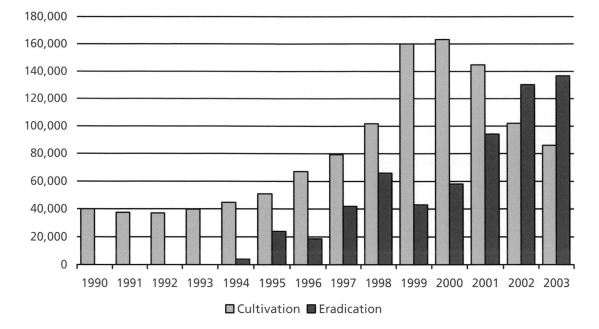

**Colombia, comparison of net opium poppy cultivation and reported cumulated sprayed area¹, in ha, 1991 - 2003**

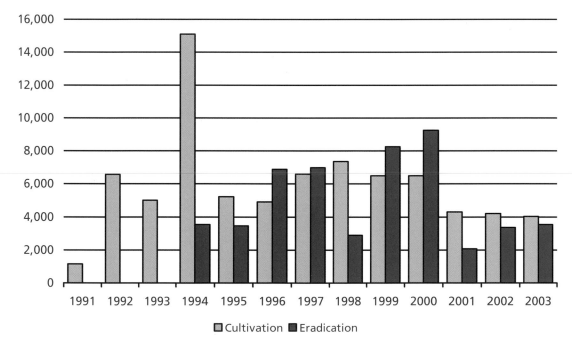

¹ Reported cumulated spraying does not take into account the effectiveness of spraying nor the fact that some spraying paths can overlap, which explains that eradicated areas are larger then cultivated areas.  Illicit crop cultivation estimates presented in this publication are net, i.e. post-eradication.

## 3.2.2 Peru

Peru is the second largest cultivator of coca. It remains well behind the first, Colombia, and levels of production in 2003 continue to remain well below those reached in the mid-1990's when it was the world's largest producer of coca. Under its Global Illicit Crop Monitoring Programme, UNODC has been assisting the Peruvian Government in the implementation and refinement of a national coca monitoring system since 1998. Annual surveys have been produced since the year 2000.

**Results of the 2003 UNODC Peru Annual Survey**

*(1) Coca Cultivation*

In the year 2003, the total area under coca cultivation in Peru was estimated at 44,200 hectares, representing a 5.4 percent decline over 2002.

*(2) Geographical Distribution*

In 2003, 32% of total coca cultivation in the country took place in Apurimac, 31% in Alto Huallaga and 28% in La Convencion – Lares. The most important decreases in cultivation were noted in the areas of Central Huallaga, where coca cultivation has virtually disappeared (750 ha were estimated in 2002), as well as in Aguaytia (- 53%) and in Alto Huallaga (-11%).

*(3) Coca Production*

The total dry coca leaf production in 2003 was estimated at 50,790 metric tons, representing an average annual dry leaf yield of about 1,100 kg per ha at the national level. The 2003 dry coca leaf production decreased by 1,759 metric tons, or 3.3%, over 2002.

*(4) Coca prices*

In 2003, the average price paid for coca leaf on the illegal market was 2.22 US$/kg, with a maximum of US$3.35 in the month of February in Monzon, and a minimum of US$1.02 in the month of April in the Apurimac valley. This represented a decline of 11% compared to last year's average coca leaf price of 2.48 US$/kg.

*(5) Opium cultivation and production*

The UNODC-supported national illicit crop monitoring system has not yet established a reliable methodology for the detection of opium poppy in Peru and no data was available for 2003.

Opium poppy cultivation is considered negligible in Peru. In 2003, DIRANDRO reported a decrease of opium poppy eradication and seizures, indicating that the level of opium poppy cultivation is not expanding.

*(6) Eradication*

In 2003, the Peruvian Government reported the eradication of 11,312 hectares of coca, of which 7,022 hectares (62 percent) under programmed illicit crop elimination campaigns and 4,291 hectares (38 percent) under farmers' voluntary coca reduction initiatives in exchange for sustainable livelihood schemes.

**Fact Sheet: Peru**

Source:UNODC survey report, available at www.unodc.org/unodc/en/crop_monitoring

| | |
|---|---|
| Coca cultivation: | 44,200 ha against 46,700 ha in 2002 (or a 5.4% decline) |

2002-2003 trends in some areas:

| | |
|---|---|
| Upper Huallaga: - | 11% |
| Aguaytia: - | 52% |
| Apurimac: | +1% |
| La convención - Lares: | + 1% |
| Central Sleva: | -29% |
| Others | -64% |

| | |
|---|---|
| Total dry coca leaf production in 2003: | 50,790 metric tons (3.3% increase over 2002) |
| Potential coca base/cocaine production in 2003: | 155 metric tons against 160 metric tons in 2002 |
| Average annual coca base price in 2003: | US$305/kg |
| Total potential farm-gate value of coca leaf: | US$112 million |
| Opium poppy cultivation : | no estimate, but probably low level |
| Reported eradication (CORAH and DEVIDA) | in 2002: Coca bush: 7,200 ha    (+ 13% from 2001) in 2003: Coca bush: 11, 300 ha (+57% from 2002) |

*Graphs, tables and maps: Peru 2003*

**Peru, coca cultivation, in ha, 1990 – 2003**

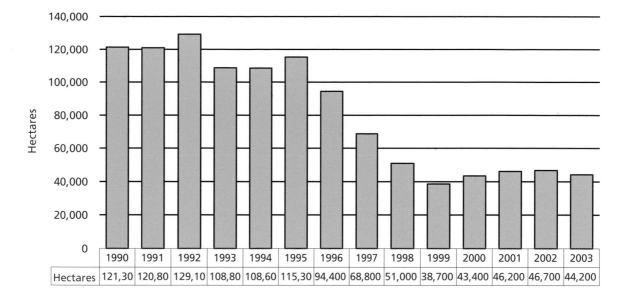

| | 1990 | 1991 | 1992 | 1993 | 1994 | 1995 | 1996 | 1997 | 1998 | 1999 | 2000 | 2001 | 2002 | 2003 |
|---|---|---|---|---|---|---|---|---|---|---|---|---|---|---|
| Hectares | 121,30 | 120,80 | 129,10 | 108,80 | 108,60 | 115,30 | 94,400 | 68,800 | 51,000 | 38,700 | 43,400 | 46,200 | 46,700 | 44,200 |

**Peru, main areas of coca cultivation 2001 – 2003**

| Area | 2002 | 2003 | Change 2002 - 2003 | Percentage of 2003 Total |
|---|---|---|---|---|
| Alto Huallaga | 15,290 | 13,650 | -11% | 31% |
| Aguaytia | 1,070 | 510 | -52% | 1% |
| Apurimac | 14,170 | 14,300 | 1% | 32% |
| La Convencion - Lares | 12,170 | 12,340 | 1% | 28% |
| Central Selva | 350 | 250 | -29% | 1% |
| Inambari - Tambopata | 2,430 | 2,260 | -7% | 5% |
| San Gaban | n.a. | 470 | | 1% |
| Others | 1,250 | 450 | -64% | 1% |
| Total | 46,700 | 44,200 | -5% | 100% |

**Peru, potential cocaine production, 1990-2003**

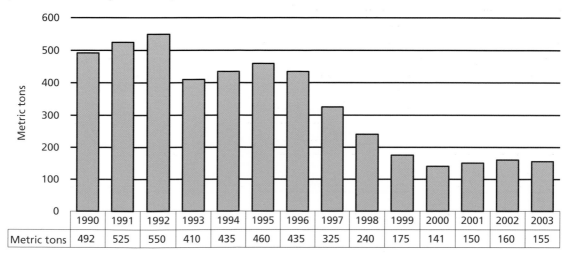

| | 1990 | 1991 | 1992 | 1993 | 1994 | 1995 | 1996 | 1997 | 1998 | 1999 | 2000 | 2001 | 2002 | 2003 |
|---|---|---|---|---|---|---|---|---|---|---|---|---|---|---|
| Metric tons | 492 | 525 | 550 | 410 | 435 | 460 | 435 | 325 | 240 | 175 | 141 | 150 | 160 | 155 |

241

## Peru coca cultivation in 2002

Source: UNODC Peru Coca Survey 2003

**Peru, farmgate prices of coca leaf 1990-2003 (US$/kg)**

|  | 1990 | 1991 | 1992 | 1993 | 1994 | 1995 | 1996 | 1997 | 1998 | 1999 | 2000 | 2001 | 2002 | 2003 |
|---|---|---|---|---|---|---|---|---|---|---|---|---|---|---|
| January | 0.7 | 0.8 | 1.1 | 4.4 | 1.5 | 3.0 | 0.4 | 0.6 | 0.6 | 1.8 | 1.6 | 2.0 | 2.6 | 2.3 |
| February | 0.9 | 1.6 | 1.7 | 3.5 | 1.6 | 3.0 | 0.4 | 0.6 | 0.7 | 1.4 | 1.3 | 2.1 | 2.6 | 2.4 |
| March | 0.8 | 1.6 | 1.7 | 1.7 | 1.6 | 2.6 | 0.4 | 0.6 | 0.7 | 1.7 | 1.6 | 2.1 | 2.3 | 2.0 |
| April | 0.5 | 1.5 | 2.6 | 1.3 | 1.6 | 1.7 | 0.5 | 0.6 | 0.6 | 1.6 | 1.7 | 2.3 | 2.2 | 1.9 |
| May | 0.5 | 1.5 | 1.9 | 1.7 | 1.6 | 0.9 | 0.5 | 0.6 | 1.0 | 1.6 | 1.9 | 2.4 | 2.3 | 1.9 |
| June | 0.4 | 1.7 | 2.2 | 1.3 | 1.8 | 0.7 | 0.7 | 0.6 | 1.0 | 1.4 | 2.0 | 2.5 | 2.5 | 1.8 |
| July | 0.4 | 1.6 | 2.2 | 1.0 | 2.6 | 0.4 | 0.9 | 0.9 | 1.1 | 1.3 | 2.1 | 2.5 | 2.3 | 2.1 |
| August | 0.4 | 1.5 | 3.0 | 1.9 | 3.0 | 0.4 | 1.0 | 1.3 | 2.1 | 1.8 | 2.3 | 2.7 | 2.9 | 2.1 |
| September | 1.2 | 1.7 | 4.4 | 2.1 | 3.0 | 0.4 | 1.0 | 1.3 | 2.0 | 2.2 | 2.7 | 2.7 | 2.8 | 2.2 |
| October | 1.6 | 1.7 | 2.6 | 2.1 | 3.9 | 0.4 | 1.0 | 0.9 | 1.5 | 2.5 | 2.8 | 2.5 | 2.5 | 2.4 |
| November | 0.9 | 1.3 | 2.6 | 1.3 | 4.4 | 0.4 | 0.6 | 0.7 | 1.4 | 2.0 | 2.2 | 2.0 | 2.4 | 2.2 |
| December | 0.9 | 1.0 | 3.5 | 1.3 | 3.0 | 0.4 | 0.6 | 0.7 | 1.7 | 1.6 | 1.9 | 1.9 | 2.3 | 1.9 |
| Annual Average US$/kg | 0.8 | 1.5 | 2.5 | 2.0 | 2.5 | 1.2 | 0.7 | 0.8 | 1.2 | 1.7 | 2.0 | 2.3 | 2.5 | 2.1 |
| In constant US$ of 2003 | 1.1 | 2.0 | 3.3 | 2.5 | 3.1 | 1.4 | 0.8 | 0.9 | 1.6 | 2.4 | 2.2 | 2.5 | 2.5 | 2.1 |

**Peru, Upper Huallaga, farmgate prices of coca leaf 1991-2003 (US$/kg)**

|  | 1991 | 1992 | 1993 | 1994 | 1995 | 1996 | 1997 | 1998 | 1999 | 2000 | 2001 | 2002 | 2003 |
|---|---|---|---|---|---|---|---|---|---|---|---|---|---|
| January | 1.1 | 1.3 | 3.8 | 1.5 | 3.0 | 0.4 | 0.6 | 0.7 | 1.9 | 2.6 | 2.2 | 3.9 | 2.2 |
| February | 1.3 | 1.5 | 3.2 | 1.6 | 2.9 | 0.4 | 0.6 | 0.7 | 2.1 | 2.5 | 2.2 | 3.5 | 2.4 |
| March | 1.6 | 2.0 | 2.2 | 1.6 | 2.4 | 0.4 | 0.6 | 0.7 | 2.0 | 2.4 | 2.3 | 2.7 | 1.9 |
| April | 1.5 | 2.1 | 1.6 | 1.6 | 1.7 | 0.5 | 0.6 | 0.9 | 2.1 | 1.9 | 2.6 | 3.0 | 2.1 |
| May | 1.6 | 2.2 | 1.5 | 1.7 | 1.1 | 0.6 | 0.6 | 1.1 | 1.8 | 2.2 | 2.5 | 3.2 | 2.0 |
| June | 1.6 | 2.1 | 1.4 | 2.0 | 0.7 | 0.7 | 0.7 | 1.3 | 1.6 | 2.3 | 2.7 | 3.8 | 2.2 |
| July | 1.6 | 2.5 | 1.4 | 2.5 | 0.5 | 0.8 | 0.9 | 1.9 | 1.7 | 2.3 | 2.6 | 3.0 | 2.4 |
| August | 1.6 | 3.2 | 1.7 | 2.9 | 0.4 | 1.0 | 1.2 | 2.2 | 2.1 | 2.6 | 2.9 | 3.3 | 2.4 |
| September | 1.6 | 3.3 | 2.0 | 3.3 | 0.4 | 1.0 | 1.2 | 2.4 | 2.8 | 3.0 | 3.1 | 3.1 | 2.5 |
| October | 1.6 | 3.2 | 1.8 | 3.8 | 0.4 | 0.9 | 1.0 | 2.0 | 3.1 | 3.0 | 2.8 | 2.2 | 2.6 |
| November | 1.4 | 2.9 | 1.6 | 3.8 | 0.4 | 0.8 | 0.8 | 1.8 | 3.0 | 2.4 | 1.8 | 2.4 | 2.5 |
| December | 1.2 | 3.5 | 1.4 | 3.5 | 0.4 | 0.6 | 0.7 | 1.9 | 2.8 | 1.9 | 1.9 | 2.4 | 1.9 |
| Annual Average US$/kg | 1.5 | 2.5 | 2.0 | 2.5 | 1.2 | 0.7 | 0.8 | 1.5 | 2.3 | 2.4 | 2.5 | 3.0 | 2.3 |
| In constant US$ of 2003 | 2.0 | 3.3 | 2.5 | 3.1 | 1.4 | 0.8 | 0.9 | 1.6 | 2.5 | 2.6 | 2.6 | 3.1 | 2.3 |

**Peru, average dry coca leaf prices for Peru and for Upper Huallaga, US$/kg, 1990-2003**

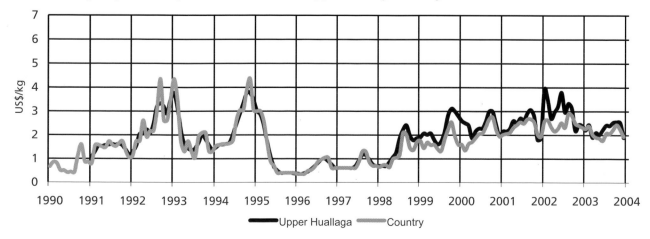

**Peru, coca cultivation and reported eradication, in ha, 1983 – 2003 (source CORAH)**

| Years | Eradication (ha) | Cultivation (ha) |
|-------|------------------|------------------|
| 1983 | 700 | 45,000 |
| 1984 | 3,100 | 60,000 |
| 1985 | 4,800 | 70,000 |
| 1986 | 2,600 | 107,500 |
| 1987 | 400 | 110,146 |
| 1988 | 5,100 | 111,875 |
| 1989 | 1,300 | 123,007 |
| 1990 | - | 121,300 |
| 1991 | - | 120,800 |
| 1992 | - | 129,100 |
| 1993 | - | 108,800 |
| 1994 | - | 108,600 |
| 1995 | - | 115,300 |
| 1996 | 1,300 | 94,400 |
| 1997 | 3,500 | 68,800 |
| 1998 | 7,800 | 51,000 |
| 1999 | 14,700 | 38,700 |
| 2000 | 6,200 | 43,400 |
| 2001 | 6,400 | 46,200 |
| 2002 | 7,200 | 46,700 |
| 2003 | 11,300 | 44,200 |

**Peru, cultivation and reported eradication, in ha, 1983 - 2003**

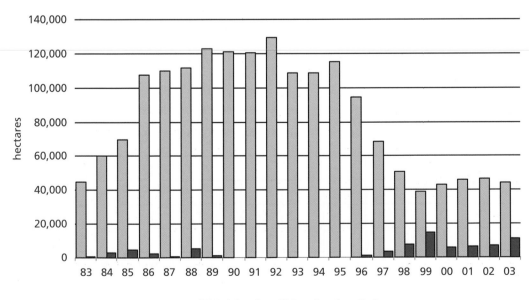

## 3.2.3. Bolivia

Under its Illicit Crop Monitoring Programme, UNODC has been assisting the Bolivian Government in the implementation of a national coca monitoring system. For the first time, in 2003, the Bolivian project was extended to the national level and consequently, able to provide estimates for coca cultivation at the national level. Bolivia is the third largest producer of coca in the world. It trails far behind Colombia, the world's largest producer.

**Results of the 2003 UNODC Bolivia Annual Survey**

### (1) Coca Cultivation

The results of the first national survey revealed that 23,600 hectares of coca bush were cultivated in Bolivia in 2003. This was 9% of the world's coca cultivation in 2003.

### (2) Geographical Distribution

Most of the coca cultivatin in Bolivia takes place in the Yungas of La Paz. Between 2002 and 2003, coca cultivation showed a +18% increase in this area, which accounted for 71% of the total coca cultivation in 2003. It is also in this area that most of the traditional coca cultivation takes place. The remaining 29% of coca cultivation was grown in the Chapare area of the Cochabamba department. Comparison with 2002 is not possible over the Chapare area. However, reports from DIRECO supported by anecdotal information indicated that coca cultivation was on the decrease following the sustained eradication campaign in this area.

### (3) Coca Production

The overall estimate of 23,600 ha for cultivation quoted above includes the 12,000 ha permitted by Bolivian Law No 1008, "Law on the Regime Applicable to Coca and Controlled Substances," 1988, for traditional uses. The overall area under coca cultivation produced an estimated 28,300 metric tons of drug coca leaf, of which 17,100 metric tons were estimated to have been used for cocaine production. The potential cocaine production in Bolivia amounted to 60 metric tons in 2003.

### (4) Coca prices

Prices of dry coca leaf remained stable throughout 2003, averaging US$5.4 per kilogram.

### (5) Eradication

The eradication of coca crops is done manually and takes place mainly in Chapare. In 2003, the Government of Bolivia eradicated 10,100 ha of coca fields, similar to the levels reported since 1998.

**Fact Sheet:**

Source:UNODC survey report, available at www.unodc.org/unodc/en/crop_monitoring

| | | |
|---|---|---|
| Coca cultivation including 12,000ha cultivation allowed by law: | | 23,600 ha |
| Distribution of Coca Cultivation in Bolivia 2003: | Yungas of La Paz | 16,200 ha (69%) |
| | Chapare area | 7,300 ha (31%) |
| | Apolo | 50 ha (0.2%) |
| Detailed by provinces in Yungas of La Paz: | Caranavi | +81% |
| | North Yungas | +14% |
| | South Yungas | +16% |
| | Inquisivi | +8% |
| | Murillo | +39% |
| Dry coca leaf yield: | traditional area: | 936 kg/ha/year |
| | Elsewhere (mainly Chapare): | 1,798 kg/ha/year |
| Average dry coca leaf price: | | 5.4US$/kg |
| Potential farm-gate value of coca leaf production: | | US$ 153 million |
| Potential cocaine production: | | 60 metric tons |
| Data communicated by DIRECO: | | |
| Eradication at country level: | | |
| | in 2002: | 11,853 ha |
| | in 2003: | 10,087 ha |

*Graphs, tables and maps: Bolivia*

**Bolivia, coca cultivation, in ha, 1990 – 2003**

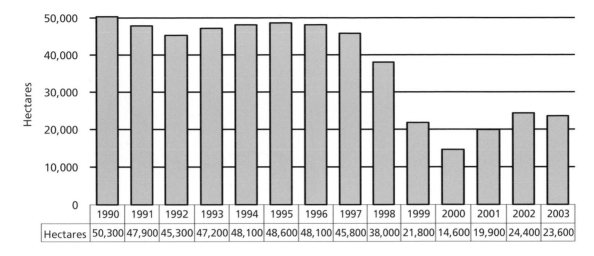

| Hectares | 1990 | 1991 | 1992 | 1993 | 1994 | 1995 | 1996 | 1997 | 1998 | 1999 | 2000 | 2001 | 2002 | 2003 |
|---|---|---|---|---|---|---|---|---|---|---|---|---|---|---|
| | 50,300 | 47,900 | 45,300 | 47,200 | 48,100 | 48,600 | 48,100 | 45,800 | 38,000 | 21,800 | 14,600 | 19,900 | 24,400 | 23,600 |

**Bolivia, Distribution of coca cultivation (2003 UNODC survey)**

| Area | 2003 Coca Cultivation | % of 2003 total |
|---|---|---|
| Yungas of La Paz | 16,200 | 69% |
| Chapare area | 7,300 | 31% |
| Apolo | 50 | 0.2% |
| Rounded total | 23,600 | |

**Bolivia, coca cultivation by municipalities (2002 UNODC survey)**

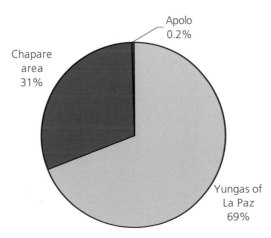

Coca cultivation for 2003 in the Yungas of La Paz by municipality

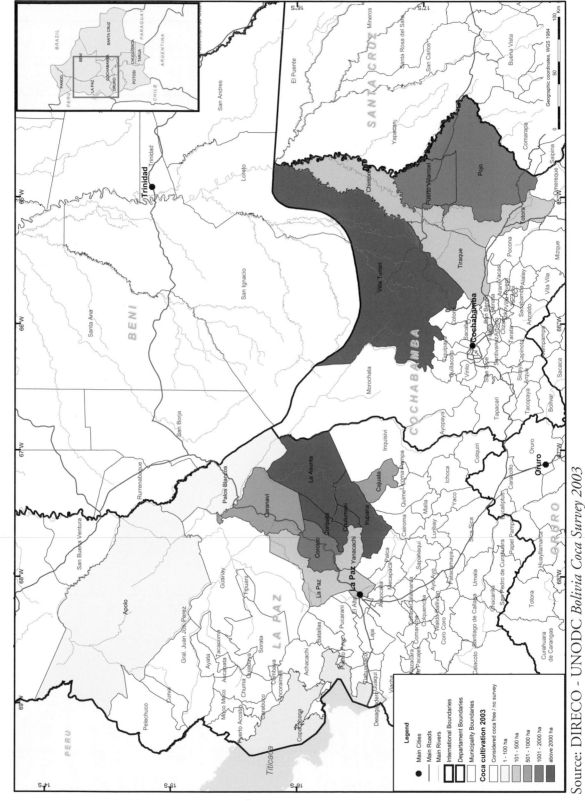

Source: DIRECO - UNODC *Bolivia Coca Survey 2003*

## Bolivia, potential cocaine production, 1990 - 2003

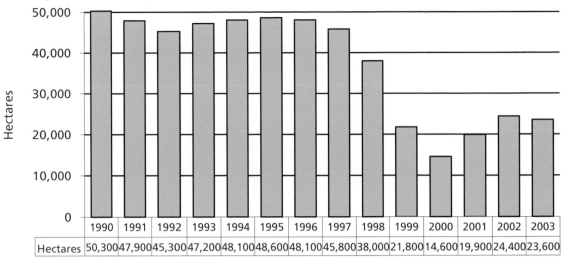

| | 1990 | 1991 | 1992 | 1993 | 1994 | 1995 | 1996 | 1997 | 1998 | 1999 | 2000 | 2001 | 2002 | 2003 |
|---|---|---|---|---|---|---|---|---|---|---|---|---|---|---|
| Hectares | 50,300 | 47,900 | 45,300 | 47,200 | 48,100 | 48,600 | 48,100 | 45,800 | 38,000 | 21,800 | 14,600 | 19,900 | 24,400 | 23,600 |

## Bolivia, farmgate prices of coca leaf, 1991-2003 (US$/kg)

| | 1990 | 1991 | 1992 | 1993 | 1994 | 1995 | 1996 | 1997 | 1998 | 1999 | 2000 | 2001 | 2002 | 2003 |
|---|---|---|---|---|---|---|---|---|---|---|---|---|---|---|
| January | 0.3 | 0.5 | | 1.0 | 1.1 | 1.5 | 0.9 | 1.3 | 2.1 | 1.5 | 6.0 | 5.4 | 6.1 | 5.4 |
| February | 0.3 | 1.2 | 0.9 | 1.0 | 1.1 | 1.7 | 1.4 | 1.2 | 2.0 | 1.5 | 5.1 | 5.3 | 5.8 | 5.3 |
| March | 0.3 | 1.5 | 1.0 | 1.0 | 0.6 | 1.5 | 0.9 | 1.1 | 1.3 | 1.7 | 5.4 | 5.3 | 5.7 | 5.2 |
| April | 0.2 | 1.1 | 0.8 | 1.1 | 0.9 | 1.3 | 0.9 | 1.0 | 1.4 | 2.0 | 5.7 | 5.5 | 5.7 | 5.2 |
| May | 0.4 | 0.8 | 0.9 | 1.0 | 0.9 | 1.4 | 0.9 | 1.1 | 1.3 | 2.0 | 5.9 | 5.4 | 5.6 | 5.3 |
| June | 0.6 | 1.2 | 1.0 | 1.4 | 0.9 | 1.3 | 1.3 | 1.2 | 1.5 | 2.4 | 6.0 | 5.5 | 5.6 | 5.4 |
| July | 0.8 | 0.8 | 0.8 | 1.8 | 0.7 | 1.3 | 0.8 | 1.4 | 1.5 | 2.4 | 6.0 | 5.6 | 5.7 | 5.5 |
| August | 1.0 | 1.0 | 0.9 | 1.5 | 0.8 | 1.4 | 1.1 | 1.9 | 1.4 | 3.7 | 6.0 | 5.6 | 5.7 | 5.5 |
| September | 1.1 | 1.2 | 1.2 | 1.5 | 1.2 | 1.4 | 1.7 | 2.2 | 1.5 | 4.8 | 5.3 | 5.3 | 5.4 | 5.4 |
| October | 0.7 | 0.9 | 0.9 | 1.4 | 1.6 | 1.4 | 1.4 | 2.2 | 1.4 | 4.9 | 4.8 | 5.6 | 5.4 | 5.4 |
| November | 0.5 | 1.1 | 0.9 | 1.2 | 1.8 | 1.4 | 1.3 | 2.3 | 1.4 | 4.9 | 5.3 | 5.6 | 5.4 | 5.4 |
| December | 0.3 | 0.8 | 0.9 | 1.2 | 1.7 | 1.4 | 1.2 | 2.1 | 1.4 | 5.0 | 5.3 | 5.7 | 5.5 | 5.5 |
| Annual Average | 0.5 | 1.0 | 0.9 | 1.3 | 1.1 | 1.4 | 1.1 | 1.6 | 1.5 | 3.1 | 5.6 | 5.5 | 5.6 | 5.4 |

## Bolivia, coca leaf prices, US$/kg, 1990-2003

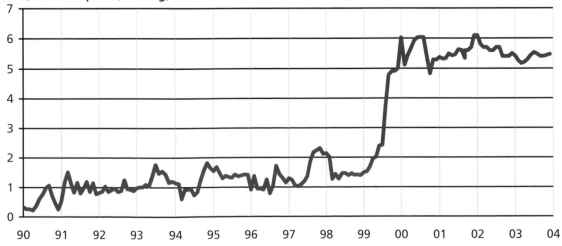

**Bolivia, reported eradication and cultivation, in ha, 1997-2003**

| Year | Eradicated (ha) | Cultivated (ha) |
|------|-----------------|-----------------|
| 1997 | 7,026 | 45,800 |
| 1998 | 11,621 | 38,000 |
| 1999 | 16,999 | 21,800 |
| 2000 | 7,953 | 19,600 |
| 2001 | 9,435 | 19,900 |
| 2002 | 11,853 | 24,400 |
| 2003 | 10,087 | 23,600 |

Source: DIRECO

**Bolivia, reported eradication and cultivation, in ha, 1997-2003**

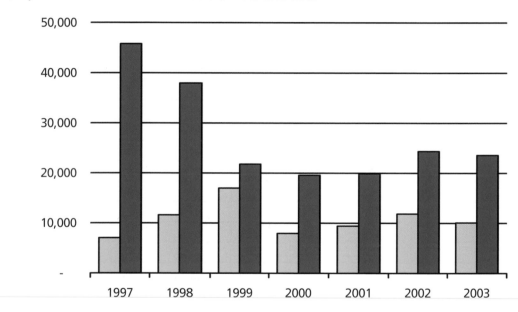

## 3.2.4. Seizure of Illicit laboratories

**MANUFACTURE**

**SEIZURES OF ILLICIT LABORATORIES**

**REPORTED FOR 2001 - 2002**

Remark: For convenience, an attempt was made to group the reported estimates by drug categories. however, due to inconsistencies and gaps in the reporting, no overall analysis of the data set was performed. Numbers are presented as reported to UNODC and should be interpreted with caution.

Source: Annual Report Questionnaire if not otherwise indicated

| Country or Territory | Year | Name of drug seized | Number of laboratories (and quantity of drug) | Source |
|---|---|---|---|---|
| | | **COCA GROUP** | | |
| **Americas** | | | | |
| North America | | | | |
| Canada | 2001 | Coca paste | 1 Lab. | |
| United States | 2001 | Cocaine | 3 Lab.(0.456 kg) | |
| | 2002 | Cocaine | 5 Lab.(1.000 kg) | |
| Subtotal North America | | | 9 Lab.(1.456 kg) | |
| South America | | | | |
| Argentina | 2001 | Cocaine | 6 Lab. | |
| | 2002 | Cocaine | 9 Lab. | |
| Bolivia | 2001 | Cocaine | 5 Lab.(334.100 kg) | F.O |
| | 2001 | Cocaine base | 1006 Lab.(4280.400 kg) | F.O |
| | 2002 | | 1 Lab.(24.500 kg) | |
| Chile | 2002 | | 1 Lab. | |
| Colombia | 2001 | Cocaine base | 470 Lab.(5229.000 kg) | |
| | 2001 | Cocaine | 1085 Lab.(5335.000 kg) | |
| | 2002 | Cocaine base | 1273 Lab. | |
| | 2002 | Cocaine | 161 Lab. | |
| Peru | 2001 | Cocaine base | 64 Lab. | |
| | 2001 | Cocaine | 2 Lab.(3000.000 kg) | |
| Venezuela | 2001 | Cocaine | 2 Lab. | |
| Subtotal South America | | | 4085 Lab.(18203.000 kg) | |
| Total Americas | | | 4094 Lab.(18204.456 kg) | |
| **Asia** | | | | |
| East and South-East Asia | | | | |
| Hong Kong SAR, China | 2001 | Cocaine (crack) | 2 Lab. | |
| | 2002 | Cocaine | 2 Lab. | |
| Thailand | 2001 | Cocaine | 1 Lab. | Govt. |
| Subtotal East and South-East Asia | | | 5 Lab. | |
| Total Asia | | | 5 Lab. | |
| **Europe** | | | | |
| Eastern Europe | | | | |
| Slovenia | 2002 | Cocaine base | 1 Lab. | |
| Subtotal Eastern Europe | | | 1 Lab. | |
| Western Europe | | | | |
| France | 2002 | Cocaine | 1 Lab. | |
| Germany | 2001 | Cocaine | 1 Lab. | |
| | 2002 | | 1 Lab. | |
| Spain | 2001 | Synthetic cocaine | 1 Lab. | |
| | 2001 | Cocaine | 4 Lab. | |
| Subtotal Western Europe | | | 8 Lab. | |
| Total Europe | | | 9 Lab. | |
| Coca group | | | 4108 Lab.(18204.456 kg) | |

# 3.3. Cannabis

## 3.3.1. Morocco

Until recently, the information available on cannabis cultivation in Morocco pointed to the fact that it had been increasing since the 1980's. However, estimates of the actual size of the area under cannabis cultivation and of the production of hashish in Morocco have been a debated and, at times, controversial. In February 2003, however, the Moroccan government signed a cooperation agreement with UNODC to conduct a survey on illicit drug production (cannabis) and organized crime in Morocco. The first survey on cannabis production was launched in July 2003.

**Results of the 2003 UNODC Morocco Cannabis Survey**

### (1) Cannabis Cultivation

The survey estimated cannabis cultivation at about 134,000 hectares over the total area covered by the survey (14,000km$^2$, five provinces of the Northern Region). This represents 10% of the area surveyed, 27% of the arable lands of the surveyed territory, and 1.5% of Morocco's total arable land (8.7 million ha).

### (2) Cannabis and cannabis resin production

The total potential production of raw cannabis was estimated to be around 47,000 metric tons and the potential cannabis resin production was estimated at 3,080 metric tons.

### (3) Cannabis producers

In the cannabis production area, 75% of the douars (villages) and 96,600 farms were found to produce cannabis in 2003, representing a total population of about 800,000 persons (the 1994 census gave a figure of 1.65 million for the rural population in the area), i.e. 2.5% of Morocco's total population, estimated at 29.6 million in 2002.

### (4) Cannabis producers' revenues

The average income per family generated by cannabis was estimated at Dh 20,900 (US$ 2,200) and represented on average half (51%) of the total annual income of a cannabis producing family in 2003 (Dh 41,335, US$ 4,351). By comparison, the average annual income of the 1,496,000 farms in Morocco was Dh 42,874 (US$ 4,513) i.e. more or less similar to the annual income of a cannabis producing family.

The total income per capita generated by cannabis was estimated at Dh 2,237 (US$ 267) for a total annual income of Dh 4,970 (US$ 523). In comparison, the GDP per capita was about Dh 12,000 (US$ 1,260) in Morocco in 2002.

### (6) Trafficking and overall turnover of the market of cannabis resin (hashish) of Moroccan origin

In 2001, cannabis resin seizures by the Moroccan authorities amounted to 61.35 metric tons and ranked third after Spain and Pakistan. It represented 7% of the total cannabis resin seizures in the world. The fact that Spain came first (57% of the world seizures and 75% of the European seizures in 2001) is evidence of the importance of the Spanish territory as a transit zone for Moroccan hashish sold on the European market.

In 2002, around 735 mt of cannabis resins were seized in western Europe and 66 mt in Morocco (801 mt in total). Assuming roughly the same amount of cannabis resin would have been seized in 2003, around 2,300 metric tons would be left from the 2003 Moroccan cannabis resin production for consumption. Based on an average retail price of US$ 5.4 per gram in Western Europe in 2003, the total market turnover of Moroccan cannabis resin could be estimated at US$ 12 billion (i.e. Dh 114 billion, or 10 billion). Most of this turn-over is generated by the trafficking networks operating in the European markets. Because of the large degree of assumption, these estimates should be treated with caution.

**Fact Sheet : Morocco 2003**

Source: UNODC survey report, available at www.unodc.org/unodc/en/crop_monitoring

| | |
|---|---|
| Cannabis cultivation: | 134,000 ha (of which 12% on irrigated land) |
| Gross cannabis production: | 47,400 metric tons |
| Potential resin production: | 3,080 metric tons |
| Number of households cultivating cannabis: | 96,600 households<br>(66 % of the 146,000 rural households in the study area and 6.5 % of the 1,496,000 agricultural households in Morocco) |
| Total population involved in cannabis cultivation: | 800,000 people<br>(2.7 % of the country's population of 29.6 million in 2002) |
| Cannabis cultivation in % of the total arable land in the study area: | 27 % (and 1.5 % of the 8.7 million of ha of arable land in Morocco) |
| Total farmers' income from cannabis: | Dh 2 billion / US$ 214 million |
| Average annual household income from cannabis: | Dh 20,900 / US$ 2,200 (out of a total annual household income of 41,335 Dh /US$ 4 352, or 51%) |
| Average cannabis income per capita: | Dh 2,536 / US$ 267 (out of a total annual income per capita of 4,970 Dh / US$ 523). (2002 GDP per capita: Dh 13,445 / US$ 1,260 ) |
| In % of 2002 Moroccan GDP : | 0,57 % (with a GDP of US$ 37,3 billion) |
| 2002 seizure of cannabis resin: | 735 mt in Western Europe (¾ in Spain)<br>66 mt in Morocco |
| Annual turn-over of international trade in cannabis resin: | €10 billion (equivalent to Dh 114 billion or about US$ 12 billion) |

*Graphs, tables, maps: Morocco 2003*

## Morocco, provincial cannabis cultivation

| Province | Total area (ha) | Area surveyed (ha) | Cannabis cultivation (ha) | Cannabis cultivation in % of surveyed area % |
|---|---|---|---|---|
| Al Hoceima | 375,008 | 346,022 | 22,831 | 7% |
| Chefchaouen | 529,503 | 529,503 | 66,699 | 13% |
| Larache | 278,968 | 195,888 | 11,966 | 6% |
| Taounate | 527,568 | 211,252 | 25,720 | 12% |
| Tétouan | 245,771 | 94,157 | 6,889 | 7% |
| Total | 1,956,818 | 1,376,822 | 134,105 | 10% |

**Morocco, provincial cannabis cultivation (ha) 2003**

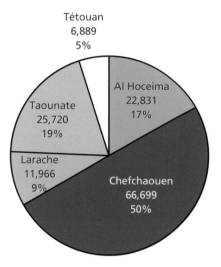

**Morocco, provincial raw cannabis production (mt) 2003**

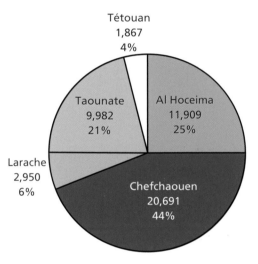

## Morocco, provincial raw cannabis production 2003

| Province | Cannabis Yield (kg/ha) | |
|---|---|---|
| | Rainfed | Irrigated |
| Al Hoceima | 428 | 945 |
| Chefchaouen | 292 | 504 |
| Larache | 239 | 295 |
| Taounate | 361 | 589 |
| Tetouan | 256 | 370 |
| Average | 330 | 638 |

**Morocco, potential farmers income from cannabis 2003**

| Production | Raw cannabis (metric tons) | Equivalent in powder cannabis (metric tons) | Price (Dh / kg) | Estimated value (Dh) | Estimated value (US$) |
|---|---|---|---|---|---|
| 66% raw cannabis | 31,279 | *2,033* | 35 | 1,094,778,300 | 115,239,821 |
| 34% cannabis powder (sandouk) | 16,113 | 1,046 | 900 | 941,705,065 | 99,126,849 |
| Total (rounded) | 47,400 | 3,080 | | 2,036,000,000 | 214,000,000 |

**Morocco, number of farms and farmers cultivating cannabis 2003**

| Province | Total number of farmers surveyed | Number of farmers cultivating cannabis | % of farmers cultivating cannabis | Total number of farmers in the surveyed area | Estimated number of farmers cultivating cannabis | Average househ old size | Total population benefiting from cannabis cultivation |
|---|---|---|---|---|---|---|---|
| Al Hoceima | 490 | 272 | 56 | 30,500 | 16,931 | 9.32 | 157,793 |
| Chefchaouen | 724 | 680 | 94 | 52,317 | 49,138 | 8.32 | 408,824 |
| Larache | 253 | 96 | 38 | 21,524 | 8,167 | 7.39 | 60,356 |
| Taounate | 463 | 229 | 49 | 33,965 | 16,799 | 8.11 | 136,241 |
| Tetouan | 177 | 113 | 64 | 8,735 | 5,577 | 7.3 | 40,709 |
| Total | 2,107 | 1,390 | 66 | 147,041 | 96,612 | 8.03 | 803,923 |

**Morocco, share of cannabis in the household cannabis farmer's income (in %) 2003**

| Provinces | Cannabis | Cereales | Other agricultural productions | Livestock | Other incomes |
|---|---|---|---|---|---|
| Al Hoceima | 62 | 11 | 7 | 8 | 11 |
| Chefchaouen | 62 | 11 | 6 | 8 | 12 |
| Larache | 15 | 12 | 26 | 30 | 17 |
| Taounate | 33 | 10 | 18 | 6 | 32 |
| Tetouan | 39 | 13 | 14 | 16 | 18 |
| Average | 51 | 11 | 11 | 11 | 16 |

**Morocco, share of cannabis in the cannabis farmer's household income 2003**

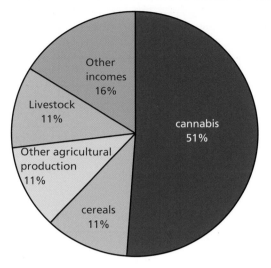

**Morocco, average cannabis parcel size (ha) 2003**

| Province | Ha |
|---|---|
| Al Hoceima | 0,19 |
| Chefchaouen | 0,37 |
| Larache | 0,77 |
| Taounate | 0,32 |
| Tetouan | 0,40 |
| **Five provinces** | **0,30** |

**Morocco, average cannabis area per farmer 2003**

| Province | Average cannabis area per farmer | |
|---|---|---|
| | Rainfed (ha) | Irrigated (ha) |
| Al Hoceima | 1,9 | 0,5 |
| Chefchaouen | 1,4 | 0,2 |
| Larache | 1,4 | 0,2 |
| Taounate | 0,8 | 0,1 |
| Tetouan | 0,8 | 0,2 |
| Moyenne | 1,3 | 0,3 |

**Morocco, comparing incomes from rainfed cannabis and rainfed barley per hectare 2003**

| Province | Cannabis price (Dh /kg) | Yield rainfed cannabis (kg /ha ) | Income rainfed cannabis (Dh/ha) | Barley price (Dh/kg) | Yield rainfed barley (kg/ha) | Income rainfed barley (Dh/ha) |
|---|---|---|---|---|---|---|
| Al Hoceima | 38.11 | 428 | 16,311 | 2 | 870 | 1,740 |
| Chefchaouen | 31.34 | 292 | 9,151 | 2 | 690 | 1,380 |
| Larache | 30.00 | 239 | 7,170 | 2 | 550 | 1,100 |
| Taounate | 41.76 | 361 | 15,075 | 2 | 700 | 1,400 |
| Tetouan | 42.66 | 256 | 10,920 | 2 | 690 | 1,380 |
| **Average** | 35.26 | 330 | 11,635 | 2 | 730 | 1,460 |

**Morocco, Northern Provinces: Cannabis cultivation in 2003 (per commune)**

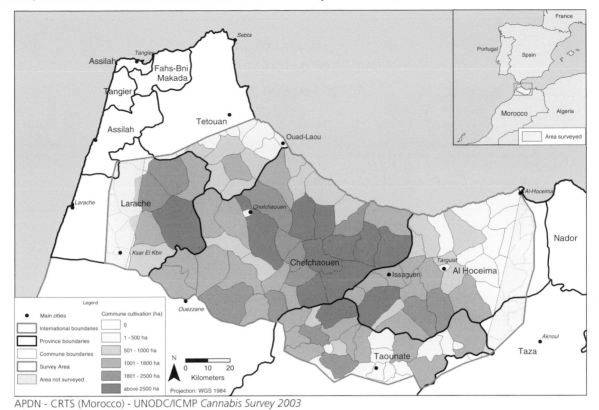

APDN - CRTS (Morocco) - UNODC/ICMP *Cannabis Survey 2003*

**Morocco, Northern Provinces: Cannabis production in 2003 (per commune)**

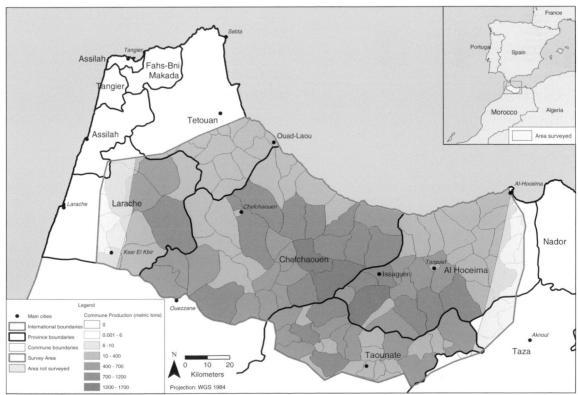

APDN - CRTS (Morocco ) - UNODC/ICMP *Cannabis Survey 2003*

## 3.3.2. Seizure of Illicit laboratories

**MANUFACTURE**

**SEIZURES OF ILLICIT LABORATORIES**

**REPORTED FOR 2001 - 2002**

Remark: For convenience, an attempt was made to group the reported estimates by drug categories. however, due to inconsistencies and gaps in the reporting, no overall analysis of the data set was performed. Numbers are presented as reported to UNODC and should be interpreted with caution.

Source: Annual Report Questionnaire if not otherwise indicated

| Country or Territory | Year | Name of drug seized | Number of laboratories (and quantity of drug) | Source |
|---|---|---|---|---|
| | | **CANNABIS GROUP** | | |
| **Americas** | | | | |
| North America | | | | |
| Canada | 2002 | | 1 Lab. | |
| Subtotal North America | | | 1 Lab. | |
| Total Americas | | | 1 Lab. | |
| **Europe** | | | | |
| Eastern Europe | | | | |
| Bulgaria | 2001 | Cannabis liquid | 1 Lab. | |
| Poland | 2002 | Cannabis | 32 Lab. | |
| Russian Federation | 2001 | Cannabis herb | 137 Lab.(920.549 kg) | |
| | 2002 | Cannabis herb | 121 Lab. | |
| Subtotal Eastern Europe | | | 291 Lab.(920.549 kg) | |
| Western Europe | | | | |
| Denmark | 2001 | Cannabis resin | 1 Lab. | |
| Subtotal Western Europe | | | 1 Lab. | |
| Total Europe | | | 292 Lab.(920.549 kg) | |
| Cannabis group | | | 293 Lab.(920.549 kg) | |

# 3.4. Amphetamine-type stimulants

## 3.4.1. Seizure of Illicit laboratories

**MANUFACTURE**

**SEIZURES OF ILLICIT LABORATORIES**

**REPORTED FOR 2001 - 2002**

Remark: For convenience, an attempt was made to group the reported estimates by drug categories. however, due to inconsistencies and gaps in the reporting, no overall analysis of the data set was performed. Numbers are presented as reported to UNODC and should be interpreted with caution.

Source: Annual Report Questionnaire if not otherwise indicated

| Country or Territory | Year | Name of drug seized | Number of laboratories (and quantity of drug) | Source |
|---|---|---|---|---|
| **COMBINED AMPHETAMINE, METHAMPHETAMINE GROUP** | | | | |
| **Europe** | | | | |
| Eastern Europe | | | | |
| Lithuania | 2002 | Amphetamine, methamphetamine | 2 Lab.(1460.000 kg) | |
| Russian Federation | 2001 | Methamphetamine, methcathinone and amphetamine | 71 Lab.(0.061 kg) | |
| Subtotal Eastern Europe | | | 73 Lab.(1460.061 kg) | |
| Total Europe | | | 73 Lab.(1460.061 kg) | |
| **Oceania** | | | | |
| Oceania | | | | |
| Australia | 2001 | Methamphetamine, amphetamine | 201 Lab*. | |
| | 2002 | Methamphetamine, amphetamine | 240 Lab*. | |
| Subtotal Oceania | | | 441 Lab. | |
| Total Oceania | | | 441 Lab. | |
| Combined amphetamine, methamphetamine group | | | 514 Lab.(1460.061 kg) | |
| **AMPHETAMINE GROUP** | | | | |
| **Americas** | | | | |
| North America | | | | |
| United States | 2001 | Amphetamine | 52 Lab.(5.300 kg) | |
| | 2002 | Amphetamine | 0 Lab.(0.000 kg) | |
| Subtotal North America | | | 52 Lab.(5.300 kg) | |
| South America | | | | |
| Chile | 2002 | Amphetamine | 1 Lab. | |
| Subtotal South America | | | 1 Lab. | |
| Total Americas | | | 53 Lab.(5.300 kg) | |
| **Europe** | | | | |
| Eastern Europe | | | | |
| Bulgaria | 2002 | Amphetamine | 2 Lab.(1500.000 kg) | |
| Estonia | 2002 | Amphetamine | 1 Lab. | |
| Poland | 2001 | Amphetamine | 12 Lab.(86.000 kg) | |
| | 2002 | Amphetamine | 15 Lab. | |
| Russian Federation | 2002 | Amphetamine | 97 Lab. | |
| Subtotal Eastern Europe | | | 127 Lab.(1586.000 kg) | |

\* Fiscal year 2001: July 2000 - June 2001; \*\* Fiscal year 2002: July 2001 - June 2002

259

| Country or Territory | Year | Name of drug seized | Number of laboratories (and quantity of drug) | Source |
|---|---|---|---|---|
| **Western Europe** | | | | |
| Belgium | 2001 | Amphetamine | 1 Lab. | |
| | 2002 | Amphetamine | 1 Lab. | |
| | 2002 | | 1 Lab. | |
| Denmark | 2001 | Amphetamine | 1 Lab. | |
| France | 2002 | Amphetamine | 1 Lab. | |
| Germany | 2001 | Amphetamine | 1 Lab. | |
| | 2002 | | 2 Lab. | |
| Netherlands | 2001 | Amphetamine | 10 Lab. | |
| | 2002 | Amphetamine | 10 Lab. | |
| Sweden | 2001 | Amphetamine | 3 Lab. | |
| United Kingdom | 2001 | Amphetamine | 5 Lab. | |
| | 2002 | Amphetamine | 1 Lab. | |
| Subtotal Western Europe | | | 37 Lab. | |
| Total Europe | | | 164 Lab.(1586.000 kg) | |
| Amphetamine group | | | 217 Lab.(1591.300 kg) | |

## METHAMPHETAMINE GROUP

| Country or Territory | Year | Name of drug seized | Number of laboratories (and quantity of drug) | Source |
|---|---|---|---|---|
| **Africa** | | | | |
| Southern Africa | | | | |
| South Africa | 2002 | Methamphetamine | 1 Lab. | |
| Subtotal Southern Africa | | | 1 Lab. | |
| Total Africa | | | 1 Lab. | |
| **Americas** | | | | |
| North America | | | | |
| Canada | 2001 | Methamphetamine | 13 Lab. | |
| | 2002 | Methamphetamine | 14 Lab. | |
| Mexico | 2001 | Methamphetamine | 19 Lab. | |
| | 2002 | Methamphetamine | 10 Lab. | |
| United States | 2001 | Methamphetamine | 7990 Lab.(865.400 kg) | |
| | 2002 | Methamphetamine | 9024 Lab.(3367.000 kg) | |
| Subtotal North America | | | 17070 Lab.(4232.400 kg) | |
| Total Americas | | | 17070 Lab.(4232.400 kg) | |
| **Asia** | | | | |
| East and South-East Asia | | | | |
| China | 2001 | Methamphetamine | 44 Lab. | |
| | 2002 | Methamphetamine | 13 Lab. | |
| Korea (Republic of) | 2001 | Methamphetamine | 1 Lab.(10.000 kg) | |
| Myanmar | 2001 | Methamphetamine | 5 Lab. | |
| | 2002 | Methamphetamine | 4 Lab. | |
| Philippines | 2001 | Methamphetamine | 3 Lab. | |
| | 2002 | Methamphetamine | 4 Lab. | |
| Thailand | 2001 | Methamphetamine | 10 Lab. | Govt. |
| Subtotal East and South-East Asia | | | 84 Lab.(10.000 kg) | |
| Total Asia | | | 84 Lab.(10.000 kg) | |
| **Europe** | | | | |
| Eastern Europe | | | | |
| Bulgaria | 2001 | Methamphetamine | 1 Lab. | INCB |
| Czech Republic | 2001 | Methamphetamine | 28 Lab. | |

| Country or Territory | Year | Name of drug seized | Number of laboratories (and quantity of drug) | Source |
|---|---|---|---|---|
| Czech Republic | 2002 | Methamphetamine | 104 Lab. | |
| Slovakia | 2001 | Methamphetamine | 10 Lab. | |
| Subtotal Eastern Europe | | | 143 Lab. | |
| Western Europe | | | | |
| Germany | 2001 | Methamphetamine | 3 Lab. | |
| | 2002 | Methamphetamine | 2 Lab. | |
| Subtotal Western Europe | | | 5 Lab. | |
| Total Europe | | | 148 Lab. | |
| **Oceania** | | | | |
| Oceania | | | | |
| New Zealand | 2001 | Methamphetamine | 39 Lab. | |
| | 2002 | Methamphetamine | 147 Lab. | |
| Subtotal Oceania | | | 186 Lab. | |
| Total Oceania | | | 186 Lab. | |
| Methamphetamine group | | | 17489 Lab.(4242.400 kg) | |

## ECSTASY GROUP

| Country or Territory | Year | Name of drug seized | Number of laboratories (and quantity of drug) | Source |
|---|---|---|---|---|
| **Africa** | | | | |
| Southern Africa | | | | |
| South Africa | 2001 | MDMA | 5 Lab.(857.000 kg) | |
| Subtotal Southern Africa | | | 5 Lab.(857.000 kg) | |
| Total Africa | | | 5 Lab.(857.000 kg) | |
| **Americas** | | | | |
| North America | | | | |
| Canada | 2001 | MDA | 2 Lab. | |
| | 2002 | MDMA | 8 Lab. | |
| Mexico | 2002 | MDMA | 1 Lab. | |
| United States | 2001 | MDMA | 17 Lab.(4.400 kg) | |
| | 2002 | MDMA | 9 Lab.(1.500 kg) | |
| Subtotal North America | | | 37 Lab.(5.900 kg) | |
| Total Americas | | | 37 Lab.(5.900 kg) | |
| **Asia** | | | | |
| East and South-East Asia | | | | |
| China | 2002 | | 11 Lab. | |
| *Hong Kong SAR, China* | 2001 | MDMA | 3 Lab. | |
| Indonesia | 2001 | MDMA (Ecstasy) | 9 Lab. | |
| | 2002 | | 2 Lab. | |
| Subtotal East and South-East Asia | | | 25 Lab. | |
| Total Asia | | | 25 Lab. | |
| **Europe** | | | | |
| Eastern Europe | | | | |
| Estonia | 2002 | MDMA | 1 Lab. | |
| Subtotal Eastern Europe | | | 1 Lab. | |
| Western Europe | | | | |
| Belgium | 2001 | MDMA (Ecstasy) | 3 Lab. | |
| | 2001 | MDMA powder | 1 Lab. | |
| | 2002 | | 4 Lab. | |
| France | 2002 | MDMA | 1 Lab. | |

| Country or Territory | Year | Name of drug seized | Number of laboratories (and quantity of drug) | Source |
|---|---|---|---|---|
| Germany | 2001 | MDMA | 2 Lab. | |
| Netherlands | 2001 | MDMA | 25 Lab. | |
| | 2002 | MDMA | 18 Lab. | |
| United Kingdom | 2001 | MDMA (Ecstasy) | 1 Lab. | |
| | 2002 | | 1 Lab. | |
| | 2002 | MDMA | 2 Lab.( 4160000 u.) | |
| Subtotal Western Europe | | | 58 Lab.( 4160000 u.) | |
| Total Europe | | | 59 Lab.( 4160000 u.) | |
| **Oceania** | | | | |
| <u>Oceania</u> | | | | |
| New Zealand | 2001 | MDMA (Ecstasy) | 2 Lab. | |
| Subtotal Oceania | | | 2 Lab. | |
| Total Oceania | | | 2 Lab. | |
| Ecstasy group | | | 128 Lab.(862.900 kg)( 4160000 u.) | |

# 3.5. Other Drugs

## 3.5.1. Seizures of Illicit Laboratories

**MANUFACTURE**
**SEIZURES OF ILLICIT LABORATORIES**
**REPORTED FOR 2001 - 2002**

Remark: For convenience, an attempt was made to group the reported estimates by drug categories. however, due to inconsistencies and gaps in the reporting, no overall analysis of the data set was performed. Numbers are presented as reported to UNODC and should be interpreted with caution.

Source: Annual Report Questionnaire if not otherwise indicated

| Country or Territory | Year | Name of drug seized | Number of laboratories (and quantity of drug) | Source |
|---|---|---|---|---|
| **OTHER SYNTHETIC STIMULANTS** | | | | |
| **Africa** | | | | |
| Southern Africa | | | | |
| South Africa | 2002 | Methcathinone | 13 Lab. | |
| Subtotal Southern Africa | | | 13 Lab. | |
| Total Africa | | | 13 Lab. | |
| **Americas** | | | | |
| North America | | | | |
| United States | 2001 | Methcathinone | 4 Lab.(0.172 kg) | |
| | 2002 | Methcathinone | 9 Lab.(1.190 kg) | |
| Subtotal North America | | | 13 Lab.(1.362 kg) | |
| South America | | | | |
| Colombia | 2001 | Synthetic drugs | 1 Lab. | |
| | 2002 | | 1 Lab. | |
| Subtotal South America | | | 2 Lab. | |
| Total Americas | | | 15 Lab.(1.362 kg) | |
| **Europe** | | | | |
| Western Europe | | | | |
| Netherlands | 2002 | | 1 Lab. | |
| Subtotal Western Europe | | | 1 Lab. | |
| Total Europe | | | 1 Lab. | |
| Other synthetic stimulants | | | 29 Lab.(1.362 kg) | |
| **DEPRESSANT GROUP** | | | | |
| **Africa** | | | | |
| Southern Africa | | | | |
| South Africa | 2001 | Methaqualone | 5 Lab.( 198419 u.) | |
| | 2002 | Methaqualone | 4 Lab. | |
| | 2002 | GHB | 1 Lab. | |
| Subtotal Southern Africa | | | 10 Lab.( 198419 u.) | |
| Total Africa | | | 10 Lab.( 198419 u.) | |
| **Americas** | | | | |
| North America | | | | |
| Canada | 2002 | | 2 Lab. | |
| United States | 2002 | GHB | 7 Lab.(1.360 kg) | |
| Subtotal North America | | | 9 Lab.(1.360 kg) | |

263

| Country or Territory | Year | Name of drug seized | Number of laboratories (and quantity of drug) | Source |
|---|---|---|---|---|
| Total Americas | | | 9 Lab.(1.360 kg) | |
| **Asia** | | | | |
| *East and South-East Asia* | | | | |
| China | 2002 | Methaqualone | 1 Lab. | |
| Subtotal East and South-East Asia | | | 1 Lab. | |
| *South Asia* | | | | |
| India | 2002 | Methaqualone | 1 Lab.(442.000 kg) | |
| Subtotal South Asia | | | 1 Lab.(442.000 kg) | |
| Total Asia | | | 2 Lab.(442.000 kg) | |
| **Europe** | | | | |
| *Eastern Europe* | | | | |
| Estonia | 2002 | GHB | 1 Lab. | |
| Subtotal Eastern Europe | | | 1 Lab. | |
| Total Europe | | | 1 Lab. | |
| Depressant group | | | 22 Lab.(443.360 kg)( 198419 u.) | |

## HALLUCINOGEN GROUP

| Country or Territory | Year | Name of drug seized | Number of laboratories (and quantity of drug) | Source |
|---|---|---|---|---|
| **Americas** | | | | |
| *North America* | | | | |
| Canada | 2002 | | 2 Lab. | |
| United States | 2001 | Phencyclidine (PCP) | 4 Lab. | |
| | 2002 | | 6 Lab.(8.000 kg) | |
| Subtotal North America | | | 12 Lab.(8.000 kg) | |
| Total Americas | | | 12 Lab.(8.000 kg) | |
| **Europe** | | | | |
| *Western Europe* | | | | |
| Denmark | 2001 | LSD | 1 Lab. | |
| Germany | 2002 | | 1 Lab. | |
| Subtotal Western Europe | | | 2 Lab. | |
| Total Europe | | | 2 Lab. | |
| Hallucinogen group | | | 14 Lab.(8.000 kg) | |

## OTHER

| Country or Territory | Year | Name of drug seized | Number of laboratories (and quantity of drug) | Source |
|---|---|---|---|---|
| **Europe** | | | | |
| *Eastern Europe* | | | | |
| Estonia | 2002 | | 1 Lab. | |
| Russian Federation | 2001 | Other drugs | 300 Lab. | |
| Subtotal Eastern Europe | | | 301 Lab. | |
| Total Europe | | | 301 Lab. | |
| Other | | | 301 Lab. | |

## UNSPECIFIED

| Country or Territory | Year | Name of drug seized | Number of laboratories (and quantity of drug) | Source |
|---|---|---|---|---|
| **Americas** | | | | |
| *South America* | | | | |
| Peru | 2002 | unknown | 238 Lab. | |
| Subtotal South America | | | 238 Lab. | |
| Total Americas | | | 238 Lab. | |
| **Europe** | | | | |

| Country or Territory | Year | Name of drug seized | Number of laboratories (and quantity of drug) | Source |
|---|---|---|---|---|
| **Western Europe** | | | | |
| Netherlands | 2002 | Unspecified | 15 Lab. | Govt |
| Spain | 2002 | Unspecified | 8 Lab. | |
| Subtotal Western Europe | | | 23 Lab. | |
| Total Europe | | | 23 Lab. | |
| Unspecified | | | 261 Lab. | |

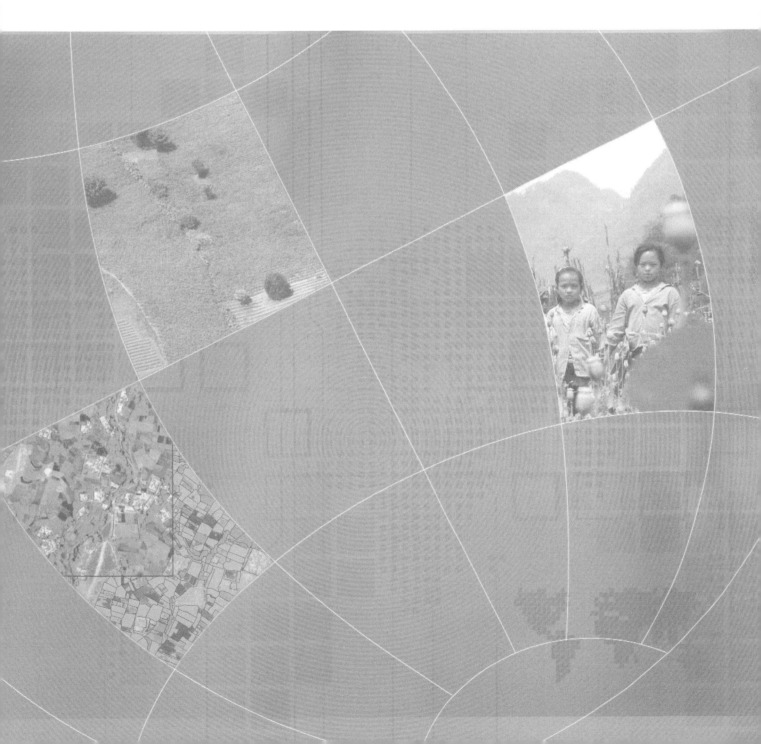

# 4. SEIZURES

# 4.1. Opiates: Seizures 1997-2002

| Region/country or territory | SEIZURES, 1997 - 2002 Opium (raw and prepared) | | | | | |
|---|---|---|---|---|---|---|
| | 1997 | 1998 | 1999 | 2000 | 2001 | 2002 |
| **AFRICA** | | | | | | |
| **East Africa** | | | | | | |
| Mauritius | No Report | No Report | No Report | No Report | 0.001 kg | No Report |
| Sub-Total | | | | | 0.001 kg | |
| **North Africa** | | | | | | |
| Egypt | 31.156 kg | 25.894 kg | 24.702 kg | 75.283 kg | 40.000 kg | 33.000 kg |
| Tunisia | No Report | No Report | No Report | 0.017 kg [ICPO] | No Report | No Report |
| Sub-Total | 31.156 kg | 25.894 kg | 24.702 kg | 75.300 kg | 40.000 kg | 33.000 kg |
| **Southern Africa** | | | | | | |
| Zambia | 0.102 kg [Govt] | 6.770 kg [Govt] | 8.622 kg | 0.000 kg [Govt] | 0.000 kg [Govt] | No Report |
| Sub-Total | 0.102 kg | 6.770 kg | 8.622 kg | | | |
| **West and Central Africa** | | | | | | |
| Benin | No Report | No Report | No Report | No Report | 0.414 kg [ICPO] | No Report |
| Niger | No Report | No Report | 0.013 kg [ICPO] | No Report | No Report | No Report |
| Sub-Total | | | 0.013 kg | | 0.414 kg | |
| Total region | 31.258 kg | 32.664 kg | 33.337 kg | 75.300 kg | 40.415 kg | 33.000 kg |
| **AMERICAS** | | | | | | |
| **Caribbean** | | | | | | |
| *Netherlands Antilles* | No Report | No Report | No Report | No Report | No Report | 0.440 kg [ICPO] |
| Sub-Total | | | | | | 0.440 kg |
| **North America** | | | | | | |
| Canada | 11.925 kg | 61.310 kg | 57.000 kg 10061 u. | 18.788 kg 140 u. | 27.307 kg | 12.320 kg 1313 u. |
| Mexico [*] | 342.081 kg | 149.640 kg | 801.180 kg | 469.445 kg | 516.369 kg | 309.902 kg |
| United States | 39.010 kg | No Report | 68.970 kg | No Report | 24.500 kg | 95.779 kg |
| Sub-Total | 393.016 kg | 210.950 kg | 927.150 kg 10061 u. | 488.233 kg 140 u. | 568.176 kg | 418.001 kg 1313 u. |
| **South America** | | | | | | |
| Colombia | 121.550 kg | 99.950 kg | 29.203 kg | 16.063 kg | 3.700 kg | 110.000 kg |
| Peru | No Report | 11.528 kg | No Report | No Report | 146.950 kg | 244.753 kg |
| Sub-Total | 121.550 kg | 111.478 kg | 29.203 kg | 16.063 kg | 150.650 kg | 354.753 kg |
| Total region | 514.566 kg | 322.428 kg | 956.353 kg 10061 u. | 504.296 kg 140 u. | 718.826 kg | 773.194 kg 1313 u. |
| **ASIA** | | | | | | |
| **Central Asia and Transcaucasian countries** | | | | | | |
| Armenia | 2.054 kg | No Report | 2.032 kg [Govt.] | 2.188 kg | 0.090 kg | 0.078 kg |
| Azerbaijan | 83.328 kg [ICPO] | 48.541 kg | 52.218 kg | 87.617 kg [ICPO] | 10.500 kg | 0.127 kg |
| Georgia | No Report | No Report | 14.700 kg [ICPO] | 33.500 kg [ICPO] | No Report | No Report |
| Kazakhstan | 1000.000 kg [Govt.] | 296.574 kg | 170.236 kg | 136.000 kg [F.O] | 36.000 kg [F.O] | 13.571 kg [F.O] |

Source: Annual Report Questionnaire if not otherwise indicated
* Seizures refer to opium latex

## SEIZURES, 1997 - 2002

### Opium (raw and prepared)

| Region/country or territory | 1997 | 1998 | 1999 | 2000 | 2001 | 2002 |
|---|---|---|---|---|---|---|
| **ASIA** | | | | | | |
| **Central Asia  and Transcaucasian countries** | | | | | | |
| Kyrgyzstan | 1639.476 kg | 171.872 kg | 151.174 kg | 1405.232 kg | 469.225 kg | 109.295 kg |
| Tajikistan | 3455.510 kg [F.O] | 1190.400 kg | 1269.278 kg [F.O] | 4778.448 kg [F.O] | 3664.277 kg | 1624.101 kg |
| Turkmenistan | 1410.000 kg [Govt.] | 1412.000 kg [Govt.] | 4600.000 kg [F.O] | 2300.000 kg [F.O] | No Report | 1200.000 kg [F.O] |
| Uzbekistan | 2364.167 kg | 1935.315 kg | 3292.342 kg | 2008.200 kg | 241.680 kg [F.O] | 76.000 kg [F.O] |
| Sub-Total | 9954.535 kg | 5054.702 kg | 9551.979 kg | 10751.190 kg | 4421.772 kg | 3023.172 kg |
| **East and South-East Asia** | | | | | | |
| Cambodia | 15.006 kg [ICPO] | No Report | No Report | No Report | No Report | No Report |
| China | 1880.000 kg | 1215.000 kg | 1193.000 kg [ICPO] | 2428.000 kg [Govt.] | 2820.000 kg [Govt.] | 1219.300 kg |
| Hong Kong SAR, China | 3.400 kg | No Report | 0.100 kg | 0.090 kg | 2.500 kg | No Report |
| Indonesia | No Report | 0.030 kg [HNLP] | 3.097 kg [HNLP] | 0.034 kg [ICPO] | 0.009 kg | No Report |
| Japan | 39.061 kg | 19.811 kg | 7.688 kg | 8.979 kg | 11.020 kg | 57.700 kg<br>1 u. |
| Korea (Republic of) | 6.805 kg | 1.035 kg | 3.064 kg | 14996 u. [ICPO] | 0.218 kg | 0.258 kg [ICPO] |
| Lao People's Dem. Rep. | 200.100 kg [Govt.] | 442.000 kg [INCSR] | 225.800 kg [HNLP] | 78.000 kg [INCSR] | 372.600 kg [Govt] | 123.150 kg |
| Malaysia | 150.311 kg | 32.747 kg | 21.066 kg | 0.710 kg | 69.270 kg [ICPO] | No Report |
| Myanmar | 7883.975 kg | 5705.881 kg | 1759.538 kg | 1773.652 kg | 1770.773 kg | 1989.222 kg |
| Singapore | 1.545 kg | 22.781 kg | 98.144 kg | 4.504 kg | 13.375 kg | No Report |
| Thailand | 1150.582 kg | 1631.124 kg | 421.939 kg | 1595.000 kg [HNLP] | 2289.000 kg [HNLP] | 3458.000 kg [ICPO] |
| Viet Nam | No Report | No Report | 495.350 kg [F.O] | 460.000 kg [ICPO] | 583.005 kg | No Report |
| Sub-Total | 11330.790 kg | 9070.408 kg | 4228.786 kg | 6348.969 kg<br>14996  u. | 7931.770 kg | 6847.630 kg<br>1 u. |
| **Near and Middle East /South-West Asia** | | | | | | |
| Afghanistan | No Report | No Report | No Report | No Report | No Report | 5581.615 kg |
| Bahrain | 0.007 kg | 0.014 kg [ICPO] | 0.323 kg [ICPO] | 0.001 kg [ICPO] | No Report | 0.007 kg |
| Iran (Islamic Republic of) | 162413.953 kg | 154453.569 kg | 204485.000 kg | 179053.000 kg [NAPOL] | 81061.000 kg | 72856.000 kg [Govt] |
| Iraq | 4.815 kg | No Report | No Report | 10.511 kg | 0.993 kg | No Report |
| Israel | 5.100 kg | 0.556 kg | 0.005 kg [ICPO] | 0.194 kg | 4.405 kg | 0.006 kg |
| Jordan | 22.671 kg | No Report | 61.700 kg | No Report | 0.327 kg | 19.326 kg |
| Kuwait | 11.710 kg [ICPO] | 4.720 kg | 14.000 kg [INCB] | 32.500 kg [ICPO] | No Report | 6.367 kg [ICPO] |
| Lebanon | 7.625 kg | No Report | 44.226 kg | 0.052 kg | 7.028 kg | 0.762 kg |
| Oman | 0.060 kg [INCB] | No Report | No Report | 1.647 kg [ICPO] | 0.308 kg | 0.591 kg |
| Pakistan | 7300.000 kg [Govt.] | 5021.712 kg | 16319.918 kg | 8867.407 kg | 5175.000 kg [F.O] | 2686.257 kg |
| Qatar | 0.962 kg [ICPO] | 0.030 kg [ICPO] | 0.100 kg [ICPO] | 2.700 kg [ICPO] | No Report | 0.225 kg |
| Saudi Arabia | 16.127 kg [ICPO] | 16.721 kg [(1] | No Report | 13.472 kg | 0.954 kg | 4.561 kg [ICPO] |
| Syrian Arab Republic | 6.003 kg [Govt] | 1.200 kg [Govt] | 5.876 kg [Govt] | 35.400 kg [Govt] | 1.862 kg [Govt] | 16.066 kg |
| United Arab Emirates | 3.822 kg | 9.717 kg | 8.389 kg | 27.236 kg | 8.899 kg | 22.669 kg |

Source: Annual Report Questionnaire if not otherwise indicated

## SEIZURES, 1997 - 2002
### Opium (raw and prepared)

| Region/country or territory | 1997 | 1998 | 1999 | 2000 | 2001 | 2002 |
|---|---|---|---|---|---|---|
| **ASIA** | | | | | | |
| **Near and Middle East /South-West Asia** | | | | | | |
| Sub-Total | 169792.800 kg | 159508.300 kg | 220939.500 kg | 188044.100 kg | 86260.770 kg | 81194.470 kg |
| **South Asia** | | | | | | |
| Bangladesh | No Report | No Report | 0.072 kg [F.O] | No Report | 11.535 kg [ICPO] | 0.023 kg |
| India | 3316.000 kg | 2031.000 kg | 1588.000 kg | 2684.000 kg | 2533.000 kg | 1867.000 kg |
| Nepal | No Report | 0.950 kg | 1.440 kg | No Report | No Report | No Report |
| Sri Lanka | 1571 u. | 0.020 kg | 0.008 kg | 36.452 kg | 1.658 kg | 16.800 kg |
| Sub-Total | 3316.000 kg 1571 u. | 2031.970 kg | 1589.520 kg | 2720.452 kg | 2546.193 kg | 1883.823 kg |
| Total region | 194394.200 kg 1571 u. | 175665.300 kg | 236309.800 kg | 207864.700 kg 14996 u. | 101160.500 kg | 92949.090 kg 1 u. |
| **EUROPE** | | | | | | |
| **Eastern Europe** | | | | | | |
| Albania | No Report | No Report | 0.026 kg [ICPO] | No Report | No Report | No Report |
| Belarus | 1.124 kg [INCB] | 0.001 kg | 0.033 kg | 0.090 kg | 1381.000 kg [ICPO] | 0.056 kg |
| Bosnia Herzegovina | No Report | No Report | No Report | No Report | No Report | 0.074 kg [ICPO] |
| Bulgaria | 8.240 kg | 1.970 kg | 4.466 kg | No Report | 1.980 kg | 1.440 kg |
| Croatia | 0.001 kg | [2] | 0.103 kg | 0.011 kg | No Report | No Report |
| Estonia | No Report | No Report | No Report | 19.426 kg 20 u. | No Report | 169.509 kg [ICPO] |
| FYR of Macedonia | 44.783 kg [NAPOL] | 19.985 kg | 12.239 kg [NAPOL] | 27.395 kg [NAPOL] | 3.494 kg [Govt] | 22.930 kg |
| Hungary | No Report | No Report | 2.149 kg | 17.905 kg | 0.003 kg | 0.892 kg |
| Latvia | 0.230 kg | 0.755 kg | 0.005 kg | 0.005 kg | No Report | No Report |
| Lithuania | 0.236 kg | 0.101 kg | 0.190 kg | 0.129 kg | 436.505 kg | 261.373 kg |
| Poland | No Report | No Report | No Report | 55.000 kg | No Report | 16.000 kg |
| Republic of Moldova | 20.000 kg | No Report | 28.000 kg [ICPO] | 1485.000 kg [ICPO] 98.550 lt. | 1891.000 kg | 1505.000 kg [Govt] |
| Romania | 2.488 kg [ICPO] | 0.728 kg | 2.470 kg | 0.060 kg | 15.530 kg | 0.794 kg |
| Russian Federation | 222.706 kg | 1803.700 kg [F.O] | 1506.966 kg | 2186.000 kg [F.O] | 862.645 kg | 445.254 kg [F.O] |
| Serbia and Montenegro | No Report | No Report | No Report | No Report | No Report | 0.587 kg |
| Ukraine | No Report | No Report | No Report | 166.056 kg [ICPO] | 151.009 kg | 42.000 kg |
| Sub-Total | 299.808 kg | 1827.240 kg | 1556.647 kg | 3957.077 kg 98.550 lt. 20 u. | 4743.166 kg | 2465.909 kg |
| **Western Europe** | | | | | | |
| Austria | 9.041 kg | 10.447 kg | 33.646 kg | 69.873 kg | 4.488 kg | 25.160 kg |
| Belgium | No Report | 0.011 kg | 0.200 kg | No Report | No Report | |
| Cyprus | 1.913 kg | 0.021 kg | 0.062 kg | 0.575 kg | 0.367 kg | No Report |
| Denmark | 0.105 kg | 5.428 kg | 0.330 kg | 1.405 kg | 5.000 kg | 5.274 kg |
| Finland | No Report | 0.007 kg | No Report | No Report | No Report | No Report |

Source: Annual Report Questionnaire if not otherwise indicated

## SEIZURES, 1997 - 2002
### Opium (raw and prepared)

| Region/country or territory | 1997 | 1998 | 1999 | 2000 | 2001 | 2002 |
|---|---|---|---|---|---|---|
| **EUROPE** | | | | | | |
| **Western Europe** | | | | | | |
| France | 2.696 kg | 3.194 kg | 0.503 kg | 18.701 kg | 2.720 kg | 1.376 kg |
| Germany | 41.656 kg | 286.074 kg | 79.500 kg | 30.900 kg | 4.115 kg | 62.674 kg |
| Greece | 2.559 kg | No Report | 46.208 kg [ICPO] | 1.742 kg | 0.955 kg | No Report |
| Italy | 9.821 kg 54 u. | 2.895 kg | 0.401 kg [ICPO] | 28.672 kg | 0.189 kg 6 u. | 0.539 kg 17 u. |
| Norway | 0.023 kg | 2.498 kg | 1.661 kg | 9.800 kg | 3.214 kg | 0.121 kg |
| Portugal | 0.012 kg | 0.001 kg | No Report | 2.850 kg [ICPO] | 0.015 kg 77 u. | 0.082 kg 1014 u. |
| Spain | 26.287 kg | 0.002 kg | 1.080 kg | 5.264 kg | 84.900 kg | 0.153 kg |
| Sweden | 7.709 kg 139 u. | 15.641 kg | 9.867 kg | 24.030 kg | 16.153 kg | 10.100 kg |
| Switzerland | 0.042 kg | 0.015 kg | 0.775 kg | 0.009 kg [ICPO] | No Report | 0.005 kg |
| Turkey | 93.356 kg | 141.665 kg | 318.624 kg | 362.950 kg [Govt.] | 261.176 kg | 161.054 kg |
| United Kingdom | 17.800 kg | 54.263 kg | 37.700 kg [NCIS] | 18.481 kg | 34.971 kg | 34.971 kg [3] |
| Sub-Total | 213.020 kg 193 u. | 522.162 kg | 530.557 kg | 575.252 kg | 418.263 kg 83 u. | 301.509 kg 1031 u. |
| Total region | 512.828 kg 193 u. | 2349.402 kg | 2087.204 kg | 4532.329 kg 98.550 lt. 20 u. | 5161.429 kg 83 u. | 2767.418 kg 1031 u. |
| **OCEANIA** | | | | | | |
| **Oceania** | | | | | | |
| Australia | 2.095 kg | No Report | 3.000 kg [INCB] | 2.279 kg | 68.410 kg 397 u. | 12.535 kg |
| New Zealand | 0.016 kg [INCB] | 0.006 kg | No Report | No Report | 0.008 kg | 0.004 kg |
| Sub-Total | 2.111 kg | 0.006 kg | 3.000 kg | 2.279 kg | 68.418 kg 397 u. | 12.539 kg |
| Total region | 2.111 kg | 0.006 kg | 3.000 kg | 2.279 kg | 68.418 kg 397 u. | 12.539 kg |
| **TOTAL** | 195454.900 kg 1764 u. | 178369.800 kg | 239389.700 kg 10061 u. | 212978.900 kg 98.550 lt. 15156 u. | 107149.600 kg 480 u. | 96535.250 kg 2345 u. |

1) Including other opiates. 2) Small quantity. 3) Due to unavailability of 2002 data, year 2001 data were used for analysis purposes.

Source: Annual Report Questionnaire if not otherwise indicated

## SEIZURES, 1997 - 2002
### Opium (liquid)

| Region/country or territory | 1997 | 1998 | 1999 | 2000 | 2001 | 2002 |
|---|---|---|---|---|---|---|
| **AFRICA** | | | | | | |
| **North Africa** | | | | | | |
| Egypt | 0.009 lt. | 0.030 lt. | 0.001 lt. | 0.005 lt. | No Report | No Report |
| Sub-Total | 0.009 lt. | 0.030 lt. | 0.001 lt. | 0.005 lt. | | |
| Total region | 0.009 lt. | 0.030 lt. | 0.001 lt. | 0.005 lt. | | |
| **AMERICAS** | | | | | | |
| **Caribbean** | | | | | | |
| *Cayman Islands* | No Report | No Report | No Report | 0.628 kg 1 u. | No Report | No Report |
| Sub-Total | | | | 0.628 kg 1 u. | | |
| **South America** | | | | | | |
| Peru | No Report | No Report | 66.088 kg | 508.358 kg | No Report | No Report |
| Sub-Total | | | 66.088 kg | 508.358 kg | | |
| Total region | | | 66.088 kg | 508.986 kg 1 u. | | |
| **ASIA** | | | | | | |
| **Central Asia and Transcaucasian countries** | | | | | | |
| Armenia | No Report | 2.000 kg | No Report | 0.002 kg | No Report | No Report |
| Kazakhstan | No Report | 1.265 kg | No Report | No Report | No Report | No Report |
| Kyrgyzstan | 15000 u. | No Report | No Report | No Report | No Report | No Report |
| Sub-Total | 15000 u. | 3.265 kg | | 0.002 kg | | |
| **East and South-East Asia** | | | | | | |
| *Hong Kong SAR, China* | No Report | No Report | No Report | 2 u. | No Report | No Report |
| Indonesia | No Report | 0.030 kg | 3.097 kg | 0.034 kg | No Report | No Report |
| Japan | No Report | 0.130 lt. | No Report | No Report | No Report | No Report |
| Lao People's Dem. Rep. | No Report | No Report | No Report | No Report | No Report | 98.000 lt. |
| Myanmar | 1027.685 kg | 383.251 kg | 332.495 kg | 16.086 kg | 18.684 kg | 18.025 kg |
| Sub-Total | 1027.685 kg | 383.281 kg 0.130 lt. | 335.592 kg | 16.120 kg 2 u. | 18.684 kg | 18.025 kg 98.000 lt. |
| **Near and Middle East /South-West Asia** | | | | | | |
| Jordan | No Report | No Report | No Report | 41.150 kg | No Report | No Report |
| Lebanon | No Report | 35.840 kg | No Report | 0.000 kg [1 | No Report | No Report |
| Sub-Total | | 35.840 kg | | 41.150 kg | | |
| Total region | 1027.685 kg 15000 u. | 422.386 kg 0.130 lt. | 335.592 kg | 57.272 kg 2 u. | 18.684 kg | 18.025 kg 98.000 lt. |

Source: Annual Report Questionnaire if not otherwise indicated

273

## SEIZURES, 1997 - 2002

### Opium (liquid)

| Region/country or territory | 1997 | 1998 | 1999 | 2000 | 2001 | 2002 |
|---|---|---|---|---|---|---|
| **EUROPE** | | | | | | |
| **Eastern Europe** | | | | | | |
| Belarus | No Report | 330.882 kg | 244.034 kg [2 | 220.520 kg | No Report | 334.225 kg [3 |
| Croatia | 2.000 lt. | 8.600 lt. | No Report | 1.500 kg | No Report | No Report |
| Estonia | No Report | 19.200 kg | 0.276 kg | 0.027 kg | No Report | No Report |
| | | 293 u. | 61 u. | 19 u. | | |
| Latvia | 0.133 lt. | 64.800 kg | 17.300 kg | 7.170 kg | No Report | No Report |
| Lithuania | 86.000 lt. | 49.490 lt. | 190.000 lt. | 77.000 lt. | No Report | No Report |
| Republic of Moldova | No Report | 13.480 kg | No Report | No Report | No Report | No Report |
| Ukraine | 171.200 kg | 127.000 kg | No Report | No Report | No Report | No Report |
| Sub-Total | 171.200 kg | 555.362 kg | 261.610 kg | 229.217 kg | | 334.225 kg |
| | 88.133 lt. | 58.090 lt. | 190.000 lt. | 77.000 lt. | | |
| | | 293 u. | 61 u. | 19 u. | | |
| **Western Europe** | | | | | | |
| Austria | No Report | No Report | No Report | 0.075 kg | No Report | No Report |
| Denmark | 0.030 kg | 0.004 kg | 2.640 kg | No Report | No Report | No Report |
| Italy | No Report | No Report | No Report | 35 u. | No Report | No Report |
| Sweden | No Report | 0.326 lt. | 16.000 lt. | 0.018 kg | No Report | No Report |
| Sub-Total | 0.030 kg | 0.004 kg | 2.640 kg | 0.093 kg | | |
| | | 0.326 lt. | 16.000 lt. | 35 u. | | |
| Total region | 171.230 kg | 555.366 kg | 264.250 kg | 229.310 kg | | 334.225 kg |
| | 88.133 lt. | 58.416 lt. | 206.000 lt. | 77.000 lt. | | |
| | | 293 u. | 61 u. | 54 u. | | |
| **OCEANIA** | | | | | | |
| **Oceania** | | | | | | |
| Australia | 1.630 kg | No Report | No Report | No Report | No Report | No Report |
| Sub-Total | 1.630 kg | | | | | |
| Total region | 1.630 kg | | | | | |
| TOTAL | 1200.545 kg | 977.752 kg | 665.930 kg | 795.568 kg | 18.684 kg | 352.250 kg |
| | 88.142 lt. | 58.576 lt. | 206.001 lt. | 77.005 lt. | | 98.000 lt. |
| | 15000 u. | 293 u. | 61 u. | 57 u. | | |

1) Small quantity. 2) Includes liquid heroin (1.160kg) 3) poppy brew

Source: Annual Report Questionnaire if not otherwise indicated

## SEIZURES, 1997 - 2002
### Opium (plant,capsule)

| Region/country or territory | 1997 | 1998 | 1999 | 2000 | 2001 | 2002 |
|---|---|---|---|---|---|---|
| **AFRICA** | | | | | | |
| **North Africa** | | | | | | |
| Egypt | No Report | 0.352 kg 30214000 u. | 14.552 kg | No Report | No Report | No Report |
| Sub-Total | | 0.352 kg 30214000 u. | 14.552 kg | | | |
| **West and Central Africa** | | | | | | |
| Niger | No Report | 0.040 kg [ICPO] | No Report | No Report | No Report | No Report |
| Sao Tome and Principe | 0.300 kg | No Report | 0.300 kg | No Report | No Report | No Report |
| Sub-Total | 0.300 kg | 0.040 kg | 0.300 kg | | | |
| Total region | 0.300 kg | 0.392 kg 30214000 u. | 14.852 kg | | | |
| **AMERICAS** | | | | | | |
| **Central America** | | | | | | |
| Guatemala | 2.600 kg [Govt.] 69119 u. | 114238 u. | 23100 u. | 20619 u. | No Report | No Report |
| Sub-Total | 2.600 kg 69119 u. | 114238 u. | 23100 u. | 20619 u. | | |
| **North America** | | | | | | |
| Canada | 18 u. | 2.016 kg | 15000 u. | No Report | No Report | No Report |
| United States | 50.685 kg 0.109 lt. | No Report | No Report | No Report | No Report | No Report |
| Sub-Total | 50.685 kg 0.109 lt. 18 u. | 2.016 kg | 15000 u. | | | |
| **South America** | | | | | | |
| Argentina | 2.470 kg | 408 u. | No Report | No Report | No Report | No Report |
| Colombia | 104818496 u. | No Report | No Report | No Report | No Report | No Report |
| Ecuador | No Report | 100873 u. | No Report | No Report | No Report | No Report |
| Peru | 1754 u. | 964 u. | 63703.614 kg | 20837.016 kg | No Report | No Report |
| Sub-Total | 2.470 kg 104820200 u. | 102245 u. | 63703.610 kg | 20837.020 kg | | |
| Total region | 55.755 kg 0.109 lt. 104889400 u. | 2.016 kg 216483 u. | 63703.610 kg 38100 u. | 20837.020 kg 20619 u. | | |
| **ASIA** | | | | | | |
| **Central Asia and Transcaucasian countries** | | | | | | |
| Armenia | 4.460 kg | 18.725 kg | No Report | No Report | No Report | No Report |
| Azerbaijan | 38750.000 kg [ICPO] | 6.200 kg | No Report | No Report | No Report | No Report |
| Georgia | No Report | 7.500 kg [ICPO] | No Report | No Report | No Report | No Report |

Source: Annual Report Questionnaire if not otherwise indicated

## SEIZURES, 1997 - 2002

### Opium (plant,capsule)

| Region/country or territory | 1997 | 1998 | 1999 | 2000 | 2001 | 2002 |
|---|---|---|---|---|---|---|
| **ASIA** | | | | | | |
| **Central Asia  and Transcaucasian countries** | | | | | | |
| Kazakhstan | No Report | 113.895 kg | No Report | No Report | No Report | No Report |
| Tajikistan | No Report | No Report | No Report | No Report | No Report | 143.141 kg[(1] |
| Uzbekistan | 118.285 kg | 54.496 kg | No Report | 14.700 kg | No Report | No Report |
| Sub-Total | 38872.750 kg | 200.816 kg | | 14.700 kg | | 143.141 kg |
| **East and South-East Asia** | | | | | | |
| *Hong Kong SAR, China* | No Report | No Report | 32  u. | 3.001 kg | No Report | No Report |
| Indonesia | 1620  u. | 0.030 kg | No Report | No Report | No Report | No Report |
| Japan | 6803  u. | 0.063 kg 6807  u. | No Report | 0.022 kg 11571  u. | No Report | 0.091 kg 1424  u. |
| Korea (Republic of) | 24301  u. | 21944  u. | No Report | No Report | No Report | No Report |
| Malaysia | 321  u. | No Report | No Report | No Report | No Report | No Report |
| Thailand | 205.234 kg | No Report | 312.837 kg | No Report | No Report | No Report |
| Viet Nam | 919.000 kg[ICPO] | 1.100 kg[ICPO] | No Report | No Report | No Report | No Report |
| Sub-Total | 1124.234 kg 33045  u. | 1.193 kg 28751  u. | 312.837 kg 32  u. | 3.023 kg 11571  u. | | 0.091 kg 1424  u. |
| **Near and Middle East /South-West Asia** | | | | | | |
| Pakistan | No Report | No Report | No Report | No Report | No Report | 21757.000 kg |
| United Arab Emirates | 129  u. | No Report | No Report | No Report | No Report | No Report |
| Yemen | No Report | [ICPO] | No Report | No Report | No Report | No Report |
| Sub-Total | 129  u. | | | | | 21757.000 kg |
| **South Asia** | | | | | | |
| Nepal | 0.693 kg[ICPO] | No Report | No Report | No Report | No Report | No Report |
| Sub-Total | 0.693 kg | | | | | |
| Total region | 39997.670 kg 33174  u. | 202.009 kg 28751  u. | 312.837 kg 32  u. | 17.723 kg 11571  u. | | 21900.230 kg 1424  u. |
| **EUROPE** | | | | | | |
| **Eastern Europe** | | | | | | |
| Belarus | 327.744 kg[INCB] | 1621.000 kg | 1056.000 kg | 1084.000 kg | No Report | No Report |
| Bulgaria | No Report | No Report | No Report | No Report | 1415.000 kg | No Report |
| Croatia | 769  u. | 3504  u. | 6206  u. | 1.607 kg 519  u. | No Report | No Report |
| Estonia | 165.800 kg | 36.011 kg 111  u. | No Report | 37.883 kg 69  u. | No Report | No Report |
| Latvia | 218.000 kg | 192.000 kg | 30.200 kg | 145.950 kg | No Report | No Report |
| Lithuania | 1291.000 kg | 1525.000 kg | 744.000 kg | 623.000 kg | No Report | No Report |
| Poland | 8500.000 kg | 4000.000 kg | 3553.000 kg | No Report | No Report | No Report |
| Republic of Moldova | 597.000 kg | 406.550 kg | No Report | No Report | No Report | 3635.000 kg[Govt] |
| Russian Federation | 853.019 kg | 16511.359 kg | 18366.055 kg | No Report | No Report | No Report |

Source: Annual Report Questionnaire if not otherwise indicated

## SEIZURES, 1997 - 2002
### Opium (plant,capsule)

| Region/country or territory | 1997 | 1998 | 1999 | 2000 | 2001 | 2002 |
|---|---|---|---|---|---|---|
| **EUROPE** | | | | | | |
| **Eastern Europe** | | | | | | |
| Ukraine | 34003.262 kg | 26632.801 kg | No Report | No Report | No Report | 23115.000 kg |
| Sub-Total | 45955.820 kg | 50924.720 kg | 23749.260 kg | 1892.440 kg | 1415.000 kg | 26750.000 kg |
| | 769 u. | 3615 u. | 6206 u. | 588 u. | | |
| **Western Europe** | | | | | | |
| Austria | 1.193 kg | 9.367 kg | 9.349 kg | No Report | No Report | No Report |
| Finland | No Report | 1.000 kg | No Report | No Report | No Report | No Report |
| Greece | 640 u. | No Report | No Report | No Report | No Report | No Report |
| Italy | 1448 u. | 5991 u. | No Report | 4449 u. [2] | No Report | No Report |
| Norway | 0.115 kg | 0.070 kg | No Report | 0.001 kg | No Report | No Report |
| Portugal | No Report | 28848 u. | 351 u. | 2.850 kg | No Report | No Report |
| | | | | 1348 u. | | |
| Spain | 862.112 kg [3] | 4.800 kg | 1003.004 kg | 22755.700 kg | No Report | 49.737 kg |
| Sweden | | No Report | 3615 u. | No Report | No Report | No Report |
| Turkey | No Report | No Report | No Report | 1820.000 kg | No Report | No Report |
| | | | | 3550 u. | | |
| Sub-Total | 863.420 kg | 15.237 kg | 1012.353 kg | 24578.550 kg | | 49.737 kg |
| | 2088 u. | 34839 u. | 3966 u. | 9347 u. | | |
| Total region | 46819.250 kg | 50939.960 kg | 24761.610 kg | 26470.990 kg | 1415.000 kg | 26799.740 kg |
| | 2857 u. | 38454 u. | 10172 u. | 9935 u. | | |
| **OCEANIA** | | | | | | |
| **Oceania** | | | | | | |
| Australia | 0.095 kg | No Report | No Report | 0.407 kg | No Report | 79.533 kg |
| | | | | 2083 u. | | |
| New Zealand | No Report | 20249 u. | 338 u. | No Report | No Report | No Report |
| Sub-Total | 0.095 kg | 20249 u. | 338 u. | 0.407 kg | | 79.533 kg |
| | | | | 2083 u. | | |
| Total region | 0.095 kg | 20249 u. | 338 u. | 0.407 kg | | 79.533 kg |
| | | | | 2083 u. | | |
| TOTAL | 86873.060 kg | 51144.380 kg | 88792.910 kg | 47326.130 kg | 1415.000 kg | 48779.500 kg |
| | 0.109 lt. | 30517940 u. | 48642 u. | 44208 u. | | 1424 u. |
| | 104925400 u. | | | | | |

1) Poppystraw, heads,stems & leaves 2) 221buds(1), 4,228 plants(6) 3) Including depressants.

Source: Annual Report Questionnaire if not otherwise indicated

## SEIZURES, 1997 - 2002
### Heroin

| Region/country or territory | 1997 | 1998 | 1999 | 2000 | 2001 | 2002 |
|---|---|---|---|---|---|---|
| **AFRICA** | | | | | | |
| **East Africa** | | | | | | |
| Burundi | No Report | No Report | 0.006 kg [ICPO] 260 u. | No Report | No Report | No Report |
| Ethiopia | 36.112 kg | 8.987 kg | 12.582 kg | 18.042 kg | 5.650 kg | 33.505 kg |
| Kenya | 7.787 kg | 9.954 kg | 17.459 kg | 28.657 kg | 19.438 kg [Govt] | 41.272 kg |
| Madagascar | No Report | No Report | 0.005 kg [ICPO] | No Report | No Report | No Report |
| Mauritius | 6.920 kg | 6.060 kg | 3.067 kg | 4.062 kg | 24.532 kg | 6.973 kg |
| Rwanda | No Report | No Report | No Report | No Report | No Report | 0.500 kg |
| Uganda | No Report | 1.302 kg | 14.170 kg | 3.400 kg | 5.772 kg | 11.190 kg |
| United Republic of Tanzania | 4.852 kg | 2.745 kg | 7.583 kg | 5.322 kg [ICPO] | 7.997 kg [Govt] | 1.458 kg [ICPO] |
| Sub-Total | 55.671 kg | 29.048 kg | 54.872 kg 260 u. | 59.483 kg | 63.389 kg | 94.898 kg |
| **North Africa** | | | | | | |
| Algeria | No Report | 0.256 kg [ICPO] | 0.002 kg | No Report | 0.006 kg [ICPO] | 0.024 kg |
| Egypt | 51.222 kg 0.225 lt. | 24.416 kg 0.266 lt. | 23.627 kg | 37.114 kg | 38.000 kg 385 u. | 55.000 kg |
| Libyan Arab Jam. | 0.851 kg [F.O] | 4.809 kg | 4.809 kg [F.O] | 15.000 kg [F.O] | 12.000 kg [F.O] | No Report |
| Morocco | 0.318 kg [Govt.] | 1.282 kg | 0.437 kg | 0.152 kg | 3.971 kg 110 u. | 3.528 kg 18 u. |
| Sudan | No Report | No Report | 0.250 kg [Govt] | No Report | 0.505 kg [Govt] | No Report |
| Tunisia | 0.308 kg [ICPO] | 0.474 kg | 1.391 kg | 1.020 kg [ICPO] | No Report | 0.254 kg |
| Sub-Total | 52.699 kg 0.225 lt. | 31.237 kg 0.266 lt. | 30.516 kg | 53.286 kg | 54.482 kg 495 u. | 58.806 kg 18 u. |
| **Southern Africa** | | | | | | |
| Angola | 0.010 kg [ICPO] | No Report | (1 | 0.005 kg [ICPO] | 21.500 kg [ICPO] | No Report |
| Botswana | 0.228 kg [ICPO] | No Report | No Report | No Report | No Report | No Report |
| Lesotho | No Report | No Report | 0.500 kg [ICPO] | No Report | No Report | No Report |
| Malawi | No Report | 0.200 kg | 0.500 kg | No Report | No Report | No Report |
| Mozambique | No Report | No Report | No Report | 232 u. [ICPO] | 0.005 kg [ICPO] | No Report |
| Namibia | No Report | No Report | 0.003 kg [ICPO] | 0.100 kg | 0.003 kg | 0.002 kg |
| South Africa | 1.548 kg | 5.383 kg | 7.435 kg [ICPO] | 15.386 kg | 8.465 kg | 15.020 kg |
| Swaziland | 1.041 kg [ICPO] | 0.010 kg | 0.097 kg | 1.919 kg | 0.093 kg | 0.004 kg |
| Zambia | 0.000 kg [Govt] | 0.001 kg [Govt] | 0.369 kg | 0.005 kg | 0.002 kg [Govt] | 0.360 kg |
| Zimbabwe | No Report | 0.740 kg | No Report | No Report | No Report | 0.077 kg |
| Sub-Total | 2.827 kg | 6.334 kg | 8.904 kg | 17.415 kg 232 u. | 30.068 kg | 15.463 kg |
| **West and Central Africa** | | | | | | |
| Benin | 0.143 kg [Govt] | 0.888 kg | 18.670 kg [Govt] | 7.572 kg [F.O] | 0.079 kg [ICPO] | 0.014 kg [ICPO] |
| Burkina Faso | 222.000 kg [Govt.] | No Report | No Report | No Report | 0.038 kg | No Report |
| Cameroon | No Report | 2.150 kg | 0.400 kg | No Report | No Report | No Report |

Source: Annual Report Questionnaire if not otherwise indicated

## SEIZURES, 1997 - 2002
### Heroin

| Region/country or territory | 1997 | 1998 | 1999 | 2000 | 2001 | 2002 |
|---|---|---|---|---|---|---|
| **AFRICA** | | | | | | |
| **West and Central Africa** | | | | | | |
| Chad | No Report | No Report | 1.800 kg [ICPO] | No Report | No Report | No Report |
| Congo | 0.070 kg | No Report | No Report | No Report | 0.010 kg | 0.016 kg |
| Côte d'Ivoire | 0.538 kg | 0.060 kg 16 u. | 1.889 kg 19 u. | 3.035 kg [ICPO] | 10.394 kg | 34.085 kg |
| Gabon | No Report | No Report | 0.106 kg [ICPO] | No Report | No Report | No Report |
| Gambia | 0.088 kg [ICPO] | 0.590 kg [ICPO] | 0.039 kg | No Report | 4.000 kg | No Report |
| Ghana | 0.005 kg | 18.023 kg | 21.020 kg | No Report | No Report | 19.060 kg |
| Guinea | No Report | No Report | No Report | 2.215 kg [ICPO] | 0.592 kg [ICPO] | 0.057 kg [ICPO] |
| Mauritania | 0.005 kg [Govt] | 0.005 kg [Govt] | No Report | No Report | No Report | No Report |
| Niger | 0.100 kg [ICPO] | 0.412 kg [ICPO] | No Report | No Report | No Report | No Report |
| Nigeria | 10.490 kg | 362.000 kg [Govt] | 81.035 kg | 55.100 kg | 46.639 kg | 55.626 kg |
| Senegal | No Report | 0.234 kg [ICPO] | 0.071 kg [ICPO] 382 u. | 198 u. [ICPO] | No Report | 0.336 kg [ICPO] |
| Togo | 81.601 kg [Govt.] | No Report | No Report | 10.808 kg | 15.253 kg | 4.727 kg |
| Sub-Total | 315.040 kg | 384.362 kg 16 u. | 125.030 kg 401 u. | 78.730 kg 198 u. | 77.005 kg | 113.921 kg |
| Total region | 426.237 kg 0.225 lt. | 450.981 kg 0.266 lt. 16 u. | 219.322 kg 661 u. | 208.914 kg 430 u. | 224.944 kg 495 u. | 283.089 kg 18 u. |
| **AMERICAS** | | | | | | |
| **Caribbean** | | | | | | |
| *Aruba* | 3.298 kg [INCB] | No Report | 6.000 kg [F.O] | 78.000 kg [F.O] | 65.000 kg [F.O] | 25.677 kg [ICPO] |
| Barbados | No Report | No Report | 3.230 kg [HONLC] | No Report | No Report | No Report |
| *Bermuda* | 0.398 kg | No Report | 0.836 kg | 0.292 kg | 2.000 kg [F.O] | 2.630 kg |
| *British Virgin Islands* | No Report | No Report | No Report | No Report | 1.200 kg 1 u. | No Report |
| *Cayman Islands* | No Report | No Report | No Report | 1.000 kg [F.O] | 0.213 kg | No Report |
| Cuba | 0.700 kg [ICPO] | No Report | 3.000 kg [F.O] | No Report | No Report | No Report |
| Dominican Republic | 11.328 kg | 6.891 kg | 11.909 kg | 24.000 kg [F.O] | 33.003 kg | 67.000 kg [HONLC] |
| *Guadeloupe* | No Report | No Report | No Report | No Report | 4.000 kg [F.O] | No Report |
| Jamaica | No Report | No Report | No Report | No Report | 0.450 kg | No Report |
| *Netherlands Antilles* | No Report | No Report | 2.000 kg [INCB] | 2.032 kg [ICPO] | 72.000 kg [F.O] | 62.622 kg [ICPO] |
| *Puerto Rico* | No Report | No Report | No Report | 24.000 kg [F.O] | 42.000 kg [F.O] | 12.070 kg [ICPO] 24619 u. |
| Saint Lucia | No Report | No Report | No Report | 2.000 kg | No Report | No Report |
| Trinidad Tobago | No Report | No Report | No Report | 5.000 kg [INCSR] | No Report | 10.380 kg [ICPO] |
| Sub-Total | 15.724 kg | 6.891 kg | 26.975 kg | 136.324 kg | 219.866 kg 1 u. | 180.379 kg 24619 u. |
| **Central America** | | | | | | |
| Belize | No Report | No Report | No Report | No Report | 3.399 kg | No Report |

Source: Annual Report Questionnaire if not otherwise indicated

## SEIZURES, 1997 - 2002

### Heroin

| Region/country or territory | 1997 | 1998 | 1999 | 2000 | 2001 | 2002 |
|---|---|---|---|---|---|---|
| **AMERICAS** | | | | | | |
| **Central America** | | | | | | |
| Costa Rica | 26.000 kg [CICAD] | 13.500 kg | 2.400 kg | 7.787 kg | 20.280 kg [*] | 58.770 kg* |
| El Salvador | 2.151 kg [ICPO] | 0.697 kg [ICPO] | 0.099 kg | 6.900 kg [ICPO] | 9.368 kg | 13.229 kg |
| Guatemala | 17.420 kg [Govt.] | 3.650 kg | 53.000 kg | 9.740 kg | 21.170 kg | 0.050 kg |
| Nicaragua | 2.000 kg | No Report | 2.000 kg [CICAD] | 2.000 kg [CICAD] | 8.422 kg [ICPO] | 53.189 kg |
| Panama | 33.307 kg | 22.825 kg | 46.456 kg | 39.045 kg | 87.000 kg | 101.100 kg [HONLC] |
| Sub-Total | 80.878 kg | 40.672 kg | 103.954 kg | 65.472 kg | 149.639 kg | 226.338 kg |
| **North America** | | | | | | |
| Canada | 95.000 kg | 22.295 kg<br>0.176 lt.<br>994 u. | 88.000 kg<br>91 u. | 6.970 kg<br>0.117 lt.<br>2 u. | 73.979 kg | 3.295 kg |
| Mexico | 114.903 kg | 120.896 kg | 260.191 kg | 299.102 kg | 263.152 kg [**] | 282.692 kg |
| United States | 1542.000 kg | 1580.700 kg [Govt.] | 1200.000 kg<br>437 u. | 1705.188 kg<br>1.850 lt.<br>593 u. | 1983.700 kg | 2765.600 kg |
| Sub-Total | 1751.903 kg | 1723.891 kg<br>0.176 lt.<br>994 u. | 1548.191 kg<br>528 u. | 2011.260 kg<br>1.967 lt.<br>595 u. | 2320.831 kg | 3051.587 kg |
| **South America** | | | | | | |
| Argentina | 38.580 kg | 31.040 kg | 7.962 kg | 47.664 kg | 84.683 kg | 32.296 kg |
| Bolivia | No Report | 0.760 kg | No Report | No Report | No Report | No Report |
| Brazil | No Report | 0.950 kg | No Report | [ICPO] | 12.500 kg [Govt] | 56.600 kg [F.O] |
| Chile | No Report | No Report | No Report | 21.088 kg | 33.234 kg | 13.649 kg |
| Colombia | 129.735 kg | 239.154 kg | 514.592 kg | 563.054 kg | 787.600 kg | 775.000 kg |
| Ecuador | 53.096 kg | 58.248 kg | 80.559 kg | 108.715 kg [ICPO] | 254.639 kg | No Report |
| Peru | No Report | No Report | No Report | 2.186 kg | 0.004 kg | 15.793 kg |
| Suriname | No Report | 0.030 kg | No Report | No Report | No Report | No Report |
| Uruguay | No Report | No Report | No Report | No Report | 5.872 kg [ICPO] | 7.200 kg |
| Venezuela | 16.086 kg [CICAD] | No Report | 41.514 kg | 195.580 kg | 228.430 kg | 562.950 kg |
| Sub-Total | 237.497 kg | 330.182 kg | 644.627 kg | 938.287 kg | 1406.962 kg | 1463.488 kg |
| Total region | 2086.002 kg | 2101.636 kg<br>0.176 lt.<br>994 u. | 2323.748 kg<br>528 u. | 3151.343 kg<br>1.967 lt.<br>595 u. | 4097.298 kg<br>1 u. | 4921.792 kg<br>24619 u. |
| **ASIA** | | | | | | |
| **Central Asia and Transcaucasian countries** | | | | | | |
| Armenia | 0.429 kg | 0.065 kg | 0.191 kg | 0.109 kg | 0.016 kg | 0.175 kg |
| Azerbaijan | 0.170 kg [ICPO] | 4.332 kg | 4.018 kg | 9.917 kg [ICPO] | 4.000 kg | 0.704 kg |
| Georgia | No Report | 0.083 kg [ICPO] | 2.300 kg [ICPO] | 3.993 kg [ICPO] | 5.518 kg [ICPO] | No Report |
| Kazakhstan | 43.000 kg [Govt.] | 24.196 kg | 54.264 kg | 262.400 kg [F.O] | 136.700 kg [F.O] | 167.690 kg [F.O] |
| Kyrgyzstan | 4.404 kg | 24.732 kg | 26.870 kg | 216.780 kg | 170.898 kg | 271.250 kg |
| Tajikistan | 60.000 kg | 271.471 kg | 708.820 kg | 1882.929 kg [F.O] | 4239.005 kg | 3958.182 kg |

Source: Annual Report Questionnaire if not otherwise indicated

* Reported figures at the time of the preparation of the report; revised figures by the Gov. of Costa Rica show seizures of heroin of 61.77 kg in 2002 and 121.3 kg in 2003.

** Reported figures at the time of the preparation of the report, revised figures by the Gov. of Mexico show seizures of heroin of 269.614 kg in 2001.

## SEIZURES, 1997 - 2002
### Heroin

| Region/country or territory | 1997 | 1998 | 1999 | 2000 | 2001 | 2002 |
|---|---|---|---|---|---|---|
| **ASIA** | | | | | | |
| **Central Asia and Transcaucasian countries** | | | | | | |
| Turkmenistan | 1948.000 kg [Govt.] | 495.000 kg [Govt.] | 240.000 kg [F.O] | 200.000 kg [F.O] | 71.000 kg [NAPOL] | 400.000 kg [F.O] |
| Uzbekistan | 70.269 kg | 194.679 kg | 324.843 kg | 675.000 kg | 466.601 kg [F.O] | 256.320 kg |
| Sub-Total | 2126.272 kg | 1014.558 kg | 1361.306 kg | 3251.128 kg | 5093.738 kg | 5054.322 kg |
| **East and South-East Asia** | | | | | | |
| Brunei Darussalam | 0.001 kg | 0.003 kg | No Report | 0.001 kg | No Report | 0.004 kg [ICPO] |
| Cambodia | 16.000 kg [ICPO] | No Report | No Report | No Report | No Report | No Report |
| China | 5477.000 kg | 7358.000 kg | 5364.000 kg [ICPO] | 6281.000 kg [Govt.] | 13200.000 kg | 9290.800 kg |
| Hong Kong SAR, China | 202.200 kg | 209.000 kg [Govt.] | 284.001 kg  0.003 lt. | 339.003 kg | 156.400 kg | 105.590 kg |
| Indonesia | 20.433 kg | 27.761 kg | 14.049 kg | 22.655 kg | 16.641 kg | 20.004 kg |
| Japan | 5.990 kg | 3.947 kg | 2.150 kg | 7.006 kg | 4.944 kg | 20.900 kg  0.000 lt. |
| Korea (Republic of) | 0.599 kg | 2.126 kg | 0.342 kg | No Report | 0.567 kg | 1.078 kg [ICPO] |
| Lao People's Dem. Rep. | 72.300 kg [Govt.] | 80.000 kg [INCSR] | 14.750 kg [HNLP] | 20.000 kg [INCSR] | 49.700 kg [Govt] | 21.245 kg  30 u. |
| Macau SAR, China | 0.231 kg [ICPO] | 2.217 kg [ICPO] | 1.000 kg [INCB] | 0.147 kg | 0.069 kg | 0.052 kg |
| Malaysia | 276.154 kg | 289.664 kg | 200.937 kg | 109.170 kg | 227.058 kg [ICPO] | 294.471 kg [ICPO] |
| Myanmar | 1401.079 kg | 403.805 kg | 273.193 kg | 158.921 kg | 96.744 kg | 333.888 kg |
| Philippines | 3.014 kg [ICPO] | 1.741 kg [ICPO] | 0.022 kg | No Report | 0.010 kg | No Report |
| Singapore | 82.613 kg | 141.852 kg | 56.730 kg | 52.083 kg | 106.678 kg | 63.420 kg |
| Taiwan province, China | No Report | No Report | No Report | 273.000 kg [PRESS] | 153.000 kg [PRESS] | No Report |
| Thailand | 323.287 kg | 507.769 kg | 405.034 kg | 384.000 kg [HNLP] | 501.000 kg [F.O] | 697.000 kg [F.O] |
| Viet Nam | 24.300 kg [ICPO] | 60.000 kg [ICPO] | 66.663 kg [F.O] | 49.320 kg [ICPO]  70000 u. | 40.300 kg | No Report |
| Sub-Total | 7905.201 kg | 9087.884 kg | 6682.871 kg  0.003 lt. | 7696.305 kg  70000 u. | 14553.110 kg | 10848.450 kg  30 u. |
| **Near and Middle East /South-West Asia** | | | | | | |
| Afghanistan | No Report | No Report | No Report | No Report | No Report | 1291.700 kg |
| Bahrain | 4.165 kg | 3.982 kg [ICPO] | 2.856 kg [ICPO] | 1.643 kg [ICPO] | 0.001 kg [ICPO] | 2.473 kg |
| Iran (Islamic Republic of) | 1986.042 kg | 2894.462 kg | 6030.000 kg | 6189.000 kg [NAPOL] | 4001.000 kg | 3977.000 kg [Govt] |
| Iraq | No Report | 8.300 kg | No Report | 1.020 kg | No Report | No Report |
| Israel | 75.100 kg | 137.800 kg | 111.830 kg [ICPO] | 80.000 kg | 67.625 kg | 66.590 kg |
| Jordan | 82.449 kg | 52.397 kg | 41.397 kg | 127.712 kg | 35.545 kg | 14.666 kg |
| Kuwait | 23.590 kg [ICPO] | 21.601 kg | 35.000 kg [INCB] | No Report | No Report | 17.186 kg [ICPO] |
| Lebanon | 2.361 kg | 3.093 kg | 8.149 kg | 2.363 kg | 13.002 kg | 2.005 kg |
| Oman | 0.756 kg [INCB] | No Report | 54.109 kg | 14.008 kg [ICPO] | 8.485 kg | 28.734 kg |
| Pakistan | 6156.000 kg [ICPO] | 3363.723 kg | 4973.711 kg | 9492.029 kg | 6931.470 kg | 5870.498 kg |

Source: Annual Report Questionnaire if not otherwise indicated

## SEIZURES, 1997 - 2002

### Heroin

| Region/country or territory | 1997 | 1998 | 1999 | 2000 | 2001 | 2002 |
|---|---|---|---|---|---|---|
| **ASIA** | | | | | | |
| **Near and Middle East /South-West Asia** | | | | | | |
| Qatar | No Report | 1.480 kg [ICPO] | 0.108 kg [ICPO] | 0.534 kg [ICPO] | 0.404 kg [ICPO] | 7.045 kg |
| Saudi Arabia | 115.667 kg [ICPO] | 63.107 kg | No Report | 200.922 kg | 178.825 kg | 28.564 kg [ICPO] |
| Syrian Arab Republic | 12.263 kg [Govt] | 36.204 kg [Govt] | 57.659 kg [Govt] | 50.441 kg [Govt] | 30.342 kg [Govt] | 27.663 kg |
| United Arab Emirates | 35.767 kg | 34.450 kg | 65.909 kg | 82.176 kg | 40.100 kg | 115.031 kg |
| Yemen | No Report | 0.027 kg [ICPO] | No Report | No Report | No Report | No Report |
| Sub-Total | 8494.159 kg | 6620.626 kg | 11380.730 kg | 16241.850 kg | 11306.800 kg | 11449.160 kg |
| **South Asia** | | | | | | |
| Bangladesh | No Report | No Report | 28.840 kg [F.O] | 8.031 kg | 42.290 kg [ICPO] | 15.746 kg |
| India | 1332.000 kg | 655.000 kg | 839.000 kg | 1240.000 kg | 889.000 kg | 933.000 kg [Govt] |
| Maldives | No Report | 1.142 kg | 0.357 kg | No Report | 0.167 kg | 0.300 kg [ICPO] |
| Nepal | 11.117 kg [Govt] | 9.400 kg [Govt] | 1.515 kg [Govt] | 1.705 kg [Govt] | 9.360 kg [ICPO] | 10.493 kg |
| Sri Lanka | 55.015 kg | 56.942 kg | 68.500 kg | 94.150 kg | 102.216 kg | 62.545 kg |
| Sub-Total | 1398.132 kg | 722.484 kg | 938.212 kg | 1343.886 kg | 1043.033 kg | 1022.084 kg |
| Total region | 19923.770 kg | 17445.550 kg | 20363.120 kg  0.003 lt. | 28533.170 kg  70000 u. | 31996.680 kg | 28374.010 kg  30 u. |
| **EUROPE** | | | | | | |
| **Eastern Europe** | | | | | | |
| Albania | No Report | No Report | 7.122 kg [ICPO] | 47.000 kg [Govt] | 4.500 kg [Govt] | 71.714 kg |
| Belarus | 0.635 kg [INCB] | 0.907 kg | 1.977 kg | 3.442 kg | 3.257 kg [ICPO] | 6.171 kg |
| Bosnia Herzegovina | 0.017 kg [NAPOL] | 0.686 kg [NAPOL] | 1.125 kg [ICPO] | 0.375 kg [NAPOL] | 1.900 kg [ICPO]  5 u. | 3.265 kg [ICPO] |
| Bulgaria | 322.691 kg | 219.632 kg | 265.249 kg | 2067.201 kg | 1550.629 kg | 535.090 kg |
| Croatia | 3.040 kg | 50.095 kg | 13.232 kg | 7.041 kg | 19.569 kg | 46.359 kg |
| Czech Republic | 21.442 kg | 240.000 kg | 108.380 kg | 114.520 kg | 88.590 kg  478 u. | 34.033 kg  40 u. |
| Estonia | No Report | 0.091 kg  129 u. | 0.518 kg  1269 u. | 0.438 kg  2129 u. | 1.163 kg | 3.783 kg |
| FYR of Macedonia | 15.425 kg [NAPOL] | 91.672 kg | 14.375 kg [NAPOL] | 90.789 kg [NAPOL] | 110.882 kg [Govt] | 28.572 kg |
| Hungary | 206.160 kg [Govt.] | 634.613 kg | 172.703 kg | 819.000 kg | 154.410 kg | 320.129 kg |
| Latvia | 0.011 kg | 0.098 kg | 0.768 kg | 0.775 kg | 0.465 kg | No Report |
| Lithuania | 0.089 kg | 0.423 kg | 0.923 kg | 0.943 kg | 2.740 kg | 2.761 kg |
| Poland | 142.812 kg | 67.405 kg | 44.947 kg | 120.063 kg [(2]  388.000 lt. | 208.106 kg | 293.207 kg |
| Republic of Moldova | 10.000 kg | No Report | No Report | 1.313 kg [ICPO] | 0.041 kg | No Report |
| Romania | 117.922 kg [ICPO] | 412.327 kg | 63.630 kg | 52.940 kg | 41.770 kg | 202.180 kg |
| Russian Federation | 24.027 kg | 442.900 kg | 695.085 kg | 984.000 kg [F.O] | 1287.226 kg | 842.163 kg [F.O] |
| Serbia and Montenegro | 15.425 kg [ICPO] | No Report | No Report | No Report | 62.518 kg | 43.462 kg |

Source: Annual Report Questionnaire if not otherwise indicated

## SEIZURES, 1997 - 2002
### Heroin

| Region/country or territory | 1997 | 1998 | 1999 | 2000 | 2001 | 2002 |
|---|---|---|---|---|---|---|
| **EUROPE** | | | | | | |
| **Eastern Europe** | | | | | | |
| Slovakia | 90.450 kg | 13.671 kg | 5.808 kg | 98.507 kg | 15.680 kg | 15.400 kg |
| Slovenia | 29.828 kg | 46.106 kg | 32.270 kg | 392.065 kg | 88.930 kg | 68.670 kg |
| Ukraine | 3.728 kg | 8.940 kg | 21.530 kg [ICPO.] | 21.743 kg [ICPO] | 8.669 kg | 206.600 kg |
| Sub-Total | 1003.702 kg | 2229.566 kg 129 u. | 1449.642 kg 1269 u. | 4822.155 kg 388.000 lt. 2129 u. | 3651.045 kg 483 u. | 2723.559 kg 40 u. |
| **Western Europe** | | | | | | |
| Andorra | 0.005 kg [ICPO] | 0.003 kg [ICPO] | 0.013 kg | 0.009 kg [ICPO] | 0.009 kg | [1] |
| Austria | 102.138 kg | 118.213 kg | 78.914 kg | 230.747 kg | 288.312 kg | 59.473 kg |
| Belgium | 55.000 kg | 75.790 kg | 73.537 kg | 187.739 kg | 187.739 kg [UNODC (3] | 262.000 kg |
| Cyprus | No Report | 0.035 kg | 2.193 kg | 4.949 kg | 1.638 kg | 0.283 kg |
| Denmark | 37.900 kg | 55.136 kg | 96.040 kg | 32.080 kg | 25.125 kg | 62.495 kg |
| Finland | 2.532 kg | 1.965 kg | 2.884 kg | 6.026 kg | 7.500 kg | |
| France | 415.453 kg | 343.783 kg | 203.313 kg | 443.935 kg | 351.055 kg | 476.149 kg |
| Germany | 722.211 kg | 685.920 kg | 796.400 kg | 796.000 kg | 835.836 kg | 519.598 kg |
| Greece | 146.311 kg 38 u. | 232.110 kg 6 u. | 98.401 kg 10 u. | 1179.526 kg 14 u. | 329.725 kg | 201.176 kg [4] |
| Iceland | No Report | No Report | 0.001 kg | No Report | No Report | [1] |
| Ireland | 8.184 kg | 36.963 kg | 15.921 kg | 23.942 kg | 29.527 kg | 16.606 kg |
| Italy | 470.335 kg 5360 u. | 703.335 kg 3069 u. | 1313.708 kg [ICPO] | 980.379 kg 1678 u. | 2004.588 kg 1423 u. | 2584.564 kg 1697 u. |
| Liechtenstein | 18.680 kg | No Report | 14.388 kg | 0.005 kg | 0.003 kg | 0.004 kg |
| Luxembourg | 2.525 kg | 3.592 kg | 1.914 kg | 11.358 kg [ICPO] | No Report | 2.956 kg [ICPO] |
| Malta | 4.535 kg | 0.498 kg | 1.724 kg | 5.912 kg | 2.599 kg | 1.218 kg [ICPO] |
| Monaco | 0.011 kg | | No Report | No Report | No Report | No Report |
| Netherlands | 999.000 kg [Govt] | 784.000 kg [Govt] | 770.000 kg [Govt] | 896.000 kg [Govt] | 739.000 kg | 1122.000 kg |
| Norway | 55.509 kg | 37.347 kg | 45.810 kg | 51.500 kg | 67.905 kg | 59.106 kg |
| Portugal | 57.389 kg | 96.666 kg | 76.417 kg | 567.577 kg [6] | 316.039 kg 5.000 lt. | 96.315 kg |
| Spain | 479.450 kg | 444.243 kg | 1159.297 kg | 484.854 kg | 630.600 kg | 274.777 kg |
| Sweden | 11.509 kg | 70.927 kg 0.011 lt. | 63.009 kg 0.509 lt. | 27.649 kg | 32.627 kg | 58.600 kg |
| Switzerland | 209.261 kg | 403.680 kg | 397.527 kg | 372.061 kg | 227.515 kg | 208.510 kg |
| Turkey | 3509.851 kg | 4651.486 kg | 3605.123 kg | 6052.582 kg [Govt.] | 4392.103 kg | 2557.778 kg |
| United Kingdom | 2234.900 kg | 1345.804 kg | 2341.700 kg [NCIS] | 3382.392 kg | 3928.976 kg | 3928.976 kg [7] |
| Sub-Total | 9542.689 kg 5398 u. | 10091.500 kg 0.011 lt. 3075 u. | 11158.230 kg 0.509 lt. 10 u. | 15737.220 kg 1692 u. | 14398.420 kg 5.000 lt. 1423 u. | 12492.580 kg 1697 u. |
| Total region | 10546.390 kg 5398 u. | 12321.060 kg 0.011 lt. 3204 u. | 12607.880 kg 0.509 lt. 1279 u. | 20559.380 kg 388.000 lt. 3821 u. | 18049.470 kg 5.000 lt. 1906 u. | 15216.140 kg 1737 u. |

Source: Annual Report Questionnaire if not otherwise indicated

## SEIZURES, 1997 - 2002

### Heroin

| Region/country or territory | 1997 | 1998 | 1999 | 2000 | 2001 | 2002 |
|---|---|---|---|---|---|---|
| **OCEANIA** | | | | | | |
| **Oceania** | | | | | | |
| Australia | 365.370 kg | 298.690 kg [Govt. (8] | 360.145 kg | 583.456 kg | 82.729 kg | 459.368 kg |
| Fiji | No Report | No Report | No Report | 357.700 kg [ICPO] | No Report | No Report |
| New Zealand | 0.171 kg [INCB] | 10.859 kg | 0.544 kg | 0.066 kg | 5.536 kg | 0.809 kg |
| Sub-Total | 365.541 kg | 309.549 kg | 360.689 kg | 941.222 kg | 88.265 kg | 460.177 kg |
| Total region | 365.541 kg | 309.549 kg | 360.689 kg | 941.222 kg | 88.265 kg | 460.177 kg |
| TOTAL | 33347.930 kg | 32628.780 kg | 35874.750 kg | 53394.020 kg | 54456.660 kg | 49255.210 kg |
| | 0.225 lt. | 0.453 lt. | 0.512 lt. | 389.967 lt. | 5.000 lt. | 26404 u. |
| | 5398 u. | 4214 u. | 2468 u. | 74846 u. | 2402 u. | |

1) Small quantity. 2) 388 lt. Polish heroin 3) Due to unavailability of 2001 data, year 2000 data were used for analysis purposes. 4) including morphine 5) Including depressants. 6) heroin with 44gm of cocaine 7) Due to unavailability of 2002 data, year 2001 data were used for analysis purposes. 8) Provisional figures.

Source: Annual Report Questionnaire if not otherwise indicated

## SEIZURES, 1997 - 2002
### Morphine

| Region/country or territory | 1997 | 1998 | 1999 | 2000 | 2001 | 2002 |
|---|---|---|---|---|---|---|
| **AFRICA** | | | | | | |
| **East Africa** | | | | | | |
| Ethiopia | No Report | 0.001 kg 6 u. | No Report | No Report | No Report | No Report |
| United Republic of Tanzania | 0.283 kg | No Report | 0.020 kg | No Report | 3.338 kg [Govt] | 0.850 kg [ICPO] |
| Sub-Total | 0.283 kg | 0.001 kg 6 u. | 0.020 kg | | 3.338 kg | 0.850 kg |
| **North Africa** | | | | | | |
| Egypt | 0.001 kg | 0.012 lt. | 0.007 kg | No Report | 4 u. | No Report |
| Morocco | 0.318 kg | 0.997 kg | No Report | No Report | 247 u. | No Report |
| Sudan | No Report | No Report | No Report | No Report | 18408 u. [Govt] | No Report |
| Sub-Total | 0.319 kg | 0.997 kg 0.012 lt. | 0.007 kg | | 18659 u. | |
| **Southern Africa** | | | | | | |
| Mozambique | No Report | No Report | 0.085 kg [ICPO] | No Report | No Report | No Report |
| Zambia | 0.000 kg [Govt] | 3.200 kg [Govt] | 0.028 kg | 0.061 kg | 0.860 kg [Govt] | No Report |
| Sub-Total | | 3.200 kg | 0.113 kg | 0.061 kg | 0.860 kg | |
| **West and Central Africa** | | | | | | |
| Benin | No Report | 3.190 kg | No Report | No Report | No Report | No Report |
| Chad | No Report | No Report | No Report | 0.090 kg | No Report | No Report |
| Nigeria | 0.130 kg | No Report | No Report | 21.120 kg | No Report | No Report |
| Sub-Total | 0.130 kg | 3.190 kg | | 21.210 kg | | |
| Total region | 0.732 kg | 7.388 kg 0.012 lt. 6 u. | 0.140 kg | 21.271 kg | 4.198 kg 18659 u. | 0.850 kg |
| **AMERICAS** | | | | | | |
| **Caribbean** | | | | | | |
| *Aruba* | No Report | No Report | No Report | No Report | No Report | 0.509 kg [ICPO] |
| Cuba | No Report | No Report | No Report | No Report | No Report | 63 u. [ICPO] |
| Dominican Republic | No Report | No Report | No Report | 19.000 kg [CICAD] | No Report | No Report |
| Sub-Total | | | | 19.000 kg | | 0.509 kg 63 u. |
| **Central America** | | | | | | |
| Guatemala | 0.720 kg [Govt.] | No Report | No Report | No Report | No Report | No Report |
| Sub-Total | 0.720 kg | | | | | |
| **North America** | | | | | | |
| Canada | 1.076 kg 2468 u. | 1.662 kg 0.433 lt. 1166 u. | 1.000 kg 1.016 lt. 1826 u. | 0.751 kg 1.285 lt. 1842 u. | 0.267 kg 3807 u. | 0.239 kg 3591 u. |
| Mexico | 2.068 kg | No Report | 1.130 kg | 4.480 kg | 0.539 kg | 0.002 kg |

Source: Annual Report Questionnaire if not otherwise indicated

## SEIZURES, 1997 - 2002
### Morphine

| Region/country or territory | 1997 | 1998 | 1999 | 2000 | 2001 | 2002 |
|---|---|---|---|---|---|---|
| **AMERICAS** | | | | | | |
| **North America** | | | | | | |
| United States | 0.006 lt.<br>560 u. | No Report | 3.134 kg<br>998 u. | 180.108 kg<br>15.723 lt.<br>134 u. | 812 u. | 652 u. |
| Sub-Total | 3.144 kg<br>0.006 lt.<br>3028 u. | 1.662 kg<br>0.433 lt.<br>1166 u. | 5.264 kg<br>1.016 lt.<br>2824 u. | 185.339 kg<br>17.008 lt.<br>1976 u. | 0.806 kg<br>4619 u. | 0.241 kg<br>4243 u. |
| **South America** | | | | | | |
| Argentina | No Report | No Report | 650.000 kg | No Report | No Report | No Report |
| Brazil | No Report | No Report | 0.150 kg | No Report | No Report | No Report |
| Chile | No Report | 29 u. | 1 u. <sup>ICPO</sup> | No Report | No Report | 5 u. |
| Colombia | 87.122 kg | 79.111 kg | 154.023 kg | 91.017 kg | 47.300 kg | 20.000 kg |
| Peru | No Report | No Report | No Report | 11.979 kg | 0.492 kg | 6.230 kg |
| Sub-Total | 87.122 kg | 79.111 kg<br>29 u. | 804.173 kg<br>1 u. | 102.996 kg | 47.792 kg | 26.230 kg<br>5 u. |
| Total region | 90.986 kg<br>0.006 lt.<br>3028 u. | 80.773 kg<br>0.433 lt.<br>1195 u. | 809.437 kg<br>1.016 lt.<br>2825 u. | 307.335 kg<br>17.008 lt.<br>1976 u. | 48.598 kg<br>4619 u. | 26.980 kg<br>4311 u. |
| **ASIA** | | | | | | |
| **Central Asia and Transcaucasian countries** | | | | | | |
| Armenia | 3 u. | [1] | No Report | 0.000 kg [1] | 0.351 kg | [1] |
| Azerbaijan | No Report | No Report | 0.085 kg | No Report | No Report | No Report |
| Georgia | No Report | No Report | 0.003 kg <sup>ICPO</sup> | 0.262 kg <sup>ICPO</sup> | 0.107 kg <sup>ICPO</sup> | No Report |
| Kazakhstan | No Report | 4.172 kg | 1.493 kg | No Report | No Report | No Report |
| Uzbekistan | 8 u. | 0.030 kg | 3.400 kg <sup>ICPO</sup> | No Report | No Report | No Report |
| Sub-Total | 11 u. | 4.202 kg | 4.981 kg | 0.262 kg | 0.458 kg | |
| **East and South-East Asia** | | | | | | |
| Brunei Darussalam | No Report | No Report | No Report | No Report | No Report | 0.004 kg |
| China | 358.000 kg | 146.000 kg | No Report | No Report | No Report | No Report |
| Hong Kong SAR, China | No Report | No Report | [1] | No Report | 1462 u. | No Report |
| Indonesia | 0.320 kg | No Report | 3.174 kg<br>202 u. | 0.223 kg | 0.001 kg | No Report |
| Japan | 0.011 kg<br>1.107 lt.<br>229 u. | 0.363 kg<br>0.002 lt.<br>146 u. | 0.002 kg | 200 u. | 1.275 kg<br>117 u. | 0.001 lt. |
| Lao People's Dem. Rep. | No Report | No Report | No Report | No Report | No Report | 18.100 kg |
| Mongolia | No Report | No Report | No Report | 0.270 kg <sup>ICPO</sup> | No Report | No Report |
| Myanmar | 45.728 kg<br>200 u. | 95.087 kg | 24.001 kg | 22.696 kg | 6.052 kg<br>107 u. | 314.004 kg<br>177 u. |

Source: Annual Report Questionnaire if not otherwise indicated

## SEIZURES, 1997 - 2002
### Morphine

| Region/country or territory | 1997 | 1998 | 1999 | 2000 | 2001 | 2002 |
|---|---|---|---|---|---|---|
| **ASIA** | | | | | | |
| **East and South-East Asia** | | | | | | |
| Singapore | No Report | No Report | No Report | No Report | 0.076 kg 24 u. | No Report |
| Thailand | 0.005 kg | No Report | 0.200 kg [ICPO] | 0.005 kg [ICPO] | No Report | No Report |
| Sub-Total | 404.064 kg 1.107 lt. 429 u. | 241.450 kg 0.002 lt. 146 u. | 27.377 kg 202 u. | 23.194 kg 200 u. | 7.404 kg 1710 u. | 332.108 kg 0.001 lt. 177 u. |
| **Near and Middle East /South-West Asia** | | | | | | |
| Iran (Islamic Republic of) | 18949.754 kg | 22291.102 kg | 22764.000 kg | 20764.000 kg [NAPOL] | 8668.000 kg | 9521.000 kg [Govt] |
| Israel | No Report | No Report | 0.028 kg [ICPO] | 18 u. | 0.041 kg | 50 u. |
| Kuwait | No Report | No Report | 34.813 kg [ICPO] | 10.611 kg [ICPO] | No Report | No Report |
| Oman | No Report | No Report | 1.006 kg | No Report | No Report | No Report |
| Pakistan | No Report | No Report | No Report | No Report | 1824.000 kg 7850 u. | 6839.260 kg |
| Qatar | 0.133 kg [ICPO] | No Report | No Report | No Report | No Report | No Report |
| Saudi Arabia | No Report | No Report | 149.491 kg [ICPO] | No Report | No Report | No Report |
| United Arab Emirates | No Report | 0.018 kg | 0.030 kg | No Report | No Report | 0.015 kg |
| Sub-Total | 18949.890 kg | 22291.120 kg | 22949.370 kg | 20774.610 kg 18 u. | 10492.040 kg 7850 u. | 16360.270 kg 50 u. |
| **South Asia** | | | | | | |
| Bangladesh | No Report | No Report | No Report | No Report | 108 u. [ICPO] | No Report |
| India | 128.000 kg | 19.000 kg | 30.000 kg | 39.000 kg | 26.000 kg | 66.000 kg |
| Nepal | 11.126 kg [ICPO] | No Report | No Report | No Report | No Report | No Report |
| Sub-Total | 139.126 kg | 19.000 kg | 30.000 kg | 39.000 kg | 26.000 kg 108 u. | 66.000 kg |
| Total region | 19493.080 kg 1.107 lt. 440 u. | 22555.770 kg 0.002 lt. 146 u. | 23011.720 kg 202 u. | 20837.070 kg 218 u. | 10525.900 kg 9668 u. | 16758.380 kg 0.001 lt. 227 u. |
| **EUROPE** | | | | | | |
| **Eastern Europe** | | | | | | |
| Albania | No Report | No Report | No Report | 10 u. [ICPO] | No Report | 10 u. |
| Belarus | 0.001 kg [INCB] | 0.154 kg | 0.005 kg | 0.078 kg | 192.000 kg [ICPO] | 0.032 kg |
| Bulgaria | 4.000 kg | No Report | 16 u. | No Report | No Report | No Report |
| Croatia | No Report | 79 u. | 652 u. | 27 u. | No Report | No Report |
| Czech Republic | No Report | No Report | No Report | No Report | 0.049 kg | 1.739 lt. |
| Estonia | [(2] | 0.003 kg 5 u. | No Report | 0.011 kg 40 u. | 1.066 kg | 0.039 kg |
| Hungary | 0.686 kg [Govt.] | No Report | 0.200 kg | No Report | 10 u. | 1.802 kg |
| Poland | No Report | No Report | No Report | 0.588 kg [ICPO] 174 u. | No Report | No Report |

Source: Annual Report Questionnaire if not otherwise indicated

## SEIZURES, 1997 - 2002
### Morphine

| Region/country or territory | 1997 | 1998 | 1999 | 2000 | 2001 | 2002 |
|---|---|---|---|---|---|---|
| **EUROPE** | | | | | | |
| **Eastern Europe** | | | | | | |
| Republic of Moldova | 31 u. | No Report | No Report | No Report | No Report | No Report |
| Romania | 71 u. [ICPO] | 86 u. | 132 u. | 0.112 kg | 248 u. | 414 u. |
| Russian Federation | 6.037 kg<br>8 u. | 15.000 kg [F.O] | 2.427 kg | 2.000 kg [F.O] | 11.024 kg | 1.896 kg [ICPO] |
| Slovakia | No Report | 3 u. | | 0.288 kg | | 0.600 kg |
| Sub-Total | 10.724 kg<br>110 u. | 15.157 kg<br>173 u. | 2.632 kg<br>800 u. | 3.077 kg<br>251 u. | 204.139 kg<br>258 u. | 4.369 kg<br>1.739 lt.<br>424 u. |
| **Western Europe** | | | | | | |
| Austria | 0.327 kg | 1.522 kg | 0.328 kg | 0.220 kg | 0.200 kg | 0.280 kg |
| Belgium | 10.000 kg | 0.098 kg | | 17.400 kg [ICPO] | 17.400 kg [UNODC (3] | |
| Cyprus | No Report | No Report | No Report | No Report | 15 u. | 0.013 kg |
| Denmark | 1.560 lt. | 3.000 kg | No Report | 1.405 kg [ICPO] | No Report | 20000 u. [ICPO] |
| Finland | 0.005 kg | No Report | 0.910 kg<br>60 u. | 0.054 kg<br>60 u. | No Report | No Report |
| France | 0.020 kg | 0.088 kg | 1.566 kg | 0.222 kg | 0.218 kg | 5.459 kg |
| Ireland | 0.003 kg<br>528 u. | 0.004 kg | 90 u. [ICPO] | No Report | No Report | No Report |
| Italy | 0.095 kg<br>9 u. | 2.270 kg<br>12 u. | 1.314 kg [ICPO] | 0.752 kg<br>5 u. | 0.015 kg<br>452 u. | 3.332 kg<br>5 u. |
| Norway | 0.011 kg | 0.008 kg<br>33 u. | 0.001 kg<br>1219 u. | 2005 u. | 1963 u. | 0.003 kg<br>1859 u. |
| Portugal | No Report | 0.005 kg | 85 u. | 241 u. | 0.043 kg<br>97 u. | 35 u. |
| Spain | 8 u. | 3 u. | 13 u. | 33 u. | 16 u. | 15 u. |
| Sweden | 0.003 kg<br>104 u. | 0.154 lt. | 0.011 kg<br>0.202 lt.<br>120 u. | 0.074 kg<br>320 u. | 0.070 kg | 0.300 kg<br>621 u. |
| Switzerland | No Report | 0.054 kg | 0.537 kg | 0.135 kg | 0.492 kg | 0.146 kg |
| Turkey | 662.816 kg * | 754.494 kg | 1010.328 kg | 2484.934 kg [Govt.] | 797.493 kg | 7889.741 kg |
| United Kingdom | 0.400 kg | 41.251 kg | 1.300 kg [NCIS] | 3.278 kg | 4.015 kg | 4.015 kg [(4] |
| Sub-Total | 673.680 kg<br>1.560 lt.<br>649 u. | 802.794 kg<br>0.154 lt.<br>48 u. | 1016.295 kg<br>0.202 lt.<br>1587 u. | 2508.474 kg<br>2664 u. | 819.946 kg<br>2543 u. | 7903.289 kg<br>22535 u. |
| Total region | 684.404 kg<br>1.560 lt.<br>759 u. | 817.951 kg<br>0.154 lt.<br>221 u. | 1018.927 kg<br>0.202 lt.<br>2387 u. | 2511.552 kg<br>2915 u. | 1024.085 kg<br>2801 u. | 7907.658 kg<br>1.739 lt.<br>22959 u. |
| **OCEANIA** | | | | | | |
| **Oceania** | | | | | | |
| Australia | 2.049 kg | No Report | No Report | 3.205 kg<br>104 u. | 0.036 kg<br>73 u. | 4.097 kg |

Source: Annual Report Questionnaire if not otherwise indicated

* Reported figures at the time of the preparation of the report; revised figures by the Gov. of Turkey show seizures of morphine of 562.8 kg in 1997.

## SEIZURES, 1997 - 2002
### Morphine

| Region/country or territory | 1997 | 1998 | 1999 | 2000 | 2001 | 2002 |
|---|---|---|---|---|---|---|
| **OCEANIA** | | | | | | |
| **Oceania** | | | | | | |
| New Zealand | 1.422 kg [INCB] | 1.166 kg | 0.312 kg | 0.713 lt.<br>396 u. | 0.954 kg<br>1285 u. | 0.887 kg<br>370 u. |
| Sub-Total | 3.471 kg | 1.166 kg | 0.312 kg | 3.205 kg<br>0.713 lt.<br>500 u. | 0.990 kg<br>1358 u. | 4.984 kg<br>370 u. |
| Total region | 3.471 kg | 1.166 kg | 0.312 kg | 3.205 kg<br>0.713 lt.<br>500 u. | 0.990 kg<br>1358 u. | 4.984 kg<br>370 u. |
| TOTAL | 20272.670 kg<br>2.673 lt.<br>4227 u. | 23463.050 kg<br>0.601 lt.<br>1568 u. | 24840.540 kg<br>1.218 lt.<br>5414 u. | 23680.430 kg<br>17.721 lt.<br>5609 u. | 11603.770 kg<br>37105 u. | 24698.860 kg<br>1.740 lt.<br>27867 u. |

1) Small quantity. 2) Including depressants. 3) Due to unavailability of 2001 data, year 2000 data were used for analysis purposes.
4) Due to unavailability of 2002 data, year 2001 data were used for analysis purposes.

Source: Annual Report Questionnaire if not otherwise indicated

## SEIZURES, 1997 - 2002
### Other opiates

| Region/country or territory | 1997 | 1998 | 1999 | 2000 | 2001 | 2002 |
|---|---|---|---|---|---|---|
| **AFRICA** | | | | | | |
| **East Africa** | | | | | | |
| Ethiopia | No Report | No Report | No Report | No Report | No Report | 0.826 kg |
| Mauritius | 26 u. [ICPO] | No Report | No Report | No Report | No Report | 204 u. [ICPO] |
| Sub-Total | 26 u. | | | | | 0.826 kg<br>204 u. |
| **North Africa** | | | | | | |
| Egypt | 0.060 lt. [(1] | No Report | 0.030 lt. [(1] | 1.140 lt. [ICPO] | No Report | No Report |
| Sub-Total | 0.060 lt. | | 0.030 lt. | 1.140 lt. | | |
| **West and Central Africa** | | | | | | |
| Benin | No Report | No Report | No Report | 1.650 kg [ICPO] | No Report | No Report |
| Nigeria | No Report | No Report | No Report | No Report | No Report | 0.756 kg [ICPO]<br>68421 u. |
| Sub-Total | | | | 1.650 kg | | 0.756 kg<br>68421 u. |
| Total region | 0.060 lt.<br>26 u. | | 0.030 lt. | 1.650 kg<br>1.140 lt. | | 1.582 kg<br>68625 u. |
| **AMERICAS** | | | | | | |
| **Caribbean** | | | | | | |
| *Cayman Islands* | No Report | No Report | 0.003 kg [ICPO] | 2 u. | No Report | No Report |
| Dominican Republic | No Report | No Report | 8.000 kg [ICPO] | No Report | No Report | No Report |
| *Puerto Rico* | No Report | No Report | No Report | No Report | No Report | 0.036 lt. [ICPO]<br>4 u. |
| Sub-Total | | | 8.003 kg | 2 u. | | 0.036 lt.<br>4 u. |
| **North America** | | | | | | |
| Canada | 0.912 kg<br>0.301 lt.<br>4826 u. | 1.446 kg<br>0.093 lt.<br>8880 u. | 0.594 kg<br>8805 u. | 0.682 kg<br>1.050 lt.<br>4784 u. | 1.124 kg<br>22045 u. | 0.918 kg<br>28238 u. |
| Mexico | No Report | No Report | No Report | No Report | No Report | 8053.635 kg |
| United States | No Report | No Report | 9338 u. [ICPO (1] | No Report | 10778580 u. | 78081 u. |
| Sub-Total | 0.912 kg<br>0.301 lt.<br>4826 u. | 1.446 kg<br>0.093 lt.<br>8880 u. | 0.594 kg<br>18143 u. | 0.682 kg<br>1.050 lt.<br>4784 u. | 1.124 kg<br>10800630 u. | 8054.553 kg<br>106319 u. |
| **South America** | | | | | | |
| Argentina | No Report | No Report | No Report | No Report | 0.200 kg | No Report |
| Chile | No Report | 25 u. | No Report | No Report | No Report | 13 u. |
| Colombia | No Report | No Report | 3.500 kg [(1] | No Report | 1.000 kg [(1] | No Report |
| Peru | No Report | No Report | 38.693 kg [ICPO] | No Report | No Report | No Report |
| Sub-Total | | 25 u. | 42.193 kg | | 1.200 kg | 13 u. |

Source: Annual Report Questionnaire if not otherwise indicated

## SEIZURES, 1997 - 2002
### Other opiates

| Region/country or territory | 1997 | 1998 | 1999 | 2000 | 2001 | 2002 |
|---|---|---|---|---|---|---|
| **AMERICAS** | | | | | | |
| Total region | 0.912 kg | 1.446 kg | 50.790 kg | 0.682 kg | 2.324 kg | 8054.553 kg |
| | 0.301 lt. | 0.093 lt. | 18143 u. | 1.050 lt. | 10800630 u. | 0.036 lt. |
| | 4826 u. | 8905 u. | | 4786 u. | | 106336 u. |
| **ASIA** | | | | | | |
| **Central Asia and Transcaucasian countries** | | | | | | |
| Armenia | No Report | No Report | 0.017 kg [ICPO] | 1.679 kg | No Report | No Report |
| Azerbaijan | No Report | No Report | No Report | 72.590 kg [ICPO] | No Report | No Report |
| Georgia | No Report | No Report | 25.003 kg [ICPO (2] | 12.871 kg [ICPO] | No Report | No Report |
| Kazakhstan | No Report | 3.219 kg | 7.944 kg | No Report | No Report | No Report |
| Uzbekistan | 0.019 kg | No Report | No Report | 288.000 kg [ICPO] | No Report | No Report |
| Sub-Total | 0.019 kg | 3.219 kg | 32.964 kg | 375.140 kg | | |
| **East and South-East Asia** | | | | | | |
| Brunei Darussalam | 85.173 kg | 0.057 kg | 12.970 lt. | 23.000 lt. | 1413 u. | 0.003 lt. [(1] |
| | 554 u. | 474 u. | 2377 u. | | | 2565 u. |
| Hong Kong SAR, China | No Report | No Report | 187 u. [(2] | 7.600 lt. [ICPO] | 5.200 lt. | 4930 u. |
| | | | | 1873 u. | 3306 u. | |
| Indonesia | No Report | 7179 u. | 564 u. [ICPO (1] | No Report | No Report | No Report |
| Japan | 0.141 kg | 0.006 kg | 0.005 kg | No Report | No Report | 579 u. [ICPO] |
| | 1809 u. | 0.030 lt. | | | | |
| | | 5557 u. | | | | |
| Macau SAR, China | 64 u. [ICPO] | 8.000 lt. [ICPO] | No Report | 2.000 lt. [ICPO] | No Report | 52 u. [ICPO] |
| | | 45 u. | | 1 u. | | |
| Malaysia | No Report | No Report | 18453 u. | 17982.480 lt. [(1] | No Report | No Report |
| Myanmar | 194.377 kg | No Report | 555.000 kg | 222.089 lt. [(3] | No Report | 338.454 lt. [(3] |
| | | | 121.000 lt. | | | |
| Singapore | 136 u. | 301 u. | 0.438 kg [(2] | 1127 u. [(4] | 6382.000 kg | No Report |
| Thailand | No Report | No Report | 381.600 lt. [ICPO (1] | 569.505 kg [ICPO] | No Report | 1057.000 kg [ICPO] |
| Sub-Total | 279.691 kg | 0.063 kg | 555.443 kg | 569.505 kg | 6382.000 kg | 1057.000 kg |
| | 2563 u. | 8.030 lt. | 515.570 lt. | 18237.170 lt. | 5.200 lt. | 338.457 lt. |
| | | 13556 u. | 21581 u. | 3001 u. | 4719 u. | 8126 u. |
| **Near and Middle East /South-West Asia** | | | | | | |
| Bahrain | No Report | No Report | No Report | No Report | No Report | 58 u. |
| Iran (Islamic Republic of) | 255.065 kg | No Report | 1088.000 kg | 1459.000 kg [ICPO] | No Report | No Report |
| Iraq | No Report | No Report | No Report | No Report | 1.000 kg [(1] | No Report |
| Israel | No Report | No Report | 2.121 lt. [ICPO (1] | 3.843 kg [ICPO] | No Report | 2.600 kg [ICPO] |
| | | | 7 u. | 15 u. | | |
| Jordan | 894.738 kg | No Report | No Report | No Report | No Report | No Report |
| Lebanon | No Report | No Report | No Report | 0.300 kg [ICPO] | No Report | No Report |
| Pakistan | No Report | No Report | No Report | No Report | No Report | 21757.000 kg [ICPO] |

Source: Annual Report Questionnaire if not otherwise indicated

## SEIZURES, 1997 - 2002
### Other opiates

| Region/country or territory | 1997 | 1998 | 1999 | 2000 | 2001 | 2002 |
|---|---|---|---|---|---|---|
| **ASIA** | | | | | | |
| **Near and Middle East /South-West Asia** | | | | | | |
| United Arab Emirates | No Report | No Report | No Report | No Report | No Report | 0.030 kg[(1] |
| Sub-Total | 1149.803 kg | | 1088.000 kg<br>2.121 lt.<br>7 u. | 1463.143 kg<br>15 u. | 1.000 kg | 21759.630 kg<br>58 u. |
| **South Asia** | | | | | | |
| Bangladesh | No Report | No Report | No Report | No Report | No Report | 290.475 kg<br>108356 u. |
| Nepal | 4971 u.[ICPO] | 3676 u. | No Report | No Report | No Report | 35.000 lt.[ICPO] |
| Sub-Total | 4971 u. | 3676 u. | | | | 290.475 kg<br>35.000 lt.<br>108356 u. |
| Total region | 1429.513 kg<br>7534 u. | 3.282 kg<br>8.030 lt.<br>17232 u. | 1676.407 kg<br>517.691 lt.<br>21588 u. | 2407.788 kg<br>18237.170 lt.<br>3016 u. | 6383.000 kg<br>5.200 lt.<br>4719 u. | 23107.100 kg<br>373.457 lt.<br>116540 u. |
| **EUROPE** | | | | | | |
| **Eastern Europe** | | | | | | |
| Albania | No Report | No Report | No Report | 0.480 lt.[ICPO]<br>7 u. | No Report | 21 u.[(5] |
| Belarus | No Report | No Report | No Report | No Report | No Report | 0.361 kg[ICPO] |
| Bosnia Herzegovina | No Report | 1 u.[ICPO] | No Report | No Report | No Report | No Report |
| Bulgaria | No Report | No Report | No Report | 3650 u.[ICPO] | No Report | No Report |
| Croatia | No Report | No Report | No Report | 29 u. | No Report | 4047 u.[ICPO] |
| Estonia | 23.332 lt. | No Report | 2 u. | 0.003 kg<br>20 u. | No Report | 0.076 kg |
| FYR of Macedonia | No Report | No Report | 3.988 kg[ICPO]<br>2.250 lt.<br>135 u. | No Report | No Report | No Report |
| Hungary | No Report | 438 u. | 120 u.[ICPO (2] | No Report | 262 u. | 222 u. |
| Latvia | 0.134 kg | No Report | No Report | No Report | No Report | No Report |
| Lithuania | No Report | 13 u. | 0.210 kg<br>92 u. | 0.888 lt.[(2] | No Report | 0.001 kg[ICPO] |
| Poland | 1004.000 lt. | 395.000 lt. | 389.000 lt.[(6] | 3.500 lt.[ICPO]<br>174 u. | No Report | 193.000 kg[(6] |
| Republic of Moldova | 1000 u. | 2100 u. | 682 u.[ICPO] | 0.858 kg[ICPO] | No Report | 171.720 kg[Govt (7] |
| Romania | No Report | 19494 u. | 26 u.[(2] | 0.840 lt.[(2]<br>387 u. | No Report | 0.046 kg[ICPO] |
| Russian Federation | 4.925 kg<br>11 u. | 167.700 kg[F.O] | 54.575 kg | 18.000 kg[F.O] | 21469.675 kg | 93.446 kg[ICPO] |
| Slovakia | No Report | 922 u. | 278 u. | 38 u.[ICPO] | No Report | 21 u. |
| Slovenia | No Report | No Report | 0.552 lt. | 1.545 lt.[ICPO]<br>245 u. | No Report | No Report |

Source: Annual Report Questionnaire if not otherwise indicated

## SEIZURES, 1997 - 2002
### Other opiates

| Region/country or territory | 1997 | 1998 | 1999 | 2000 | 2001 | 2002 |
|---|---|---|---|---|---|---|
| **EUROPE** | | | | | | |
| **Eastern Europe** | | | | | | |
| Ukraine | No Report | No Report | 11600 u. [ICPO (1] | No Report | No Report | 20.000 kg |
| Sub-Total | 5.059 kg | 167.700 kg | 58.773 kg | 18.861 kg | 21469.680 kg | 478.650 kg |
| | 1027.332 lt. | 395.000 lt. | 391.802 lt. | 7.253 lt. | 262 u. | 4311 u. |
| | 1011 u. | 22968 u. | 12935 u. | 4550 u. | | |
| **Western Europe** | | | | | | |
| Austria | 0.083 kg | No Report | No Report | No Report | No Report | No Report |
| Belgium | No Report | 0.109 kg | 9.100 kg [ICPO] | 15.070 kg [ICPO] | 15.070 kg [UNODC (8] | No Report |
| | | | 0.200 lt. | | | |
| | | | 307500 u. | | | |
| Cyprus | No Report | No Report | 55 u. [ICPO] | No Report | No Report | 0.200 kg [ICPO] |
| | | | | | | 70 u. |
| Denmark | No Report | 6.000 kg | No Report | No Report | No Report | No Report |
| Finland | No Report | No Report | 46 u. [ICPO] | 13808 u. | 31967 u. | 18700 u. |
| France | No Report | No Report | 521 u. [ICPO (2] | 4134 u. [ICPO] | No Report | No Report |
| Greece | 2.308 kg | 1.529 kg | 0.132 kg | 0.472 kg | 0.070 kg | 1576 u. |
| | 15322 u. | 6774 u. | 7795 u. | 5162 u. | 1466 u. | |
| Ireland | No Report | No Report | 0.320 kg [ICPO (2] | No Report | No Report | 6.895 lt. [ICPO] |
| | | | 579 u. | | | 252 u. |
| Italy | 0.002 kg | 0.554 kg | 2.426 kg [ICPO (2] | 2.967 kg [(9] | No Report | 5.447 kg [ICPO] |
| | 7 u. | 7538 u. | | 7220 u. | | 22442 u. |
| Luxembourg | No Report | No Report | 0.180 lt. [ICPO (2] | 0.098 lt. [ICPO] | No Report | No Report |
| Malta | No Report | 77 u. | No Report | 98 u. | No Report | 0.230 lt. [ICPO] |
| Monaco | No Report | No Report | No Report | No Report | No Report | 0.003 lt. [ICPO] |
| Netherlands | 2.000 kg [Govt (2] | 4093 u. [Govt (2] | 50.000 kg [Govt (2] | 16.000 kg [Govt (2] | No Report | No Report |
| | 16748 u. | | 186437 u. | 5543 u. | | |
| Norway | No Report | No Report | 0.017 kg | 0.001 kg | 0.255 kg | 0.756 kg |
| | | | 9657 u. | 8007 u. | 18879 u. | 68421 u. |
| Portugal | 21 u. | 35 u. | 21 u. | 15 u. [(10] | 20.910 kg | 0.009 kg |
| | | | | | 22 u. | 2 u. |
| Spain | 1159 u. | No Report | 966 u. [ICPO] | No Report | 7708 u. | 742 u. [ICPO] |
| Sweden | No Report | 0.003 kg | 0.053 kg | 0.052 kg | No Report | 4629 u. |
| | | 1.312 lt. | 783 u. | 631 u. | | |
| Switzerland | 0.010 kg | No Report | 5006 u. | 5472 u. [(2] | No Report | 4079 u. [ICPO] |
| Turkey | No Report | No Report | 34090 u. [ICPO (2] | 0.234 kg [Govt. (2] | No Report | No Report |
| United Kingdom | 1.000 kg | 0.064 kg | 60.600 kg [NCIS (2] | 0.548 kg | 1146.641 kg | 1146.641 kg [(11] |
| | 1.000 lt. | | | | | |
| | 1 u. | | | | | |
| Sub-Total | 5.403 kg | 8.259 kg | 122.648 kg | 35.344 kg | 1182.946 kg | 1153.053 kg |
| | 1.000 lt. | 1.312 lt. | 0.380 lt. | 0.098 lt. | 60042 u. | 7.128 lt. |
| | 33258 u. | 18517 u. | 553456 u. | 50090 u. | | 120913 u. |

Source: Annual Report Questionnaire if not otherwise indicated

## SEIZURES, 1997 - 2002
### Other opiates

| Region/country or territory | 1997 | 1998 | 1999 | 2000 | 2001 | 2002 |
|---|---|---|---|---|---|---|
| **EUROPE** | | | | | | |
| Total region | 10.462 kg | 175.959 kg | 181.421 kg | 54.205 kg | 22652.620 kg | 1631.703 kg |
| | 1028.332 lt. | 396.312 lt. | 392.182 lt. | 7.351 lt. | 60304 u. | 7.128 lt. |
| | 34269 u. | 41485 u. | 566391 u. | 54640 u. | | 125224 u. |
| **OCEANIA** | | | | | | |
| **Oceania** | | | | | | |
| Australia | (12 | 22.243 kg Govt. (13 | 6.792 kg Govt. (13 | 0.384 kg | 6.786 kg Govt. (14 | No Report |
| New Zealand | No Report | No Report | 0.100 kg | No Report | No Report | 0.461 kg |
| | | | | | | 1301 u. |
| Sub-Total | | 22.243 kg | 6.892 kg | 0.384 kg | 6.786 kg | 0.461 kg |
| | | | | | | 1301 u. |
| Total region | | 22.243 kg | 6.892 kg | 0.384 kg | 6.786 kg | 0.461 kg |
| | | | | | | 1301 u. |
| TOTAL | 1440.887 kg | 202.930 kg | 1915.510 kg | 2464.709 kg | 29044.730 kg | 32795.400 kg |
| | 1028.693 lt. | 404.435 lt. | 909.903 lt. | 18246.710 lt. | 5.200 lt. | 380.621 lt. |
| | 46655 u. | 67622 u. | 606122 u. | 62442 u. | 10865650 u. | 418026 u. |

1) Codeine 2) Methadone 3) Phensedyl 4) Methadone and dihydrocodeine 5) pethidine 6) Polish heroin (also called "compot") 7) Poppy solution 8) Due to unavailability of 2001 data, year 2000 data were used for analysis purposes. 9) 2.933 kg,7208 u. methadone 10) 15 u. liquid heroin, 92 u. methadone 11) Due to unavailability of 2002 data, year 2001 data were used for analysis purposes. 12) Small quantity. 13) Provisional figures. 14) Fiscal year

Source: Annual Report Questionnaire if not otherwise indicated

## 4.2. Cocaine: Seizures 1997-2002

### SEIZURES, 1997 - 2002
#### Cocaine (base and salts)

| Region/country or territory | 1997 | 1998 | 1999 | 2000 | 2001 | 2002 |
|---|---|---|---|---|---|---|
| **AFRICA** | | | | | | |
| **East Africa** | | | | | | |
| Kenya | 0.410 kg | 1.240 kg | 0.110 kg | 4.017 kg | 0.207 kg [Govt] | 18.584 kg [Govt] |
| Rwanda | No Report | No Report | No Report | No Report | No Report | 4.000 kg |
| Uganda | No Report | No Report | 0.412 kg | 1.910 kg | No Report | No Report |
| United Republic of Tanzania | 0.200 kg | No Report | 1.161 kg | 2.103 kg [ICPO] | 7.389 kg [Govt] | 2.461 kg [ICPO] |
| Sub-Total | 0.610 kg | 1.240 kg | 1.683 kg | 8.030 kg | 7.596 kg | 25.045 kg |
| **North Africa** | | | | | | |
| Algeria | No Report | No Report | No Report | No Report | 0.288 kg [ICPO] | 0.268 kg |
| Egypt | 0.914 kg | 1.860 kg | 0.792 kg | 14.288 kg | No Report | 4.001 kg |
| Libyan Arab Jam. | No Report | 0.136 kg | 0.070 kg [F.O] | 0.531 kg [F.O] | 0.173 kg [F.O] | No Report |
| Morocco | 6055.550 kg | 30.111 kg | 1.742 kg | 0.898 kg | 4.298 kg 103 u. | 15.801 kg 15 u. |
| Sudan | 0.130 kg [Govt] | No Report | No Report | 0.001 kg 2 u. | 0.587 kg [Govt] | No Report |
| Tunisia | 0.047 kg [ICPO] | 0.127 kg | 0.017 kg [ICPO] | No Report | No Report | 1.055 kg |
| Sub-Total | 6056.641 kg | 32.234 kg | 2.621 kg | 15.718 kg 2 u. | 5.346 kg 103 u. | 21.125 kg 15 u. |
| **Southern Africa** | | | | | | |
| Angola | 536.000 kg [ICPO] | 38.007 kg [ICPO] | 15.901 kg | 173.724 kg [ICPO] | 20.745 kg [ICPO] | No Report |
| Botswana | 0.982 kg [ICPO] | 0.700 kg [ICPO] | 1.696 kg [ICPO] | No Report | No Report | No Report |
| Lesotho | 2.346 kg [ICPO] | No Report | 0.632 kg [ICPO] | No Report | No Report | No Report |
| Malawi | No Report | 1.500 kg | 1.200 kg | No Report | 0.250 kg | No Report |
| Mozambique | No Report | 2.134 kg [ICPO] | 0.385 kg [ICPO] | 0.100 kg [ICPO] | 0.012 kg [ICPO] | No Report |
| Namibia | 23.932 kg [INCB] | 2.110 kg | No Report | 0.093 kg | 3.036 kg 100 u. | 0.189 kg 89 u. |
| South Africa | 151.519 kg | 635.908 kg 3825 u. | 345.549 kg [ICPO] 12940 u. | 91.202 kg | 155.305 kg 3470 u. | 436.499 kg |
| Swaziland | 9.650 kg [ICPO] | No Report | 3.609 kg | 6.832 kg | 1.006 kg | 1.058 kg |
| Zambia | 6.498 kg [Govt] | 0.000 kg [Govt] | 1.116 kg | 0.005 kg 27 u. | [Govt (1] | 17.300 kg |
| Zimbabwe | No Report | 0.501 kg | 0.166 kg | 0.593 kg | No Report | No Report |
| Sub-Total | 730.927 kg | 680.860 kg 3825 u. | 370.254 kg 12940 u. | 272.549 kg 27 u. | 180.354 kg 3570 u. | 455.046 kg 89 u. |
| **West and Central Africa** | | | | | | |
| Benin | 0.015 kg [Govt] | 0.628 kg | No Report | 21.494 kg [F.O] | 31.741 kg [ICPO] | 0.050 kg [ICPO] |
| Burkina Faso | 278.000 kg [Govt.] | No Report | No Report | No Report | No Report | No Report |
| Cameroon | No Report | 3.780 kg | No Report | No Report | No Report | No Report |
| Chad | No Report | No Report | 0.015 kg [ICPO] | 0.028 kg | No Report | No Report |
| Congo | No Report | No Report | No Report | 40.010 kg | 0.020 kg | 0.611 kg |
| Côte d'Ivoire | 22.028 kg | 19.015 kg | 9.287 kg 16 u. | 3.442 kg [ICPO] | 1.048 kg | 3.150 kg |

Source: Annual Report Questionnaire if not otherwise indicated

## SEIZURES, 1997 - 2002

### Cocaine (base and salts)

| Region/country or territory | 1997 | 1998 | 1999 | 2000 | 2001 | 2002 |
|---|---|---|---|---|---|---|
| **AFRICA** | | | | | | |
| **West and Central Africa** | | | | | | |
| Gabon | No Report | No Report | 0.216 kg [ICPO] | No Report | No Report | No Report |
| Gambia | 0.057 kg [ICPO] | 0.074 kg [ICPO] | 0.060 kg | No Report | 7.000 kg | No Report |
| Ghana | 6.350 kg [F.O.] | 5.035 kg | 7.062 kg | No Report | No Report | 10.400 kg |
| Niger | 28.866 kg [ICPO] | 0.233 kg [ICPO] | No Report | No Report | No Report | No Report |
| Nigeria | 31.900 kg [CICAD] | 9.260 kg [Govt.] | 15.064 kg | 53.950 kg | 195.823 kg | 35.347 kg |
| Sao Tome and Principe | 0.100 kg | No Report | 0.100 kg | No Report | No Report | No Report |
| Senegal | No Report | 5.321 kg [ICPO] | 31.564 kg [ICPO] 110 u. | 0.207 kg [ICPO] | No Report | 0.837 kg [ICPO] |
| Togo | 13.873 kg [Govt.] | No Report | No Report | 6.213 kg | 29.927 kg | 3.051 kg |
| Sub-Total | 381.189 kg | 43.346 kg | 63.368 kg 126 u. | 125.344 kg | 265.559 kg | 53.446 kg |
| Total region | 7169.367 kg | 757.680 kg 3825 u. | 437.926 kg 13066 u. | 421.641 kg 29 u. | 458.855 kg 3673 u. | 554.662 kg 104 u. |
| **AMERICAS** | | | | | | |
| **Caribbean** | | | | | | |
| Anguilla | 0.003 kg 8 u. | 0.108 kg | 0.020 kg [F.O] | No Report | 926.000 kg [F.O] | No Report |
| Antigua and Barbuda | 126.000 kg [F.O] | 1.000 kg [F.O] | 26.000 kg [F.O] | 24.000 kg [F.O] | 767.000 kg [F.O] | No Report |
| Aruba | 408.307 kg [INCB] | 794.000 kg [NAPOL] | 465.000 kg [F.O] | 346.000 kg [F.O] | 266.000 kg [F.O] | 490.681 kg [ICPO] |
| Bahamas | 2579.040 kg [ICPO] | 3343.054 kg | 1857.000 kg [F.O] | 2759.510 kg | 1469.000 kg 3238 u. | 2477.273 kg |
| Barbados | 88.050 kg [INCB] | 35.000 kg [NAPOL] | 132.760 kg [HONLC] | 81.000 kg [F.O] | 83.000 kg [F.O] | No Report |
| Bermuda | 4.516 kg | 4.330 kg | 8.076 kg | 11.574 kg | 667.000 kg [F.O] | 8.860 kg |
| British Virgin Islands | 838.000 kg [NAPOL] | 20.000 kg [NAPOL] | 432.000 kg [F.O] | 534.000 kg [F.O] | 2159.040 kg 34 u. | No Report |
| Cayman Islands | 1054.000 kg 319 u. | 1195.142 kg 1824 u. | 1926.129 kg | 1813.000 kg [F.O] | 1006.817 kg 40874 u. | 404.825 kg 28199 u. |
| Cuba | 1444.000 kg [F.O] | 669.000 kg [NAPOL] | 2444.000 kg [F.O] | 3145.000 kg [F.O] | 1278.000 kg [F.O] | 406.001 kg [ICPO] |
| Dominica | 101.000 kg [F.O] | 29.000 kg [F.O] | 82.769 kg [ICPO] | 10.000 kg [F.O] | 6.000 kg [F.O] | 4.526 kg [ICPO] |
| Dominican Republic | 1234.206 kg | 2341.916 kg | 1075.953 kg | 1310.000 kg [CICAD] | 1913.944 kg | 2295.200 kg [HONLC] |
| French Guiana | 213.000 kg [F.O] | 3.000 kg [F.O] | 446.000 kg [F.O] | 25.000 kg [F.O] | No Report | No Report |
| Grenada | 6.995 kg [INCB] | 26.500 kg | 43.000 kg [F.O] | 103.000 kg [F.O] | 53.389 kg | 77.320 kg [ICPO] |
| Guadeloupe | 66.000 kg [F.O] | 3222.000 kg [F.O] | 593.000 kg [F.O] | 292.000 kg [F.O] | 593.000 kg [F.O] | No Report |
| Haiti | 2100.000 kg [NAPOL] | 1272.000 kg [NAPOL] | 436.000 kg | 594.000 kg [F.O] | 414.000 kg | 272.760 kg |
| Jamaica | 414.680 kg [ICPO] 6296 u. | 1143.000 kg [F.O] | 2455.000 kg [ICPO] 3543 u. | 1656.000 kg [F.O] | 2950.910 kg 3099 u. | 3725.000 kg [ICPO] 2750 u. |
| Martinique | 37.000 kg [F.O] | 46.000 kg [F.O] | 36.000 kg [F.O] | 15.000 kg [F.O] | No Report | No Report |
| Montserrat | 0.130 kg 1 u. | No Report | No Report | No Report | No Report | No Report |

Source: Annual Report Questionnaire if not otherwise indicated

## SEIZURES, 1997 - 2002
### Cocaine (base and salts)

| Region/country or territory | 1997 | 1998 | 1999 | 2000 | 2001 | 2002 |
|---|---|---|---|---|---|---|
| **AMERICAS** | | | | | | |
| **Caribbean** | | | | | | |
| *Netherlands Antilles* | 1302.000 kg [F.O] | 639.000 kg [NAPOL] | 18.000 kg [F.O] | 965.353 kg [ICPO] | 1043.000 kg [F.O] | 2455.168 kg [ICPO] |
| *Puerto Rico* | 15153.000 kg [F.O] | 10344.000 kg [F.O] | 9977.000 kg [F.O] | 5516.000 kg [F.O] | 2831.000 kg [F.O] | 208.280 kg [ICPO] 76637 u. |
| Saint Kitts and Nevis | 150.000 kg [F.O] | 1.000 kg [F.O] | 10.000 kg [F.O] | 53.000 kg [INCSR] | 20.000 kg [F.O] | No Report |
| Saint Lucia | 7.782 kg | 78.137 kg | 133.000 kg [CICAD] | 110.473 kg | 63.000 kg [F.O] | No Report |
| Saint Vincent and the Grenadines | 1.000 kg [F.O] | 13.000 kg [F.O] | 15.000 kg [F.O] | 51.000 kg [INCSR] | 207.000 kg [F.O] | No Report |
| Trinidad Tobago | 71.000 kg [CICAD] | 77.680 kg | 137.000 kg [CICAD] | 203.000 kg [INCSR] | 821.880 kg | 172.769 kg |
| *Turks and Caicos Islands* | 1.500 kg | 2075.000 kg | 3.000 kg | 0.136 kg [ICPO] | 4.000 kg [F.O] | 1.689 kg |
| *US Virgin Islands* | No Report | No Report | 432.028 kg [ICPO] | No Report | No Report | No Report |
| Sub-Total | 27401.210 kg 6624 u. | 27372.870 kg 1824 u. | 23183.730 kg 3543 u. | 19618.050 kg | 19542.980 kg 47245 u. | 13000.350 kg 107586 u. |
| **Central America** | | | | | | |
| Belize | 2691.000 kg [CICAD] | 1221.000 kg [NAPOL] | 39.515 kg [ICPO] | 13.000 kg [F.O] | 3854.857 kg | 7.549 kg [ICPO] |
| Costa Rica* | 7857.000 kg [ICPO] 52170 u. | 7387.140 kg 102844 u. | 1998.720 kg 56514 u. | 5780.730 kg 64998 u. | 1747.960 kg 45283 u. | 2994.540 kg 100 u. |
| El Salvador | 234.431 kg [ICPO] | 45.256 kg [ICPO] | 38.649 kg | 434.700 kg [ICPO] | 31.544 kg | 2075.154 kg |
| Guatemala | 5098.466 kg [Govt.] 17 u. | 9217.070 kg | 9964.788 kg | 1537.360 kg | 4107.913 kg | 2934.265 kg |
| Honduras | 2187.673 kg 209 u. | 1804.000 kg [CICAD] 603 u. | 709.000 kg [CICAD] 662 u. | 1215.000 kg [CICAD] 1031 u. | No Report | 79.023 kg 708 u. |
| Nicaragua | 2790.200 kg 7109 u. | 4750.265 kg 21235 u. | 833.000 kg [CICAD] | 963.000 kg [CICAD] | 2717.971 kg [ICPO] | 2208.437 kg 12739 u. |
| Panama | 11324.740 kg | 11828.085 kg | 3139.889 kg | 7413.455 kg | 2660.000 kg | 2587.700 kg [HONLC] |
| Sub-Total | 32183.510 kg 59505 u. | 36252.820 kg 124682 u. | 16723.560 kg 57176 u. | 17357.240 kg 66029 u. | 15120.250 kg 45283 u. | 12886.670 kg 13547 u. |
| **North America** | | | | | | |
| Canada | 2090.000 kg 312 u. | 562.983 kg 0.007 lt. | 1650.518 kg 0.407 lt. 19 u. | 280.866 kg 5.156 lt. 26 u. | 1678.488 kg 167 u. | 181.391 kg 75 u. |
| Mexico | 34952.714 kg | 22597.072 kg | 34622.602 kg | 23195.942 kg [(2] | 29988.684 kg | 12639.347 kg |
| United States | 102000.000 kg [Govt.] | 117000.000 kg [Govt.] | 132318.000 kg | 99700.000 kg 1514.386 lt. 5326 u. | 106212.500 kg | 101904.500 kg [(2] |
| Sub-Total | 139042.700 kg 312 u. | 140160.100 kg 0.007 lt. | 168591.100 kg 0.407 lt. 19 u. | 123176.800 kg 1519.542 lt. 5352 u. | 137879.700 kg 167 u. | 114725.200 kg 75 u. |
| **South America** | | | | | | |
| Argentina | 5192.570 kg | 1766.900 kg | 1660.776 kg | 2351.359 kg | 2286.858 kg | 1638.281 kg |
| Bolivia | 12325.000 kg [F.O] | 11346.000 kg [F.O] | 7712.000 kg [F.O] | 5599.000 kg [F.O] | 4615.000 kg [F.O] | 5103.030 kg |

Source: Annual Report Questionnaire if not otherwise indicated

* Reported figures at the time of the preparation of the report; revised figures by the Gov. of Costa Rica show seizures of cocaine for the year 2000 of 5,871 kg; for 2001 1,748.6 kg; for 2002 2,955 kg and for 2003 4,291.2 kg.

## SEIZURES, 1997 - 2002
### Cocaine (base and salts)

| Region/country or territory | 1997 | 1998 | 1999 | 2000 | 2001 | 2002 |
|---|---|---|---|---|---|---|
| **AMERICAS** | | | | | | |
| **South America** | | | | | | |
| Brazil | 4309.378 kg | 6560.414 kg | 7646.103 kg | 5555.925 kg | 9137.265 kg Govt | 9415.200 kg F.O |
| Chile | 2660.720 kg | 2952.471 kg | 2930.000 kg CICAD | 2076.100 kg | 2428.090 kg | 2262.311 kg |
| Colombia | 42044.000 kg | 107480.000 kg | 63945.000 kg (3 | 110428.000 kg | 73863.500 kg | 118867.000 kg |
| | | | 36411.949 lt. | | | |
| Ecuador | 3697.160 kg | 3854.229 kg | 10161.831 kg | 3308.420 kg ICPO | 12242.329 kg | 5137.800 kg HONLC |
| Guyana | 167.000 kg F.O | 3222.000 kg NAPOL | 40.163 kg ICPO | 167.000 kg CICAD | 73.000 kg ICPO | No Report |
| Paraguay | 77.083 kg | 222.352 kg | 95.058 kg | 96.000 kg CICAD | No Report | 230.152 kg |
| Peru | 8795.617 kg | 9936.968 kg | 11307.116 kg | 11847.611 kg | 9189.362 kg | 14568.175 kg |
| Suriname | 116.099 kg | 283.444 kg | 185.000 kg CICAD | 207.000 kg INCSR | 2253.000 kg | 340.000 kg |
| Uruguay | 27.968 kg Govt. | 23.604 kg | 18.698 kg | 20.642 kg | 24.758 kg ICPO | 43.013 kg |
| Venezuela | 16741.000 kg CICAD | 8159.000 kg CICAD | 12418.839 kg | 15063.194 kg | 13950.940 kg | 17828.940 kg |
| Sub-Total | 96153.600 kg | 155807.400 kg | 118120.600 kg | 156720.300 kg | 130064.100 kg | 175433.900 kg |
| | | | 36411.950 lt. | | | |
| Total region | 294781.000 kg | 359593.100 kg | 326619.000 kg | 316872.300 kg | 302607.000 kg | 316046.200 kg |
| | 66441 u. | 0.007 lt. | 36412.360 lt. | 1519.542 lt. | 92695 u. | 121208 u. |
| | | 126506 u. | 60738 u. | 71381 u. | | |
| **ASIA** | | | | | | |
| **Central Asia and Transcaucasian countries** | | | | | | |
| Azerbaijan | No Report | No Report | 0.005 kg | No Report | No Report | No Report |
| Georgia | No Report | No Report | 0.002 kg ICPO | No Report | No Report | No Report |
| Kazakhstan | No Report | 20.000 kg | 0.035 kg | No Report | 0.054 kg F.O | 0.119 kg F.O |
| Turkmenistan | No Report | 1.000 kg Govt. | No Report | No Report | No Report | No Report |
| Sub-Total | | 21.000 kg | 0.042 kg | | 0.054 kg | 0.119 kg |
| **East and South-East Asia** | | | | | | |
| Hong Kong SAR, China | 31.300 kg | 167.700 kg Govt. | 11.990 kg | 9.004 kg | 29.700 kg | 8.300 kg |
| Indonesia | 3.301 kg | 4.748 kg | 0.500 kg | 17.415 kg | 30.793 kg | 2.314 kg |
| Japan | 25.455 kg | 20.846 kg | 10.349 kg | 15.580 kg | 23.716 kg | 16.900 kg |
| Korea (Republic of) | 11.218 kg | 2.080 kg | 2.251 kg | No Report | 0.111 kg | 1.170 kg ICPO |
| Macau SAR, China | No Report | No Report | No Report | 0.008 kg | No Report | 0.027 kg |
| Malaysia | No Report | No Report | No Report | No Report | 0.017 kg ICPO | No Report |
| Mongolia | No Report | No Report | 2.800 kg ICPO | No Report | 0.400 kg | No Report |
| Philippines | 1.000 kg ICPO | 1.080 kg ICPO | 0.227 kg | 0.588 kg | No Report | 8.026 kg |
| Singapore | No Report | 1.050 kg | No Report | No Report | No Report | No Report |
| Thailand | 2.426 kg | 3.555 kg | 0.619 kg ICPO | 4.003 kg HNLP | 4.625 kg HNLP | 14.730 kg ICPO |
| Sub-Total | 74.700 kg | 201.059 kg | 28.736 kg | 46.598 kg | 89.362 kg | 51.467 kg |
| **Near and Middle East /South-West Asia** | | | | | | |
| Bahrain | No Report | No Report | No Report | 0.010 kg ICPO | No Report | 0.002 kg |

Source: Annual Report Questionnaire if not otherwise indicated

## SEIZURES, 1997 - 2002
### Cocaine (base and salts)

| Region/country or territory | 1997 | 1998 | 1999 | 2000 | 2001 | 2002 |
|---|---|---|---|---|---|---|
| **ASIA** | | | | | | |
| **Near and Middle East /South-West Asia** | | | | | | |
| Iran (Islamic Republic of) | 1.700 kg | No Report | No Report | No Report | No Report | No Report |
| Israel | 43.700 kg | 99.800 kg | 28.229 kg [ICPO] | 11.659 kg | 23.617 kg | 96.012 kg |
| Jordan | No Report | 0.940 kg | 1.912 kg | 0.803 kg | 0.505 kg | 0.188 kg |
| Kuwait | 0.010 kg [ICPO] | 0.003 kg | No Report | 36.000 kg [ICPO] | No Report | 0.002 kg [ICPO] |
| Lebanon | 4.804 kg | 11.898 kg | 32.013 kg | 0.466 kg | 7.207 kg | 7.839 kg |
| Pakistan | No Report | 0.100 kg | 1.100 kg | No Report | No Report | No Report |
| Saudi Arabia | 0.347 kg [ICPO] | 2.202 kg | 4.908 kg [ICPO] | 0.708 kg 3 u. | 0.046 kg | 1.528 kg [ICPO] |
| Syrian Arab Republic | 0.240 kg [Govt] | 0.235 kg [Govt] | 32.102 kg [Govt] | 7.177 kg [Govt] | 1031.880 kg [Govt] | 57.237 kg |
| United Arab Emirates | No Report | 0.146 kg | 0.840 kg | 0.537 kg | 0.007 kg | 0.013 kg |
| Sub-Total | 50.801 kg | 115.324 kg | 101.104 kg | 57.360 kg 3 u. | 1063.262 kg | 162.821 kg |
| **South Asia** | | | | | | |
| Bangladesh | No Report | No Report | No Report | 0.550 kg | No Report | No Report |
| India | 24.000 kg | 1.000 kg | 1.000 kg [ICPO] | 0.350 kg [F.O] | 2.000 kg | 2.000 kg |
| Maldives | No Report | No Report | No Report | No Report | No Report | 15.801 kg [ICPO] 15 u. |
| Nepal | 24.000 kg [ICPO] | No Report | No Report | No Report | No Report | No Report |
| Sri Lanka | No Report | No Report | No Report | No Report | 0.640 kg | No Report |
| Sub-Total | 48.000 kg | 1.000 kg | 1.000 kg | 0.900 kg | 2.640 kg | 17.801 kg 15 u. |
| Total region | 173.501 kg | 338.383 kg | 130.882 kg | 104.858 kg 3 u. | 1155.318 kg | 232.209 kg 15 u. |
| **EUROPE** | | | | | | |
| **Eastern Europe** | | | | | | |
| Albania | No Report | No Report | 2.159 kg [ICPO] | 4.000 kg [Govt] | 0.266 kg [Govt] | 0.006 kg |
| Belarus | 2.074 kg [INCB] | No Report | No Report | No Report | 142.000 kg [ICPO] | 0.003 kg |
| Bosnia Herzegovina | No Report | 0.014 kg [ICPO] | No Report | 164.392 kg [NAPOL] | No Report | 0.240 kg [ICPO] |
| Bulgaria | 2.011 kg | 685.585 kg | 17.010 kg | 4.333 kg | 12.752 kg | 36.282 kg |
| Croatia | 563.009 kg | 6.426 kg | 1.807 kg | 913.127 kg | 1.487 kg | 3.365 kg |
| Czech Republic | 66.828 kg | 42.000 kg | 140.800 kg | 14.712 kg | 5.170 kg 9 u. | 6.042 kg |
| Estonia | 0.006 kg | 2.565 kg 71 u. | 0.128 kg 139 u. | 0.108 kg 37 u. | 0.137 kg | 2.286 kg |
| FYR of Macedonia | 0.011 kg [NAPOL] | 0.040 kg | 2.955 kg [NAPOL] | 4.689 kg [NAPOL] | 5.860 kg [Govt] | 0.342 kg |
| Hungary | 6.995 kg [Govt.] | 26.385 kg | 121.147 kg | 9.200 kg | 6.015 kg | 58.928 kg |
| Latvia | 0.024 kg 0.895 lt. | 0.063 kg | 1.915 kg | 0.027 kg | 1.024 kg | No Report |

Source: Annual Report Questionnaire if not otherwise indicated

## SEIZURES, 1997 - 2002
### Cocaine (base and salts)

| Region/country or territory | 1997 | 1998 | 1999 | 2000 | 2001 | 2002 |
|---|---|---|---|---|---|---|
| **EUROPE** | | | | | | |
| **Eastern Europe** | | | | | | |
| Lithuania | 2.049 kg | 10.133 kg | 0.275 kg | 1.841 kg | 0.129 kg | 0.732 kg |
| Poland | 15.501 kg | 21.157 kg | 20.082 kg | 5.664 kg | No Report | 422.179 kg |
| Republic of Moldova | No Report | No Report | No Report | No Report | 0.001 kg | No Report |
| Romania | 69.556 kg [ICPO] | 1.203 kg | 9.670 kg | 13.140 kg | 2.524 kg | 2.720 kg |
| Russian Federation | 70.825 kg | 100.340 kg | 12.749 kg | 65.000 kg [F.O] | 82.502 kg | 58.155 kg [ICPO] |
| Serbia and Montenegro | No Report | No Report | No Report | No Report | 3.623 kg | 1.926 kg [ICPO] |
| Slovakia | 9.580 kg [ICPO] | 1.642 kg | 2.508 kg | 0.166 kg | No Report | 0.069 kg |
| Slovenia | 3.573 kg | 3.522 kg | 1.580 kg | 0.098 kg | 1.080 kg | 55.380 kg |
| Ukraine | 625.010 kg | 250.586 kg | 26.263 kg [ICPO] | 0.520 kg [ICPO] | 0.018 kg | 0.012 kg |
| Sub-Total | 1437.052 kg 0.895 lt. | 1151.661 kg 71 u. | 361.048 kg 139 u. | 1201.017 kg 37 u. | 264.589 kg 9 u. | 648.666 kg |
| **Western Europe** | | | | | | |
| Andorra | 0.108 kg [ICPO] | 0.064 kg [ICPO] | 0.060 kg | 0.023 kg [ICPO] | 0.086 kg | 0.270 kg [ICPO] |
| Austria | 86.902 kg | 99.140 kg | 63.377 kg | 20.375 kg | 108.278 kg | 36.896 kg |
| Belgium | 3329.000 kg | 2088.312 kg | 1761.709 kg | 2813.991 kg | 2813.991 kg [UNODC (4] | 3589.000 kg |
| Cyprus | 0.020 kg | 0.018 kg | 5.361 kg | 57.599 kg | 0.123 kg | 1.944 kg |
| Denmark | 58.000 kg | 44.133 kg | 24.200 kg | 35.910 kg | 25.624 kg | 14.152 kg |
| Finland | 0.121 kg | 1.987 kg | 1.703 kg | 38.575 kg | 6.500 kg | 0.442 kg |
| France | 860.599 kg | 1076.000 kg | 3697.372 kg | 1333.119 kg | 2102.257 kg | 3660.183 kg |
| Germany | 1721.189 kg | 1133.243 kg | 1979.100 kg | 915.600 kg | 1290.087 kg | 2142.894 kg |
| Greece | 16.734 kg | 283.971 kg | 45.485 kg 8 u. | 156.245 kg 2 u. | 227.287 kg | 18.035 kg |
| Iceland | No Report | No Report | 0.955 kg | 0.942 kg | 0.257 kg | 1.870 kg |
| Ireland | 11.044 kg | 334.230 kg | 85.553 kg | 18.041 kg | 5.325 kg | 30.467 kg |
| Italy | 1639.542 kg 887 u. | 2143.804 kg 1341 u. | 2997.611 kg [ICPO] 14 u. | 2359.715 kg 2329 u. | 1808.910 kg 612 u. | 4039.991 kg 646 u. |
| Liechtenstein | 1.065 kg | 0.151 kg | 0.003 kg | 0.010 kg | 0.750 kg | 0.014 kg |
| Luxembourg | 8.983 kg | 5.995 kg | 0.327 kg | 10.757 kg [ICPO] | No Report | 2.486 kg [ICPO] |
| Malta | 0.301 kg | 0.058 kg | 1.366 kg | 0.028 kg | 2.542 kg | 4.535 kg [ICPO] |
| Monaco | 0.001 kg | 0.012 kg | 0.056 kg [ICPO] | 0.001 kg [ICPO] | No Report | 0.010 kg |
| Netherlands | 11495.000 kg [Govt] | 8998.000 kg [Govt] | 10361.000 kg [Govt] | 6472.000 kg [Govt] | 8382.000 kg | 7968.000 kg |
| Norway | 4.633 kg | 93.020 kg | 60.477 kg | 12.215 kg | 20.753 kg | 35.828 kg |
| Portugal | 3162.641 kg | 624.949 kg | 822.560 kg | 3075.374 kg | 5574.658 kg | 3140.103 kg |
| Spain | 18418.760 kg | 11687.623 kg | 18110.883 kg | 6164.770 kg | 33681.091 kg | 17617.749 kg |
| Sweden | 33.920 kg | 18.505 kg | 413.945 kg 1.944 lt. 430 u. | 52.257 kg | 47.388 kg | 41.000 kg |
| Switzerland | 349.435 kg | 251.616 kg | 288.013 kg | 207.476 kg | 168.637 kg | 185.940 kg |
| Turkey | 9.637 kg | 604.880 kg | 13.153 kg | 8.444 kg [Govt.] | 1.010 kg | 7.734 kg |

Source: Annual Report Questionnaire if not otherwise indicated

## SEIZURES, 1997 - 2002
### Cocaine (base and salts)

| Region/country or territory | 1997 | 1998 | 1999 | 2000 | 2001 | 2002 |
|---|---|---|---|---|---|---|
| **EUROPE** | | | | | | |
| **Western Europe** | | | | | | |
| United Kingdom | 2350.200 kg | 2985.323 kg [5 | 2972.700 kg [NCIS] | 3970.220 kg | 2897.441 kg | 2897.441 kg [6 |
| Sub-Total | 43557.830 kg | 32475.040 kg | 43706.970 kg | 27723.690 kg | 59165.000 kg | 45436.990 kg |
| | 887 u. | 1341 u. | 1.944 lt. | 2331 u. | 612 u. | 646 u. |
| | | | 452 u. | | | |
| Total region | 44994.880 kg | 33626.700 kg | 44068.020 kg | 28924.700 kg | 59429.590 kg | 46085.660 kg |
| | 0.895 lt. | 1412 u. | 1.944 lt. | 2368 u. | 621 u. | 646 u. |
| | 887 u. | | 591 u. | | | |
| **OCEANIA** | | | | | | |
| **Oceania** | | | | | | |
| Australia | 81.944 kg | 103.162 kg [Govt. (7] | 70.725 kg | 1437.869 kg | 1151.255 kg | 105.874 kg |
| Fiji | No Report | No Report | No Report | 0.347 kg [ICPO] | 2.000 kg [ICPO] | No Report |
| New Zealand | 0.037 kg [INCB] | 0.015 kg | 0.454 kg | 0.249 kg | 0.008 kg | 0.267 kg |
| Tonga | 0.001 kg [INCB] | No Report | No Report | No Report | No Report | No Report |
| Sub-Total | 81.982 kg | 103.177 kg | 71.179 kg | 1438.465 kg | 1153.263 kg | 106.141 kg |
| Total region | 81.982 kg | 103.177 kg | 71.179 kg | 1438.465 kg | 1153.263 kg | 106.141 kg |
| TOTAL | 347200.800 kg | 394419.100 kg | 371327.000 kg | 347762.000 kg | 364804.000 kg | 363024.800 kg |
| | 0.895 lt. | 0.007 lt. | 36414.300 lt. | 1519.542 lt. | 96989 u. | 121973 u. |
| | 67328 u. | 131743 u. | 74395 u. | 73781 u. | | |

1) Small quantity. 2) Includes crack. 3) The 36411.949 litres correspond to 4,737 gallons coca base liquid and 4,882 gallons cocaine liquid 4) Due to unavailability of 2001 data, year 2000 data were used for analysis purposes. 5) Included in cannabis seeds. 6) Due to unavailability of 2002 data, year 2001 data were used for analysis purposes. 7) Provisional figures.

Source: Annual Report Questionnaire if not otherwise indicated

## SEIZURES, 1997 - 2002
### Coca leaf

| Region/country or territory | 1997 | 1998 | 1999 | 2000 | 2001 | 2002 |
|---|---|---|---|---|---|---|
| **AMERICAS** | | | | | | |
| **North America** | | | | | | |
| Canada | 0.192 kg | No Report | 0.316 kg | 0.056 kg | 0.050 kg | 3.405 kg |
| United States | No Report | No Report | 58.436 kg | 45.608 kg [(1] 2.181 lt. | 0.600 kg | No Report |
| Sub-Total | 0.192 kg | | 58.752 kg | 45.664 kg 2.181 lt. | 0.650 kg | 3.405 kg |
| **South America** | | | | | | |
| Argentina | 49754.102 kg | 47847.961 kg | 68492.192 kg | 95901.272 kg | 91352.081 kg | 45570.390 kg |
| Bolivia | 80090.000 kg [F.O] | 110202.000 [F.O] kg | 63911.000 kg [F.O] | 59704.000 kg [F.O] | 8072.056 kg | 103176.037 kg |
| Brazil | 0.035 kg | No Report | No Report | 0.018 kg [ICPO] | No Report | No Report |
| Chile | No Report | No Report | No Report | No Report | No Report | 0.249 kg [ICPO] |
| Colombia | 117817.000 kg | 340564.000 kg | 307783.000 [(2] kg | 897911.000 kg | 583.165 kg | 368000.000* kg |
| Ecuador | No Report | 0.050 kg | 5000 u. | No Report | No Report | No Report |
| Peru | 146824.953 kg | 132209.875 kg | 34792.500 kg | 48609.597 kg | 29324.293 kg | 39921.738 kg |
| Uruguay | No Report | No Report | No Report | No Report | No Report | 0.646 kg |
| Venezuela | No Report | No Report | No Report | No Report | 180.000 kg | No Report |
| Sub-Total | 394486.100 kg | 630823.900 kg | 474978.700 kg 5000 u. | 1102126.000 kg | 129511.600 kg | 556669.100 kg |
| Total region | 394486.300 kg | 630823.900 kg | 475037.400 kg 5000 u. | 1102172.000 kg 2.181 lt. | 129512.200 kg | 556672.400 kg |
| **ASIA** | | | | | | |
| **Central Asia and Transcaucasian countries** | | | | | | |
| Armenia | No Report | 0.163 kg | No Report | No Report | No Report | No Report |
| Sub-Total | | 0.163 kg | | | | |
| Total region | | 0.163 kg | | | | |
| **EUROPE** | | | | | | |
| **Eastern Europe** | | | | | | |
| Hungary | No Report | No Report | No Report | No Report | 1.049 kg | 0.632 kg |
| Poland | No Report | No Report | No Report | No Report | 45.298 kg | No Report |
| Serbia and Montenegro | No Report | No Report | No Report | No Report | No Report | 1.226 kg |
| Sub-Total | | | | | 46.347 kg | 1.858 kg |
| **Western Europe** | | | | | | |
| Denmark | No Report | No Report | No Report | 0.043 kg | 0.000 kg | No Report |
| France | No Report | No Report | 11.133 kg | No Report | No Report | 0.203 kg |
| Italy | No Report | 0.049 kg | 0.109 kg [ICPO] | 0.445 kg | 0.055 kg | 2.255 kg |
| Norway | No Report | 0.001 kg | 3.420 kg | No Report | No Report | 0.030 kg |

Source: Annual Report Questionnaire if not otherwise indicated

* Reported figures at the time of the preparation of the report; revised figures by the Gov. of Colombia show seizures of coca leaf of 638,000 kg for 2002.

## SEIZURES, 1997 - 2002
### Coca leaf

| Region/country or territory | 1997 | 1998 | 1999 | 2000 | 2001 | 2002 |
|---|---|---|---|---|---|---|
| **EUROPE** | | | | | | |
| **Western Europe** | | | | | | |
| Portugal | 0.043 kg | 0.020 kg | No Report | No Report | No Report | 1 u. |
| Sweden | No Report | No Report | No Report | 0.268 kg | No Report | No Report |
| Sub-Total | 0.043 kg | 0.070 kg | 14.662 kg | 0.756 kg | 0.055 kg | 2.488 kg 1 u. |
| Total region | 0.043 kg | 0.070 kg | 14.662 kg | 0.756 kg | 46.402 kg | 4.346 kg 1 u. |
| **OCEANIA** | | | | | | |
| **Oceania** | | | | | | |
| Australia | 0.590 kg | No Report | No Report | No Report | 0.019 kg | 10.443 kg |
| New Zealand | No Report | 0.019 kg | 0.011 kg | No Report | 4.253 kg | 0.013 kg |
| Sub-Total | 0.590 kg | 0.019 kg | 0.011 kg | | 4.272 kg | 10.456 kg |
| Total region | 0.590 kg | 0.019 kg | 0.011 kg | | 4.272 kg | 10.456 kg |
| TOTAL | 394486.900 kg | 630824.100 kg | 475052.100 kg 5000 u. | 1102172.000 kg 2.181 lt. | 129562.900 kg | 556687.300 kg 1 u. |

1) Includes cocaine other 2) Do not include 9702 gallons (36726 litres) of coca leaf in process

Source: Annual Report Questionnaire if not otherwise indicated

## 4.3. Cannabis: Seizures 1997-2002

| Region/country or territory | SEIZURES, 1997 - 2002 Cannabis herb | | | | | |
|---|---|---|---|---|---|---|
| | 1997 | 1998 | 1999 | 2000 | 2001 | 2002 |
| **AFRICA** | | | | | | |
| **East Africa** | | | | | | |
| Burundi | No Report | No Report | 45.847 kg [ICPO] | No Report | No Report | No Report |
| Ethiopia | 135.346 kg | 331.561 kg | 807.364 kg | 181.821 kg | 152.064 kg | 155.568 kg |
| Kenya | 11250.000 kg | 2375.240 kg | 8762.033 kg | 5649.000 kg | 383253.486 kg [Govt (1] | 77737.711 kg |
| Madagascar | 510.460 kg [INCB] | No Report | 1265.332 kg [ICPO] | No Report | No Report | No Report |
| Mauritius | 18435.000 kg | 3.090 kg | 5.592 kg | 21.931 kg | 66.985 kg | 43.492 kg |
| Rwanda | No Report | No Report | No Report | No Report | No Report | 6215.000 kg |
| Seychelles | No Report | 2.056 kg [ICPO] | 1.005 kg | 22.014 kg | 0.067 kg [ICPO] | 1.042 kg |
| Somalia | No Report | No Report | No Report | No Report | No Report | 1000.000 kg |
| Uganda | No Report | 5530.000 kg | 5530.000 kg [ICPO] | 6100.000 kg | 50000.000 kg | 100.000 kg |
| United Republic of Tanzania | 82539.539 kg | 4617.862 kg | 6021.273 kg | 24293.304 kg [ICPO] | 249639.026 kg [Govt] | 90410.857 kg [ICPO] |
| Sub-Total | 112870.300 kg | 12859.810 kg | 22438.450 kg | 36268.070 kg | 683111.600 kg | 175663.700 kg |
| **North Africa** | | | | | | |
| Algeria | No Report | 58.300 kg [ICPO] | No Report | No Report | No Report | No Report |
| Egypt | 10185.538 kg | 31078.387 kg | 22588.505 kg | 30397.591 kg | 50037.000 kg | No Report |
| Morocco | 27955.979 kg | 37160.879 kg | No Report | No Report | 73.810 kg [ICPO] | 93506.730 kg [ICPO] |
| Sudan | No Report | No Report | No Report | 1887.805 kg | No Report | No Report |
| Tunisia | 18.163 kg [ICPO] | 2.000 kg | 1893.381 kg [ICPO] | No Report | No Report | No Report |
| Sub-Total | 38159.680 kg | 68299.560 kg | 24481.890 kg | 32285.400 kg | 50110.810 kg | 93506.730 kg |
| **Southern Africa** | | | | | | |
| Angola | 518.006 kg [ICPO] | 1.975 kg [ICPO] | 2829.167 kg | 4733.667 kg [ICPO] | 621.278 kg [ICPO] | No Report |
| Botswana | 1446.153 kg [ICPO] | 1186.000 kg [ICPO] | 1229.000 kg [ICPO] | No Report | No Report | 1000.000 kg [ICPO] |
| Lesotho | 10472.073 kg [ICPO] | 21583.824 kg [ICPO] | 7243.697 kg [ICPO] | No Report | No Report | 6513.350 kg [ICPO] |
| Malawi | 10320.105 kg | 5201.971 kg | 27141.583 kg | 312471.845 kg | 8663.694 kg | 7131.989 kg |
| Mozambique | 184.024 kg [ICPO] | 462.000 kg [ICPO] | 894.406 kg [ICPO] | 1700.562 kg [ICPO] | 6721.550 kg [ICPO] | 5798.000 kg [ICPO] |
| Namibia | 298.830 kg [INCB] | 361.395 kg | 282.363 kg | 302.981 kg | 5386.189 kg | 949.448 kg [ICPO] |
| South Africa | 171929.328 kg | 197116.297 kg | 289943.561 kg [ICPO] | 717701.918 kg | 123964.058 kg | 104977.750 kg |
| Swaziland | 11302.505 kg [ICPO] | 5943.293 kg | 33283.707 kg | 14946.718 kg | 15064.342 kg | 10196.081 kg |
| Zambia | 11176.308 kg [Govt] | 3256.366 kg [Govt] | 7000.653 kg | 7318.199 kg | 14.600 kg [Govt] | 1605.194 kg |
| Zimbabwe | 4667.320 kg [ICPO] | 6117.086 kg | 1816.001 kg | 3045.908 kg | 1530.254 kg | 3722.538 kg |
| Sub-Total | 222314.600 kg | 241230.200 kg | 371664.200 kg | 1062222.000 kg | 161966.000 kg | 141894.300 kg |
| **West and Central Africa** | | | | | | |
| Benin | 26.862 kg [Govt] | 611.077 kg [Govt] | 25.138 kg [Govt] | 971.781 kg [F.O] | 809.408 kg [ICPO] | 2126.210 kg [ICPO] |
| Burkina Faso | 2402.734 kg [Govt.] | No Report | No Report | No Report | 2404.713 kg | No Report |
| Cameroon | No Report | 112.875 kg | 1154.560 kg | No Report | No Report | 443.245 kg 180 u. |
| Central African Republic | No Report | 57.551 kg [ICPO] | No Report | No Report | No Report | 6.650 kg [Govt] |

Source: Annual Report Questionnaire if not otherwise indicated

## SEIZURES, 1997 - 2002
### Cannabis herb

| Region/country or territory | 1997 | 1998 | 1999 | 2000 | 2001 | 2002 |
|---|---|---|---|---|---|---|
| **AFRICA** | | | | | | |
| **West and Central Africa** | | | | | | |
| Chad | No Report | No Report | 686.000 kg [ICPO] | 378.000 kg | No Report | No Report |
| Congo | No Report | No Report | 1.000 kg | 259.000 kg | 222.000 kg | 1147.830 kg |
| Côte d'Ivoire | 853.871 kg | 898.960 kg | 1650.189 kg | 1236.644 kg [ICPO] | 1876.658 kg | 4397.968 kg |
| Equatorial Guinea | 3.500 kg [INCB] | 24.000 kg 6 u. | 26.000 kg 46 u. | No Report | No Report | No Report |
| Gabon | 24.255 kg [ICPO] | 114.336 kg [ICPO] | 45.648 kg [ICPO] | No Report | No Report | No Report |
| Gambia | 566.971 kg [ICPO] | 376.145 kg [ICPO] | No Report | No Report | 700.000 kg | 638.959 kg [ICPO] |
| Ghana | 1409.470 kg [F.O.] | 4375.098 kg | 4080.049 kg | No Report | No Report | 5418.140 kg |
| Guinea | No Report | No Report | No Report | 640.345 kg [ICPO] | No Report | No Report |
| Guinea-Bissau | No Report | No Report | No Report | No Report | 367.000 kg | No Report |
| Mali | 404.270 kg [ICPO] | No Report | No Report | No Report | No Report | No Report |
| Mauritania | 92.006 kg [Govt] | 17.200 kg [Govt] | No Report | No Report | No Report | No Report |
| Niger | 499.887 kg [ICPO] | 682.173 kg [ICPO] | 1356.162 kg [ICPO] | No Report | No Report | No Report |
| Nigeria | 15904.721 kg | 16170.500 kg [Govt.] | 17691.014 kg | 272260.020 kg | 317950.204 kg | 506846.009 kg |
| *Saint Helena* | 3.009 kg | 0.183 kg | No Report | 0.075 kg | | No Report |
| Sao Tome and Principe | 0.200 kg | No Report | No Report | No Report | 15.000 kg | No Report |
| Senegal | 13627.390 kg [F.O.] | 69652.000 kg [F.O.] | 7165.830 kg [ICPO] | No Report | No Report | 4888.080 kg [ICPO] |
| Togo | 1066.189 kg [Govt.] | No Report | No Report | 429.056 kg | 655.247 kg | 234.641 kg |
| Sub-Total | 36885.330 kg | 93092.090 kg 6 u. | 33881.590 kg 46 u. | 276174.900 kg | 325000.200 kg | 526147.700 kg 180 u. |
| Total region | 410230.000 kg | 415481.700 kg 6 u. | 452466.100 kg 46 u. | 1406950.000 kg | 1220189.000 kg | 937212.400 kg 180 u. |
| **AMERICAS** | | | | | | |
| **Caribbean** | | | | | | |
| *Anguilla* | 0.644 kg | 5.037 kg | 8.000 kg [F.O] | No Report | 1.000 kg [F.O] | No Report |
| Antigua and Barbuda | 628.000 kg [F.O] | 105.000 kg [F.O] | 94.000 kg [F.O] | 67.000 kg [F.O] | 662.000 kg [F.O] | No Report |
| *Aruba* | 13.000 kg [F.O] | No Report | 142.000 kg [F.O] | 12.000 kg [F.O] | 1159.000 kg [F.O] | 434.247 kg [ICPO] |
| Bahamas | 3763.000 kg [F.O] | 2591.065 kg | 3610.000 kg [F.O] | 4093.000 kg | 4174.000 kg 9203 u. | 11515.000 kg |
| Barbados | 1132.027 kg [INCB] | 1650.000 kg [CICAD] | 333.580 kg [HONLC] | 2948.000 kg [F.O] | 5748.925 kg [ICPO] | No Report |
| *Bermuda* | 91.800 kg | 91.800 kg | 87.067 kg | 136.579 kg | 32.000 kg [F.O] | 360.000 kg |
| *British Virgin Islands* | 85.000 kg [F.O] | 84.000 kg [F.O] | 354.000 kg [F.O] | 26.000 kg [F.O] | 151.950 kg 80 u. | No Report |
| *Cayman Islands* | 3422.073 kg 427 u. | 4063.009 kg 650 u. | 5100.371 kg | 6621.000 kg | 11818.000 kg | 6681.000 kg |
| Cuba | 6023.000 kg [F.O] | 4610.000 kg [F.O] | 5559.000 kg [F.O] | 8802.000 kg [F.O] | 6121.000 kg [F.O] | 6023.428 kg [ICPO] |
| Dominica | 404.000 kg [F.O] | 361.000 kg [F.O] | 192.000 kg [F.O] | 468.000 kg [CICAD] | 521.000 kg [F.O] | No Report |

Source: Annual Report Questionnaire if not otherwise indicated

## SEIZURES, 1997 - 2002
### Cannabis herb

| Region/country or territory | 1997 | 1998 | 1999 | 2000 | 2001 | 2002 |
|---|---|---|---|---|---|---|
| **AMERICAS** | | | | | | |
| **Caribbean** | | | | | | |
| Dominican Republic | 800.660 kg | 110.298 kg | 184.333 kg | 1526.000 kg [CICAD] | 3815.900 kg | 1749.000 kg [HONLC] |
| French Guiana | 123.000 kg [F.O] | 127.000 kg [F.O] | 134.000 kg [F.O] | 58.000 kg [F.O] | No Report | No Report |
| Grenada | 123.199 kg [INCB] | 84.000 kg | 219.000 kg [F.O] | 103.000 kg [INCSR] | 133.690 kg | 379.280 kg [ICPO] 547 u. |
| Guadeloupe | 20179.000 kg [F.O] | 8860.000 kg [F.O] | 515.000 kg [F.O] | 1017.000 kg [F.O] | 516.000 kg [F.O] | No Report |
| Haiti | 9000.000 kg [F.O] | 9255.000 kg [F.O] | 71.030 kg | 401.000 kg [F.O] | 1705.000 kg [F.O] | 149.050 kg |
| Jamaica | 24729.000 kg [F.O] | 35911.000 kg [F.O] | 56226.940 kg [ICPO] | 55870.000 kg [F.O] | 74044.000 kg | 27137.000 kg [ICPO] |
| Martinique | 355.000 kg [F.O] | 136.000 kg [F.O] | 199.000 kg [F.O] | 749.000 kg [F.O] | No Report | No Report |
| Montserrat | 3.285 kg 14090 u. | No Report | 2677.000 kg [F.O] | 0.497 kg | No Report | No Report |
| Netherlands Antilles | 1553.310 kg [INCB] | No Report | 541.000 kg [F.O] | 39.782 kg [ICPO] | 3772.000 kg [F.O] | 5691.000 kg [ICPO] |
| Puerto Rico | 1337.000 kg [F.O] | 1285.000 kg [F.O] | 12605.000 kg [F.O] | 1982.000 kg [F.O] | 24.000 kg [F.O] | 49536.000 kg [ICPO] 1177 u. |
| Saint Kitts and Nevis | 67.000 kg [F.O] | 31.000 kg [F.O] | 14124.000 kg [F.O] | 119.000 kg [INCSR] | 330.000 kg [F.O] | No Report |
| Saint Lucia | 621.684 kg | 363.663 kg | 267.000 kg [CICAD] | 1803.610 kg | 753.000 kg [F.O] | No Report |
| Saint Vincent and the Grenadines | 527.000 kg [F.O] | 1321.000 kg [F.O] | 7180.000 kg [F.O] | 1709.000 kg [INCSR] | 1962.000 kg [F.O] | No Report |
| Trinidad Tobago | 1430.000 kg [CICAD] | 3483.545 kg | 8287.000 kg [CICAD] | 1546.000 kg [F.O] | 2393.950 kg | 1135.404 kg |
| Turks and Caicos Islands | 22.000 kg | 8.000 kg | 68.500 kg | 27.000 kg [F.O] | 24.000 kg [F.O] | 12.802 kg |
| US Virgin Islands | No Report | No Report | 48.123 kg [ICPO] | No Report | No Report | No Report |
| Sub-Total | 76433.690 kg 14517 u. | 74536.420 kg 650 u. | 118826.900 kg | 90124.470 kg | 119862.400 kg 9283 u. | 110803.200 kg 1724 u. |
| **Central America** | | | | | | |
| Belize | 263.000 kg [CICAD] | 1557.000 kg [F.O] | 392.000 kg [F.O] | 249.000 kg [F.O] | 269.909 kg | 392.468 kg [ICPO] |
| Costa Rica* | 107.000 kg [CICAD] | 469.340 kg | 1693.550 kg | 1140.650 kg | 2848.620 kg | 688.130 kg |
| El Salvador | 971.247 kg [ICPO] | 291.202 kg [ICPO] | 604.581 kg | 455.700 kg [ICPO] | 463.917 kg | 666.059 kg |
| Guatemala | 256.222 kg [Govt.] | 193.970 kg | 814.212 kg | 158.450 kg | 584.550 kg | 1098.310 kg |
| Honduras | 2.147 kg | 1293.000 kg [CICAD] | 1583.000 kg [CICAD] | 1112.000 kg [CICAD] | No Report | 416.142 kg 1127 u. |
| Nicaragua | 285.198 kg | 613.027 kg | 754.000 kg [CICAD] | 737.000 kg [CICAD] | 586.560 kg [ICPO] | 631.028 kg |
| Panama | 14102.067 kg | 16536.006 kg | 3477.268 kg | 3657.498 kg | 1639.000 kg | 1842.000 kg [HONLC] |
| Sub-Total | 15986.880 kg | 20953.550 kg | 9318.610 kg | 7510.298 kg | 6392.556 kg | 5734.137 kg 1127 u. |
| **North America** | | | | | | |
| Canada | 50624.000 kg | 27299.990 kg 8 u. | 44541.000 kg 52 u. | 70221.600 kg 738 u. | 6833.524 kg 18 u. | 13278.116 kg |
| Mexico | 1038470.414 kg | 1062143.980 kg | 1471959.958 kg | 2050402.078 kg | 1837524.728 kg | 1633326.209 kg [**] |
| United States | 684745.375 kg | 799000.875 kg [Govt.] | 1175373.000 kg | 218256.453 kg | 682574.100 kg | 1110525.400 kg |

Source: Annual Report Questionnaire if not otherwise indicated

\* Reported figures at the time of the preparation of the report; revised figures by the Gov. of Costa Rica show seizures of cannabis herb of 553.08 kg in 1997; 2,887 kg in 2001; 728.76 kg in 2002 and 1,764.93 in 2003.

\* \* Reported figures at the time of the preparation of the report, revised figures by the Gov. of Mexico show seizures of cannabis herb of 1839357.121 Kg in 2001.

## SEIZURES, 1997 - 2002
### Cannabis herb

| Region/country or territory | 1997 | 1998 | 1999 | 2000 | 2001 | 2002 |
|---|---|---|---|---|---|---|
| **AMERICAS** | | | | | | |
| **North America** | | | | | | |
| Sub-Total | 1773840.000 kg | 1888445.000 kg 8 u. | 2691874.000 kg 52 u. | 2338880.000 kg 738 u. | 2526932.000 kg 18 u. | 2757130.000 kg |
| **South America** | | | | | | |
| Argentina | 13709.620 kg | 10920.230 kg | 18301.339 kg | 25538.966 kg | 33052.239 kg | 44823.951 kg |
| Bolivia | 3617.000 kg [F.O] | 320.000 kg [F.O] | 2160.000 kg [F.O] | 3745.000 kg [F.O] | 7054.500 kg [F.O] | 8753.957 kg |
| Brazil | 31828.432 kg | 28982.492 kg | 69171.506 kg | 159073.232 kg | 146279.636 kg [Govt] | 194080.000 kg [F.O] |
| Chile | 784.430 kg | 2238.325 kg | 2105.000 kg [CICAD] | 3277.341 kg [(2] | 2418.496 kg | 8832.672 kg |
| Colombia | 178132.000 kg [Govt.] | 70025.000 kg | 70124.000 kg | 75465.000 kg | 86610.000 kg | 76998.000 kg |
| Ecuador | 224.206 kg | 17734.697 kg | 2976.910 kg | 18263.357 kg [ICPO] | 3079.376 kg | 1571.000 kg [HONLC] |
| Guyana | 40.000 kg [F.O] | 51.000 kg [F.O] | 3528.000 kg [F.O] | 4387.000 kg [F.O] | 243.000 kg [ICPO] | No Report |
| Paraguay | 17218.105 kg | 80077.914 kg | 199282.319 kg | 51081.000 kg [CICAD] | No Report | 48140.946 kg |
| Peru | 20910.326 kg | 19880.324 kg | 4055.732 kg | 1635.419 kg | 2601.446 kg | 2888.717 kg |
| Suriname | 65.000 kg [F.O] | 104.754 kg | 177.000 kg [CICAD] | 107.000 kg [INCSR] | 46.000 kg | 205.000 kg |
| Uruguay | 25601.006 kg [Govt.] | 424.778 kg | 493.783 kg | 805.843 kg | 1115.222 kg [ICPO] | 899.704 kg |
| Venezuela | No Report | 4500.000 kg [CICAD] | 13055.778 kg | 14999.634 kg | 14431.800 kg | 20919.610 kg |
| Sub-Total | 292130.100 kg | 235259.500 kg | 385431.300 kg | 358378.800 kg | 296931.700 kg | 408113.600 kg |
| Total region | 2158391.000 kg 14517 u. | 2219195.000 kg 658 u. | 3205451.000 kg 52 u. | 2794894.000 kg 738 u. | 2950119.000 kg 9301 u. | 3281781.000 kg 2851 u. |
| **ASIA** | | | | | | |
| **Central Asia and Transcaucasian countries** | | | | | | |
| Armenia | No Report | 0.888 kg | 46.675 kg [Govt.] | 53.798 kg | 14.081 kg | 76.084 kg |
| Azerbaijan | 37.475 kg [ICPO] | 40.287 kg | 55.395 kg | 2773.104 kg [ICPO] | 61.500 kg | 2212.550 kg |
| Georgia | No Report | No Report | 31972.800 kg [ICPO] | No Report | 32397.000 kg [ICPO] | No Report |
| Kazakhstan | 11800.000 kg [Govt.] | 716.236 kg | 10481.505 kg | No Report | 11789.000 kg [F.O] | 17072.230 kg [F.O] |
| Kyrgyzstan | 694.100 kg [F.O] | 1569.243 kg [F.O] | 1716.475 kg [(3] | 3748.220 kg [(4] | 2250.663 kg [(4] | 2525.915 kg |
| Tajikistan | 336.311 kg [F.O] | 323.331 kg [F.O] | No Report | No Report | 750.486 kg | 998.956 kg |
| Uzbekistan | 374.496 kg | 358.558 kg | 288.689 kg | No Report | No Report | 417.900 kg |
| Sub-Total | 13242.380 kg | 3008.543 kg | 44561.540 kg | 6575.122 kg | 47262.730 kg | 23303.630 kg |
| **East and South-East Asia** | | | | | | |
| Brunei Darussalam | 0.139 kg | 3.288 kg | 0.364 kg | 0.054 kg | 0.007 kg | 1.132 kg |
| Cambodia | 53751.000 kg [ICPO] | No Report | No Report | No Report | No Report | No Report |
| China | 2408.000 kg | 5079.000 kg | No Report | 4493.000 kg [Govt.] | 751.000 kg [Govt.] | 1300.000 kg [Govt.] |
| Hong Kong SAR, China | 1002.100 kg | 585.000 kg [Govt.] | 24.727 kg | 226.007 kg | No Report | 665.910 kg |
| Indonesia | 715.735 kg | 1071.862 kg | 3741.068 kg | 6332.908 kg | 27390.075 kg | 61291.436 kg |
| Japan | 155.246 kg | 120.884 kg | 565.904 kg | 310.246 kg | 1070.248 kg | 256.500 kg 24 u. |

Source: Annual Report Questionnaire if not otherwise indicated

307

## SEIZURES, 1997 - 2002
### Cannabis herb

| Region/country or territory | 1997 | 1998 | 1999 | 2000 | 2001 | 2002 |
|---|---|---|---|---|---|---|
| **ASIA** | | | | | | |
| **East and South-East Asia** | | | | | | |
| Korea (Republic of) | 59.548 kg | 32.751 kg | 39.442 kg | 39.371 kg [ICPO] | 283.869 kg | 194.795 kg [ICPO] |
| Lao People's Dem. Rep. | 7026.000 kg [Govt.] | 410.000 kg [INCSR] | 2187.000 kg [HNLP] | 1860.000 kg [INCSR] | 1702.000 kg [Govt] | 1932.200 kg |
| *Macau SAR, China* | 5.519 kg [ICPO] | 1.661 kg [ICPO] | 3.000 kg [INCB] | 16.381 kg | 0.519 kg | 0.124 kg |
| Malaysia | 3889.132 kg | 1781.010 kg | 2064.498 kg | 1885.450 kg | 1570.526 kg [ICPO] | 1734.133 kg [ICPO] |
| Mongolia | No Report | No Report | 5.000 kg [ICPO] | 5.800 kg [ICPO] | No Report | No Report |
| Myanmar | 288.034 kg | 380.970 kg | 274.282 kg | 601.508 kg | 284.387 kg | 281.988 kg |
| Philippines | 2172.452 kg [Govt (5] | 2057.974 kg [Govt (5] | 1187.870 kg | 1429.474 kg [Govt (5] | 706.418 kg [Govt (5] | 1361.507 kg |
| Singapore | 4363.452 kg | 21.831 kg [(3] | 7.432 kg [(3] | 23.903 kg | 8.843 kg | 2.637 kg [ICPO] |
| Thailand | 9141.927 kg | 5581.840 kg | 14706.198 kg | 10320.000 kg [HNLP] | 10921.000 kg [F.O] | 12095.000 kg [F.O] |
| Viet Nam | 7986.000 kg [ICPO] | 379.000 kg [ICPO] | 400.100 kg [F.O] | 2139.000 kg [ICPO] | 1289.005 kg | No Report |
| Sub-Total | 92964.290 kg | 17507.070 kg | 25206.890 kg | 29683.100 kg | 45977.900 kg | 81117.370 kg 24 u. |
| **Near and Middle East /South-West Asia** | | | | | | |
| Bahrain | 7.382 kg | 0.041 kg [ICPO] | 0.042 kg [ICPO] | 7.417 kg [ICPO] | No Report | 0.008 kg |
| Iran (Islamic Republic of) | No Report | No Report | No Report | 1495.000 kg [ICPO] | No Report | No Report |
| Iraq | No Report | No Report | 270.000 kg [INCB] | 569.970 kg [ICPO] | No Report | No Report |
| Israel | 10635.000 kg | 3581.000 kg | 3400.000 kg [ICPO] | 9855.000 kg | 11685.000 kg | 12382.000 kg |
| Jordan | 0.106 kg | No Report | No Report | No Report | 55.034 kg | 1.440 kg |
| Kuwait | 28.580 kg [ICPO] | 0.246 kg | [ICPO] | 3.099 kg [ICPO] | No Report | 715.060 kg [ICPO] |
| Lebanon | No Report | No Report | 1.379 kg | 0.017 kg | 0.011 kg | 0.091 kg |
| Oman | No Report | No Report | 0.269 kg | 6823.000 kg [ICPO] | 0.001 kg | 0.306 kg |
| Pakistan | No Report | No Report | No Report | 1223.205 kg [ICPO] | No Report | 68346.000 kg [F.O] |
| Qatar | No Report | 146.250 kg [ICPO] | 3.297 kg [ICPO] | 0.300 kg [ICPO] | No Report | 0.003 kg |
| Saudi Arabia | No Report | No Report | No Report | No Report | No Report | 5591.000 kg [ICPO] |
| Syrian Arab Republic | 1714.634 kg [Govt] | 231.759 kg [Govt] | 819.058 kg [Govt] | 222.016 kg [Govt] | 379.957 kg [Govt] | No Report |
| United Arab Emirates | No Report | 0.095 kg | 0.341 kg | No Report | 2.566 kg | 0.425 kg |
| Yemen | 0.569 kg [ICPO] | 11.350 kg [ICPO] | No Report | 24.990 kg [ICPO] | No Report | No Report |
| Sub-Total | 12386.270 kg | 3970.741 kg | 4494.386 kg | 20224.010 kg | 12122.570 kg | 87036.330 kg |
| **South Asia** | | | | | | |
| Bangladesh | No Report | No Report | 724.070 kg [F.O] | 2657.899 kg | 1421.200 kg [ICPO] | 1721.816 kg |
| India | 80866.000 kg | 68221.000 kg | 38610.000 kg | 100056.000 kg | 75943.000 kg [Govt (6] | 93477.000 kg [Govt] |
| Maldives | No Report | 0.001 kg | 0.022 kg | No Report | 0.004 kg | 0.072 kg [ICPO] |
| Nepal | 2040.894 kg [ICPO] | 6409.669 kg | 4064.650 kg | 8025.308 kg [ICPO] | No Report | 850.031 kg |
| Sri Lanka | 63338.734 kg | 3450.686 kg | 4062.421 kg | 5026.336 kg | 113238.733 kg | 555.135 kg [ICPO] |
| Sub-Total | 146245.600 kg | 78081.360 kg | 47461.160 kg | 115765.500 kg | 190602.900 kg | 96604.050 kg |

Source: Annual Report Questionnaire if not otherwise indicated

## SEIZURES, 1997 - 2002
### Cannabis herb

| Region/country or territory | 1997 | 1998 | 1999 | 2000 | 2001 | 2002 |
|---|---|---|---|---|---|---|
| **ASIA** | | | | | | |
| Total region | 264838.600 kg | 102567.700 kg | 121724.000 kg | 172247.800 kg | 295966.100 kg | 288061.400 kg<br>24 u. |
| **EUROPE** | | | | | | |
| **Eastern Europe** | | | | | | |
| Albania | No Report | No Report | 4395.156 kg [ICPO] | 6604.000 kg [Govt] | 6915.000 kg [Govt] | 13717.898 kg |
| Belarus | 90.802 kg [INCB] | No Report | 425.000 kg | 124.000 kg | 103.000 kg [ICPO] | 89.000 kg |
| Bosnia Herzegovina | 1.002 kg [NAPOL] | 53.815 kg [NAPOL] | 59.144 kg [ICPO] | 127.982 kg [NAPOL] | 467.585 kg [ICPO] | 919.545 kg [ICPO] |
| Bulgaria | 227.440 kg | 1527.562 kg | 29365.000 kg | 295.947 kg | 183.061 kg | 1308.970 kg |
| Croatia | 135.868 kg | 20342.877 kg | 200.898 kg | 797.501 kg | 737.911 kg | 608.070 kg |
| Czech Republic | 5.403 kg | 5.500 kg | 111.200 kg | 16.648 kg | 190.450 kg | 100.728 kg |
| Estonia | 3.439 kg | 4.789 kg<br>358 u. | 1.468 kg<br>491 u. | 4.190 kg<br>673 u. | 0.903 kg | 1.747 kg |
| FYR of Macedonia | 57.989 kg [NAPOL] | 1136.752 kg | 698.098 kg [NAPOL] | 1333.399 kg [NAPOL] | 99.115 kg [Govt] | 29.234 kg |
| Hungary | 2140.000 kg [Govt.] | 42.930 kg | 65.725 kg | 51.000 kg | 131.030 kg | 114.755 kg |
| Latvia | 22.000 kg | 2.480 kg | 231.200 kg | 6.780 kg | 193.580 kg | No Report |
| Lithuania | 8.063 kg | 30.357 kg | 25.667 kg | 14.428 kg | 15.540 kg | 5.300 kg |
| Poland | 62.476 kg | 62.146 kg | 847.901 kg | 139.000 kg | 74.306 kg | 495.700 kg |
| Republic of Moldova | 435.500 kg | No Report | 416.000 kg [ICPO] | No Report | No Report | No Report |
| Romania | 40.186 kg [ICPO] | 7.478 kg | 4.530 kg [ICPO] | 321.000 kg [ICPO] | 155.000 kg | 14904.710 kg [ICPO] |
| Russian Federation | 22976.000 kg | 23510.650 kg | 33801.919 kg | 23313.000 kg [F.O] | 43877.267 kg | 29847.879 kg [ICPO] |
| Serbia and Montenegro | No Report | No Report | No Report | No Report | 1230.224 kg | 1729.501 kg |
| Slovakia | 865.615 kg | 12539.934 kg | 156.000 kg | 168.196 kg | No Report | 151.500 kg |
| Slovenia | 47.555 kg | 2772.604 kg | 249.156 kg | 3413.025 kg | 177.880 kg | 1099.940 kg |
| Ukraine | No Report | No Report | 4045.000 kg [ICPO. (6] | 11609.932 kg [ICPO] | 8195.320 kg | 80.000 kg |
| Sub-Total | 27119.340 kg | 62039.880 kg<br>358 u. | 75099.070 kg<br>491 u. | 48340.030 kg<br>673 u. | 62747.170 kg | 65204.480 kg |
| **Western Europe** | | | | | | |
| Andorra | 1.892 kg [ICPO] | 0.116 kg [ICPO] | 0.046 kg | 0.237 kg [ICPO] | 0.200 kg | 0.111 kg |
| Austria | 668.071 kg | 1211.031 kg | 341.402 kg | 1562.828 kg | 282.255 kg | 450.289 kg |
| Belgium | 39072.000 kg | 2463.270 kg | 2914.749 kg | 8206.746 kg | 8206.746 kg [UNODC (7] | 23920.000 kg |
| Cyprus | 17.582 kg | 128.905 kg | 30.108 kg | 28.875 kg | 37.537 kg | 9.169 kg |
| Denmark | No Report | No Report | 52.830 kg | 739.819 kg<br>14032 u. | 762.262 kg | 50.671 kg |
| Finland | 12.153 kg | 8.014 kg | 18.167 kg | 13.825 kg | 16.100 kg | 32.000 kg |
| France | 3452.210 kg | 3521.790 kg | 3382.205 kg | 4865.558 kg | 3922.370 kg | 6146.700 kg |
| Germany | 4167.282 kg | 14897.189 kg | 15021.800 kg | 5870.900 kg | 2078.703 kg | 6130.199 kg |
| Greece | 12409.776 kg<br>482 u. | 17510.434 kg | 12038.938 kg<br>10 u. | 14908.448 kg | 11653.193 kg | 6021.447 kg |
| Iceland | No Report | No Report | 0.503 kg | 5.092 kg | 0.030 kg | 1.439 kg |
| Ireland | 34.824 kg | 38.909 kg | 68.290 kg | 207.954 kg | 11590.057 kg | 6105.710 kg |

Source: Annual Report Questionnaire if not otherwise indicated

309

## SEIZURES, 1997 - 2002
### Cannabis herb

| Region/country or territory | 1997 | 1998 | 1999 | 2000 | 2001 | 2002 |
|---|---|---|---|---|---|---|
| **EUROPE** | | | | | | |
| **Western Europe** | | | | | | |
| Italy | 45011.035 kg 2675 u. | 38785.988 kg 1192 u. | 21248.982 kg [ICPO] | 26071.488 kg 2068 u. | 36622.637 kg 967 u. | 16397.838 kg 823 u. |
| Liechtenstein | 1.530 kg | No Report | No Report | 0.972 kg [3] | 422.470 kg | 1.442 kg |
| Luxembourg | 34.387 kg | 4.956 kg | 3.932 kg | 8.383 kg [ICPO] | No Report | 18.196 kg [ICPO] |
| Malta | 0.163 kg | 0.069 kg | 0.161 kg | No Report | 0.022 kg | 0.846 kg [ICPO] |
| Monaco | 0.028 kg | 0.032 kg | 0.013 kg [ICPO] | 0.024 kg [ICPO] | No Report | 0.093 kg |
| Netherlands | 35315.000 kg [Govt] | 55463.000 kg [Govt] | 49115.000 kg [Govt] | 10330.000 kg [Govt] | 21139.000 kg | 42675.000 kg [3] |
| Norway | 44.095 kg | 88.172 kg | 16.471 kg | 20.905 kg | 35.384 kg | 105.654 kg |
| Portugal | 72.240 kg | 7.115 kg | 65.766 kg | 223.212 kg | 234.533 kg | 361.026 kg |
| Spain | 24890.311 kg | 412.866 kg | 761.342 kg | 353.292 kg | 532.420 kg | 380.733 kg |
| Sweden | 30.705 kg | 98.431 kg | 28.228 kg 4 u. | 45.597 kg | 13.981 kg | 76.000 kg |
| Switzerland | 6634.843 kg | 13163.982 kg | 7800.229 kg | 18313.602 kg | 11106.537 kg | 21893.240 kg |
| Turkey | No Report | No Report | 5458.350 kg [ICPO] | 1.000 kg | 4561.533 kg | 5524.179 kg |
| United Kingdom | 31120.199 kg | 21660.666 kg | 15410.048 kg [ICPO] 20 u. | 25473.979 kg | 26740.984 kg | 26740.984 kg [8] |
| Sub-Total | 202990.300 kg 3157 u. | 169464.900 kg 1192 u. | 133777.600 kg 34 u. | 117252.700 kg 16100 u. | 139959.000 kg 967 u. | 163043.000 kg 823 u. |
| Total region | 230109.700 kg 3157 u. | 231504.800 kg 1550 u. | 208876.600 kg 525 u. | 165592.800 kg 16773 u. | 202706.100 kg 967 u. | 228247.500 kg 823 u. |
| **OCEANIA** | | | | | | |
| **Oceania** | | | | | | |
| Australia | 4398.986 kg [9] | 15996.628 kg [Govt. (6] | 3340.917 kg [Govt. (6] | 4365.089 kg [Govt. (10] | 6918.357 kg | 5310.996 kg [11] |
| Fiji | No Report | No Report | 45.618 kg [ICPO] | 106.200 kg [ICPO] | 316.750 kg [ICPO] | 14.414 kg [ICPO] |
| *New Caledonia* | 133.610 kg [INCB] | No Report | 132.000 kg [INCB] | No Report | No Report | No Report |
| New Zealand | 285.012 kg | 389.182 kg [9] | 323.649 kg | 332.396 kg | 1847.000 kg | 593.078 kg |
| Tonga | 0.297 kg [INCB] | No Report | No Report | No Report | No Report | No Report |
| Sub-Total | 4817.905 kg | 16385.810 kg | 3842.184 kg | 4803.685 kg | 9082.107 kg | 5918.488 kg |
| Total region | 4817.905 kg | 16385.810 kg | 3842.184 kg | 4803.685 kg | 9082.107 kg | 5918.488 kg |
| TOTAL | 3068387.000 kg 17674 u. | 2985135.000 kg 2214 u. | 3992360.000 kg 623 u. | 4544489.000 kg 17511 u. | 4678062.000 kg 10268 u. | 4741221.000 kg 3878 u. |

1) Includes plants,resin & seeds 2) No. of seizures include seizures of cannabis plant 3) Including cannabis resin. 4) Including cannabis resin and plants 5) Including cannabis resin 6) Provisional figures. 7) Due to unavailability of 2001 data,  year 2000 data were used  for analysis purposes. 8) Due to unavailability of 2002 data,  year 2001 data were used  for analysis purposes. 9) Including cannabis resin, liquid cannabis. 10) Fiscal year 11) Includes 1855.237kg of Cannabis unspecified

Source: Annual Report Questionnaire if not otherwise indicated

## SEIZURES, 1997 - 2002
### Cannabis resin

| Region/country or territory | 1997 | 1998 | 1999 | 2000 | 2001 | 2002 |
|---|---|---|---|---|---|---|
| **AFRICA** | | | | | | |
| **East Africa** | | | | | | |
| Kenya | 7.007 kg | No Report | 3.200 kg [ICPO] | 6356.000 kg | 21.000 kg [ICPO] | 17.172 kg |
| Mauritius | No Report | 0.130 kg | [(1] | 0.007 kg | 0.040 kg | 0.027 kg |
| Seychelles | No Report | 1.073 kg [Govt.] | 72.883 kg | 32.962 kg | 17.934 kg [ICPO] | 2.986 kg |
| Uganda | No Report | 25.000 kg | 8.797 kg | No Report | No Report | No Report |
| United Republic of Tanzania | No Report | 42.162 kg | No Report | 15.000 kg [ICPO] | 12.500 kg [Govt] | 1865.614 kg [ICPO] |
| Sub-Total | 7.007 kg | 68.365 kg | 84.880 kg | 6403.969 kg | 51.474 kg | 1885.799 kg |
| **North Africa** | | | | | | |
| Algeria | No Report | 1217.179 kg [ICPO] | 4080.662 kg | 1694.127 kg [ICPO] | 1728.258 kg [ICPO] | 2148.379 kg |
| Egypt | 441.588 kg | 628.434 kg | 626.000 kg | 525.000 kg | 486.000 kg | 1080.000 kg |
| Libyan Arab Jam. | 310.000 kg [F.O] | 471.955 kg | 1.476 kg [F.O] | 3.418 kg [F.O] | 7.044 kg [F.O] | No Report |
| Morocco | 71887.469 kg | 55519.734 kg | 54755.235 kg | 143946.033 kg | 61355.736 kg | 66394.000 kg |
| Tunisia | 201.074 kg [ICPO] | 806.324 kg | 1893.381 kg | 536.684 kg [ICPO] | 1288.877 kg | 977.730 kg |
| Sub-Total | 72840.130 kg | 58643.630 kg | 61356.760 kg | 146705.300 kg | 64865.920 kg | 70600.100 kg |
| **Southern Africa** | | | | | | |
| Lesotho | 3.942 kg [ICPO] | No Report | No Report | No Report | No Report | No Report |
| Malawi | No Report | 3.000 kg | 3.000 kg | No Report | No Report | No Report |
| Mozambique | 12000.000 kg [ICPO] | 14.160 kg [ICPO] | 11.000 kg [ICPO] | 15542.000 kg [ICPO] | 0.200 kg [ICPO] | No Report |
| South Africa | 2.150 kg | 20.568 kg | 22.612 kg [ICPO] | 11500.000 kg | 534.146 kg | 696.170 kg |
| Swaziland | No Report | No Report | No Report | No Report | 5.056 kg | No Report |
| Zambia | 40.269 kg [Govt] | 3.111 kg [Govt] | 4.201 kg | 14.604 kg | 0.016 kg [Govt] | 1037.000 kg |
| Zimbabwe | No Report | 3.191 kg | No Report | No Report | 0.081 kg | 11.000 kg |
| Sub-Total | 12046.360 kg | 44.030 kg | 40.813 kg | 27056.600 kg | 539.499 kg | 1744.170 kg |
| **West and Central Africa** | | | | | | |
| Benin | No Report | No Report | No Report | 350.000 kg [ICPO] | 13.000 kg [ICPO] | No Report |
| Burkina Faso | 4647.000 kg [Govt.] | No Report | No Report | No Report | No Report | No Report |
| Gambia | 0.048 kg [ICPO] | 0.420 kg [ICPO] | 0.007 kg | No Report | No Report | 1.966 kg [ICPO] |
| *Saint Helena* | No Report | No Report | No Report | No Report | No Report | 1 u. |
| Sao Tome and Principe | 4.000 kg | No Report | No Report | No Report | No Report | No Report |
| Senegal | No Report | No Report | No Report | 5390.000 kg [ICPO] | No Report | No Report |
| Sub-Total | 4651.048 kg | 0.420 kg | 0.007 kg | 5740.000 kg | 13.000 kg | 1.966 kg 1 u. |
| Total region | 89544.540 kg | 58756.440 kg | 61482.460 kg | 185905.800 kg | 65469.890 kg | 74232.040 kg 1 u. |
| **AMERICAS** | | | | | | |
| **Caribbean** | | | | | | |
| Antigua and Barbuda | 1944.900 kg [ICPO] | No Report | 1000.000 kg [CICAD] | No Report | No Report | No Report |

Source: Annual Report Questionnaire if not otherwise indicated

## SEIZURES, 1997 - 2002

### Cannabis resin

| Region/country or territory | 1997 | 1998 | 1999 | 2000 | 2001 | 2002 |
|---|---|---|---|---|---|---|
| **AMERICAS** | | | | | | |
| **Caribbean** | | | | | | |
| *Aruba* | 0.004 kg [INCB] | No Report | No Report | No Report | No Report | No Report |
| Bahamas | 5.030 kg [ICPO] | 16.082 kg | 2.095 kg [ICPO] | 27.900 kg | 14.220 kg 31 u. | 61.690 kg [ICPO] |
| Barbados | No Report | No Report | 1.270 kg [HONLC] | No Report | No Report | No Report |
| *Bermuda* | 0.609 kg | 0.609 kg | 171.002 kg | 1.136 kg | No Report | 1.550 kg |
| Cuba | No Report | No Report | 66.200 kg [F.O] | No Report | No Report | 0.192 kg [ICPO] |
| Dominica | No Report | No Report | 0.015 kg [ICPO] | No Report | 51.580 kg [ICPO] | No Report |
| Dominican Republic | No Report | No Report | 184.000 kg [ICPO] | No Report | 0.008 kg | 0.007 kg [ICPO] |
| Jamaica | 67.590 kg [ICPO] | No Report | 61.450 kg [ICPO] | 20.000 kg [CICAD] | 8.100 kg | 497.000 kg [ICPO] |
| *Netherlands Antilles* | 0.354 kg [INCB] | No Report | No Report | 0.061 kg [ICPO] | 0.104 kg [ICPO] | 0.060 kg [ICPO] |
| Saint Lucia | [(2] | No Report | No Report | 0.071 kg | No Report | No Report |
| Trinidad Tobago | No Report | 2725.305 kg | No Report | No Report | No Report | No Report |
| *Turks and Caicos Islands* | No Report | No Report | No Report | 0.202 kg [ICPO] | No Report | No Report |
| Sub-Total | 2018.487 kg | 2741.996 kg | 1486.032 kg | 49.370 kg | 74.012 kg 31 u. | 560.499 kg |
| **Central America** | | | | | | |
| Honduras | No Report | No Report | 1027 u. [CICAD] | No Report | No Report | No Report |
| Panama | No Report | No Report | No Report | 0.002 kg [ICPO] | No Report | No Report |
| Sub-Total | | | 1027 u. | 0.002 kg | | |
| **North America** | | | | | | |
| Canada | 6178.000 kg | 15925.320 kg 0.002 lt. 97 u. | 6477.000 kg 1.000 lt. 5 u. | 16317.600 kg 31 u. | 1755.997 kg | 158.893 kg |
| Mexico | 115.155 kg | 1.743 kg | 0.329 kg | 0.005 kg | 29.507 kg | 0.035 kg |
| United States | 1072.600 kg | No Report | 761.000 kg | 945.137 kg | 56.500 kg | 620.900 kg |
| Sub-Total | 7365.755 kg | 15927.060 kg 0.002 lt. 97 u. | 7238.330 kg 1.000 lt. 5 u. | 17262.740 kg 31 u. | 1842.004 kg | 779.828 kg |
| **South America** | | | | | | |
| Argentina | 0.060 kg | 1.880 kg | 5006 u. | 9.114 kg | 1.219 kg | 1.891 kg |
| Brazil | 12.160 kg | No Report | 37.550 kg | 41.009 kg | 43.519 kg [Govt] | 36.100 kg [F.O] |
| Chile | No Report | No Report | No Report | 0.001 kg | No Report | No Report |
| Colombia | 7.000 kg | No Report | 338.000 kg | 38.000 lt. [CICAD] | 0.200 kg | No Report |
| *Falkland Islands* | 0.122 kg | No Report | 0.063 kg | 0.120 kg | No Report | No Report |
| Paraguay | 1.780 kg | 3.702 kg | 2.337 kg | No Report | No Report | 1301.000 kg |
| Suriname | No Report | 0.529 kg | No Report | No Report | No Report | No Report |
| Uruguay | No Report | No Report | 1.136 kg | 0.045 kg | No Report | 2.387 kg |
| Sub-Total | 21.122 kg | 6.111 kg | 379.085 kg 5006 u. | 50.289 kg 38.000 lt. | 44.938 kg | 1341.378 kg |

Source: Annual Report Questionnaire if not otherwise indicated

## SEIZURES, 1997 - 2002
### Cannabis resin

| Region/country or territory | 1997 | 1998 | 1999 | 2000 | 2001 | 2002 |
|---|---|---|---|---|---|---|
| **AMERICAS** | | | | | | |
| Total region | 9405.364 kg | 18675.170 kg | 9103.447 kg | 17362.400 kg | 1960.954 kg | 2681.705 kg |
| | | 0.002 lt. | 1.000 lt. | 38.000 lt. | 31 u. | |
| | | 97 u. | 6038 u. | 31 u. | | |
| **ASIA** | | | | | | |
| **Central Asia and Transcaucasian countries** | | | | | | |
| Armenia | No Report | No Report | 0.178 kg [ICPO] | 0.169 kg | 0.112 kg | 0.914 kg |
| Azerbaijan | No Report | 23.256 kg | 0.832 kg | No Report | 15.500 kg | 0.169 kg |
| Georgia | No Report | No Report | 0.003 kg [ICPO] | 0.009 kg [ICPO] | No Report | No Report |
| Kazakhstan | 4100.000 kg [Govt.] | 298.635 kg | 145.462 kg | No Report | 276.160 kg [F.O] | 192.650 kg [F.O] |
| Tajikistan | 630.311 kg [F.O] | 726.449 kg [F.O] | 560.000 kg [F.O] | 429.981 kg [F.O] | No Report | No Report |
| Turkmenistan | No Report | 22249.000 kg [Govt.] | 10413.000 kg [F.O] | No Report | No Report | No Report |
| Uzbekistan | 316.055 kg | No Report | 694.000 kg [F.O] | 65.100 kg | 86.000 kg [F.O] | 44.700 kg |
| Sub-Total | 5046.366 kg | 23297.340 kg | 11813.480 kg | 495.259 kg | 377.772 kg | 238.433 kg |
| **East and South-East Asia** | | | | | | |
| Hong Kong SAR, China | 38.900 kg | No Report | 14.376 kg | 6.004 kg | 0.700 kg | 0.370 kg |
| Indonesia | No Report | 0.690 kg | 300.005 kg [HNLP] | 3.885 kg | 5.632 kg | 0.687 kg |
| | | 230 u. | | | | |
| Japan | 107.421 kg | 214.560 kg | 200.297 kg | 185.416 kg | 73.499 kg | 275.300 kg |
| Korea (Republic of) | 0.635 kg | 0.884 kg | 1.963 kg | No Report | 4.254 kg | 158.968 kg [ICPO] |
| Macau SAR, China | No Report | 0.995 kg [ICPO] | No Report | 0.043 kg | 0.499 kg | No Report |
| Mongolia | No Report | No Report | No Report | No Report | 2 u. | No Report |
| Philippines | 0.283 kg [ICPO] | No Report | No Report | 1.770 kg | 8.015 kg | 265.000 kg |
| | | | | 2 u. | | |
| Thailand | 45.169 kg | 20.592 kg | 121.220 kg | 91.903 kg [ICPO] | No Report | 52.170 kg [ICPO] |
| Sub-Total | 192.408 kg | 237.721 kg | 637.860 kg | 289.021 kg | 92.599 kg | 752.495 kg |
| | | 230 u. | | 2 u. | 2 u. | |
| **Near and Middle East /South-West Asia** | | | | | | |
| Afghanistan | No Report | No Report | No Report | No Report | No Report | 50314.044 kg |
| Bahrain | 0.012 kg | 1.036 kg [ICPO] | 1263.049 kg [ICPO] | No Report | No Report | 3.700 kg |
| Iran (Islamic Republic of) | 11095.789 kg | 14376.364 kg | 18907.000 kg | 31581.000 kg [NAPOL] | 46084.000 kg | 64166.000 kg [Govt] |
| Iraq | No Report | No Report | No Report | 569.970 kg | 2343.796 kg | No Report |
| Israel | 133.000 kg | 60.900 kg | 70.000 kg [ICPO] | 30.218 kg | 143.000 kg | 2893.000 kg |
| Jordan | No Report | 166.737 kg | 112.410 kg | 298.456 kg | 785.542 kg | 864.966 kg |
| Kuwait | 0.530 kg [ICPO] | 214.103 kg | 972.878 kg [ICPO] | 3488.000 kg [F.O] | No Report | No Report |
| Lebanon | 1876.281 kg | 2492.609 kg | 76.698 kg | 358.000 kg [ICPO] | 307.820 kg | 28670.335 kg |
| Oman | 1979.000 kg [INCB] | No Report | 14335.695 kg | No Report | 2382.645 kg | 49.934 kg |
| Pakistan | 107000.000 kg [ICPO] | 65909.234 kg | 81458.142 kg | 129181.626 kg | 75161.024 kg | 85126.407 kg |
| Qatar | 361.692 kg [ICPO] | 374.526 kg [ICPO] | 680.869 kg [ICPO] | 134.586 kg [ICPO] | 144.820 kg [ICPO] | 65.969 kg |

Source: Annual Report Questionnaire if not otherwise indicated

313

## SEIZURES, 1997 - 2002
### Cannabis resin

| Region/country or territory | 1997 | 1998 | 1999 | 2000 | 2001 | 2002 |
|---|---|---|---|---|---|---|
| **ASIA** | | | | | | |
| **Near and Middle East /South-West Asia** | | | | | | |
| Saudi Arabia | 1321.285 kg [ICPO] | 2357.874 kg | 2003.000 kg [ICPO] | 2719.091 kg 18 u. | 1767.430 kg | No Report |
| Syrian Arab Republic | No Report | No Report | No Report | No Report | No Report | 907.427 kg |
| United Arab Emirates | 3505.585 kg | 7087.219 kg | 2530.511 kg | 943.405 kg | 6113.923 kg | 3127.065 kg |
| Yemen | No Report | No Report | No Report | No Report | No Report | 26.125 kg |
| Sub-Total | 127273.200 kg | 93040.600 kg | 122410.300 kg | 169304.400 kg 18 u. | 135234.000 kg | 236215.000 kg |
| **South Asia** | | | | | | |
| Bangladesh | No Report | No Report | 0.700 kg [F.O] | 0.001 kg | 133.020 kg [ICPO] | 6.054 kg |
| India | 3281.000 kg | 10106.000 kg | 3290.000 kg | 5041.000 kg | 5664.000 kg | 4487.000 kg [Govt] |
| Maldives | No Report | No Report | 0.004 kg | No Report | No Report | 0.007 kg [ICPO] |
| Nepal | 981.892 kg [Govt] | 2585.886 kg [Govt] | 1671.413 kg [Govt] | 2539.936 kg [Govt] | No Report | 850.031 kg [ICPO] |
| Sri Lanka | 17.756 kg | No Report | [(1] | 0.011 kg | 0.015 kg | 19979.000 kg [ICPO] |
| Sub-Total | 4280.648 kg | 12691.890 kg | 4962.117 kg | 7580.948 kg | 5797.035 kg | 25322.090 kg |
| Total region | 136792.600 kg | 129267.500 kg 230 u. | 139823.700 kg | 177669.600 kg 20 u. | 141501.400 kg 2 u. | 262528.000 kg |
| **EUROPE** | | | | | | |
| **Eastern Europe** | | | | | | |
| Belarus | 5.380 kg [INCB] | 0.509 kg | 1.949 kg | 0.639 kg | 669.000 kg [ICPO] | 2.174 kg |
| Bosnia Herzegovina | 0.500 kg [NAPOL] | No Report | 0.002 kg [NAPOL] | No Report | 0.060 kg [ICPO] | No Report |
| Bulgaria | 533.570 kg | 0.680 kg | 0.010 kg | 514.017 kg | 422.584 kg | 88.476 kg |
| Croatia | 3.257 kg | 2.878 kg | 6.555 kg | 1.041 kg | 4.559 kg | 2.107 kg |
| Czech Republic | 0.324 kg | No Report | 1.200 kg | 23.099 kg | 6.850 kg | 11.391 kg |
| Estonia | 0.316 kg | 0.133 kg 52 u. | 1.191 kg 191 u. | 9.913 kg 58 u. | 0.199 kg | 1.067 kg |
| FYR of Macedonia | No Report | 1.164 kg [NAPOL] | 0.089 kg [NAPOL] | 427.519 kg [NAPOL] | 309.846 kg [Govt] | 258.406 kg |
| Hungary | 21.739 kg [Govt.] | 6.803 kg | 5.242 kg | 22.538 kg | 0.880 kg | 4.181 kg |
| Latvia | 0.646 kg | 3.150 kg | 0.685 kg | 0.495 kg | 0.191 kg | No Report |
| Lithuania | 0.078 kg | 3.780 kg | 1.054 kg | 0.169 kg | 0.260 kg | 0.569 kg |
| Poland | 628.000 kg | 8.176 kg | 49.203 kg | No Report | 9.426 kg | 217.346 kg |
| Republic of Moldova | No Report | 228.000 kg | No Report | 523.000 kg [ICPO] | 358.130 kg | No Report |
| Romania | 1309.792 kg [ICPO] | 1.673 kg | 43.530 kg | 340.810 kg [(3] | 13871.000 kg | 38.580 kg |
| Russian Federation | 887.500 kg [Govt.] | 1588.700 kg | 710.895 kg | 845.000 kg [F.O] | 1335.671 kg | 1424.257 kg [ICPO] |
| Serbia and Montenegro | No Report | No Report | No Report | No Report | 4.534 kg | 6.814 kg |
| Slovakia | 0.038 kg | 0.015 kg | No Report | 2.085 kg | 0.635 kg | No Report |
| Slovenia | 0.938 kg | 1.958 kg | 64.622 kg | 1.022 kg | 2.360 kg | 0.120 kg |
| Ukraine | 9.500 kg | 6150.100 kg | 14.000 kg [ICPO. (4] | 49.316 kg [ICPO] | 11.130 kg | 7.092 kg [ICPO] |

Source: Annual Report Questionnaire if not otherwise indicated

## SEIZURES, 1997 - 2002
### Cannabis resin

| Region/country or territory | 1997 | 1998 | 1999 | 2000 | 2001 | 2002 |
|---|---|---|---|---|---|---|
| **EUROPE** | | | | | | |
| **Eastern Europe** | | | | | | |
| Sub-Total | 3401.578 kg | 7997.719 kg<br>52 u. | 900.227 kg<br>191 u. | 2760.663 kg<br>58 u. | 17007.310 kg | 2062.580 kg |
| **Western Europe** | | | | | | |
| Andorra | No Report | 1.372 kg ICPO | 1.422 kg | 3.061 kg ICPO | 3.790 kg | 3.076 kg |
| Austria | 243.909 kg | 124.718 kg | 109.996 kg | 243.673 kg | 137.987 kg | 133.209 kg |
| Belgium | 8980.000 kg | 817.622 kg | 3130.812 kg ICPO | 532.163 kg | 532.163 kg UNODC (5 | 5298.000 kg |
| Cyprus | 3.413 kg | 1.201 kg | 7.291 kg | 9.525 kg | 1.443 kg | 1.456 kg |
| Denmark | 467.100 kg | 1572.455 kg | 14021.300 kg | 2914.419 kg | 1762.742 kg | 2635.235 kg |
| Finland | 197.659 kg | 160.972 kg | 492.316 kg | 196.540 kg | 590.000 kg | 482.300 kg |
| France | 51664.367 kg | 52176.426 kg | 64096.665 kg | 48710.697 kg | 58195.515 kg | 50836.113 kg |
| Germany | 7327.560 kg | 6109.549 kg | 4885.200 kg | 8525.200 kg | 6863.057 kg | 5003.001 kg |
| Greece | 6825.727 kg | 30.817 kg | 55.819 kg | 56.120 kg | 270.780 kg | 67.711 kg |
| Iceland | No Report | No Report | 41.622 kg | 26.626 kg | 44.140 kg | 57.564 kg |
| Ireland | 1247.244 kg | 3179.178 kg | 2514.975 kg | 379.800 kg | 567.026 kg | 3314.938 kg |
| Italy | 14740.517 kg<br>1954 u. | 15412.128 kg<br>711 u. | 46780.319 kg ICPO | 20725.364 kg<br>818 u. | 16455.477 kg<br>811 u. | 28600.257 kg<br>947 u. |
| Liechtenstein | 0.008 kg | 2.770 kg | No Report | No Report | 0.012 kg | 0.013 kg |
| Luxembourg | 0.868 kg | 1.974 kg | 1.270 kg | 1.174 kg ICPO | No Report | 0.697 kg ICPO |
| Malta | 1.788 kg | 25.116 kg | 1.606 kg | 3.913 kg | 3.562 kg | 8.801 kg ICPO |
| Monaco | 0.170 kg | 0.396 kg | 0.111 kg ICPO | 0.512 kg ICPO | No Report | 0.095 kg |
| Netherlands | 30272.000 kg Govt | 70696.000 kg Govt | 61226.000 kg Govt | 29590.000 kg Govt | 10972.000 kg | * |
| Norway | 904.059 kg | 1874.136 kg | 1254.762 kg | 632.647 kg | 808.541 kg | 1097.980 kg |
| Portugal | 9621.183 kg | 5747.793 kg | 10636.075 kg | 30467.121 kg | 6472.688 kg | 7022.029 kg |
| Spain | 315328.000 kg ICPO | 428236.375 kg | 431165.280 kg | 474504.785 kg | 514181.600 kg | 564808.966 kg |
| Sweden | 627.994 kg | 390.930 kg | 1065.387 kg<br>26 u. | 1206.709 kg | 772.462 kg | 729.000 kg |
| Switzerland | 653.467 kg | 1837.480 kg | 651.548 kg | 1258.307 kg ICPO | 317.550 kg | 1317.640 kg |
| Turkey | 10439.201 kg | 9434.290 kg | 11085.546 kg | 28637.130 kg | 268.477 kg | 1220.725 kg |
| United Kingdom | 118849.203 kg | 82837.533 kg | 33727.243 kg ICPO<br>194 u. | 48346.903 kg | 58996.761 kg | 58996.761 kg (6 |
| Sub-Total | 578395.400 kg<br>1954 u. | 680671.300 kg<br>711 u. | 686952.600 kg<br>220 u. | 696972.400 kg<br>818 u. | 678217.800 kg<br>811 u. | 731635.600 kg<br>947 u. |
| Total region | 581797.000 kg<br>1954 u. | 688669.100 kg<br>763 u. | 687852.900 kg<br>411 u. | 699733.100 kg<br>876 u. | 695225.100 kg<br>811 u. | 733698.100 kg<br>947 u. |
| **OCEANIA** | | | | | | |
| **Oceania** | | | | | | |
| Australia | 537.289 kg | No Report | 4.129 kg | 17.972 kg | 3266.944 kg | 55.795 kg |
| *New Caledonia* | 0.003 kg INCB | No Report | No Report | No Report | No Report | No Report |

Source: Annual Report Questionnaire if not otherwise indicated

* Data was not available at the time of the preparation of the report; latest information received indicates amount of 32,717 kg (previously included in overall cannabis seizures of the Netherlands for 2002).

## SEIZURES, 1997 - 2002
### Cannabis resin

| Region/country or territory | 1997 | 1998 | 1999 | 2000 | 2001 | 2002 |
|---|---|---|---|---|---|---|
| **OCEANIA** | | | | | | |
| **Oceania** | | | | | | |
| New Zealand | 2.198 kg [INCB] | 3.632 kg | 0.676 kg | No Report | 0.435 kg | 0.482 kg |
| Sub-Total | 539.490 kg | 3.632 kg | 4.805 kg | 17.972 kg | 3267.379 kg | 56.277 kg |
| Total region | 539.490 kg | 3.632 kg | 4.805 kg | 17.972 kg | 3267.379 kg | 56.277 kg |
| TOTAL | 818079.000 kg | 895371.900 kg | 898267.300 kg | 1080689.000 kg | 907424.700 kg | 1073196.000 kg |
| | 1954 u. | 0.002 lt. | 1.000 lt. | 38.000 lt. | 844 u. | 948 u. |
| | | 1090 u. | 6449 u. | 927 u. | | |

1) Small quantity. 2) Including depressants. 3) Including cannabis herb. 4) Provisional figures. 5) Due to unavailability of 2001 data, year 2000 data were used for analysis purposes. 6) Due to unavailability of 2002 data, year 2001 data were used for analysis purposes.

Source: Annual Report Questionnaire if not otherwise indicated

## SEIZURES, 1997 - 2002
### Cannabis oil

| Region/country or territory | 1997 | 1998 | 1999 | 2000 | 2001 | 2002 |
|---|---|---|---|---|---|---|
| **AFRICA** | | | | | | |
| **East Africa** | | | | | | |
| Kenya | No Report | No Report | 4.057 kg | No Report | No Report | No Report |
| Sub-Total | | | 4.057 kg | | | |
| **North Africa** | | | | | | |
| Morocco | 1.060 kg [Govt.] | 14.473 kg | 19.000 lt. | 0.693 kg | 0.008 kg | No Report |
| Sub-Total | 1.060 kg | 14.473 kg | 19.000 lt. | 0.693 kg | 0.008 kg | |
| **Southern Africa** | | | | | | |
| Zambia | 0.000 kg [Govt] | 0.000 kg [Govt] | 0.000 kg [Govt] | 0.000 kg [Govt] | 8.500 kg [Govt] | No Report |
| Sub-Total | | | | | 8.500 kg | |
| **West and Central Africa** | | | | | | |
| Benin | No Report | 26.863 kg | No Report | No Report | No Report | No Report |
| Sub-Total | | 26.863 kg | | | | |
| Total region | 1.060 kg | 41.336 kg | 4.057 kg 19.000 lt. | 0.693 kg | 8.508 kg | |
| **AMERICAS** | | | | | | |
| **Caribbean** | | | | | | |
| *Aruba* | No Report | No Report | 0.002 kg [ICPO] | No Report | No Report | No Report |
| Bahamas | 0.020 kg [ICPO] | No Report | 104.089 kg [ICPO] | 0.450 kg | No Report | No Report |
| *Cayman Islands* | 46.036 kg 2 u. | No Report | No Report | No Report | No Report | No Report |
| Haiti | | 11.000 kg [CICAD] | No Report | No Report | No Report | No Report |
| Jamaica | 383.820 kg [ICPO] | No Report | 371.490 kg [ICPO] | 579.091 kg [ICPO] | 210.980 kg | No Report |
| Saint Vincent and the Grenadines | No Report | No Report | No Report | 28375 u. [INCSR] | No Report | No Report |
| Trinidad Tobago | 1430.000 kg [CICAD] | No Report | No Report | No Report | No Report | No Report |
| Sub-Total | 1859.876 kg 2 u. | 11.000 kg | 475.581 kg | 579.541 kg 28375 u. | 210.980 kg | |
| **Central America** | | | | | | |
| Panama | No Report | No Report | 11.360 lt. | No Report | No Report | No Report |
| Sub-Total | | | 11.360 lt. | | | |
| **North America** | | | | | | |
| Canada | 824.000 kg | 524.937 kg 20.166 lt. 2 u. | 434.000 kg 55.302 lt. 6 u. | 28.000 kg 187.392 lt. 13 u. | 120.191 kg 16 u. | 168.830 kg 66.000 lt. |
| United States | No Report | No Report | 490.685 kg | 66.152 kg | 59.700 kg | |
| Sub-Total | 824.000 kg | 524.937 kg 20.166 lt. 2 u. | 924.685 kg 55.302 lt. 6 u. | 94.152 kg 187.392 lt. 13 u. | 179.891 kg 16 u. | 168.830 kg 66.000 lt. |
| **South America** | | | | | | |
| Chile | No Report | No Report | 0.025 kg [ICPO] | No Report | No Report | 0.320 kg [ICPO] |

Source: Annual Report Questionnaire if not otherwise indicated

## SEIZURES, 1997 - 2002
### Cannabis oil

| Region/country or territory | 1997 | 1998 | 1999 | 2000 | 2001 | 2002 |
|---|---|---|---|---|---|---|
| **AMERICAS** | | | | | | |
| **South America** | | | | | | |
| Colombia | 8.000 lt. | No Report | No Report | No Report | No Report | No Report |
| Suriname | No Report | No Report | No Report | No Report | 0.217 kg | No Report |
| Uruguay | No Report | No Report | No Report | No Report | No Report | 2.386 kg [ICPO] |
| Venezuela | 8003.000 kg [CICAD] | No Report | No Report | No Report | No Report | No Report |
| Sub-Total | 8003.000 kg 8.000 lt. | | 0.025 kg | | 0.217 kg | 2.706 kg |
| Total region | 10686.880 kg 8.000 lt. 2 u. | 535.937 kg 20.166 lt. 2 u. | 1400.291 kg 66.662 lt. 6 u. | 673.693 kg 187.392 lt. 28388 u. | 391.088 kg 16 u. | 171.536 kg 66.000 lt. |
| **ASIA** | | | | | | |
| **Central Asia and Transcaucasian countries** | | | | | | |
| Armenia | No Report | 22.353 kg | 0.002 kg [ICPO] | 0.000 kg [(1] | 0.007 kg | No Report |
| Azerbaijan | 1.793 kg [ICPO] | No Report | No Report | No Report | No Report | No Report |
| Kyrgyzstan | 603.554 kg | 1569.238 kg | No Report | No Report | No Report | No Report |
| Sub-Total | 605.347 kg | 1591.591 kg | 0.002 kg | 0.000 kg | 0.007 kg | |
| **East and South-East Asia** | | | | | | |
| Brunei Darussalam | No Report | No Report | No Report | No Report | 0.260 lt. | No Report |
| Indonesia | 4.017 kg | No Report | 300.005 kg | 3.886 kg [ICPO] | No Report | No Report |
| Japan | 0.143 lt. | 3.750 kg | 0.002 kg 0.002 lt. | | 0.000 lt. | 0.003 lt. |
| Korea (Republic of) | 0.027 kg | No Report | No Report | No Report | No Report | 0.765 kg [ICPO] |
| Thailand | No Report | No Report | No Report | 0.516 kg [ICPO] | No Report | No Report |
| Sub-Total | 4.044 kg 0.143 lt. | 3.750 kg | 300.007 kg 0.002 lt. | 4.402 kg | 0.260 lt. | 0.765 kg 0.003 lt. |
| **Near and Middle East /South-West Asia** | | | | | | |
| Iran (Islamic Republic of) | No Report | No Report | 68.000 kg [ICPO] | No Report | No Report | No Report |
| Jordan | 0.145 kg | No Report | No Report | No Report | No Report | No Report |
| Lebanon | 58.000 kg | No Report | No Report | 10.000 kg | No Report | 119.600 kg |
| Sub-Total | 58.145 kg | | 68.000 kg | 10.000 kg | | 119.600 kg |
| **South Asia** | | | | | | |
| Maldives | No Report | No Report | 0.001 kg | No Report | 0.003 kg | No Report |
| Nepal | 1342.492 kg [ICPO] | No Report | 2.100 kg | No Report | No Report | No Report |
| Sub-Total | 1342.492 kg | | 2.101 kg | | 0.003 kg | |
| Total region | 2010.028 kg 0.143 lt. | 1595.341 kg | 370.110 kg 0.002 lt. | 14.402 kg | 0.010 kg 0.260 lt. | 120.365 kg 0.003 lt. |
| **EUROPE** | | | | | | |
| **Eastern Europe** | | | | | | |
| Albania | No Report | No Report | 13.000 lt. [ICPO] | 2.100 lt. [ICPO] | No Report | 0.600 lt. |

Source: Annual Report Questionnaire if not otherwise indicated

## SEIZURES, 1997 - 2002
### Cannabis oil

| Region/country or territory | 1997 | 1998 | 1999 | 2000 | 2001 | 2002 |
|---|---|---|---|---|---|---|
| **EUROPE** | | | | | | |
| **Eastern Europe** | | | | | | |
| Belarus | No Report | No Report | 0.002 kg | No Report | No Report | 2.401 kg |
| Bulgaria | No Report | No Report | 0.100 kg | 0.080 kg | 6 u. | No Report |
| Croatia | No Report | 0.008 kg | No Report | No Report | No Report | No Report |
| Estonia | No Report | No Report | No Report | 0.300 kg 2 u. | No Report | No Report |
| Romania | No Report | No Report | No Report | No Report | No Report | 1.000 lt. |
| Russian Federation | No Report | 102.900 kg [F.O] | 141.344 kg | 291.000 kg [F.O] | 366.590 kg | No Report |
| Slovakia | No Report | No Report | No Report | 64.000 kg | No Report | No Report |
| Sub-Total | | 102.908 kg | 141.446 kg 13.000 lt. | 355.380 kg 2.100 lt. 2 u. | 366.590 kg 6 u. | 2.401 kg 1.600 lt. |
| **Western Europe** | | | | | | |
| Austria | 3.164 kg | No Report | No Report | 0.750 kg [ICPO] | 0.188 kg | 1.919 kg |
| Belgium | No Report | No Report | 5.000 kg | No Report | No Report | No Report |
| Cyprus | No Report | No Report | 30.294 kg | No Report | No Report | No Report [(1] |
| Denmark | 0.123 kg | 0.008 kg | 3.910 kg | 0.962 kg | 0.019 kg | |
| France | 5.442 kg | 0.592 kg | 1.690 kg | 2.830 kg | 3.513 kg | 5.086 kg |
| Germany | 3.510 kg | 0.538 kg | 2.300 kg | 4.500 kg | 0.044 kg | 2.062 kg |
| Greece | No Report | No Report | 0.200 kg [ICPO] | 1.205 kg | 1.910 kg | 757.000 kg |
| Italy | 6.259 kg 6 u. | 0.635 kg 3 u. | 6.772 kg [ICPO] | 13.349 kg 5 u. | 25.263 kg 171 u. | 52.646 kg 753 u. |
| Monaco | 0.029 lt. | No Report | No Report | No Report | No Report | No Report |
| Netherlands | No Report | 150.000 lt. [Govt] | 1.000 lt. [Govt] | No Report | No Report | No Report |
| Norway | 0.308 kg | 0.034 kg | 0.026 kg | 0.028 kg | 0.009 kg | 1.683 kg |
| Portugal | No Report | No Report | 0.001 kg | 0.004 kg | 0.134 kg | 0.011 kg 11 u. |
| Spain | 0.705 lt. | 74.970 lt. | 2346 u. | 0.310 lt. | 1915.500 kg | 0.001 lt. |
| Sweden | 0.019 kg | No Report | 0.006 kg | No Report | 0.203 kg | No Report |
| Switzerland | 8.607 kg | 1.541 kg | 0.609 kg | 95.082 kg | 17.577 kg | 191.654 kg |
| Turkey | No Report | 63.411 kg | No Report | 2.480 kg | 0.001 kg | No Report |
| United Kingdom | 26.600 kg | 7.366 kg | No Report | 4.491 kg | 6.862 kg | 6.862 kg [(2] |
| Sub-Total | 54.032 kg 0.734 lt. 6 u. | 74.125 kg 224.970 lt. 3 u. | 50.808 kg 1.000 lt. 2346 u. | 125.681 kg 0.310 lt. 5 u. | 1971.223 kg 171 u. | 1018.923 kg 0.001 lt. 764 u. |
| Total region | 54.032 kg 0.734 lt. 6 u. | 177.033 kg 224.970 lt. 3 u. | 192.254 kg 14.000 lt. 2346 u. | 481.061 kg 2.410 lt. 7 u. | 2337.813 kg 177 u. | 1021.324 kg 1.601 lt. 764 u. |

Source: Annual Report Questionnaire if not otherwise indicated

319

## SEIZURES, 1997 - 2002
### Cannabis oil

| Region/country or territory | 1997 | 1998 | 1999 | 2000 | 2001 | 2002 |
|---|---|---|---|---|---|---|
| **OCEANIA** | | | | | | |
| **Oceania** | | | | | | |
| Australia | 4.945 kg | No Report | 2.650 kg | 0.755 lt. | No Report | 0.251 kg<br>4 u. |
| New Zealand | No Report | 4.159 kg | 0.026 kg | 8.305 kg | 3.147 kg | 1.342 kg |
| Sub-Total | 4.945 kg | 4.159 kg | 2.676 kg | 8.305 kg<br>0.755 lt. | 3.147 kg | 1.593 kg<br>4 u. |
| Total region | 4.945 kg | 4.159 kg | 2.676 kg | 8.305 kg<br>0.755 lt. | 3.147 kg | 1.593 kg<br>4 u. |
| TOTAL | 12756.940 kg<br>8.877 lt.<br>8 u. | 2353.806 kg<br>245.136 lt.<br>5 u. | 1969.388 kg<br>99.664 lt.<br>2352 u. | 1178.154 kg<br>190.557 lt.<br>28395 u. | 2740.566 kg<br>0.260 lt.<br>193 u. | 1314.818 kg<br>67.604 lt.<br>768 u. |

1) Small quantity. 2) Due to unavailability of 2002 data, year 2001 data were used for analysis purposes.

Source: Annual Report Questionnaire if not otherwise indicated

## SEIZURES, 1997 - 2002
### Cannabis plant

| Region/country or territory | 1997 | 1998 | 1999 | 2000 | 2001 | 2002 |
|---|---|---|---|---|---|---|
| **AFRICA** | | | | | | |
| **East Africa** | | | | | | |
| Eritrea | No Report | No Report | No Report | No Report | 20.000 kg | No Report |
| Kenya | 5.565 kg 2226 u. | No Report | No Report | No Report | No Report | 23625 u. |
| Madagascar | No Report | No Report | No Report | No Report | No Report | 1050980.000 kg |
| Mauritius | 41316 u. | 43294 u. | 45444 u. | 55038 u. | 30788 u. | 22464 u. |
| Seychelles | No Report | No Report | 30.700 kg | 7.233 kg | No Report | 1.073 kg |
| Uganda | No Report | 9411 u. | 35000 u. | 54700 u. | 780000 u. | 1431.100 kg |
| Sub-Total | 5.565 kg 43542 u. | 52705 u. | 30.700 kg 80444 u. | 7.233 kg 109738 u. | 20.000 kg 810788 u. | 1052412.000 kg 46089 u. |
| **North Africa** | | | | | | |
| Egypt | 63542820 u. | 35150384 u. | No Report | No Report | 470 u. | No Report |
| Morocco | No Report | No Report | No Report | No Report | 73810.724 kg | 93206.000 kg |
| Sub-Total | 63542820 u. | 35150380 u. | | | 73810.730 kg 470 u. | 93206.000 kg |
| **Southern Africa** | | | | | | |
| Angola | No Report | No Report | 5733 u. | No Report | No Report | No Report |
| Malawi | 1116.725 kg 8313 u. | 6371.045 kg | 9428.350 kg | 61182.146 kg | 51611.136 kg | 4127.826 kg |
| Namibia | No Report | No Report | 25 u. | No Report | 67 u. | 949.448 kg |
| South Africa | 243565.688 kg | 784201.063 kg | No Report | 864234.300 kg | 608330.095 kg | 754913.307 kg |
| Swaziland | No Report | 7517.000 kg | 2528136 u. | 36665 u. | No Report | No Report |
| Zimbabwe | No Report | 300.000 kg 2936 u. | 165 u. | 3555 u. | 878 u. | 6136 u. |
| Sub-Total | 244682.400 kg 8313 u. | 798389.100 kg 2936 u. | 9428.350 kg 2534059 u. | 925416.400 kg 40220 u. | 659941.300 kg 945 u. | 759990.600 kg 6136 u. |
| **West and Central Africa** | | | | | | |
| Cameroon | No Report | No Report | No Report | No Report | 2649.008 kg | No Report |
| Congo | 3435.000 kg | No Report | 10.000 kg[(1] | No Report | No Report | No Report |
| Côte d'Ivoire | No Report | 200 u. | No Report | No Report | No Report | No Report |
| Gambia | No Report | No Report | 834.982 kg | No Report | 700.000 kg | No Report |
| Ghana | No Report | No Report | No Report | No Report | No Report | 5000.000 kg |
| Guinea-Bissau | No Report | No Report | No Report | No Report | 8.000 kg | No Report |
| Nigeria | No Report | 1712580.000 [Govt.] kg | No Report | No Report | 270250.000 kg | No Report |
| *Saint Helena* | 18 u. | 17 u. | 17 u. | 6 u. | 5 u. | 1150 u. |
| Togo | No Report | No Report | No Report | 50.000 kg | No Report | 5.500 kg |
| Sub-Total | 3435.000 kg 18 u. | 1712580.000 kg 217 u. | 844.982 kg 17 u. | 50.000 kg 6 u. | 273607.000 kg 5 u. | 5005.500 kg 1150 u. |

Source: Annual Report Questionnaire if not otherwise indicated

## SEIZURES, 1997 - 2002
### Cannabis plant

| Region/country or territory | 1997 | 1998 | 1999 | 2000 | 2001 | 2002 |
|---|---|---|---|---|---|---|
| **AFRICA** | | | | | | |
| Total region | 248123.000 kg 63594690 u. | 2510969.000 kg 35206240 u. | 10304.030 kg 2614520 u. | 925473.700 kg 149964 u. | 1007379.000 kg 812208 u. | 1910614.000 kg 53375 u. |
| **AMERICAS** | | | | | | |
| **Caribbean** | | | | | | |
| Anguilla | 48 u. | 40 u. | No Report | No Report | No Report | No Report |
| Antigua and Barbuda | No Report | No Report | 23384 u. CICAD | 9317 u. CICAD | No Report | No Report |
| Bahamas | No Report | 99 u. | No Report | 1466 u. | 10207 u. | 110 u. |
| Barbados | No Report | 400 u. CICAD | 81 u. HONLC | 1078 u. CICAD | No Report | No Report |
| Bermuda | 871 u. | No Report | 268 u. | 230 u. | No Report | 34 u. |
| British Virgin Islands | No Report | No Report | No Report | No Report | 4556 u. | No Report |
| Dominica | No Report | No Report | 55120 u. CICAD | 123032 u. CICAD | No Report | No Report |
| Dominican Republic | 116 u. | 346 u. | 1991 u. | 1114 u. CICAD | 6578 u. | 4061 u. HONLC |
| Grenada | No Report | 6212.000 kg | 12086 u. CICAD | 2091 u. INCSR | 6611 u. | No Report |
| Haiti | No Report | No Report | No Report | No Report | 1705.000 kg | No Report |
| Jamaica | 6858.300 kg ICPO | No Report | No Report | No Report | 34 u. | No Report |
| Montserrat | No Report | No Report | No Report | 1008 u. | No Report | No Report |
| Saint Kitts and Nevis | 126293 u. CICAD | 36000 u. CICAD | 63911 u. CICAD | 34057 u. INCSR | No Report | No Report |
| Saint Lucia | 26037 u. | 69200 u. | 18047 u. CICAD | 83090 u. | No Report | No Report |
| Saint Vincent and the Grenadines | No Report | 1500 u. CICAD | 4760 u. CICAD | 28375 u. CICAD | No Report | No Report |
| Trinidad Tobago | No Report | 2869850 u. | 4415958 u. CICAD | 7200000 u. INCSR | 3122894 u. | 2671600 u. |
| Sub-Total | 6858.300 kg 153365 u. | 6212.000 kg 2977435 u. | 4595606 u. | 7484858 u. | 1705.000 kg 3150880 u. | 2675805 u. |
| **Central America** | | | | | | |
| Belize | 294712.000 kg CICAD | 202803 u. CICAD | 270136 u. CICAD | 143000 u. CICAD | 70607 u. | No Report |
| Costa Rica | * | 733089 u. | 2153645 u. | 2048421 u. | 1906454 u. | 1235119 u. |
| El Salvador | No Report | No Report | 4688 u. | No Report | 1126 u. | 1158 u. |
| Guatemala | 587096 u. Govt. | 576060 u. | 594378 u. | 293897 u. | 418097 u. | No Report |
| Honduras | 337322 u. | 286414 u. CICAD | 133680 u. CICAD | 83859 u. CICAD | No Report | 41402 u. |
| Nicaragua | 24239.000 kg | 833943 u. | 13569 u. CICAD | 83070 u. CICAD | No Report | 144967 u. |
| Panama | No Report | No Report | 25102 u. | No Report | 36950 u. | No Report |
| Sub-Total | 318951.000 kg 924418 u. | 2632309 u. | 3195198 u. | 2652247 u. | 2433234 u. | 1422646 u. |
| **North America** | | | | | | |
| Canada | 776288 u. | 1025808 u. | 1304477 u. | 1199423 u. | 86456.827 kg 508039 u. | 83444.072 kg 1405304 u. |
| Mexico | No Report | No Report | No Report | No Report | No Report | 355578 u. |
| United States | No Report | No Report | 497.366 kg | 163.344 kg | 4561.900 kg | |

Source: Annual Report Questionnaire if not otherwise indicated

* No reported figures at the time of the preparation of the report for 1997; information recently received from Gov. of Costa Rica shows cannabis plant seizures of 176,117 (units) for 1997; 979,665 (units) for 2003.

## SEIZURES, 1997 - 2002
### Cannabis plant

| Region/country or territory | 1997 | 1998 | 1999 | 2000 | 2001 | 2002 |
|---|---|---|---|---|---|---|
| **AMERICAS** | | | | | | |
| **North America** | | | | | | |
| Sub-Total | 776288 u. | 1025808 u. | 497.366 kg<br>1304477 u. | 163.344 kg<br>1199423 u. | 91018.730 kg<br>508039 u. | 83444.070 kg<br>1760882 u. |
| **South America** | | | | | | |
| Argentina | 458 u. | 1296 u. | 1222 u. | 676 u. | 1687 u. | 939 u. |
| Bolivia | 3450.000 kg | No Report | No Report | No Report | 705.536 kg | No Report |
| Brazil | 2884811 u. | 3371112 u. | 3462158 u. | 3699601 u. | 3823846 u. [Govt] | 2594101 u. [F.O] |
| Chile | 34263 u. | 956.942 kg<br>759 u. | No Report | 63621 u. | 98892 u. | 69891 u. |
| Ecuador | 1 u. | 126 u. | 0.339 kg | No Report | No Report | No Report |
| *Falkland Islands* | No Report | 1 u. | No Report | No Report | No Report | No Report |
| Guyana | 18993.000 kg [ICPO] | No Report | No Report | 31698 u. [CICAD] | No Report | No Report |
| Paraguay | 2009500 u. | 1415875.000 kg | 3769000 u. | 1366500 u. [CICAD] | No Report | 4986000.000 kg |
| Peru | 140700.000 kg | No Report | 5418.300 kg | 29566.400 kg | 38106.465 kg<br><br>2 u. | 103687.000 kg |
| Suriname | 65.838 kg | 500 u. | No Report | No Report | No Report | No Report |
| Uruguay | No Report | No Report | No Report | 5 u. | No Report | 0.410 kg<br>246 u. |
| Venezuela | No Report | No Report | No Report | 26 u. | No Report | No Report |
| Sub-Total | 163208.800 kg<br>4929033 u. | 1416832.000 kg<br>3373794 u. | 5418.639 kg<br>7232380 u. | 29566.400 kg<br>5162127 u. | 38812.000 kg<br>3924427 u. | 5089688.000 kg<br>2665177 u. |
| Total region | 489018.200 kg<br>6783104 u. | 1423044.000 kg<br>10009350 u. | 5916.005 kg<br>16327660 u. | 29729.740 kg<br>16498660 u. | 131535.700 kg<br>10016580 u. | 5173132.000 kg<br>8524510 u. |
| **ASIA** | | | | | | |
| **Central Asia and Transcaucasian countries** | | | | | | |
| Armenia | No Report | 24.218 kg | No Report | No Report | No Report | No Report |
| Azerbaijan | 507380.000 kg [ICPO] | 489000.000 kg | 405669.000 kg | No Report | 317000.000 kg | No Report |
| Kazakhstan | No Report | 200.077 kg | 1869.000 kg | No Report | No Report | No Report |
| Uzbekistan | 18.930 kg | 663.316 kg | 238.772 kg | No Report | No Report | 76.000 kg |
| Sub-Total | 507398.900 kg | 489887.600 kg | 407776.800 kg | | 317000.000 kg | 76.000 kg |
| **East and South-East Asia** | | | | | | |
| Brunei Darussalam | 1 u. | No Report | No Report | 6 u. | No Report | No Report |
| *Hong Kong SAR, China* | No Report | No Report | No Report | No Report | 2103.900 kg | No Report |
| Indonesia | 200000.000 kg<br>132748 u. | 47515 u. | 78072 u. | No Report | 2061 u. | 378982 u. |
| Japan | 36.922 kg<br>2232 u. | 23.954 kg<br>1668 u. | 26.422 kg | 95.617 kg<br>50 u. | 77.020 kg<br>2022 u. | 88.900 kg<br>4917 u. |

Source: Annual Report Questionnaire if not otherwise indicated

## SEIZURES, 1997 - 2002
### Cannabis plant

| Region/country or territory | 1997 | 1998 | 1999 | 2000 | 2001 | 2002 |
|---|---|---|---|---|---|---|
| **ASIA** | | | | | | |
| **East and South-East Asia** | | | | | | |
| Korea (Republic of) | 31501 u. | 3815 u. | 10705 u. | No Report | 4255 u. | No Report |
| Lao People's Dem. Rep. | No Report | No Report | No Report | No Report | No Report | 2500.000 kg |
| Mongolia | No Report | No Report | No Report | No Report | 5 u. | No Report |
| Philippines | No Report | 518939.000 [ICPO] kg | 5005860 u. [(2] | 2599724 u. | 754223.844 kg | 4399980 u. |
| Singapore | No Report | No Report | No Report | No Report | No Report | 2.637 kg |
| Thailand | 19951.301 kg | 13401.892 kg | 42996.497 kg | No Report | No Report | No Report |
| Sub-Total | 219988.200 kg  166482 u. | 532364.900 kg  52998 u. | 43022.920 kg  5094637 u. | 95.617 kg  2599780 u. | 756404.800 kg  8343 u. | 2591.537 kg  4783879 u. |
| **Near and Middle East /South-West Asia** | | | | | | |
| Iraq | 34.812 kg | 55.905 kg | No Report | No Report | No Report | No Report |
| Jordan | No Report | 1.120 kg | 62.525 kg | 18.032 kg | No Report | No Report |
| Lebanon | No Report | No Report | 4445.880 kg | No Report | 80.000 kg | No Report |
| Qatar | No Report | No Report | No Report | No Report | No Report | 0.045 kg |
| United Arab Emirates | No Report | No Report | No Report | No Report | 0.214 kg | No Report |
| Sub-Total | 34.812 kg | 57.025 kg | 4508.405 kg | 18.032 kg | 80.214 kg | 0.045 kg |
| **South Asia** | | | | | | |
| Bangladesh | No Report | No Report | 11826 u. [F.O] | 1840 u. | No Report | 6131 u. |
| India | No Report | No Report | No Report | No Report | 174818.000 kg | No Report |
| Nepal | No Report | No Report | No Report | No Report | No Report | 3320.000 kg |
| Sri Lanka | 49900.000 kg | 21375.000 kg | 372000.000 kg | 32524.344 kg | No Report | 25834.000 kg |
| Sub-Total | 49900.000 kg | 21375.000 kg | 372000.000 kg  11826 u. | 32524.340 kg  1840 u. | 174818.000 kg | 29154.000 kg  6131 u. |
| Total region | 777321.900 kg  166482 u. | 1043685.000 kg  52998 u. | 827308.100 kg  5106463 u. | 32637.990 kg  2601620 u. | 1248303.000 kg  8343 u. | 31821.580 kg  4790010 u. |
| **EUROPE** | | | | | | |
| **Eastern Europe** | | | | | | |
| Albania | No Report | No Report | No Report | No Report | No Report | 115678 u. |
| Belarus | No Report | 117.000 kg | No Report | No Report | No Report | 7406 u. |
| Bosnia Herzegovina | 443 u. [NAPOL] | 1445 u. [NAPOL] | 16222 u. [NAPOL] | 451 u. [NAPOL] | No Report | No Report |
| Bulgaria | 127000.000 kg | 16000.000 kg  10943 u. | 2742 u. | 12713.026 kg  3448 u. | 21390.000 kg | 7457.240 kg |
| Croatia | 31710 u. | 5131 u. | 3050 u. | 1739 u. | 2843 u. | 1828 u. |
| Czech Republic | No Report | No Report | No Report | No Report | 343 u. | 3173 u. |
| Estonia | 72 u. | 23.184 kg  92 u. | 41.973 kg  175 u. | 67.647 kg  585 u. | 192.062 kg | 79.271 kg |

Source: Annual Report Questionnaire if not otherwise indicated

## SEIZURES, 1997 - 2002
### Cannabis plant

| Region/country or territory | 1997 | 1998 | 1999 | 2000 | 2001 | 2002 |
|---|---|---|---|---|---|---|
| **EUROPE** | | | | | | |
| **Eastern Europe** | | | | | | |
| FYR of Macedonia | No Report | 1457 u. | 151262 u. [NAPOL] | No Report | 606 u. [Govt] | 815 u. |
| Hungary | No Report | 1033 u. | 620.000 kg | 2217 u. | No Report | 17.069 kg 2053 u. |
| Lithuania | No Report | No Report | No Report | No Report | No Report | 68.140 kg |
| Poland | 12105.075 kg | 1904.362 kg | 900.000 kg | 1.008 kg | 15.000 kg | 1600.000 kg |
| Romania | No Report | 215.923 kg | No Report | No Report | No Report | 14904.700 kg |
| Serbia and Montenegro | No Report | No Report | No Report | No Report | No Report | 1391.066 kg |
| Slovakia | No Report | 2830.680 kg | 848.797 kg | No Report | 817.226 kg | 573.900 kg |
| Slovenia | 44944 u. | 14453 u. | 8196 u. | 6.011 kg 3354 u. | 1925 u. | 27.750 kg 9425 u. |
| Ukraine | 6091.000 kg | 5103.364 kg | No Report | No Report | No Report | 4.155 kg |
| Sub-Total | 145196.100 kg 77169 u. | 26194.510 kg 34554 u. | 2410.770 kg 181647 u. | 12787.690 kg 11794 u. | 22414.290 kg 5717 u. | 26123.290 kg 140378 u. |
| **Western Europe** | | | | | | |
| Austria | No Report | No Report | No Report | 7991 u. | 35.721 kg | 157.643 kg |
| Belgium | 653.000 kg | 6280.000 kg | 2911.166 kg | | UNODC (3 | 26476 u. |
| Cyprus | 787 u. | 276 u. | 190 u. | 493 u. | 274 u. | 248 u. |
| Denmark | 2692.300 kg | 949.969 kg | 337.290 kg | No Report | No Report | 683.201 kg |
| Finland | 82.519 kg 2328 u. | 2.334 kg 2900 u. | 5.251 kg 2789 u. | 14.041 kg 5325 u. | 16.000 kg 4900 u. | 15.500 kg 6385 u. |
| France | 38115 u. | 34266 u. | 23287 u. | 24295 u. | No Report | 96.671 kg |
| Germany | 5000.000 kg 67065 u. | 81097 u. | 168833 u. | 25277 u. | 68696 u. | 29352 u. |
| Greece | 11010 u. | 9967 u. | 46198 u. | 49985 u. | 18821 u. | 16232 u. |
| Iceland | No Report | No Report | No Report | No Report | No Report | 3.692 kg 1207 u. |
| Ireland | 753 u. | 400 u. | No Report | 98 u. | 365 u. | 467 u. |
| Italy | 379851 u. | 190240 u. | [ICPO] | 1306469 u. | 3219414 u. | 297627 u. |
| Liechtenstein | No Report | 1300.000 kg | 3.686 kg | 42.600 kg | No Report | No Report |
| Luxembourg | No Report | 222 u. | No Report | No Report | No Report | No Report |
| Malta | 153 u. | 5 u. | 35 u. | 22 u. | 11 u. | No Report |
| Netherlands | 553135 u. [Govt] | 353178 u. [Govt] | 582588 u. [Govt] | 661851 u. [Govt] | 844.000 kg 884609 u. | 900381 u. |
| Norway | 23.329 kg | 23.041 kg | 28.546 kg | 18.854 kg | 17.628 kg 123 u. | 15.922 kg |
| Portugal | 7982 u. | 17316 u. | 1184 u. | 1.936 kg 2279 u. | 3807 u. | 1.751 kg 3135 u. |
| Spain | 1734.002 kg | 3072.938 kg | 2319.031 kg | 18156.043 kg | 3907.120 kg | 5882.218 kg |
| Sweden | 2.426 kg 269 u. | 6.890 kg | 39.820 kg 249 u. | 3.213 kg 251 u. | 2.789 kg | |

Source: Annual Report Questionnaire if not otherwise indicated

## SEIZURES, 1997 - 2002
### Cannabis plant

| Region/country or territory | 1997 | 1998 | 1999 | 2000 | 2001 | 2002 |
|---|---|---|---|---|---|---|
| **EUROPE** | | | | | | |
| **Western Europe** | | | | | | |
| Switzerland | 313258 u. | 26813 u. | 79746 u. | 227476 u. | 189008 u. | 557262 u. |
| Turkey | 52100620 u. | 55655864 u. | 19736000 u. | 327.750 kg 29168530 u. | 20243988 u. | 25789062 u. |
| United Kingdom | 114988 u. | 72040 u. | 382 u.[ICPO] | 47816 u. | 71507 u. | 71507 u.[4] |
| Sub-Total | 10187.580 kg 53590320 u. | 11635.170 kg 56444580 u. | 5644.790 kg 20641480 u. | 18564.440 kg 31528160 u. | 4823.258 kg 24705520 u. | 6856.598 kg 27699340 u. |
| Total region | 155383.700 kg 53667480 u. | 37829.680 kg 56479140 u. | 8055.560 kg 20823130 u. | 31352.130 kg 31539950 u. | 27237.550 kg 24711240 u. | 32979.890 kg 27839720 u. |
| **OCEANIA** | | | | | | |
| **Oceania** | | | | | | |
| Australia | 4445.335 kg | No Report | 176.150 kg | 90060 u. | 22973 u. | 449.703 kg 295781 u. |
| New Zealand | 266867 u. | 164531 u. | 173277 u. | 10157 u. | 90857 u. | 74324 u. |
| Sub-Total | 4445.335 kg 266867 u. | 164531 u. | 176.150 kg 173277 u. | 100217 u. | 113830 u. | 449.703 kg 370105 u. |
| Total region | 4445.335 kg 266867 u. | 164531 u. | 176.150 kg 173277 u. | 100217 u. | 113830 u. | 449.703 kg 370105 u. |
| TOTAL | 1674292.000 kg 124478600 u. | 5015527.000 kg 101912200 u. | 851759.900 kg 45045050 u. | 1019194.000 kg 50890410 u. | 2414455.000 kg 35662200 u. | 7148997.000 kg 41577720 u. |

1) Including cannabis seeds. 2) Includes seedlings 3) Due to unavailability of 2001 data, year 2000 data were used for analysis purposes. 4) Due to unavailability of 2002 data, year 2001 data were used for analysis purposes.

Source: Annual Report Questionnaire if not otherwise indicated

## SEIZURES, 1997 - 2002
### Cannabis seed

| Region/country or territory | 1997 | 1998 | 1999 | 2000 | 2001 | 2002 |
|---|---|---|---|---|---|---|
| **AFRICA** | | | | | | |
| **East Africa** | | | | | | |
| Mauritius | No Report | No Report | No Report | 0.076 kg | No Report | No Report |
| Somalia | No Report | No Report | No Report | No Report | No Report | 15.000 kg |
| Uganda | No Report | 5.000 kg | No Report | 102.800 kg | No Report | No Report |
| Sub-Total | | 5.000 kg | | 102.876 kg | | 15.000 kg |
| **North Africa** | | | | | | |
| Algeria | No Report | 0.930 kg [ICPO] | No Report | No Report | No Report | No Report |
| Egypt | 33.421 kg | 11.504 kg | 115.819 kg | 24.323 kg | No Report | No Report |
| Sub-Total | 33.421 kg | 12.434 kg | 115.819 kg | 24.323 kg | | |
| **Southern Africa** | | | | | | |
| Lesotho | No Report | No Report | 35.280 kg [ICPO] | No Report | No Report | No Report |
| Swaziland | No Report | 8.096 kg | No Report | 263.840 kg | No Report | No Report |
| Zambia | 7.130 kg [Govt] | 38.597 kg [Govt] | 126.280 kg | 52.261 kg | 13.500 kg [Govt] | No Report |
| Zimbabwe | No Report | 0.200 kg | No Report | No Report | No Report | No Report |
| Sub-Total | 7.130 kg | 46.893 kg | 161.560 kg | 316.101 kg | 13.500 kg | |
| **West and Central Africa** | | | | | | |
| *Saint Helena* | No Report | 100  u. | 80  u. | No Report | No Report | No Report |
| Sub-Total | | 100  u. | 80  u. | | | |
| Total region | 40.551 kg | 64.327 kg | 277.379 kg | 443.300 kg | 13.500 kg | 15.000 kg |
| | | 100  u. | 80  u. | | | |
| **AMERICAS** | | | | | | |
| **Caribbean** | | | | | | |
| *Anguilla* | No Report | 8  u. | No Report | No Report | No Report | No Report |
| Dominican Republic | 72  u. | 1327  u. | 3642  u. | 679.000 kg [CICAD] | No Report | No Report |
| Grenada | No Report | 0.004 kg | No Report | No Report | No Report | No Report |
| Jamaica | No Report | No Report | 452.630 kg [ICPO] | No Report | No Report | No Report |
| *Montserrat* | No Report | No Report | No Report | 2500  u. | No Report | No Report |
| Saint Lucia | No Report | No Report | No Report | 0.311 kg | No Report | No Report |
| Sub-Total | 72  u. | 0.004 kg | 452.630 kg | 679.311 kg | | |
| | | 1335  u. | 3642  u. | 2500  u. | | |
| **Central America** | | | | | | |
| Guatemala | 1.840 kg [Govt.] | 5.100 kg | 78.473 kg | 24.200 kg | No Report | No Report |
| Honduras | 3.400 kg | No Report | No Report | 2.000 kg [CICAD] | No Report | No Report |
| Nicaragua | 2.063 kg | No Report | No Report | 1.000 kg [CICAD] | No Report | No Report |
| Sub-Total | 7.303 kg | 5.100 kg | 78.473 kg | 27.200 kg | | |
| **North America** | | | | | | |
| Mexico | 3968.381 kg | 4948.744 kg | 5847.545 kg | 10353.807 kg | * | * |
| United States | No Report | No Report | 412271.587 kg | 417120.258 kg | No Report | No Report |
| | | | 451  u. | 102  u. | | |

Source: Annual Report Questionnaire if not otherwise indicated

* No data had been reported at the time of the preparation of the Report; data submitted subsequently showed seizures of cannabis seed of 7660.910 Kg in 2001, and 10 214.446 Kg in 2002.

## SEIZURES, 1997 - 2002
### Cannabis seed

| Region/country or territory | 1997 | 1998 | 1999 | 2000 | 2001 | 2002 |
|---|---|---|---|---|---|---|
| **AMERICAS** | | | | | | |
| **North America** | | | | | | |
| Sub-Total | 3968.381 kg | 4948.744 kg | 418119.100 kg 451 u. | 427474.100 kg 102 u. | | |
| **South America** | | | | | | |
| Argentina | 39.440 kg | 42.790 kg 1950 u. | 0.091 kg | 0.276 kg | 1.255 kg | No Report |
| Brazil | 68.314 kg | 5.179 kg | 55.804 kg | 99.047 kg | No Report | 23.000 kg [F.O] |
| Chile | No Report | 0.377 kg | No Report | No Report | No Report | No Report |
| Colombia | 120.000 kg [Govt.] | 127.789 kg | 25.214 kg | 121.000 kg | No Report | No Report |
| Paraguay | 167.550 kg | 503.110 kg | 2130.025 kg | 668.000 kg [CICAD] | No Report | No Report |
| Peru | 9.377 kg | 0.241 kg | 19.041 kg | 2.841 kg | No Report | No Report |
| Sub-Total | 404.681 kg | 679.486 kg 1950 u. | 2230.175 kg | 891.164 kg | 1.255 kg | 23.000 kg |
| Total region | 4380.365 kg 72 u. | 5633.333 kg 3285 u. | 420880.400 kg 4093 u. | 429071.700 kg 2602 u. | 1.255 kg | 23.000 kg |
| **ASIA** | | | | | | |
| **Central Asia and Transcaucasian countries** | | | | | | |
| Uzbekistan | No Report | No Report | No Report | 222.900 kg | No Report | No Report |
| Sub-Total | | | | 222.900 kg | | |
| **East and South-East Asia** | | | | | | |
| Hong Kong SAR, China | 8.200 kg | No Report | No Report | No Report | No Report | No Report |
| Indonesia | 1.218 kg | 0.329 kg | 1.875 kg | No Report | No Report | No Report |
| Korea (Republic of) | 58.789 kg | No Report | 46.067 kg | No Report | No Report | No Report |
| Philippines | No Report | 85007.000 kg [ICPO] 223459 u. | 163.000 kg | 28.550 kg | No Report | No Report |
| Thailand | 12.127 kg | 1.225 kg | No Report | No Report | No Report | No Report |
| Sub-Total | 80.334 kg | 85008.560 kg 223459 u. | 210.942 kg | 28.550 kg | | |
| **Near and Middle East /South-West Asia** | | | | | | |
| Bahrain | No Report | No Report | 0.361 kg [ICPO] | No Report | No Report | No Report |
| Jordan | 0.770 kg | 1.412 kg | 61.461 kg | 3.589 kg | No Report | No Report |
| Lebanon | 20.000 kg | No Report | 270.000 kg | 424.000 kg | No Report | No Report |
| United Arab Emirates | No Report | No Report | No Report | 0.135 kg | No Report | No Report |
| Sub-Total | 20.770 kg | 1.412 kg | 331.822 kg | 427.724 kg | | |
| **South Asia** | | | | | | |
| Maldives | No Report | (1 | No Report | No Report | No Report | No Report |
| Sub-Total | | | | | | |

Source: Annual Report Questionnaire if not otherwise indicated

## SEIZURES, 1997 - 2002
### Cannabis seed

| Region/country or territory | 1997 | 1998 | 1999 | 2000 | 2001 | 2002 |
|---|---|---|---|---|---|---|
| **ASIA** | | | | | | |
| Total region | 101.104 kg | 85009.970 kg<br>223459 u. | 542.764 kg | 679.174 kg | | |
| **EUROPE** | | | | | | |
| **Eastern Europe** | | | | | | |
| Bulgaria | 1.250 kg | 6.556 kg | 6.768 kg [ICPO] | 1.872 kg | No Report | No Report |
| Croatia | 38037 u. | 0.053 kg<br>24133 u. | 0.868 kg<br>17054 u. | 10437 u. | No Report | No Report |
| FYR of Macedonia | No Report | 0.135 kg<br>508 u. | 0.103 kg [NAPOL]<br>696 u. | No Report | 0.120 kg [Govt]<br>186 u. | 298 u. |
| Hungary | No Report | No Report | No Report | 10.000 kg | No Report | No Report |
| Poland | 300.000 kg | No Report | 4.016 kg | 1200 u. | No Report | No Report |
| Russian Federation | 0.021 kg | No Report | No Report | No Report | No Report | No Report |
| Slovakia | No Report | No Report | No Report | No Report | No Report | 1.810 kg |
| Sub-Total | 301.271 kg<br>38037 u. | 6.744 kg<br>24641 u. | 11.755 kg<br>17750 u. | 11.872 kg<br>11637 u. | 0.120 kg<br>186 u. | 1.810 kg<br>298 u. |
| **Western Europe** | | | | | | |
| Andorra | No Report | 0.576 kg [ICPO] | 4.900 kg | No Report | No Report | No Report |
| Belgium | 75 u. | 48.190 kg | 16.250 kg | No Report | No Report | No Report |
| Finland | 0.364 kg<br>369 u. | 0.345 kg<br>1304 u. | 0.100 kg<br>1150 u. | 0.054 kg<br>1242 u. | No Report | No Report |
| Italy | 220.116 kg<br>47646 u. | No Report | No Report | No Report | No Report | No Report |
| Malta | 0.049 kg | 72 u. | 5 u. | 4 u. | No Report | No Report |
| Portugal | 53 u. | 1.563 kg | 38.377 kg<br>45 u. | 1.739 kg<br>201 u. | No Report | 4036 u. |
| Spain | 1.376 kg | No Report | No Report | No Report | No Report | No Report |
| Sub-Total | 221.905 kg<br>48143 u. | 50.674 kg<br>1376 u. | 59.627 kg<br>1200 u. | 1.793 kg<br>1447 u. | | 4036 u. |
| Total region | 523.176 kg<br>86180 u. | 57.418 kg<br>26017 u. | 71.382 kg<br>18950 u. | 13.665 kg<br>13084 u. | 0.120 kg<br>186 u. | 1.810 kg<br>4334 u. |
| **OCEANIA** | | | | | | |
| **Oceania** | | | | | | |
| Australia | No Report | No Report | 4.129 kg | 5.559 kg | No Report | No Report |
| New Zealand | No Report | 244031 u. | 253609 u. | No Report | No Report | No Report |
| Sub-Total | | 244031 u. | 4.129 kg<br>253609 u. | 5.559 kg | | |
| Total region | | 244031 u. | 4.129 kg<br>253609 u. | 5.559 kg | | |

Source: Annual Report Questionnaire if not otherwise indicated

## SEIZURES, 1997 - 2002

### Cannabis seed

| Region/country or territory | 1997 | 1998 | 1999 | 2000 | 2001 | 2002 |
|---|---|---|---|---|---|---|
| TOTAL | 5045.195 kg | 90765.060 kg | 421776.000 kg | 430213.400 kg | 14.875 kg | 39.810 kg |
| | 86252 u. | 496892 u. | 276732 u. | 15686 u. | 186 u. | 4334 u. |

1) Small quantity.

Source: Annual Report Questionnaire if not otherwise indicated

## 4.4. Amphetamine-type Stimulants: Seizures 1997-2002

| SEIZURES, 1997 - 2002 | | | | | |
|---|---|---|---|---|---|
| **Amphetamine-type Stimulants (excluding 'Ecstasy')** | | | | | |
| **Region/country or territory** | **1997** | **1998** | **1999** | **2000** | **2001** | **2002** |
|---|---|---|---|---|---|---|
| **AFRICA** | | | | | | |
| **East Africa** | | | | | | |
| Eritrea | No Report | No Report | No Report | 6.000 kg [ICPO] | No Report | No Report |
| Sub-Total | | | | 6.000 kg | | |
| **North Africa** | | | | | | |
| Egypt | 46.565 lt. 94881 u. | 15.348 lt. | 5.222 kg 19.023 lt. | 11.650 lt. 57076 u. | No Report | 10.925 lt. |
| Morocco | No Report | 49561 u. | 73917 u. | No Report | No Report | No Report |
| Sudan | No Report | No Report | No Report | 0.250 kg 38 u. | No Report | No Report |
| Tunisia | No Report | No Report | No Report | No Report | No Report | 28038 u. |
| Sub-Total | 46.565 lt. 94881 u. | 15.348 lt. 49561 u. | 5.222 kg 19.023 lt. 73917 u. | 0.250 kg 11.650 lt. 57114 u. | | 10.925 lt. 28038 u. |
| **Southern Africa** | | | | | | |
| South Africa | 0.280 kg | 527 u. | 369 u. [ICPO] | 0.013 kg [ICPO] 924 u. | 59078 u. | 1.259 kg 2294 u. |
| Zambia | 0.050 kg [Govt] | 0.000 kg [Govt] | 0.018 kg | 0.000 kg [Govt] | 270 u. [Govt] | No Report |
| Zimbabwe | No Report | 15.729 kg | No Report | No Report | No Report | No Report |
| Sub-Total | 0.330 kg | 15.729 kg 527 u. | 0.018 kg 369 u. | 0.013 kg 924 u. | 59348 u. | 1.259 kg 2294 u. |
| **West and Central Africa** | | | | | | |
| Burkina Faso | 40750 u. [ICPO] | No Report | No Report | No Report | 2.851 kg | No Report |
| Cameroon | No Report | No Report | No Report | No Report | 1000 u. | 23 u. |
| Chad | No Report | No Report | 1620 u. [ICPO] | 180000 u. | No Report | No Report |
| Côte d'Ivoire | No Report | 6385 u. | 56.131 kg | 0.200 kg [ICPO] | 0.124 kg | 66373 u. |
| Gambia | No Report | No Report | 328 u. | No Report | 3.000 kg | No Report |
| Niger | 186574 u. [ICPO] | No Report | 556537 u. [ICPO] | No Report | No Report | No Report |
| Nigeria | 309.525 kg | No Report | 322.071 kg | 0.580 kg | No Report | No Report |
| Togo | No Report | No Report | No Report | No Report | No Report | 1.160 kg |
| Sub-Total | 309.525 kg 227324 u. | 6385 u. | 378.202 kg 558485 u. | 0.780 kg 180000 u. | 5.975 kg 1000 u. | 1.160 kg 66396 u. |
| Total region | 309.855 kg 46.565 lt. 322205 u. | 15.729 kg 15.348 lt. 56473 u. | 383.442 kg 19.023 lt. 632771 u. | 7.043 kg 11.650 lt. 238038 u. | 5.975 kg 60348 u. | 2.419 kg 10.925 lt. 96728 u. |
| **AMERICAS** | | | | | | |
| **Caribbean** | | | | | | |
| Bahamas | 0.200 kg [ICPO] | No Report | No Report | 60.000 kg [CICAD] | No Report | No Report |
| *Bermuda* | No Report | No Report | No Report | No Report | No Report | 65 u. [ICPO] |
| *Cayman Islands* | No Report | 0.040 kg 120 u. | 0.001 kg [ICPO] | No Report | No Report | No Report |
| *Netherlands Antilles* | No Report | 541.000 kg [F.O] | No Report | No Report | No Report | No Report |

Source: Annual Report Questionnaire if not otherwise indicated

## SEIZURES, 1997 - 2002
### Amphetamine-type Stimulants (excluding 'Ecstasy')

| Region/country or territory | 1997 | 1998 | 1999 | 2000 | 2001 | 2002 |
|---|---|---|---|---|---|---|
| **AMERICAS** | | | | | | |
| **Caribbean** | | | | | | |
| Sub-Total | 0.200 kg | 541.040 kg<br>120 u. | 0.001 kg | 60.000 kg | | 65 u. |
| **Central America** | | | | | | |
| Costa Rica | No Report | No Report | No Report | 195 u. | 468 u. | 0.005 kg[1] |
| Sub-Total | | | | 195 u. | 468 u. | 0.005 kg |
| **North America** | | | | | | |
| Canada | 2.260 kg<br>0.225 lt. | 0.590 kg<br>54.500 lt.<br>11207 u. | 20.218 kg<br>2.306 lt.<br>4970 u. | 29.482 kg<br>2.798 lt.<br>8815 u. | 53.231 kg<br>57798 u. | 31.603 kg<br>4673 u. |
| Mexico | 38.891 kg | 98.391 kg | 926.011 kg<br>880 u. | 714.920 kg | 417.944 kg | 459.056 kg |
| United States | 1428.798 kg<br>84.942 lt.<br>3747486 u. | 1824.363 kg<br>215.776 lt.<br>411768 u. | 2641.000 kg<br>20217 u. | 2451.383 kg<br>226.682 lt.<br>43096 u. | 2857.600 kg<br>5494617 u. | 1107.205 kg<br>217437 u. |
| Sub-Total | 1469.949 kg<br>85.167 lt.<br>3747486 u. | 1923.344 kg<br>270.276 lt.<br>422975 u. | 3587.229 kg<br>2.306 lt.<br>26067 u. | 3195.785 kg<br>229.480 lt.<br>51911 u. | 3328.775 kg<br>5552415 u. | 1597.864 kg<br>222110 u. |
| **South America** | | | | | | |
| Argentina | 504 u. | 600 u. | 4103 u. | 10134 u. | 3991 u. | 430 u. |
| Brazil | No Report | No Report | No Report | No Report | No Report | 201 u.[ICPO] |
| Chile | 55686 u. | 0.011 kg<br>6973 u. | 104523 u.[CICAD] | 11287 u. | 22225 u. | 2861 u. |
| Peru | No Report | No Report | No Report | No Report | 0.063 kg<br>709 u. | No Report |
| Sub-Total | 56190 u. | 0.011 kg<br>7573 u. | 108626 u. | 21421 u. | 0.063 kg<br>26925 u. | 3492 u. |
| Total region | 1470.149 kg<br>85.167 lt.<br>3803676 u. | 2464.395 kg<br>270.276 lt.<br>430668 u. | 3587.230 kg<br>2.306 lt.<br>134693 u. | 3255.785 kg<br>229.480 lt.<br>73527 u. | 3328.838 kg<br>5579808 u. | 1597.869 kg<br>225667 u. |
| **ASIA** | | | | | | |
| **Central Asia and Transcaucasian countries** | | | | | | |
| Armenia | 0.040 lt.[ICPO] | No Report | No Report | No Report | No Report | No Report |
| Georgia | No Report | No Report | No Report | 0.013 kg[ICPO] | No Report | No Report |
| Kyrgyzstan | 0.020 kg | No Report | No Report | No Report | No Report | No Report |
| Uzbekistan | 0.430 kg[ICPO] | No Report | 0.031 kg | No Report | No Report | No Report |
| Sub-Total | 0.450 kg<br>0.040 lt. | | 0.031 kg | 0.013 kg | | |
| **East and South-East Asia** | | | | | | |
| Brunei Darussalam | 0.123 kg | 0.237 kg | 1.197 kg | 1.648 kg | 0.661 kg<br>375 u. | 0.248 kg |
| Cambodia | 13928 u.[ICPO] | No Report | No Report | No Report | No Report | No Report |

Source: Annual Report Questionnaire if not otherwise indicated

## SEIZURES, 1997 - 2002
### Amphetamine-type Stimulants (excluding 'Ecstasy')

| Region/country or territory | 1997 | 1998 | 1999 | 2000 | 2001 | 2002 |
|---|---|---|---|---|---|---|
| **ASIA** | | | | | | |
| **East and South-East Asia** | | | | | | |
| China | 1334.000 kg | 1608.000 kg | 16059.000 kg [ICPO] | 20900.000 kg [ICPO] | 4800.000 kg | 3190.000 kg |
| *Hong Kong SAR, China* | 73.600 kg | 232.700 kg [Govt.] | No Report | 87.600 kg | 63.100 kg | 71.565 kg |
| | 3461 u. | | | 7879 u. | 214776 u. | 84203 u. |
| Indonesia | 5.621 kg | 7.761 kg [HNLP] | 218.625 kg | 88.163 kg | 48.793 kg | 46.580 kg |
| | | | 29511 u. | | 5355 u. | 421246 u. |
| Japan | 173.526 kg | 549.702 kg | 1994.459 kg | 1030.580 kg [ICPO] | 419.175 kg | 446.000 kg |
| | 2.203 lt. | 0.788 lt. | 0.589 lt. | 0.471 lt. | 142 u. | 0.195 lt. |
| | 1415 u. | 1 u. | 4589 u. | 954 u. | | 51830 u. |
| Korea (Republic of) | 24.872 kg | 28.311 kg | 29.233 kg | 4.500 kg [ICPO] | 169.562 kg | 36.817 kg [ICPO] |
| | | | | 9240 u. | 2095 u. | |
| Lao People's Dem. Rep. | 774714 u. [Govt.] | No Report | 1793202 u. [HNLP] | 1957929 u. [Govt] | 851619 u. [Govt] | 151750 u. |
| *Macau SAR, China* | No Report | 0.073 kg [ICPO] | No Report | 0.272 kg [ICPO] | 0.035 kg | 1.108 kg |
| | | 187 u. | | 785 u. | 1732 u. | 3867 u. |
| Malaysia | 2.000 kg | No Report | 5.411 kg | 208.100 kg | No Report | 6.046 kg [ICPO] |
| | | | 329265 u. | 195387 u. | | 419216 u. |
| Mongolia | No Report | No Report | 0.100 kg [ICPO] | No Report | 4 u. | No Report |
| Myanmar | 5028600 u. | 16026688 u. | 22.058 kg | 6.398 kg | 33103548 u. | 431.200 kg |
| | | | 28887514 u. | 26759772 u. | | 9399794 u. |
| Philippines | 694.480 kg [ICPO] | 312.929 kg [Govt] | 943.700 kg | 989.760 kg | 1777.642 kg | 914.335 kg |
| | 2.000 lt. | 85.730 lt. | | 30.000 lt. | | |
| Singapore | 0.090 kg | 1.711 kg | 1.300 kg | 0.759 kg | 2.175 kg | 52243 u. |
| | 8141 u. | 4470 u. | 1380 u. | 24723 u. | 19935 u. | |
| *Taiwan province, China* | 2256.000 kg [PRESS] | No Report | No Report | 836.000 kg [PRESS] | 1156.000 kg [PRESS] | No Report |
| Thailand | 2183.000 kg [F.O] | 3013.000 kg [F.O] | 4517.000 kg [F.O] | 7557.000 kg [HNLP] | 8338.000 kg [F.O] | 8662.223 kg [ICPO] |
| | | | | 84000000 u. | | |
| Viet Nam | No Report | No Report | 6025 u. [ICPO] | 13876 u. [ICPO] | 72391 u. | No Report |
| Sub-Total | 6747.312 kg | 5754.424 kg | 23792.080 kg | 31710.780 kg | 16775.140 kg | 13806.120 kg |
| | 4.203 lt. | 86.518 lt. | 0.589 lt. | 30.471 lt. | 34271980 u. | 0.195 lt. |
| | 5830259 u. | 16031350 u. | 31051480 u. | 112970500 u. | | 10584150 u. |
| **Near and Middle East /South-West Asia** | | | | | | |
| Bahrain | No Report | 28 u. [ICPO] | No Report | 0.005 kg [ICPO] | No Report | 0.001 kg |
| | | | | | | 645233 u. |
| Israel | 30807 u. | No Report | 190 u. [ICPO] | 131 u. [ICPO] | 0.014 kg | 0.001 kg |
| | | | | | | 424 u. |
| Jordan | 0.290 kg [ICPO] | 262071 u. | 518813 u. | 5817798 u. | 1405872 u. | 1512750 u. |
| | 2794059 u. | | | | | |
| Kuwait | No Report | No Report | No Report | 110000 u. [ICPO] | No Report | No Report |
| Lebanon | No Report | No Report | 359 u. [ICPO] | 41616 u. [ICPO] | No Report | 989 u. [ICPO] |
| Pakistan | No Report | No Report | No Report | 20.000 kg | No Report | No Report |
| Qatar | 1026 u. [ICPO] | 220 u. [ICPO] | 14 u. [ICPO] | 448 u. [ICPO] | No Report | 6081 u. |

Source: Annual Report Questionnaire if not otherwise indicated

## SEIZURES, 1997 - 2002

### Amphetamine-type Stimulants (excluding 'Ecstasy')

| Region/country or territory | 1997 | 1998 | 1999 | 2000 | 2001 | 2002 |
|---|---|---|---|---|---|---|
| **ASIA** | | | | | | |
| **Near and Middle East /South-West Asia** | | | | | | |
| Saudi Arabia | 10852279 u. [ICPO] | 3553231 u. | 7549665 u. [ICPO] | 9698370 u. [(2] | 1.000 kg 6715652 u. | 10409161 u. [ICPO] |
| Syrian Arab Republic | 2463977 u. | No Report | 1470831 u. | 1159065 u. [(2] | 1911796 u. [Govt (2] | 3062393 u. |
| United Arab Emirates | No Report | No Report | No Report | 0.107 kg [ICPO] | 0.176 kg | 0.037 kg 2 u. |
| Yemen | 3704 u. [ICPO] | 972 u. [ICPO] | 3020 u. [ICPO] | 0.005 kg [ICPO] 3754 u. | No Report | No Report |
| Sub-Total | 0.290 kg 16145850 u. | 3816522 u. | 9542892 u. | 20.117 kg 16831180 u. | 1.190 kg 10033320 u. | 0.040 kg 15637030 u. |
| **South Asia** | | | | | | |
| India | No Report | No Report | No Report | 3.000 kg [ICPO] | 0.965 kg | No Report |
| Maldives | No Report | No Report | 0.001 kg | No Report | 6 u. | No Report |
| Nepal | No Report | No Report | No Report | No Report | No Report | 0.023 kg |
| Sub-Total | | | 0.001 kg | 3.000 kg | 0.965 kg 6 u. | 0.023 kg |
| Total region | 6748.052 kg 4.243 lt. 21976110 u. | 5754.424 kg 86.518 lt. 19847870 u. | 23792.120 kg 0.589 lt. 40594380 u. | 31733.910 kg 30.471 lt. 129801700 u. | 16777.300 kg 44305300 u. | 13806.190 kg 0.195 lt. 26221180 u. |
| **EUROPE** | | | | | | |
| **Eastern Europe** | | | | | | |
| Albania | No Report | No Report | 0.009 kg [ICPO] | No Report | No Report | 10 u. |
| Belarus | No Report | 0.282 kg | 1.644 kg | 1.267 kg [ICPO] | No Report | 18.546 kg |
| Bosnia Herzegovina | No Report | No Report | No Report | No Report | No Report | 117.000 kg [ICPO] |
| Bulgaria | 134.293 kg | 150 u. | 87.192 kg 22928 u. | 209.930 kg 18491 u. | 64.676 kg [(2] 760 u. | 173.950 kg 135347 u. |
| Croatia | 1.255 kg 1596 u. | 0.765 kg 9106 u. | 1.110 kg 15429 u. | 2.124 kg | 0.931 kg | 28.026 kg |
| Czech Republic | 0.617 kg 56 u. | 76.500 kg [ICPO.] | 21.400 kg 673 u. | 13.234 kg [ICPO] | 23.130 kg | 4.715 kg 132 u. |
| Estonia | 0.725 kg 0.078 lt. | 1.955 kg 971 u. | 11.507 kg 2707 u. | 26.692 kg 955 u. | 25.300 kg | 35.119 kg 1023 u. |
| FYR of Macedonia | No Report | No Report | No Report | No Report | No Report | 7.015 kg |
| Hungary | 12.326 kg [Govt.] | 7.605 kg | 9.257 kg | 10.000 kg | 1.740 kg 19 u. | 3.731 kg 232 u. |
| Latvia | 0.370 kg | 1.395 kg 1.700 lt. 2671 u. | 0.493 kg [ICPO] | 0.853 kg 1114 u. | 3.551 kg | No Report |
| Lithuania | 0.205 kg 1.348 lt. 5641 u. | 0.013 kg 0.994 lt. 142 u. | 0.077 kg 0.486 lt. 2297 u. | 19.492 kg 0.482 lt. 42 u. | 6.886 kg | 4.542 kg 229 u. |

Source: Annual Report Questionnaire if not otherwise indicated

## SEIZURES, 1997 - 2002

### Amphetamine-type Stimulants (excluding 'Ecstasy')

| Region/country or territory | 1997 | 1998 | 1999 | 2000 | 2001 | 2002 |
|---|---|---|---|---|---|---|
| **EUROPE** | | | | | | |
| **Eastern Europe** | | | | | | |
| Poland | 27.150 kg | 51.503 kg | 51.453 kg | 141.600 kg | 194.960 kg | 161.516 kg |
| Republic of Moldova | 20.607 kg 1034 u. | No Report | 0.105 lt. [ICPO] | No Report | No Report | No Report |
| Romania | 3289 u. [ICPO] | No Report | 10546 u. | 15874 u. | 11663 u. | 0.999 kg |
| Russian Federation | No Report | 34.000 kg [F.O] | 40.500 kg [F.O] | 9.000 kg [F.O (3] | 13.513 kg | 37.640 kg [ICPO] |
| Serbia and Montenegro | No Report | No Report | No Report | No Report | 0.087 kg | No Report |
| Slovakia | 0.094 kg | 9.717 kg 35 u. | 0.131 kg 22 u. | 0.281 kg | 0.571 kg | 0.331 kg |
| Slovenia | 1.410 kg | 0.339 kg 267 u. | 0.625 kg [ICPO] 818 u. | 0.218 kg 28546 u. | 0.064 kg 98 u. | 0.030 kg 390 u. |
| Ukraine | 39.500 kg | 2.482 kg | No Report | No Report | 0.716 kg | No Report |
| Sub-Total | 238.552 kg 1.426 lt. 11616 u. | 186.556 kg 2.694 lt. 13342 u. | 225.398 kg 0.591 lt. 55420 u. | 434.691 kg 0.482 lt. 65022 u. | 336.125 kg 12540 u. | 593.159 kg 137363 u. |
| **Western Europe** | | | | | | |
| Andorra | No Report | 143 u. [ICPO] | 43 u. | 0.004 kg [ICPO] | No Report | 0.004 kg 42 u. |
| Austria | 7895 u. | 9763 u. | 5165 u. | 0.450 kg 1452 u. | 2.918 kg | 9.491 kg |
| Belgium | 77.000 kg 511 u. | 445.000 kg 271080 u. | 325.070 kg 489566 u. | 75.140 kg [ICPO] 18397 u. | 75.140 kg [UNODC (4] 18397 u. | 500.000 kg |
| Cyprus | 0.050 kg [ICPO] | No Report | 0.012 kg | 0.005 kg [ICPO] | 0.004 kg | 0.123 kg 1 u. |
| Denmark | 119.400 kg | 25.236 kg | 31.600 kg | 57.136 kg | 160.640 kg | 35.256 kg |
| Finland | 22.189 kg 1101 u. | 24.784 kg 1003 u. | 140.464 kg 17665 u. | 79.565 kg | 137.730 kg 14967 u. | 129.200 kg |
| France | 194.047 kg 198941 u. | 165.122 kg 1142226 u. | 232.941 kg | 676.834 kg 2283620 u. | 57.420 kg | 168.050 kg |
| Germany | 233.633 kg | 309.602 kg | 360.000 kg | 271.200 kg [ICPO] | 262.539 kg | 361.720 kg |
| Greece | 0.034 kg 958 u. | 0.003 kg 5 u. | 1.380 kg 257 u. | 2.008 kg 30109 u. | 0.078 kg 8 u. | 0.500 kg 1789 u. |
| Iceland | No Report | No Report | 5.078 kg | 10.267 kg | 0.132 kg | 7.161 kg |
| Ireland | 102.585 kg 22191 u. | 43.162 kg 46538 u. | 13.300 kg [ICPO] 12015 u. | 5.040 kg 568952 u. | 17.955 kg | 16.473 kg 12728 u. |
| Italy | 0.384 kg 10950 u. | 2.454 kg 2309 u. | 5.131 kg [ICPO] 16115 u. | 0.197 kg 77299 u. | 0.924 kg 327 u. | 2.099 kg 341 u. |
| Liechtenstein | No Report | No Report | No Report | No Report | 12 u. | 0.003 kg |
| Luxembourg | 0.010 kg [ICPO] | No Report | 0.016 kg [ICPO] | 0.157 kg [ICPO] | No Report | 0.006 kg [ICPO] |
| Malta | 0.060 kg 100 u. | No Report | No Report | 45 u. [(5] | No Report | No Report |
| Netherlands | 815.000 kg [Govt] 102240 u. | 1450.000 kg [Govt] 242409 u. | 853.000 kg [Govt] 45847 u. | 293.000 kg [Govt] | 579.000 kg | 481.000 kg 1028 u. |

Source: Annual Report Questionnaire if not otherwise indicated

## SEIZURES, 1997 - 2002

### Amphetamine-type Stimulants (excluding 'Ecstasy')

| Region/country or territory | 1997 | 1998 | 1999 | 2000 | 2001 | 2002 |
|---|---|---|---|---|---|---|
| **EUROPE** | | | | | | |
| **Western Europe** | | | | | | |
| Norway | 93.241 kg | 207.999 kg | 52.110 kg | 95.506 kg | 106.936 kg | 232.566 kg |
| | | | 6056 u. | 1147 u. | 2565 u. | 11912 u. |
| Portugal | 0.019 kg | 1131 u. [6] | 0.087 kg | 0.029 kg | 0.001 kg | 0.640 kg |
| | 549 u. | | 31393 u. | 22 u. | 35 u. | 34 u. |
| Spain | 119.584 kg | 176.985 kg | 49.538 kg | 23.412 kg | 18.700 kg | 55.642 kg |
| | | | 182.000 lt. | | 29711 u. | 31427 u. |
| Sweden | 187.374 kg | 134.714 kg | 120.310 kg | 107.039 kg [ICPO] | 253.161 kg | 350.300 kg |
| | 16057 u. | | 1099 u. | | | |
| Switzerland | 7.981 kg | No Report | 10.700 kg | 39.105 kg | 4.608 kg | 10.433 kg |
| Turkey | 1020130 u. | No Report | 4244493 u. | 295037 u. | 1090486 u. [2] | 1294285 u. |
| United Kingdom | 3295.700 kg | 1807.847 kg | 1194.938 kg [ICPO] | 1772.344 kg | 1716.626 kg | 1716.626 kg [7] |
| | | | 25021 u. | 6541808 u. | | |
| Sub-Total | 5268.291 kg | 4792.908 kg | 3395.675 kg | 3508.438 kg | 3394.512 kg | 4077.293 kg |
| | 1381623 u. | 1716607 u. | 182.000 lt. | 9817888 u. | 1156508 u. | 1353587 u. |
| | | | 4894735 u. | | | |
| Total region | 5506.843 kg | 4979.464 kg | 3621.073 kg | 3943.129 kg | 3730.636 kg | 4670.453 kg |
| | 1.426 lt. | 2.694 lt. | 182.591 lt. | 0.482 lt. | 1169048 u. | 1490950 u. |
| | 1393239 u. | 1729949 u. | 4950155 u. | 9882910 u. | | |
| **OCEANIA** | | | | | | |
| **Oceania** | | | | | | |
| Australia | 202.814 kg | 182.220 kg [Govt. (8] | 276.288 kg [8] | 427.312 kg | 876.006 kg [9] | 1283.046 kg [9] |
| Fiji | No Report | No Report | No Report | 0.333 kg [ICPO] | No Report | No Report |
| New Zealand | No Report | 1.340 kg | 1.104 kg | 10.175 kg | 4.170 kg | 7.439 kg |
| | | | 1400 u. | 103 u. | | 523 u. |
| Sub-Total | 202.814 kg | 183.560 kg | 277.392 kg | 437.820 kg | 880.176 kg | 1290.485 kg |
| | | | 1400 u. | 103 u. | | 523 u. |
| Total region | 202.814 kg | 183.560 kg | 277.392 kg | 437.820 kg | 880.176 kg | 1290.485 kg |
| | | | 1400 u. | 103 u. | | 523 u. |
| TOTAL | 14237.710 kg | 13397.570 kg | 31661.250 kg | 39377.690 kg | 24722.920 kg | 21367.410 kg |
| | 137.401 lt. | 374.836 lt. | 204.509 lt. | 272.083 lt. | 51114510 u. | 11.120 lt. |
| | 27495230 u. | 22064960 u. | 46313400 u. | 139996300 u. | | 28035050 u. |

1) Ketamine 2) Captagon 3) Including other hallucinogens. 4) Due to unavailability of 2001 data, year 2000 data were used for analysis purposes. 5) Duromine 6) Small quantity. 7) Due to unavailability of 2002 data, year 2001 data were used for analysis purposes. 8) Provisional figures. 9) Includes ecstasy

Source: Annual Report Questionnaire if not otherwise indicated

## SEIZURES, 1997 - 2002
### Ecstasy (MDA, MDEA, MDMA)*

| Region/country or territory | 1997 | 1998 | 1999 | 2000 | 2001 | 2002 |
|---|---|---|---|---|---|---|
| **AFRICA** | | | | | | |
| **North Africa** | | | | | | |
| Egypt | No Report | No Report | No Report | 3372 u. | 70080 u. | 785 u. |
| Sub-Total | | | | 3372 u. | 70080 u. | 785 u. |
| **Southern Africa** | | | | | | |
| Lesotho | No Report | No Report | No Report | No Report | No Report | 1.884 kg [ICPO] |
| Namibia | No Report | No Report | 74 u. | 157 u. | 546 u. | 49 u. |
| South Africa | No Report | No Report | 30132 u. [ICPO] | 1.177 kg 297021 u. | 95792 u. | 14.540 kg 424258 u. |
| Zimbabwe | No Report | No Report | 3 u. | No Report | 6 u. | 58 u. |
| Sub-Total | | | 30209 u. | 1.177 kg 297178 u. | 96344 u. | 16.424 kg 424365 u. |
| Total region | | | 0.030 kg 31082 u. | 561.757 kg 12208530 u. | 523.613 kg 9694573 u. | 123.397 kg 8109053 u. |
| **AMERICAS** | | | | | | |
| **Caribbean** | | | | | | |
| *Aruba* | No Report | No Report | 873 u. [F.O] | 85279 u. [F.O] | 59874 u. [F.O] | 19445 u. [ICPO] |
| Bahamas | No Report | No Report | No Report | 63.000 kg | 0.023 kg 0 u. | 0.027 kg |
| *Bermuda* | No Report | No Report | No Report | No Report | 153 u. [F.O] | 65 u. |
| *Cayman Islands* | No Report | No Report | 0.030 kg | 80 u. [F.O] | No Report | 120 u. |
| Cuba | No Report | No Report | No Report | No Report | No Report | 0.001 kg [ICPO] |
| Dominican Republic | No Report | No Report | No Report | 125073 u. [F.O] | 30903 u. | 153605 u. [HONLC] |
| *Guadeloupe* | No Report | No Report | No Report | 25540 u. [F.O] | 500 u. [F.O] | No Report |
| Jamaica | No Report | No Report | No Report | No Report | 5070 u. | 79 u. [ICPO] |
| *Netherlands Antilles* | No Report | No Report | No Report | 15.464 kg [ICPO] | 20465 u. [F.O] | 94 u. [ICPO] |
| *Puerto Rico* | No Report | No Report | No Report | No Report | 1977 u. [F.O] | No Report |
| Sub-Total | | | 0.030 kg 873 u. | 78.464 kg 235972 u. | 0.023 kg 118942 u. | 0.028 kg 173408 u. |
| **Central America** | | | | | | |
| Costa Rica | No Report | No Report | No Report | 46 u. | 87 u. | 83 u. |
| Nicaragua | No Report | No Report | No Report | No Report | No Report | 19886 u. |
| Panama | No Report | No Report | No Report | 2256 u. | 22166 u. | 934 u. [HONLC] |
| Sub-Total | | | | 2302 u. | 22253 u. | 20903 u. |
| **North America** | | | | | | |
| Canada | No Report | No Report | No Report | 449.814 kg [ICPO] 2069709 u. | 421.590 kg 846973 u. | 74.992 kg 177450 u. |
| Mexico | No Report | No Report | No Report | 32.302 kg [ICPO] | 102.000 kg | 31.953 kg |
| United States | No Report | No Report | No Report | 9600000 u. | 8539981 u. | 7312142 u. |
| Sub-Total | | | | | | |

Source: Annual Report Questionnaire if not otherwise indicated

ICPO

## SEIZURES, 1997 - 2002
### Ecstasy (MDA, MDEA, MDMA)

| Region/country or territory | 1997 | 1998 | 1999 | 2000 | 2001 | 2002 |
|---|---|---|---|---|---|---|
| **AMERICAS** | | | | | | |
| **South America** | | | | | | |
| Argentina | No Report | No Report | No Report | No Report | No Report | 430 u. [ICPO] |
| Brazil | No Report | No Report | 59612 u. [ICPO] | 36796 u. | 1909 u. [Govt] | 15804 u. [F.O] |
| Chile | No Report | No Report | No Report | 140 u. [ICPO] | 2626 u. | 458 u. |
| Colombia | No Report | No Report | 1022 u. | 83.000 kg | No Report | 175382 u. |
| Ecuador | No Report | No Report | No Report | No Report | 7 u. | 185.000 kg [HONLC] |
| Guyana | No Report | No Report | 626 u. [F.O] | 124 u. [F.O] | No Report | No Report |
| Peru | No Report | No Report | No Report | No Report | 35 u. | 78 u. |
| Suriname | No Report | 3000 u. [CICAD] | No Report | 61232 u. [INCSR] | No Report | 80 u. |
| Uruguay | No Report | No Report | 84 u. | 738 u. | No Report | 31 u. |
| Venezuela | No Report | No Report | No Report | 7985 u. [CICAD] | 2 u. | 16010 u. |
| Sub-Total | | 3000 u. | 61344 u. | 83.000 kg 107015 u. | 4579 u. | 185.000 kg 208273 u. |
| Total region | | 3000 u. | 0.030 kg 62217 u. | 643.580 kg 12015000 u. | 523.613 kg 9532728 u. | 291.973 kg 7892176 u. |
| **ASIA** | | | | | | |
| **East and South-East Asia** | | | | | | |
| Brunei Darussalam | No Report | No Report | 32 u. | No Report | No Report | 10 u. |
| China | No Report | No Report | No Report | 200.000 kg [HNLP] 240000 u. | 2700000 u. | 3000000 u. [ICPO] |
| Hong Kong SAR, China | No Report | No Report | 21202 u. [ICPO] | 58.800 kg 378621 u. | 0.032 kg 170243 u. | 0.053 kg 48840 u. |
| Indonesia | No Report | No Report | 29510 u. [ICPO] | No Report | No Report | 84224 u. |
| Japan | No Report | No Report | No Report | 77528 u. [ICPO] | 0.121 kg 112542 u. | 2.600 kg 156076 u. |
| Korea (Republic of) | No Report | No Report | No Report | No Report | 1672 u. | 39011 u. [ICPO] |
| Macau SAR, China | No Report | No Report | No Report | 2453 u. [ICPO] | 1687 u. | 672 u. |
| Malaysia | No Report | No Report | 55975 u. | 49901 u. [ICPO] | No Report | 164884 u. [ICPO] |
| Philippines | No Report | No Report | No Report | 1026 u. | No Report | 246 u. |
| Singapore | No Report | No Report | 4.070 kg 17232 u. | 10339 u. | 0.257 kg 23846 u. | 7331 u. |
| Thailand | 80047 u. [HNLP] | 5878 u. [HNLP] | 30615 u. [F.O] | 72182 u. [HNLP] | 61922 u. [F.O] | 145873 u. [F.O] |
| Sub-Total | 80047 u. | 5878 u. | 4.070 kg 154566 u. | 258.800 kg 832050 u. | 0.410 kg 3071912 u. | 2.653 kg 3647167 u. |
| **Near and Middle East /South-West Asia** | | | | | | |
| Israel | No Report | No Report | 130.687 kg [ICPO] 30335 u. | 270000 u. | 1.504 kg 121695 u. | 4.454 kg 951057 u. |
| Jordan | No Report | No Report | 5000 u. [ICPO] | No Report | No Report | No Report |
| Sub-Total | | | 130.687 kg 35335 u. | 270000 u. | 1.504 kg 121695 u. | 4.454 kg 951057 u. |

Source: Annual Report Questionnaire if not otherwise indicated

## SEIZURES, 1997 - 2002
### Ecstasy (MDA, MDEA, MDMA)*

| Region/country or territory | 1997 | 1998 | 1999 | 2000 | 2001 | 2002 |
|---|---|---|---|---|---|---|
| **ASIA** | | | | | | |
| Total region | 80047 u. | 5878 u. | 134.757 kg<br>189901 u. | 258.800 kg<br>1102050 u. | 1.914 kg<br>3193607 u. | 7.107 kg<br>4598224 u. |
| **EUROPE** | | | | | | |
| **Eastern Europe** | | | | | | |
| Belarus | No Report | No Report | No Report | No Report | No Report | 0.536 kg [ICPO] |
| Bosnia Herzegovina | No Report | No Report | No Report | No Report | No Report | 1212 u. [ICPO] |
| Bulgaria | No Report | No Report | No Report | 4524 u. [Govt] | 7.900 kg<br>2361 u. | 1.500 kg<br>3135 u. |
| Croatia | No Report | No Report | 15421 u. [ICPO] | 9979 u. | 12906 u. | 110632 u. |
| Czech Republic | No Report | No Report | No Report | 17502 u. | 29.890 kg | 1.893 kg<br>88391 u. |
| Estonia | No Report | No Report | 1770 u. [ICPO] | 0.431 kg<br>1351 u. | 1.714 kg | 3.402 kg |
| FYR of Macedonia | 184 u. [NAPOL] | 787 u. [NAPOL] | 5532 u. [NAPOL] | 280 u. [NAPOL] | 45 u. [Govt] | 0.002 kg<br>18341 u. |
| Hungary | No Report | No Report | 466 u. | 13616 u. | 0.260 kg<br>18301 u. | 5.575 kg<br>23730 u. |
| Latvia | No Report | No Report | 0.749 kg [ICPO]<br>17 u. | No Report | 1620 u. | No Report |
| Lithuania | No Report | No Report | 1122 u. [ICPO] | 50724 u. [ICPO] | 0.045 kg<br>514 u. | 0.003 kg<br>1205 u. |
| Poland | No Report | No Report | 6319 u. | 129513 u. | 232735 u. | 38179 u. |
| Romania | No Report | No Report | No Report | 10945 u. [ICPO] | 67210 u. | 0.007 kg<br>19567 u. |
| Russian Federation | No Report | No Report | No Report | No Report | 0.850 kg | No Report |
| Serbia and Montenegro | No Report | No Report | No Report | No Report | 0.079 kg<br><br>10811 u. | 10000 u. |
| Slovakia | No Report | No Report | 9 u. | 493 u. [ICPO] | 0.568 kg | 435 u. |
| Slovenia | No Report | No Report | 1749 u. [ICPO] | 0.053 kg<br>27974 u. | 1852 u. | 7877 u. |
| Ukraine | No Report | No Report | 1.349 kg [ICPO]<br>18888 u. | 0.305 kg [ICPO]<br>4784 u. | 47 u. | No Report |
| Sub-Total | 184 u. | 787 u. | 2.098 kg<br>51293 u. | 0.789 kg<br>271685 u. | 41.306 kg<br>348402 u. | 12.918 kg<br>322704 u. |
| **Western Europe** | | | | | | |
| Andorra | No Report | No Report | 43 u. [ICPO] | 283 u. [ICPO] | 85 u. | 42 u. [ICPO] |
| Austria | No Report | No Report | 31129 u. | 162.093 kg | 256299 u. | 0.099 kg<br>383451 u. |
| Belgium | No Report | No Report | 266.460 kg [ICPO]<br>467477 u. | 37.000 kg [ICPO]<br>818515 u. | 37.000 kg [UNODC (1]<br>818515 u. | 1564.000 kg |
| Cyprus | No Report | No Report | 0.001 kg<br>62 u. | 0.005 kg<br>3317 u. | 0.004 kg<br>2910 u. | 0.273 kg<br>10253 u. |

Source: Annual Report Questionnaire if not otherwise indicated

## SEIZURES, 1997 - 2002
### Ecstasy (MDA, MDEA, MDMA)*

| Region/country or territory | 1997 | 1998 | 1999 | 2000 | 2001 | 2002 |
|---|---|---|---|---|---|---|
| **EUROPE** | | | | | | |
| **Western Europe** | | | | | | |
| Denmark | No Report | No Report | 26117 u. | 21608 u. | 150080 u. | 25738 u. |
| Finland | No Report | No Report | 16578 u.[ICPO] | 87393 u. | 81228 u. | 45065 u. |
| France | No Report | No Report | 1860402 u. | 2283620 u.[HNLP] | 1503773 u. | 2156937 u. |
| Germany | No Report | No Report | 1470507 u.[Govt] | 1634683 u. | 4576504 u. | 3207099 u. |
| Greece | No Report | No Report | 2815 u. | 53557 u. | 58845 u. | 28430 u. |
| Iceland | No Report | No Report | 7478 u. | 22057 u. | 93151 u. | 0.006 kg 814 u. |
| Ireland | No Report | No Report | 74.609 kg 266462 u. | 695133 u.[ICPO] | 469862 u. | 0.153 kg 117046 u. |
| Italy | No Report | No Report | 272288 u.[ICPO] | 501986 u. | 0.285 kg 308845 u. | 0.006 kg 397566 u. |
| Liechtenstein | No Report | No Report | No Report | 10 u. | No Report | 0.001 kg |
| Luxembourg | No Report | No Report | 357 u. | 318 u.[ICPO] | No Report | 1139 u.[ICPO] |
| Malta | No Report | No Report | 459 u. | 5191 u. | 2242 u. | 1012 u.[ICPO] |
| Monaco | No Report | No Report | 3 u.[ICPO] | 5 u.[ICPO] | No Report | 55 u. |
| Netherlands | 703.289 kg[Govt] 870980 u. | 1163514 u.[Govt] | 3663608 u.[Govt] | 632.000 kg[Govt] 5500000 u. | 113.000 kg 8684505 u. | 849.000 kg 6787167 u. |
| Norway | No Report | No Report | 0.025 kg 24644 u. | 0.114 kg 49208 u. | 0.117 kg 61205 u. | 0.077 kg 102409 u. |
| Portugal | No Report | No Report | 0.086 kg[Govt] 31319 u. | 1.089 kg 25499 u. | 0.088 kg 126451 u. | 1.675 kg 222466 u. |
| Spain | No Report | No Report | 357649 u. | 891562 u.[ICPO] | 860164 u. | 1396142 u. |
| Sweden | No Report | No Report | No Report | 0.262 kg[ICPO] 184161 u. | 0.314 kg 57750 u. | 96577 u. |
| Switzerland | No Report | No Report | No Report | 189569 u.[(2] | 86959 u. | 88342 u. |
| Turkey | No Report | No Report | No Report | 33894 u.[Govt.] | 121508 u. | 98989 u. |
| United Kingdom | No Report | No Report | 6323500 u.[NCIS] | 6534813 u. | 7662228 u. | 7662228 u.[(3] |
| Sub-Total | 703.289 kg 870980 u. | 1163514 u. | 341.181 kg 14822900 u. | 832.563 kg 19536380 u. | 150.808 kg 25983110 u. | 2415.290 kg 22828970 u. |
| Total region | 703.289 kg 871164 u. | 1164301 u. | 343.279 kg 14874190 u. | 833.352 kg 19808070 u. | 192.114 kg 26331510 u. | 2428.208 kg 23151670 u. |
| **OCEANIA** | | | | | | |
| **Oceania** | | | | | | |
| Australia | No Report | No Report | 55.521 kg | No Report | 338.400 kg[Govt. (4] | 722.000 kg[Govt.] |
| New Zealand | No Report | No Report | No Report | 0.072 kg 8798 u. | 3.000 lt. 83449 u. | 256350 u. |
| Sub-Total | | | 55.521 kg | 0.072 kg 8798 u. | 338.400 kg 3.000 lt. 83449 u. | 722.000 kg 256350 u. |

Source: Annual Report Questionnaire if not otherwise indicated

## SEIZURES, 1997 - 2002
### Ecstasy (MDA, MDEA, MDMA)*

| Region/country or territory | 1997 | 1998 | 1999 | 2000 | 2001 | 2002 |
|---|---|---|---|---|---|---|
| **OCEANIA** | | | | | | |
| Total region | | | 55.521 kg | 0.072 kg<br>8798 u. | 338.400 kg<br>3.000 lt.<br>83449 u. | 722.000 kg<br>256350 u. |
| TOTAL | 703.289 kg<br>951211 u. | 1173179 u. | 533.617 kg<br>15187600 u. | 2298.738 kg<br>45443000 u. | 1579.653 kg<br>3.000 lt.<br>49002290 u. | 3589.110 kg<br>44432620 u. |

1) Due to unavailability of 2001 data, year 2000 data were used for analysis purposes. 2) Includes ecstasy 3) Due to unavailability of 2002 data, year 2001 data were used for analysis purposes. 4) Fiscal year

* **General reporting of ecstasy started only in the year 2000.**

Source: Annual Report Questionnaire if not otherwise indicated

## SEIZURES, 1997 - 2002

### Depressants (excluding Methaqualone)

| Region/country or territory | 1997 | 1998 | 1999 | 2000 | 2001 | 2002 |
|---|---|---|---|---|---|---|
| **AFRICA** | | | | | | |
| **East Africa** | | | | | | |
| Kenya | No Report | 9060 u. | No Report | 272 u. | No Report | 157 u. |
| Mauritius | 1886 u. | 11694 u. | 952 u. | 1758 u. | No Report | 2781 u. |
| Sub-Total | 1886 u. | 20754 u. | 952 u. | 2030 u. | | 2938 u. |
| **North Africa** | | | | | | |
| Algeria | No Report | No Report | 110786 u. | 100555 u. [ICPO] | No Report | 244214 u. |
| Egypt | No Report | No Report | No Report | No Report | No Report | 85064 u. |
| Morocco | 36236 u. [Govt.] | No Report | No Report | 71672 u. | No Report | 60458 u. |
| Tunisia | No Report | 4439 u. | No Report | No Report | No Report | No Report |
| Sub-Total | 36236 u. | 4439 u. | 110786 u. | 172227 u. | | 389736 u. |
| **Southern Africa** | | | | | | |
| Botswana | No Report | No Report | 0.073 kg [ICPO] 500 u. | No Report | No Report | No Report |
| Mozambique | No Report | 5080 u. [ICPO] | No Report | No Report | No Report | No Report |
| South Africa | No Report | No Report | No Report | 0.025 kg [ICPO] 3026 u. | No Report | 0.316 kg 6437 u. |
| Zambia | 0.800 kg [Govt] | 0.908 kg [Govt] | 4140 u. | 0.000 kg [Govt] | 0.064 kg [Govt] 3522 u. | No Report |
| Zimbabwe | No Report | 43.640 kg | No Report | No Report | No Report | No Report |
| Sub-Total | 0.800 kg | 44.548 kg 5080 u. | 0.073 kg 4640 u. | 0.025 kg 3026 u. | 0.064 kg 3522 u. | 0.316 kg 6437 u. |
| **West and Central Africa** | | | | | | |
| Benin | 24 u. [Govt.] | No Report | No Report | No Report | No Report | No Report |
| Cameroon | No Report | No Report | No Report | No Report | No Report | 40 u. |
| Chad | No Report | No Report | 5360 u. [ICPO] | 961230 u. | No Report | No Report |
| Congo | No Report | No Report | No Report | 0.003 kg | No Report | 2 u. |
| Côte d'Ivoire | 71.500 kg 44699 u. | 23.600 kg 9367 u. | 66.690 kg | 48.646 kg [ICPO] | 298.041 kg | 247356 u. |
| Gambia | No Report | 4500 u. [ICPO] | No Report | No Report | 3.000 kg | No Report |
| Niger | No Report | 679484 u. [ICPO] | 367823 u. [ICPO] | No Report | No Report | No Report |
| Nigeria | 1426.487 kg | No Report | No Report | 134.690 kg | 282.454 kg | No Report |
| Senegal | No Report | 4063 u. [ICPO] | 4737 u. [ICPO] | 310 u. [ICPO] | No Report | No Report |
| Sub-Total | 1497.987 kg 44723 u. | 23.600 kg 697414 u. | 66.690 kg 377920 u. | 183.339 kg 961540 u. | 583.495 kg | 247398 u. |
| Total region | 1498.787 kg 82845 u. | 68.148 kg 727687 u. | 66.763 kg 494298 u. | 183.364 kg 1138823 u. | 583.559 kg 3522 u. | 0.316 kg 646509 u. |
| **AMERICAS** | | | | | | |
| **Caribbean** | | | | | | |
| *Cayman Islands* | No Report | No Report | 0.001 kg | 1 u. | No Report | No Report |
| Dominican Republic | No Report | No Report | 8 u. [ICPO] | No Report | 50 u. | No Report |

Source: Annual Report Questionnaire if not otherwise indicated

## SEIZURES, 1997 - 2002
### Depressants (excluding Methaqualone)

| Region/country or territory | 1997 | 1998 | 1999 | 2000 | 2001 | 2002 |
|---|---|---|---|---|---|---|
| **AMERICAS** | | | | | | |
| **Caribbean** | | | | | | |
| Sub-Total | | | 0.001 kg<br>8 u. | 1 u. | 50 u. | |
| **Central America** | | | | | | |
| El Salvador | No Report | 40000 u.[ICPO] | No Report | 0.010 kg[ICPO]<br>22964 u. | No Report | No Report |
| Guatemala | No Report | 52.000 kg | No Report | No Report | No Report | No Report |
| Honduras | 1 u. | No Report | No Report | No Report | No Report | No Report |
| Sub-Total | 1 u. | 52.000 kg<br>40000 u. | | 0.010 kg<br>22964 u. | | |
| **North America** | | | | | | |
| Canada | 0.880 kg<br>0.120 lt.<br>122359 u. | 0.934 kg<br>0.686 lt.<br>12033 u. | 0.726 kg<br>2.439 lt.<br>8355 u. | 173.865 kg<br>4.511 lt.<br>10921 u. | 5.321 kg<br>18684 u. | 7.497 kg[1<br>25017 u. |
| Mexico | 117104 u. | 1484000 u. | 182604 u. | 734281 u.[ICPO] | 823726 u. | 5353064 u. |
| United States | 0.026 kg<br>0.867 lt.<br>709685 u. | No Report | 2.646 kg<br>403724 u. | 0.508 kg<br>0.021 lt.<br>3338 u. | 53385 u. | 254975 u. |
| Sub-Total | 0.906 kg<br>0.987 lt.<br>949148 u. | 0.934 kg<br>0.686 lt.<br>1496033 u. | 3.372 kg<br>2.439 lt.<br>594683 u. | 174.373 kg<br>4.532 lt.<br>748540 u. | 5.321 kg<br>895795 u. | 7.497 kg<br>5633056 u. |
| **South America** | | | | | | |
| Argentina | 5759 u. | 13125 u. | 8055 u. | 11779 u. | 4795 u. | 24028 u. |
| Chile | No Report | 0.002 kg<br>2545 u. | 19813 u.[CICAD] | 6993 u. | 9341 u. | 34882 u. |
| Uruguay | No Report | No Report | No Report | No Report | No Report | 4 u. |
| Sub-Total | 5759 u. | 0.002 kg<br>15670 u. | 27868 u. | 18772 u. | 14136 u. | 58914 u. |
| Total region | 0.906 kg<br>0.987 lt.<br>954908 u. | 52.936 kg<br>0.686 lt.<br>1551703 u. | 3.373 kg<br>2.439 lt.<br>622559 u. | 174.383 kg<br>4.532 lt.<br>790277 u. | 5.321 kg<br>909981 u. | 7.497 kg<br>5691970 u. |
| **ASIA** | | | | | | |
| **Central Asia and Transcaucasian countries** | | | | | | |
| Armenia | No Report | No Report | 1209 u.[ICPO] | No Report | No Report | No Report |
| Georgia | No Report | 180 u.[ICPO] | 0.018 kg[ICPO]<br>1060 u. | 0.444 kg[ICPO] | No Report | No Report |
| Kazakhstan | No Report | No Report | 56.000 kg | No Report | No Report | No Report |
| Uzbekistan | 970 u. | No Report | No Report | No Report | No Report | 13774 u. |
| Sub-Total | 970 u. | 180 u. | 56.018 kg<br>2269 u. | 0.444 kg | | 13774 u. |
| **East and South-East Asia** | | | | | | |
| Brunei Darussalam | 3227 u. | No Report | 53 u. | 1 u. | 1 u. | 232 u. |

Source: Annual Report Questionnaire if not otherwise indicated

343

## SEIZURES, 1997 - 2002

### Depressants (excluding Methaqualone)

| Region/country or territory | 1997 | 1998 | 1999 | 2000 | 2001 | 2002 |
|---|---|---|---|---|---|---|
| **ASIA** | | | | | | |
| **East and South-East Asia** | | | | | | |
| *Hong Kong SAR, China* | 512832 u. | 162850 u. [Govt.] | 12.208 kg [(2] | 0.090 kg [ICPO] | 2.000 kg | 0.007 kg [(1] |
| | | | 1134461 u. | 77862 u. | 390550 u. | 0.020 lt. |
| | | | | | | 1155 u. |
| Indonesia | No Report | 17793 u. | 372494 u. [ICPO] | No Report | 37545 u. | No Report |
| Japan | 56895 u. | 0.024 kg | 0.003 lt. | 0.003 kg | 0.002 kg | 93733 u. |
| | | 0.010 lt. | 97310 u. | 32358 u. | 20545 u. | |
| | | 141455 u. | | | | |
| Korea (Republic of) | 681233 u. | 1452896 u. | 1030567 u. | 2176 u. [ICPO] | No Report | No Report |
| *Macau SAR, China* | No Report | 4937 u. [ICPO] | No Report | 19421 u. | 2583 u. | 2374 u. |
| Myanmar | No Report | No Report | No Report | No Report | No Report | 347662 u. |
| Philippines | No Report | No Report | No Report | 100000 u. [(3] | No Report | No Report |
| Singapore | 582 u. | 34911 u. | 13069 u. | 48061 u. | 0.074 kg | 800 u. |
| | | | | | 1807 u. | |
| Thailand | No Report | No Report | 4.630 kg [ICPO] | 10.524 kg [ICPO] | No Report | No Report |
| Viet Nam | No Report | No Report | 74274 u. [ICPO] | 115000 u. [ICPO] | 158007 u. | No Report |
| Sub-Total | 1254769 u. | 0.024 kg | 16.838 kg | 10.617 kg | 2.076 kg | 0.007 kg |
| | | 0.010 lt. | 0.003 lt. | 394879 u. | 611038 u. | 0.020 lt. |
| | | 1814842 u. | 2722228 u. | | | 445956 u. |
| **Near and Middle East /South-West Asia** | | | | | | |
| Bahrain | No Report | No Report | No Report | No Report | No Report | 8527 u. |
| Israel | No Report | No Report | 936 u. [ICPO] | No Report | No Report | No Report |
| Jordan | 2794 u. | No Report | No Report | 1014 u. | No Report | No Report |
| Kuwait | No Report | 8943 u. | No Report | No Report | No Report | No Report |
| Lebanon | 490 u. | No Report | 359 u. | 41616 u. | 859 u. | 989 u. |
| Oman | No Report | No Report | No Report | No Report | 1815.000 kg | 3554 u. |
| Pakistan | No Report | No Report | No Report | 20000 u. [ICPO] | No Report | No Report |
| Qatar | No Report | 753 u. [ICPO] | 2164 u. [ICPO] | 15 u. [ICPO] | No Report | 99 u. |
| Saudi Arabia | No Report | No Report | No Report | 854 u. [ICPO] | No Report | No Report |
| Syrian Arab Republic | No Report | No Report | 15117 u. [ICPO] | No Report | No Report | No Report |
| United Arab Emirates | No Report | No Report | No Report | No Report | 0.498 kg | No Report |
| Yemen | No Report | 169 u. [ICPO] | No Report | 1486 u. [ICPO] | No Report | No Report |
| Sub-Total | 3284 u. | 9865 u. | 18576 u. | 64985 u. | 1815.498 kg | 13169 u. |
| | | | | | 859 u. | |
| **South Asia** | | | | | | |
| Nepal | No Report | 6811 u. | No Report | 1654 u. [ICPO] | No Report | No Report |
| Sub-Total | | 6811 u. | | 1654 u. | | |
| Total region | 1259023 u. | 0.024 kg | 72.856 kg | 11.061 kg | 1817.574 kg | 0.007 kg |
| | | 0.010 lt. | 0.003 lt. | 461518 u. | 611897 u. | 0.020 lt. |
| | | 1831698 u. | 2743073 u. | | | 472898 u. |

Source: Annual Report Questionnaire if not otherwise indicated

## SEIZURES, 1997 - 2002
### Depressants (excluding Methaqualone)

| Region/country or territory | 1997 | 1998 | 1999 | 2000 | 2001 | 2002 |
|---|---|---|---|---|---|---|
| **EUROPE** | | | | | | |
| **Eastern Europe** | | | | | | |
| Belarus | No Report | No Report | 0.002 kg | 0.100 kg | No Report | 52.144 kg |
| Bulgaria | 0.627 kg | 93460 u. | 1.500 kg | 4.682 kg<br>4142 u. | No Report | 1.103 kg |
| Croatia | 4915 u. | 4358 u. | 8335 u. | 4778 u. | No Report | No Report |
| Czech Republic | No Report | No Report | 50.000 kg | 9450 u. | 1119 u. | 841 u. |
| Estonia | 9.139 kg<br>908 u. | No Report | 0.103 kg<br>138 u. | 1.525 kg[1]<br>846 u. | 0.184 kg<br>14571 u. | 27.883 kg[1] |
| FYR of Macedonia | No Report | No Report | No Report | No Report | No Report | 10 u. |
| Hungary | No Report | No Report | No Report | No Report | 0.001 kg | 192 u. |
| Latvia | 20830 u. | 11244 u. | 0.171 kg<br>13562 u. | No Report | 9011 u. | No Report |
| Lithuania | No Report | 1237 u. | 580 u. | 106 u. | No Report | 0.111 kg[1]<br>67 u. |
| Poland | No Report | No Report | No Report | No Report | 8.000 lt. | 5132 u. |
| Republic of Moldova | No Report | 1800 u. | No Report | No Report | No Report | No Report |
| Romania | No Report | No Report | No Report | No Report | 5961 u. | 33686 u. |
| Russian Federation | 975 u. | No Report | 39.500 kg[ICPO] | 2.420 kg[ICPO] | 61.574 kg | No Report |
| Slovakia | 10642 u. | 1356 u. | 1104 u. | | No Report | No Report |
| Slovenia | No Report | 5745 u. | 621 u. | 735 u. | 460 u. | 8 u. |
| Ukraine | No Report | No Report | 0.001 kg[ICPO]<br>8427 u. | 289318 u.[ICPO] | No Report | 606.000 kg |
| Sub-Total | 9.766 kg<br>38270 u. | 119200 u. | 91.277 kg<br>32767 u. | 8.727 kg<br>309375 u. | 61.759 kg<br>8.000 lt.<br>31122 u. | 687.241 kg<br>39936 u. |
| **Western Europe** | | | | | | |
| Andorra | No Report | No Report | No Report | 11 u.[ICPO] | No Report | No Report |
| Austria | No Report | No Report | No Report | 32207 u.[ICPO] | 36132 u. | 24000 u. |
| Belgium | No Report | No Report | No Report | No Report | No Report | 137009 u.[4] |
| Finland | 48395 u. | 35664 u. | 45448 u. | 32148 u. | 11700 u. | No Report |
| France | No Report | No Report | No Report | 0.039 kg | No Report | No Report |
| Germany | 6035 u. | 7071 u. | No Report | No Report | No Report | No Report |
| Greece | 10.400 kg<br>26403 u. | 2.306 kg<br>18470 u. | 80.210 kg<br>217004 u. | 3.700 kg<br>35354 u. | 22.204 kg<br>43958 u. | 39971 u. |
| Ireland | 0.248 kg<br>4935 u. | No Report | 13793 u.[ICPO] | 1.121 kg | No Report | 5040 u. |
| Italy | 14437 u. | 0.037 kg<br>1506 u. | 0.232 kg[ICPO]<br>3316 u. | 0.662 kg<br>1883 u. | No Report | No Report |
| Liechtenstein | No Report | No Report | No Report | 10280 u.[4] | 430 u. | 0.304 kg |
| Luxembourg | No Report | 145 u. | No Report | No Report | No Report | No Report |
| Malta | 212 u. | 353 u. | 8 u. | 207 u. | No Report | No Report |

Source: Annual Report Questionnaire if not otherwise indicated

## SEIZURES, 1997 - 2002

### Depressants (excluding Methaqualone)

| Region/country or territory | 1997 | 1998 | 1999 | 2000 | 2001 | 2002 |
|---|---|---|---|---|---|---|
| **EUROPE** | | | | | | |
| **Western Europe** | | | | | | |
| Norway | 130000 u. | 0.071 kg | 0.012 kg | 0.043 kg | 11.361 kg | 47.281 kg |
| | | 101295 u. | 180500 u. | 413548 u. | 848206 u. | 1251914 u. |
| Portugal | 1945 u. | 2577 u. | 2122 u. | 0.001 kg | 3689 u. | 0.007 kg |
| | | | | 4794 u. | | 1071 u. |
| Spain | 59352 u. | 99126 u. | 343974 u. | 6.825 lt.[(1] | 595619 u. | 22016 u.[(1] |
| | | | | 132951 u. | | |
| Sweden | No Report | 0.302 kg | 255000 u. | 2.320 kg[(1] | 46.570 lt. | 25.400 lt.[(1] |
| | | 293508 u. | | 16.558 lt. | 271478 u. | 965400 u. |
| | | | | 237312 u. | | |
| Switzerland | No Report | 1204104 u. | 554641 u. | 1907207 u. | No Report | No Report |
| Turkey | No Report | 3559 u. | No Report | No Report | No Report | No Report |
| United Kingdom | 6.200 kg | No Report | 12000 u.[ICPO] | 3.360 kg | 12.558 kg | 12.558 kg[(5] |
| | | | | 37 u. | 105513 u. | 105513 u. |
| Sub-Total | 16.848 kg | 2.716 kg | 80.454 kg | 11.246 kg | 46.123 kg | 60.150 kg |
| | 291714 u. | 1767378 u. | 1627806 u. | 23.383 lt. | 46.570 lt. | 25.400 lt. |
| | | | | 2807939 u. | 1916725 u. | 2551934 u. |
| Total region | 26.614 kg | 2.716 kg | 171.731 kg | 19.973 kg | 107.882 kg | 747.391 kg |
| | 329984 u. | 1886578 u. | 1660573 u. | 23.383 lt. | 54.570 lt. | 25.400 lt. |
| | | | | 3117314 u. | 1947847 u. | 2591870 u. |
| **OCEANIA** | | | | | | |
| **Oceania** | | | | | | |
| Australia | 0.380 kg | No Report | No Report | 0.117 kg | 0.038 kg | 1.049 kg[(6] |
| | | | | | | 100.000 lt. |
| New Zealand | No Report | 445 u. | 126 u. | 317 u. | No Report | 5.170 lt.[(1] |
| | | | | | | 339 u. |
| Sub-Total | 0.380 kg | 445 u. | 126 u. | 0.117 kg | 0.038 kg | 1.049 kg |
| | | | | 317 u. | | 105.170 lt. |
| | | | | | | 339 u. |
| Total region | 0.380 kg | 445 u. | 126 u. | 0.117 kg | 0.038 kg | 1.049 kg |
| | | | | 317 u. | | 105.170 lt. |
| | | | | | | 339 u. |
| TOTAL | 1526.687 kg | 123.824 kg | 314.723 kg | 388.898 kg | 2514.374 kg | 756.260 kg |
| | 0.987 lt. | 0.696 lt. | 2.442 lt. | 27.915 lt. | 54.570 lt. | 130.590 lt. |
| | 2626760 u. | 5998111 u. | 5520629 u. | 5508249 u. | 3473248 u. | 9403586 u. |

1) Including GHB 2) Includes mainly benzodiazapines 3) Diazepam 4) Rohypnol 5) Due to unavailability of 2002 data, year 2001 data were used for analysis purposes. 6) Litre amount for GHB

Source: Annual Report Questionnaire if not otherwise indicated

## SEIZURES, 1997 - 2002

### Hallucinogens (excluding LSD but incl. "Ecstasy")

| Region/country or territory | 1997 | 1998 | 1999 | 2000 | 2001 | 2002 |
|---|---|---|---|---|---|---|
| **AFRICA** | | | | | | |
| **North Africa** | | | | | | |
| Egypt | No Report | No Report | No Report | 3372 u. | 70080 u. | 785 u. |
| Sub-Total | | | | 3372 u. | 70080 u. | 785 u. |
| **Southern Africa** | | | | | | |
| Lesotho | No Report | No Report | No Report | No Report | No Report | 1.884 kg [ICPO] |
| Namibia | No Report | No Report | 74 u. | 157 u. | 546 u. | 49 u. |
| South Africa | 118784 u. | 111733 u. | 30132 u. [ICPO] | 1.177 kg 297021 u. | 95792 u. | 14.540 kg 424258 u. |
| Zimbabwe | No Report | No Report | 3 u. | No Report | 0.000 kg 6 u. | 58 u. |
| Sub-Total | 118784 u. | 111733 u. | 30209 u. | 1.177 kg 297178 u. | 0.000 kg 96344 u. | 16.424 kg 424365 u. |
| **West and Central Africa** | | | | | | |
| Central African Republic | No Report | No Report | No Report | No Report | No Report | 2.000 lt. [Govt] |
| Sub-Total | | | | | | 2.000 lt. |
| Total region | 118784 u. | 111733 u. | 0.030 kg 31111 u. | 79.641 kg 538906 u. | 0.023 kg 307619 u. | 16.452 kg 2.000 lt. 619461 u. |
| **AMERICAS** | | | | | | |
| **Caribbean** | | | | | | |
| *Aruba* | No Report | No Report | 873 u. [F.O] | 85279 u. [F.O] | 59874 u. [F.O] | 19445 u. [ICPO] |
| Bahamas | No Report | No Report | No Report | 63.000 kg | 0.023 kg 0 u. | 0.027 kg |
| *Bermuda* | No Report | No Report | No Report | No Report | 153 u. [F.O] | 65 u. |
| *Cayman Islands* | No Report | No Report | 0.030 kg | 162 u. | No Report | 120 u. |
| Cuba | No Report | No Report | No Report | No Report | No Report | 0.001 kg [ICPO] |
| Dominican Republic | No Report | No Report | 29 u. | 125073 u. [F.O] | 30903 u. | 153605 u. [HONLC] |
| *Guadeloupe* | No Report | No Report | No Report | 25540 u. [F.O] | 500 u. [F.O] | No Report |
| Jamaica | No Report | No Report | No Report | No Report | 5070 u. | 79 u. [ICPO] |
| *Netherlands Antilles* | No Report | No Report | No Report | 15.464 kg [ICPO] | 20465 u. [F.O] | 94 u. [ICPO] |
| *Puerto Rico* | No Report | No Report | No Report | No Report | 1977 u. [F.O] | No Report |
| Sub-Total | | | 0.030 kg 902 u. | 78.464 kg 236054 u. | 0.023 kg 118942 u. | 0.028 kg 173408 u. |
| **Central America** | | | | | | |
| Costa Rica | No Report | No Report | No Report | 46 u. | 87 u. | 83 u. |
| Nicaragua | No Report | No Report | No Report | No Report | No Report | 19886 u. |
| Panama | No Report | No Report | No Report | 2256 u. | 22166 u. | 934 u. [HONLC] |
| Sub-Total | | | | 2302 u. | 22253 u. | 20903 u. |

Source: Annual Report Questionnaire if not otherwise indicated

## SEIZURES, 1997 - 2002

### Hallucinogens (excluding LSD but incl. "Ecstasy")

| Region/country or territory | 1997 | 1998 | 1999 | 2000 | 2001 | 2002 |
|---|---|---|---|---|---|---|
| **AMERICAS** | | | | | | |
| **North America** | | | | | | |
| Canada | 47.703 kg | 64.019 kg | 561.837 kg | 764.514 kg | 459.025 kg | 285.733 kg |
| | 9288 u. | 0.022 lt. | 0.503 lt. | 0.155 lt. | 846973 u. | 177450 u. |
| | | 25451 u. | 3427 u. | 2136444 u. | | |
| Mexico | 611.380 kg | 93.000 kg | No Report | 32.302 kg [ICPO] | 102.000 kg | 31.953 kg |
| United States | 44.588 kg | No Report | 160.515 kg | 9600000 u. [ICPO] | 9795741 u. | 7637544 u. |
| | 59.968 lt. | | 4745097 u. | | | |
| | 151934 u. | | | | | |
| Sub-Total | 703.671 kg | 157.019 kg | 722.352 kg | 796.816 kg | 561.026 kg | 317.686 kg |
| | 59.968 lt. | 0.022 lt. | 0.503 lt. | 0.155 lt. | 10642710 u. | 7814994 u. |
| | 161222 u. | 25451 u. | 4748524 u. | 11736440 u. | | |
| **South America** | | | | | | |
| Argentina | | No Report | No Report | No Report | No Report | 430 u. [ICPO] |
| Brazil | No Report | No Report | 59612 u. [ICPO] | 36796 u. [(1] | 1909 u. [Govt] | 15804 u. [F.O] |
| Chile | No Report | 2.977 kg | No Report | 140 u. [ICPO] | 2626 u. | 583 u. |
| Colombia | No Report | No Report | 1022 u. | 83.000 kg | No Report | 175382 u. |
| Ecuador | No Report | No Report | No Report | No Report | 7 u. | 185.000 kg [HONLC] |
| Guyana | No Report | No Report | 626 u. [F.O] | 124 u. [F.O] | No Report | No Report |
| Peru | No Report | No Report | No Report | No Report | 35 u. | 78 u. |
| Suriname | No Report | 6000 u. | No Report | 61232 u. [INCSR] | No Report | 80 u. |
| Uruguay | No Report | No Report | 84 u. | 738 u. | No Report | 31 u. |
| Venezuela | No Report | No Report | No Report | 7985 u. [CICAD] | 2 u. | 16010 u. |
| Sub-Total | | 2.977 kg | 61344 u. | 83.000 kg | 4579 u. | 185.000 kg |
| | | 6000 u. | | 107015 u. | | 208398 u. |
| Total region | 703.671 kg | 159.996 kg | 722.382 kg | 958.280 kg | 561.049 kg | 502.714 kg |
| | 59.968 lt. | 0.022 lt. | 0.503 lt. | 0.155 lt. | 10788490 u. | 8217703 u. |
| | 161222 u. | 31451 u. | 4810770 u. | 12081820 u. | | |
| **ASIA** | | | | | | |
| **Central Asia and Transcaucasian countries** | | | | | | |
| Kazakhstan | No Report | No Report | 1099.000 kg | No Report | No Report | No Report |
| Sub-Total | | | 1099.000 kg | | | |
| **East and South-East Asia** | | | | | | |
| Brunei Darussalam | No Report | No Report | 32 u. | No Report | No Report | 10 u. |
| China | No Report | No Report | No Report | 200.000 kg [HNLP] | 2700000 u. | 3000000 u. [ICPO] |
| | | | | 240000 u. | | |
| Hong Kong SAR, China | 49613 u. | 265 u. [Govt.] | 21202 u. [ICPO] | 58.800 kg | 0.032 kg | 89.953 kg |
| | | | | 378621 u. | 170243 u. | 49374 u. |
| Indonesia | 5.197 kg | 119655 u. | 32361 u. | 383174 u. | No Report | 84224 u. |
| | 89413 u. | | | | | |
| Japan | 56 u. | 16 u. [(2] | 5273 u. | 0.016 kg | 0.121 kg | 2.600 kg |
| | | | | 78471 u. | 112542 u. | 156076 u. |

Source: Annual Report Questionnaire if not otherwise indicated

## SEIZURES, 1997 - 2002

### Hallucinogens (excluding LSD but incl. "Ecstasy")

| Region/country or territory | 1997 | 1998 | 1999 | 2000 | 2001 | 2002 |
|---|---|---|---|---|---|---|
| **ASIA** | | | | | | |
| **East and South-East Asia** | | | | | | |
| Korea (Republic of) | No Report | No Report | No Report | No Report | 1672 u. | 39011 u. [ICPO] |
| *Macau SAR, China* | No Report | 64 u. [ICPO] | No Report | 2453 u. [ICPO] | 1687 u. | 672 u. |
| Malaysia | 1397979 u. | 1733335 u. | 55975 u. | 49901 u. [ICPO] | No Report | 164884 u. [ICPO] |
| Philippines | No Report | No Report | No Report | 1026 u. | No Report | 246 u. |
| Singapore | No Report | 2175 u. | 5.170 kg 17232 u. | 2.566 kg 10339 u. | 0.257 kg 23846 u. | 7331 u. |
| Thailand | 13.005 kg 80047 u. | 10395 u. [Govt.] | 264.130 kg [ICPO (3] 30615 u. | 52.601 kg [ICPO] 72182 u. | 61922 u. [F.O] | 145873 u. [F.O] |
| Sub-Total | 18.202 kg 1617108 u. | 1865905 u. | 269.300 kg 162690 u. | 313.983 kg 1216167 u. | 0.410 kg 3071912 u. | 92.553 kg 3647701 u. |
| **Near and Middle East /South-West Asia** | | | | | | |
| Israel | No Report | 5.000 kg 118501 u. | 130.687 kg [ICPO] 30335 u. | 270000 u. | 1.504 kg 121695 u. | 4.454 kg 951057 u. |
| Jordan | 10178 u. | No Report | 5000 u. [ICPO] | No Report | No Report | No Report |
| Syrian Arab Republic | No Report | No Report | No Report | No Report | No Report | 19604 u. |
| Sub-Total | 10178 u. | 5.000 kg 118501 u. | 130.687 kg 35335 u. | 270000 u. | 1.504 kg 121695 u. | 4.454 kg 970661 u. |
| Total region | 18.202 kg 1627286 u. | 5.000 kg 1984406 u. | 1498.987 kg 198025 u. | 313.983 kg 1486167 u. | 1.914 kg 3193607 u. | 97.007 kg 4618362 u. |
| **EUROPE** | | | | | | |
| **Eastern Europe** | | | | | | |
| Belarus | No Report | No Report | No Report | No Report | No Report | 1.072 kg |
| Bosnia Herzegovina | No Report | 1041 u. [ICPO] | No Report | No Report | No Report | 1212 u. [ICPO] |
| Bulgaria | No Report | No Report | No Report | 4524 u. [Govt] | 7.900 kg 2361 u. | 1.500 kg 3135 u. |
| Croatia | 0.004 kg | No Report | 0.018 kg [ICPO] 15421 u. | 9979 u. | 12906 u. | 110632 u. |
| Czech Republic | 0.001 kg 4 u. | No Report | No Report | 17502 u. | 29.890 kg | 1.893 kg 88391 u. |
| Estonia | No Report | No Report | 0.000 lt. 1773 u. | 0.431 kg 1351 u. | 1.714 kg | 3.402 kg |
| FYR of Macedonia | 184 u. [NAPOL] | 1574 u. | 5532 u. [NAPOL] | 280 u. [NAPOL] | 45 u. [Govt] | 0.002 kg 18341 u. |
| Hungary | No Report | 11857 u. | 510 u. | 13616 u. | 0.260 kg 18301 u. | 6.132 kg 23730 u. |
| Latvia | 0.007 kg 23 u. | No Report | 0.749 kg [ICPO] 9625 u. | No Report | 1620 u. | No Report |
| Lithuania | 0.002 kg 1641 u. | 831 u. | 1122 u. [ICPO] | 50724 u. [ICPO] | 0.045 kg 514 u. | 0.845 kg 1205 u. |
| Poland | No Report | 1736 u. | 6319 u. | 129513 u. | 232735 u. | 3.727 kg 38179 u. |

Source: Annual Report Questionnaire if not otherwise indicated

## SEIZURES, 1997 - 2002

### Hallucinogens (excluding LSD but incl. "Ecstasy")

| Region/country or territory | 1997 | 1998 | 1999 | 2000 | 2001 | 2002 |
|---|---|---|---|---|---|---|
| **EUROPE** | | | | | | |
| **Eastern Europe** | | | | | | |
| Romania | No Report | 1093 u. | No Report | 10945 u. [ICPO] | 67210 u. | 0.017 kg |
| | | | | | | 19567 u. |
| Russian Federation | No Report | No Report | 0.153 kg | No Report | 0.850 kg | No Report |
| Serbia and Montenegro | No Report | No Report | No Report | No Report | 0.079 kg | 10000 u. |
| | | | | | 10811 u. | |
| Slovakia | No Report | No Report | 9 u. | 493 u. [ICPO] | 0.568 kg | 435 u. |
| Slovenia | 7440 u. | No Report | 1749 u. [ICPO] | 0.053 kg | 1852 u. | 7877 u. |
| | | | | 27974 u. | | |
| Ukraine | No Report | No Report | 1.349 kg [ICPO] | 0.305 kg [ICPO] | 47 u. | No Report |
| | | | 18888 u. | 4784 u. | | |
| Sub-Total | 0.014 kg | 18132 u. | 2.269 kg | 0.789 kg | 41.306 kg | 18.590 kg |
| | 9292 u. | | 0.000 lt. | 271685 u. | 348402 u. | 322704 u. |
| | | | 60948 u. | | | |
| **Western Europe** | | | | | | |
| Andorra | No Report | 88 u. [ICPO] | 0.002 kg | 0.002 kg [ICPO] | 105 u. | 42 u. [ICPO] |
| | | | 43 u. | 283 u. | | |
| Austria | 23522 u. | 114677 u. | 31129 u. | 162.093 kg | 256299 u. | 0.099 kg |
| | | | | | | 383451 u. |
| Belgium | 132.000 kg | 33.044 kg | 279.620 kg | 68.000 kg [ICPO] | 68.000 kg [UNODC (4] | 1564.000 kg |
| | 125718 u. | | 467506 u. | 818515 u. | 818515 u. | |
| Cyprus | 3 u. | 20 u. | 0.001 kg | 0.005 kg | 0.004 kg | 0.273 kg |
| | | | 62 u. | 3317 u. | 2910 u. | 10253 u. |
| Denmark | 0.102 kg | 27038 u. [(2] | 26117 u. | 0.279 kg | 150080 u. | 25738 u. |
| | 5802 u. | | | 21638 u. | | |
| Finland | 0.195 kg | 0.130 kg | 16578 u. [ICPO] | 87393 u. | 81228 u. | 45065 u. |
| | 3147 u. | 2396 u. | | | | |
| France | 1.607 kg | 4.795 kg | 14.000 kg | 13.314 kg | 7.584 kg | 2161199 u. |
| | | | 1860402 u. | 2283620 u. | 1503773 u. | |
| Germany | 694281 u. | 419329 u. | 1470507 u. [Govt] | 35.500 kg | 21.897 kg | 33.603 kg |
| | | | | 1634683 u. | 4576504 u. | 3207099 u. |
| Greece | 0.010 kg | 85 u. | 3095 u. | 53557 u. | 58845 u. | 28430 u. |
| | 136 u. | | | | | |
| Iceland | No Report | No Report | 7478 u. | 22057 u. | 93151 u. | 0.006 kg |
| | | | | | | 814 u. |
| Ireland | 9 u. | 1.087 kg | 74.609 kg | 695133 u. [ICPO] | 469862 u. | 0.153 kg |
| | | 616439 u. | 266462 u. | | | 117046 u. |
| Italy | 0.034 kg | 1.580 kg | 0.673 kg [ICPO] | 0.492 kg | 0.285 kg | 0.006 kg |
| | 161044 u. | 15 u. | 272397 u. | 502070 u. | 308845 u. | 397566 u. |
| Liechtenstein | 565 u. | 0.500 kg | No Report | 10 u. | No Report | 0.001 kg |
| Luxembourg | 367 u. | No Report | 0.167 kg | 0.122 kg [ICPO] | No Report | 1139 u. [ICPO] |
| | | | 357 u. | 318 u. | | |
| Malta | 247 u. | 153 u. | 459 u. | 5191 u. | 2242 u. | 1012 u. [ICPO] |

Source: Annual Report Questionnaire if not otherwise indicated

## SEIZURES, 1997 - 2002

### Hallucinogens (excluding LSD but incl. "Ecstasy")

| Region/country or territory | 1997 | 1998 | 1999 | 2000 | 2001 | 2002 |
|---|---|---|---|---|---|---|
| **EUROPE** | | | | | | |
| **Western Europe** | | | | | | |
| Monaco | No Report | No Report | 3 u. [ICPO] | 5 u. [ICPO] | No Report | 55 u. |
| Netherlands | 703.289 kg [Govt] 870980 u. | 1163514 u. [Govt] | 3663608 u. [Govt] | 632.000 kg [Govt] 5500000 u. | 113.000 kg 8684505 u. | 849.000 kg 6787167 u. |
| Norway | 13182 u. | 1.081 kg 15647 u. | 0.025 kg 24644 u. | 0.114 kg 49390 u. | 0.492 kg 61205 u. | 0.916 kg 102439 u. |
| Portugal | No Report | 10 u. | 0.089 kg 31319 u. | 1.089 kg 25499 u. | 0.091 kg 126451 u. | 2.240 kg 222479 u. |
| Spain | 184950 u. | 194527 u. | 357649 u. | 914974 u. [ICPO] | 860164 u. | 1396142 u. |
| Sweden | 0.135 kg 1540 u. | 0.579 kg | 0.504 kg | 0.591 kg [ICPO] 184161 u. | 0.887 kg 57750 u. | 96577 u. |
| Switzerland | 86676 u. | 73914 u. | 67353 u. | 189569 u. [5] | 86959 u. | 88342 u. |
| Turkey | No Report | 477250 u. | No Report | 33894 u. [Govt.] | 121508 u. | 98989 u. |
| United Kingdom | 1925500 u. | 2095879 u. [6] | 6323500 u. [NCIS] | 6534813 u. | 3.399 kg 7662228 u. | 3.399 kg [7] 7662228 u. |
| Sub-Total | 837.372 kg 4097669 u. | 42.796 kg 5200981 u. | 369.690 kg 14890670 u. | 913.601 kg 19560090 u. | 215.639 kg 25983130 u. | 2453.696 kg 22833270 u. |
| Total region | 837.386 kg 4106961 u. | 42.796 kg 5219113 u. | 371.959 kg 0.000 lt. 14951620 u. | 914.390 kg 19831780 u. | 256.945 kg 26331530 u. | 2472.286 kg 23155980 u. |
| **OCEANIA** | | | | | | |
| **Oceania** | | | | | | |
| Australia | 1.394 kg | 7.380 kg [Govt. (8] | 57.645 kg [9] | 0.773 kg | 343.030 kg [10] | 727.171 kg |
| New Zealand | No Report | 2665 u. | No Report | 0.530 kg [11] 8858 u. | 0.483 kg 3.000 lt. 84744 u. | 1.192 kg 256437 u. |
| Sub-Total | 1.394 kg | 7.380 kg 2665 u. | 57.645 kg | 1.303 kg 8858 u. | 343.513 kg 3.000 lt. 84744 u. | 728.363 kg 256437 u. |
| Total region | 1.394 kg | 7.380 kg 2665 u. | 57.645 kg | 1.303 kg 8858 u. | 343.513 kg 3.000 lt. 84744 u. | 728.363 kg 256437 u. |
| TOTAL | 1560.653 kg 59.968 lt. 6133037 u. | 215.172 kg 0.022 lt. 7461101 u. | 2651.003 kg 0.503 lt. 20021730 u. | 2268.774 kg 0.155 lt. 34248070 u. | 1163.443 kg 3.000 lt. 40872410 u. | 3833.247 kg 4.000 lt. 37293090 u. |

1) éxtasis 2) Small quantity. 3) Ketamine 4) Due to unavailability of 2001 data, year 2000 data were used for analysis purposes. 5) Includes ecstasy 6) Including other opiates. 7) Due to unavailability of 2002 data, year 2001 data were used for analysis purposes. 8) Provisional figures. 9) Mushrooms 10) Including LSD and excluding ecstasy 11) Psilocybine

Source: Annual Report Questionnaire if not otherwise indicated

## SEIZURES, 1997 - 2002
## LSD

| Region/country or territory | 1997 | 1998 | 1999 | 2000 | 2001 | 2002 |
|---|---|---|---|---|---|---|
| **AFRICA** | | | | | | |
| **North Africa** | | | | | | |
| Egypt | 15 u. | 514 u. | No Report | 300 u. | No Report | No Report |
| Sub-Total | 15 u. | 514 u. | | 300 u. | | |
| **Southern Africa** | | | | | | |
| Namibia | No Report | No Report | No Report | 127 u. [ICPO] | No Report | 3 u. |
| South Africa | 2730 u. | 6426 u. | 1549 u. [ICPO] | 5506 u. | 7841 u. | 1782 u. |
| Zambia | 0.080 kg [Govt] | 0.000 kg [Govt] | 0.000 kg [Govt] | 0.000 kg [Govt] | 0.000 kg [Govt] | No Report |
| Zimbabwe | No Report | No Report | 30 u. | No Report | No Report | No Report |
| Sub-Total | 0.080 kg 2730 u. | 6426 u. | 1579 u. | 5633 u. | 7841 u. | 1785 u. |
| Total region | 0.080 kg 2745 u. | 6940 u. | 1579 u. | 5933 u. | 7841 u. | 1785 u. |
| **AMERICAS** | | | | | | |
| **Caribbean** | | | | | | |
| *Bermuda* | 18 u. | No Report | No Report | No Report | No Report | No Report |
| Sub-Total | 18 u. | | | | | |
| **Central America** | | | | | | |
| Costa Rica | No Report | No Report | No Report | 1045 u. | 277 u. | No Report |
| Sub-Total | | | | 1045 u. | 277 u. | |
| **North America** | | | | | | |
| Canada | 22519 u. | 0.295 kg 8955 u. | 0.098 kg 9852 u. | 0.149 kg 5.000 lt. 1592 u. | 0.401 kg 2747 u. | 0.027 kg 2135 u. |
| Mexico | No Report | No Report | No Report | No Report | 8 u. | No Report |
| United States | 1.488 kg 0.452 lt. 79073 u. | No Report | 0.330 kg 165504 u. | 0.004 kg 1.296 lt. 28459 u. | 97057 u. | 1624 u. |
| Sub-Total | 1.488 kg 0.452 lt. 101592 u. | 0.295 kg 8955 u. | 0.428 kg 175356 u. | 0.153 kg 6.296 lt. 30051 u. | 0.401 kg 99812 u. | 0.027 kg 3759 u. |
| **South America** | | | | | | |
| Argentina | 563 u. | 1435 u. | 1085 u. | 1093 u. | 1239 u. | 468 u. |
| Brazil | 3 u. | No Report | 16 u. [Govt.] | 2368 u. | No Report | 231 u. [F.O] |
| Chile | 1764 u. | 153 u. | 11 u. [CICAD] | 33 u. | 2 u. | 30 u. |
| Uruguay | 72 u. | 1 u. | 4 u. | 143 u. | No Report | 11 u. |
| Venezuela | No Report | No Report | No Report | 1675 u. | No Report | No Report |
| Sub-Total | 2402 u. | 1589 u. | 1116 u. | 5312 u. | 1241 u. | 740 u. |
| Total region | 1.488 kg 0.452 lt. 104012 u. | 0.295 kg 10544 u. | 0.428 kg 176472 u. | 0.153 kg 6.296 lt. 36408 u. | 0.401 kg 101330 u. | 0.027 kg 4499 u. |

Source: Annual Report Questionnaire if not otherwise indicated

## SEIZURES, 1997 - 2002
### LSD

| Region/country or territory | 1997 | 1998 | 1999 | 2000 | 2001 | 2002 |
|---|---|---|---|---|---|---|
| **ASIA** | | | | | | |
| **Central Asia and Transcaucasian countries** | | | | | | |
| Uzbekistan | No Report | 40 u. | No Report | No Report | No Report | No Report |
| Sub-Total | | 40 u. | | | | |
| **East and South-East Asia** | | | | | | |
| *Hong Kong SAR, China* | 52 u. | No Report | 21 u. | 27877 u. | 6858 u. | 16 u. |
| Indonesia | No Report | 103368 u. | 53160 u. | No Report | No Report | No Report |
| Japan | 3471 u. | 4802 u. | 62618 u. | 65043 u. | 644 u. | 3973 u. |
| *Macau SAR, China* | No Report | No Report | No Report | No Report | 8 u. | No Report |
| Singapore | No Report | No Report | No Report | No Report | 807 u. | No Report |
| Thailand | 0.031 kg | No Report | No Report | No Report [ICPO] | No Report | No Report |
| Sub-Total | 0.031 kg 3523 u. | 108170 u. | 115799 u. | 92920 u. | 8317 u. | 3989 u. |
| **Near and Middle East /South-West Asia** | | | | | | |
| Israel | 0.040 lt. 7342 u. | 10337 u. | 7346 u. [ICPO] | 7769 u. | 0.003 kg 6266 u. | 0.001 kg 2491 u. |
| Kuwait | 13245 u. | No Report | No Report | No Report | No Report | No Report |
| Sub-Total | 0.040 lt. 20587 u. | 10337 u. | 7346 u. | 7769 u. | 0.003 kg 6266 u. | 0.001 kg 2491 u. |
| **South Asia** | | | | | | |
| India | No Report | 45 u. | 20 u. | No Report | No Report | No Report |
| Nepal | No Report | 9 u. | No Report | No Report | No Report | No Report |
| Sub-Total | | 54 u. | 20 u. | | | |
| Total region | 0.031 kg 0.040 lt. 24110 u. | 118601 u. | 123165 u. | 100689 u. | 0.003 kg 14583 u. | 0.001 kg 6480 u. |
| **EUROPE** | | | | | | |
| **Eastern Europe** | | | | | | |
| Croatia | 114 u. | 86 u. | 247 u. | 231 u. | 154 u. | 192 u. |
| Czech Republic | No Report | No Report | 19 u. | 1001 u. | 5 u. | 107 u. |
| Estonia | No Report | No Report | 6 u. | 0.022 kg 3 u. | 0.002 kg | 0.020 kg |
| Hungary | 1450 u. [Govt.] | 3351 u. | 1928 u. | 1242 u. | 973 u. | 969 u. |
| Latvia | 205 u. | 38 u. | 27 u. | 14 u. | 16 u. | No Report |
| Lithuania | 2 u. | 342 u. | 164 u. | 26 u. | 275 u. | No Report |
| Poland | 542 u. | 14902 u. | 14099 u. | 3659 u. | 672 u. | 797 u. |
| Romania | No Report | No Report | 1 u. | 1 u. [ICPO] | No Report | 22004 u. |
| Russian Federation | No Report | No Report | No Report | 0.380 kg [ICPO] | 1.676 kg | 2.813 kg [ICPO] |
| Serbia and Montenegro | No Report | No Report | No Report | No Report | 5 u. | No Report |
| Slovakia | 2 u. | 63 u. | 72 u. | 110 u. | 60 u. | 8 u. |

Source: Annual Report Questionnaire if not otherwise indicated

## SEIZURES, 1997 - 2002
### LSD

| Region/country or territory | 1997 | 1998 | 1999 | 2000 | 2001 | 2002 |
|---|---|---|---|---|---|---|
| **EUROPE** | | | | | | |
| **Eastern Europe** | | | | | | |
| Slovenia | 156 u. | 53 u. | 512 u. | 59 u. | No Report | No Report |
| Ukraine | 14 u. | 500 u. | 36 u. [ICPO] | No Report | No Report | 477 u. [ICPO] |
| Sub-Total | 2485 u. | 19335 u. | 17111 u. | 0.402 kg 6346 u. | 1.678 kg 2160 u. | 2.833 kg 24554 u. |
| **Western Europe** | | | | | | |
| Andorra | No Report | 28 u. [ICPO] | No Report | 47 u. [ICPO] | 9 u. | 2 u. |
| Austria | 5243 u. | 2494 u. | 2811 u. | 0.865 kg | 572 u. | 851 u. |
| Belgium | 621 u. | 2050 u. | 1047 u. | 1090 u. [ICPO] | No Report | |
| Cyprus | No Report | No Report | 2 u. | 11 u. | No Report | No Report |
| Denmark | 381 u. | 108 u. | 83 u. | 1109 u. | 156 u. | 38 u. |
| Finland | 323 u. | 301 u. | 50 u. | 2355 u. | 1026 u. | 4679 u. |
| France | 5983 u. | 18680 u. | 9991 u. | 20691 u. | 6718 u. | No Report |
| Germany | 78430 u. | 32250 u. | 22965 u. | 43924 u. | 11441 u. | 30144 u. |
| Greece | 166 u. | 44 u. | 212 u. [ICPO] | 112 u. | 577 u. | 884 u. |
| Iceland | No Report | No Report | 339 u. | 15 u. | No Report | No Report |
| Ireland | 1851 u. | 792 u. | 648 u. | No Report | 325 u. | No Report |
| Italy | 8140 u. | 0.003 kg 9752 u. | 5509 u. [ICPO] | 1980 u. | 1139 u. | 3064 u. |
| Liechtenstein | No Report | No Report | No Report | No Report | 1 u. | No Report |
| Luxembourg | 4 u. | 0.303 kg | 1 u. | 21 u. [ICPO] | No Report | 0.002 kg [ICPO] |
| Malta | 19 u. | 123 u. | 54 u. | 462 u. | No Report | No Report |
| Monaco | No Report | 10 u. | No Report | No Report | No Report | No Report |
| Netherlands | 27634 u. [Govt] | 37790 u. [Govt] | 2667 u. [Govt] | 9972 u. [Govt] | 28731 u. | 355 u. |
| Norway | 6888 u. | 2833 u. | 483 u. | 893 u. | 417 u. | 172 u. |
| Portugal | 84 u. | 261 u. | 1845 u. | 6106 u. | 3588 u. | 9785 u. |
| Spain | 25368 u. | 9068 u. | 3353 u. | 7542 u. | 26535 u. | 893 u. |
| Sweden | 1541 u. | 0.002 kg 2704 u. | 1508 u. | 0.000 kg [(1] 278 u. | 635 u. | 305 u. |
| Switzerland | 9424 u. | 2995 u. | 3130 u. | 15525 u. | 8707 u. | 1552 u. |
| Turkey | No Report | No Report | 61 u. | No Report | 105 u. | No Report |
| United Kingdom | 164100 u. | 40070 u. | 67400 u. [NCIS] | 25392 u. | 9439 u. | 9439 u. [(2] |
| Sub-Total | 336200 u. | 0.308 kg 162353 u. | 124159 u. | 0.865 kg 137525 u. | 100121 u. | 0.002 kg 62163 u. |
| Total region | 338685 u. | 0.308 kg 181688 u. | 141270 u. | 1.267 kg 143871 u. | 1.678 kg 102281 u. | 2.835 kg 86717 u. |
| **OCEANIA** | | | | | | |
| **Oceania** | | | | | | |
| Australia | | No Report | 0.108 kg | 0.007 kg | No Report | No Report |

Source: Annual Report Questionnaire if not otherwise indicated

## SEIZURES, 1997 - 2002
### LSD

| Region/country or territory | 1997 | 1998 | 1999 | 2000 | 2001 | 2002 |
|---|---|---|---|---|---|---|
| **OCEANIA** | | | | | | |
| **Oceania** | | | | | | |
| New Zealand | No Report | 37554 u. | 17437 u. | 17522 u. | 1057 u. | 0.013 kg<br>431 u. |
| Sub-Total | | 37554 u. | 0.108 kg<br>17437 u. | 0.007 kg<br>17522 u. | 1057 u. | 0.013 kg<br>431 u. |
| Total region | | 37554 u. | 0.108 kg<br>17437 u. | 0.007 kg<br>17522 u. | 1057 u. | 0.013 kg<br>431 u. |
| TOTAL | 1.599 kg<br>0.492 lt.<br>469552 u. | 0.603 kg<br>355327 u. | 0.536 kg<br>459923 u. | 1.427 kg<br>6.296 lt.<br>304423 u. | 2.082 kg<br>227092 u. | 2.876 kg<br>99912 u. |

1) 2 micrograms 2) Due to unavailability of 2002 data, year 2001 data were used for analysis purposes.

Source: Annual Report Questionnaire if not otherwise indicated

## SEIZURES, 1997 - 2002
### Methaqualone

| Region/country or territory | 1997 | 1998 | 1999 | 2000 | 2001 | 2002 |
|---|---|---|---|---|---|---|
| **AFRICA** | | | | | | |
| **East Africa** | | | | | | |
| Kenya | 5000 u. | No Report | No Report | No Report | 52693 u. [Govt] | No Report |
| United Republic of Tanzania | 57 u. | 4 u. | 7 u. | 295.000 kg [ICPO] | 2.107 kg [Govt] | 1.500 kg [ICPO] |
| Sub-Total | 5057 u. | 4 u. | 7 u. | 295.000 kg | 2.107 kg 52693 u. | 1.500 kg |
| **Southern Africa** | | | | | | |
| Angola | No Report | 1.050 kg [ICPO] | No Report | No Report | No Report | No Report |
| Lesotho | No Report | No Report | No Report | No Report | No Report | 0.652 kg [ICPO] |
| Malawi | 185.652 kg 200307 u. | 1007 u. [Govt.] | 1800 u. | No Report | No Report | 1 u. |
| Mozambique | No Report | No Report | No Report | 2200 u. [ICPO] | No Report | No Report |
| Namibia | No Report | 6318 u. | 2611 u. | 10430 u. [ICPO] | 16675 u. | 9801 u. |
| South Africa | 50.561 kg 1629531 u. | 160.000 kg 1307109 u. | 2498806 u. [ICPO] | 114.507 kg 2669813 u. | 7297.837 kg 4202835 u. | 254.080 kg 2930316 u. |
| Swaziland | 15245 u. [ICPO] | 12015 u. | 1621 u. | 6 u. [ICPO] | 258 u. | 4909 u. |
| Zambia | 0.004 kg [Govt] | 0.125 kg [Govt] | 2368 u. | 0.125 kg 724 u. | 0.020 kg [Govt] | 0.039 kg |
| Zimbabwe | No Report | 4.300 kg 4431 u. | 1701 u. | 1500 u. | No Report | No Report |
| Sub-Total | 236.217 kg 1845083 u. | 165.475 kg 1330880 u. | 2508907 u. | 114.632 kg 2684673 u. | 7297.857 kg 4219768 u. | 254.770 kg 2945027 u. |
| Total region | 236.217 kg 1850140 u. | 165.475 kg 1330884 u. | 2508914 u. | 409.632 kg 2684673 u. | 7299.964 kg 4272461 u. | 256.271 kg 2945027 u. |
| **AMERICAS** | | | | | | |
| **North America** | | | | | | |
| Canada | | 0.007 kg | 56.000 kg 123 u. | 0.139 kg 46 u. | 0.002 kg | No Report |
| United States | 1330 u. | No Report | 32030 u. | 0.002 kg 76 u. | 107 u. | 40731 u. |
| Sub-Total | 1330 u. | 0.007 kg | 56.000 kg 32153 u. | 0.141 kg 122 u. | 0.002 kg 107 u. | 40731 u. |
| **South America** | | | | | | |
| Chile | No Report | 1390 u. | No Report | No Report | No Report | No Report |
| Sub-Total | | 1390 u. | | | | |
| Total region | 1330 u. | 0.007 kg 1390 u. | 56.000 kg 32153 u. | 0.141 kg 122 u. | 0.002 kg 107 u. | 40731 u. |
| **ASIA** | | | | | | |
| **East and South-East Asia** | | | | | | |
| China | No Report | No Report | No Report | No Report | No Report | 2955.000 kg |

Source: Annual Report Questionnaire if not otherwise indicated

## SEIZURES, 1997 - 2002
### Methaqualone

| Region/country or territory | 1997 | 1998 | 1999 | 2000 | 2001 | 2002 |
|---|---|---|---|---|---|---|
| **ASIA** | | | | | | |
| **East and South-East Asia** | | | | | | |
| *Hong Kong SAR, China* | 4 u. | No Report | 187 u. [ICPO] | 25.000 kg | 0.001 kg | 0.002 kg |
| | | | | | 1 u. | 4 u. |
| Indonesia | No Report | No Report | 2018 u. | No Report | No Report | No Report |
| Sub-Total | 4 u. | | 2205 u. | 25.000 kg | 0.001 kg | 2955.002 kg |
| | | | | | 1 u. | 4 u. |
| **Near and Middle East /South-West Asia** | | | | | | |
| United Arab Emirates | 6000.815 kg | No Report | No Report | No Report | No Report | No Report |
| Sub-Total | 6000.815 kg | | | | | |
| **South Asia** | | | | | | |
| India | 1740.000 kg | 2257.000 kg | 474.000 kg | 1095.000 kg | 2024.000 kg | 7458.000 kg [Govt] |
| Sub-Total | 1740.000 kg | 2257.000 kg | 474.000 kg | 1095.000 kg | 2024.000 kg | 7458.000 kg |
| Total region | 7740.815 kg | 2257.000 kg | 474.000 kg | 1120.000 kg | 2024.001 kg | 10413.000 kg |
| | 4 u. | | 2205 u. | | 1 u. | 4 u. |
| **EUROPE** | | | | | | |
| **Eastern Europe** | | | | | | |
| FYR of Macedonia | No Report | No Report | No Report | No Report | No Report | 3 u. |
| Romania | No Report | 1924 u. | 8487 u. [ICPO] | 3981 u. [ICPO] | 3 u. | No Report |
| Sub-Total | | 1924 u. | 8487 u. | 3981 u. | 3 u. | 3 u. |
| **Western Europe** | | | | | | |
| Belgium | No Report | 11.000 kg | No Report | No Report | No Report | No Report |
| | | 52 u. | | | | |
| Greece | 41 u. | No Report | No Report | No Report | No Report | No Report |
| Switzerland | No Report | 4620 u. | No Report | No Report | No Report | No Report |
| United Kingdom | | | No Report | No Report | No Report | No Report |
| Sub-Total | 41 u. | 11.000 kg | | | | |
| | | 4672 u. | | | | |
| Total region | 41 u. | 11.000 kg | 8487 u. | 3981 u. | 3 u. | 3 u. |
| | | 6596 u. | | | | |
| TOTAL | 7977.032 kg | 2433.482 kg | 530.000 kg | 1529.773 kg | 9323.966 kg | 10669.270 kg |
| | 1851515 u. | 1338870 u. | 2551759 u. | 2688776 u. | 4272572 u. | 2985765 u. |

Source: Annual Report Questionnaire if not otherwise indicated

## SEIZURES, 1997 - 2002
### Psychotropic substances

| Region/country or territory | 1997 | 1998 | 1999 | 2000 | 2001 | 2002 |
|---|---|---|---|---|---|---|
| **AFRICA** | | | | | | |
| **East Africa** | | | | | | |
| Kenya | No Report | 9060 u.[Govt] | No Report | 272 u.[Govt] | No Report | No Report |
| Mauritius | No Report | No Report | No Report | No Report | 897 u. | No Report |
| Sub-Total | | 9060 u. | | 272 u. | 897 u. | |
| **North Africa** | | | | | | |
| Libyan Arab Jam. | 33770 u.[F.O] | No Report | 127512 u.[F.O] | 245455 u.[F.O] | 87047 u.[F.O] | No Report |
| Morocco | No Report | No Report | No Report | No Report | 135769 u. | No Report |
| Sub-Total | 33770 u. | | 127512 u. | 245455 u. | 222816 u. | |
| **West and Central Africa** | | | | | | |
| Mauritania | 147 u.[Govt] | 135 u.[Govt] | No Report | No Report | No Report | No Report |
| Sub-Total | 147 u. | 135 u. | | | | |
| Total region | 33917 u. | 9195 u. | 127512 u. | 245727 u. | 223713 u. | |
| **AMERICAS** | | | | | | |
| **Caribbean** | | | | | | |
| Dominican Republic | No Report | No Report | No Report | No Report | No Report | 99 u.[HONLC] |
| Sub-Total | | | | | | 99 u. |
| **North America** | | | | | | |
| Mexico | No Report | 1484078 u. | 1490152 u. | 3418369 u. | 8313151 u.[Govt] | No Report |
| Sub-Total | | 1484078 u. | 1490152 u. | 3418369 u. | 8313151 u. | |
| **South America** | | | | | | |
| Brazil | No Report | No Report | No Report | 4862 u.[Govt] | No Report | 39398 u.[F.O] |
| Sub-Total | | | | 4862 u. | | 39398 u. |
| Total region | | 1484078 u. | 1490152 u. | 3423231 u. | 8313151 u. | 39497 u. |
| **ASIA** | | | | | | |
| **Central Asia and Transcaucasian countries** | | | | | | |
| Uzbekistan | No Report | No Report | 0.639 kg | No Report | No Report | No Report |
| Sub-Total | | | 0.639 kg | | | |
| **Near and Middle East /South-West Asia** | | | | | | |
| United Arab Emirates | No Report | No Report | 14460 u. | 23246 u. | No Report | No Report |
| Sub-Total | | | 14460 u. | 23246 u. | | |
| Total region | | | 0.639 kg 14460 u. | 23246 u. | | |
| **EUROPE** | | | | | | |
| **Eastern Europe** | | | | | | |
| Russian Federation | No Report | 673.400 kg[F.O] | 905.500 kg[F.O] | 835.000 kg[F.O] | No Report | No Report |
| Sub-Total | | 673.400 kg | 905.500 kg | 835.000 kg | | |

Source: Annual Report Questionnaire if not otherwise indicated

## SEIZURES, 1997 - 2002
### Psychotropic substances

| Region/country or territory | 1997 | 1998 | 1999 | 2000 | 2001 | 2002 |
|---|---|---|---|---|---|---|
| **EUROPE** | | | | | | |
| **Western Europe** | | | | | | |
| Spain | No Report | No Report | No Report | No Report | No Report | 118452 u. |
| Sub-Total | | | | | | 118452 u. |
| Total region | | 673.400 kg | 905.500 kg | 835.000 kg | | 118452 u. |
| TOTAL | 33917 u. | 673.400 kg | 906.139 kg | 835.000 kg | 8536864 u. | 157949 u. |
| | | 1493273 u. | 1632124 u. | 3692204 u. | | |

Source: Annual Report Questionnaire if not otherwise indicated

359

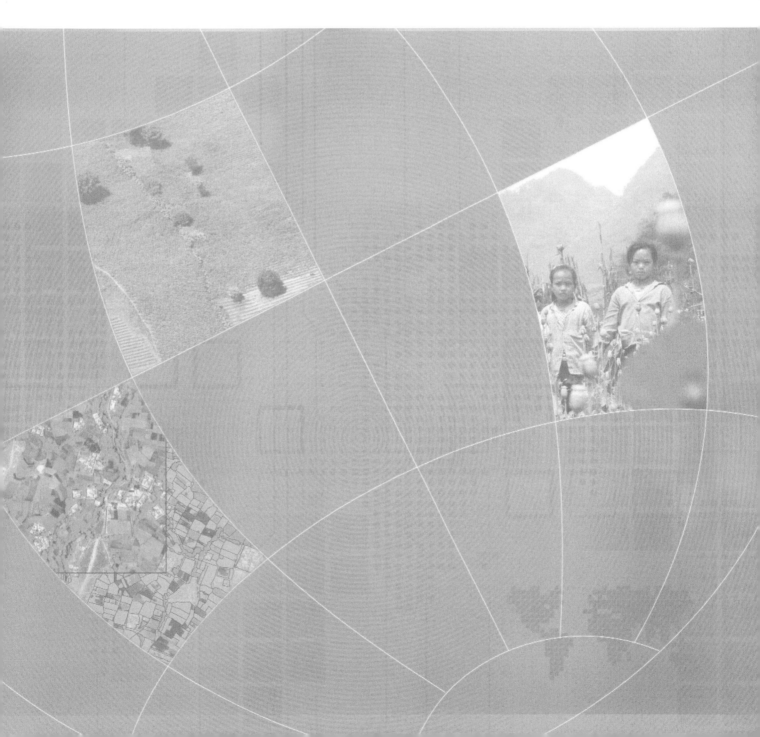

# 5. PRICES

# 5.1. Opiates: Wholesale and Street Prices and Purity Levels

## Prices in Europe and in USA, 1990-2003

### Retail prices (street price), US$/gram

| EUROPE | 1990 | 1991 | 1992 | 1993 | 1994 | 1995 | 1996 | 1997 | 1998 | 1999 | 2000 | 2001 | 2002 | 2003 |
|---|---|---|---|---|---|---|---|---|---|---|---|---|---|---|
| Austria | 270 | 250 | 203 | 132 | 138 | 103 | 87 | 70 | 94 | 57 | 75 | 44 | 92 | 68 |
| Belgium | 90 | 105 | 105 | 77 | 75 | 75 | 56 | 37 | 41 | 41 | 37 | 27 | 29 | 31 |
| Denmark | 287 | 265 | 151 | 139 | 228 | 191 | 157 | 188 | 147 | 175 | 116 | 111 | 126 | 118 |
| Finland | 800 | 696 | 770 | 724 | 606 | 455 | 414 | 257 | 254 | 250 | 207 | 121 | 188 | 197 |
| France | 145 | 153 | 150 | 135 | 144 | 170 | 156 | 113 | 119 | 111 | 32 | 34 | 47 | 57 |
| Germany | 105 | 75 | 96 | 74 | 91 | 90 | 74 | 51 | 43 | 45 | 39 | 38 | 38 | 46 |
| Greece | 120 | 175 | 63 | 44 | 105 | 88 | 77 | 80 | 55 | 55 | 55 | 53 | 45 | 26 |
| Italy | 167 | 148 | 140 | 29 | 55 | 41 | 115 | 98 | 120 | 95 | 71 | 68 | 59 | 70 |
| Luxembourg | 172 | 150 | 150 | 150 | 172 | 202 | 138 | 141 | 133 | 126 | 69 | 67 | 67 | 45 |
| Netherlands | 49 | 50 | 55 | 49 | 55 | 61 | 48 | 55 | 34 | 30 | 25 | 43 | 35 | 41 |
| Norway | 1,680 | 525 | 510 | 275 | 349 | 300 | 282 | 198 | 186 | 166 | 128 | 157 | 165 | 147 |
| Iceland | 184 | 376 | 374 | 407 | 380 | 410 | 377 | 372 | 372 | 372 | 372 | 372 | 372 | 372 |
| Portugal | 83 | 82 | 72 | 63 | 65 | 79 | 68 | 55 | 74 | 37 | 45 | 45 | 41 | 47 |
| Spain | 175 | 185 | 180 | 126 | 132 | 120 | 112 | 88 | 82 | 75 | 59 | 57 | 61 | 75 |
| Sweden | 225 | 210 | 195 | 180 | 165 | 337 | 346 | 135 | 130 | 126 | 113 | 136 | 128 | 120 |
| Switzerland | 312 | 221 | 248 | 126 | 164 | 190 | 116 | 81 | 96 | 167 | 53 | 45 | 39 | 45 |
| United Kingdom | 157 | 144 | 144 | 134 | 129 | 125 | 108 | 118 | 120 | 108 | 107 | 86 | 91 | 97 |
| Ireland | 196 | 180 | 180 | 168 | 161 | 179 | 275 | 228 | 213 | 204 | 176 | 170 | 179 | 216 |
| Average unweighted | 290 | 222 | 210 | 168 | 179 | 179 | 167 | 131 | 128 | 124 | 99 | 93 | 100 | 101 |
| inflation adjustment | 408 | 300 | 276 | 215 | 222 | 216 | 196 | 151 | 145 | 137 | 106 | 97 | 102 | 100 |
| Weighted average | 173 | 149 | 147 | 107 | 118 | 119 | 118 | 93 | 94 | 87 | 64 | 59 | 62 | 69 |
| Adjusted for inflation | 244 | 202 | 192 | 136 | 147 | 144 | 138 | 107 | 106 | 96 | 68 | 61 | 64 | 69 |

Sources: ARQ or EUROPOL, except 2003 EUROPOL, and in italic UNODC

| | 1990 | 1991 | 1992 | 1993 | 1994 | 1995 | 1996 | 1997 | 1998 | 1999 | 2000 | 2001 | 2002 | 2003 |
|---|---|---|---|---|---|---|---|---|---|---|---|---|---|---|
| USA | 281 | 279 | 268 | 268 | 204 | 196 | 170 | 151 | 162 | 137 | 126 | 110 | 88 | 130 |
| Adjusted for inflation | 396 | 377 | 351 | 341 | 253 | 236 | 200 | 173 | 183 | 151 | 135 | 114 | 90 | 130 |

Sources: ONDCP 1990-2000 data, ARQ 2001 - 2002 data. UNODC 2003 estimates based on STRIDE graph

### Wholesale, US$/kg

| EUROPE | 1990 | 1991 | 1992 | 1993 | 1994 | 1995 | 1996 | 1997 | 1998 | 1999 | 2000 | 2001 | 2002 | 2003 |
|---|---|---|---|---|---|---|---|---|---|---|---|---|---|---|
| Austria | 55,244 | 46,145 | 63,000 | 36,000 | 37,752 | 30,491 | 30,222 | 28,831 | 34,565 | 31,087 | 25,026 | 19,553 | 23,547 | 33,962 |
| Belgium | 30,000 | 30,000 | 28,500 | 26,600 | 29,586 | 32,580 | 24,307 | 21,761 | 20,847 | 18,557 | 18,360 | 20,292 | 22,229 | 16,981 |
| Denmark | 110,000 | 100,000 | 85,000 | 95,000 | 117,625 | 106,805 | 86,806 | 100,465 | 65,693 | 61,507 | 23,585 | 32,889 | 20,803 | 24,738 |
| Finland | 353,774 | 353,774 | 353,774 | 353,774 | 353,774 | 353,774 | 321,586 | 199,442 | 197,856 | 194,357 | 161,034 | 44,840 | 51,804 | 51,804 |
| France | 180,000 | 72,250 | 80,000 | 63,750 | 75,000 | 66,035 | 46,603 | 32,230 | 25,885 | 25,596 | 22,158 | 26,906 | 23,547 | 28,302 |
| Germany | 45,244 | 36,145 | 41,667 | 35,206 | 36,448 | 35,256 | 27,890 | 25,686 | 25,608 | 24,770 | 20,263 | 17,816 | 20,325 | 21,838 |
| Greece | 90,000 | 70,000 | 35,000 | 28,000 | 29,536 | 34,362 | 39,090 | 28,775 | 21,020 | 20,714 | 17,320 | 16,592 | 17,425 | 15,283 |
| Italy | 67,500 | 60,000 | 108,000 | 42,581 | 47,690 | 35,786 | 48,152 | 37,795 | 36,459 | 36,894 | 31,163 | 32,979 | 33,669 | 32,150 |
| Luxembourg | 86,000 | 75,000 | 75,000 | 45,000 | 86,000 | 57,079 | 59,852 | 54,786 | 52,630 | 50,368 | 48,000 | 50,369 | 50,369 | 24,700 |
| Netherlands | 23,850 | 25,000 | 26,550 | 23,850 | 23,850 | 24,384 | 20,572 | 13,810 | 14,056 | 16,985 | 14,703 | 15,757 | 29,199 | 17,759 |
| Norway | 220,000 | 200,000 | 212,500 | 151,099 | 101,744 | 85,000 | 72,520 | 62,209 | 64,918 | 49,872 | 44,561 | 35,874 | 37,676 | 48,296 |
| Portugal | 50,000 | 55,000 | 46,667 | 31,500 | 32,428 | 43,171 | 45,902 | 38,841 | 30,483 | 29,339 | 25,398 | 31,310 | 25,839 | 31,057 |
| Spain | 160,000 | 125,000 | 122,500 | 91,000 | 74,418 | 79,880 | 84,395 | 63,880 | 52,755 | 53,820 | 43,596 | 32,000 | 41,202 | 48,504 |
| Sweden | 140,000 | 130,000 | 115,000 | 95,000 | 117,625 | 62,655 | 64,829 | 65,771 | 63,191 | 61,025 | 41,620 | 47,083 | 48,536 | 56,989 |
| Switzerland | 124,000 | 153,800 | 228,875 | 47,460 | 52,823 | 54,850 | 41,665 | 37,234 | 34,294 | 33,422 | 29,568 | 16,082 | 19,149 | 19,149 |
| United Kingdom | 53,940 | 43,940 | 43,500 | 43,210 | 42,500 | 42,004 | 34,846 | 39,491 | 41,667 | 29,126 | 26,718 | 25,926 | 30,620 | 34,003 |
| Ireland | 63,940 | 53,940 | 53,500 | 53,210 | 52,500 | 81,479 | 77,643 | 36,531 | 34,396 | 43,478 | 37,600 | 36,441 | 36,441 | 36,441 |
| Average unweighted | 109,029 | 95,882 | 101,120 | 74,514 | 77,135 | 72,094 | 66,287 | 52,208 | 48,019 | 45,936 | 37,098 | 29,571 | 31,316 | 31,880 |
| inflation adjusted | 153,604 | 129,638 | 132,646 | 94,917 | 95,755 | 87,046 | 77,753 | 59,850 | 54,174 | 50,733 | 39,631 | 30,720 | 32,037 | 31,880 |
| Weighted average | 93,610 | 68,153 | 77,357 | 54,889 | 56,346 | 52,544 | 47,963 | 39,449 | 36,497 | 34,252 | 28,484 | 26,092 | 28,488 | 30,607 |
| inflation adjusted (kg) | 131,882 | 92,146 | 101,474 | 69,918 | 69,948 | 63,442 | 56,260 | 45,223 | 41,175 | 37,829 | 30,428 | 27,106 | 29,143 | 30,607 |
| Inflation adjusted (gram) | 132 | 92 | 101 | 70 | 70 | 63 | 56 | 45 | 41 | 38 | 30 | 27 | 29 | 31 |

Sources: ARQ, expect 2003 EUROPOL and in italic UNODC
Note: Calculation as of 1995 is based on brown heroin price x by 80% plus white heroin x by 20%

| USA | 1,990 | 1,991 | 1,992 | 1,993 | 1,994 | 1,995 | 1,996 | 1,997 | 1,998 | 1,999 | 2,000 | 2,001 | 2,002 | 2,003 |
|---|---|---|---|---|---|---|---|---|---|---|---|---|---|---|
| Average | 162,500 | 155,000 | 150,000 | 146,000 | 142,500 | 146,000 | 141,875 | 129,375 | 125,000 | 107,000 | 81,200 | 59,500 | 50,750 | 80,000 |
| Inflation adjusted (kg) | 228,937 | 209,568 | 196,765 | 185,977 | 176,899 | 176,281 | 166,416 | 148,313 | 141,021 | 118,174 | 86,743 | 61,811 | 51,917 | 80,000 |
| Inflation adjusted (gram) | 229 | 210 | 197 | 186 | 177 | 176 | 166 | 148 | 141 | 118 | 87 | 62 | 52 | 80 |

Sources: ARQ 1990-2002. UNODC 2003 estimate based on STRIDE graph for retail prices.

363

## OPIUM
### Retail and wholesale prices and purity levels:
### breakdown by drug, region and country or territory
(prices expressed in US$ or converted equivalent, and purity levels in percentage)

| Region / country or territory | RETAIL PRICE (per gram) | | | | WHOLESALE PRICE (per kilogram) | | | |
|---|---|---|---|---|---|---|---|---|
| | Typical | Range | Purity | Year | Typical | Range | Purity | Year |
| **Africa** | | | | | | | | |
| North Africa | | | | | | | | |
| Egypt | 1.6 | | - | 2001 | 6,730.0 | 5,860.0 - 7,600.0 | - | 2002 |
| East Africa | | | | | | | | |
| Uganda | 23.5 | 17.0 - 30.0 | - | 1996 | | | | |
| Southern Africa | | | | | | | | |
| Zambia | 10.7 | | - | 1999 | | | | |
| **Americas** | | | | | | | | |
| Central America | | | | | | | | |
| Guatemala | | | | | 1,888.7 | | - | 1996 |
| North America | | | | | | | | |
| Canada | 31.9 | 31.9 - 114.8 | - | 2002 | 14,030.0 | 14,030.0 - 22,320.0 | - | 2002 |
| United States | 55.0 | 30.0 - 80.0 | - | 2002 | 25,000.0 | 20,000.0 - 30,000.0 | - | 2002 |
| South America | | | | | | | | |
| Colombia | 0.3 | | - | 2001 | 190.0 | | - | 2002 |
| Peru | | | | | 3,500.0 | 3,000.0 - 4,000.0 | 80.0 | 2001 |
| **Asia** | | | | | | | | |
| Central Asia and Transcaucasia | | | | | | | | |
| Armenia | 10.0 | | - | 2000 | 1,000.0 | | - | 1999 |
| Azerbaijan | 2.0 | 1.8 - 2.2 | - | 2002 | 1,800.0 | 1,700.0 - 2,000.0 | - | 2002 |
| Kazakhstan | | | | | 1,170.0 | | - | 2002 |
| Kyrgyzstan | 4.0 | 3.0 - 5.0 | 14.0 - 22.0 | 2002 | 800.0 | 600.0 - 1,000.0 | 14.0 - 22.0 | 2002 |
| Tajikistan | 3.0 | 2.0 - 4.0 | - | 2002 | 480.0 | 100.0 - 850.0 | - | 2002 |
| Turkmenistan | 1.7 | 0.7 - 2.7 | - | 2001 | 3,720.0 | | - | 2002 |
| Uzbekistan | 1.8 | 1.0 - 2.5 | - | 2001 | 3,410.0 | | - | 2002 |
| East and South-East Asia | | | | | | | | |
| China | | | | | 1,250.0 | 870.0 - 2,500.0 | - | 2002 |
| Japan | 32.0 | | - | 2002 | | | | |
| Malaysia | | | | | 513.3 | | - | 1998 |
| Myanmar | 0.5 | 0.4 - 0.7 | - | 2002 | 241.3 | | - | 1999 |
| Republic of Korea | 90.8 | | - | 2001 | 78,980.0 | | - | 2001 |
| Singapore | 7.8 | 5.6 - 10.0 | - | 2002 | 4,460.0 | | - | 2002 |
| Viet Nam | | | | | 953.3 | 400.0 - 1,506.7 | - | 2001 |
| Near and Middle East /South-West Asia | | | | | | | | |
| Afghanistan | 0.5 | 0.4 - 0.5 | 80.0 - 95.0 | 2002 | 460.0 | 430.0 - 490.0 | 88.0 | 2002 |
| Bahrain | 2.3 | | - | 1996 | | | | |
| Iran ( Islamic Republic of) | 2.7 | 2.4 - 2.9 | - | 2000 | 1,300.0 | | - | 2002 |
| Jordan | 9.9 | 8.5 - 11.3 | - | 2002 | 11,300.0 | 9,890.0 - 12,710.0 | - | 2002 |
| Lebanon | | | | | 10.000.0 | 15,000.0 - 20,000.0 | - | 2002 |
| Oman | 2.0 | | - | 2002 | | | | |
| Pakistan | 1.3 | 1.2 - 1.4 | - | 2002 | 440.0 | 460.0 - 590.0 | - | 2002 |
| Qatar | 4.0 | | - | 2002 | 3,300.0 | 3,200.0 - 4,190.0 | - | 2002 |
| Saudi Arabia | | | | | 133,300.0 | 14,700.0 - 152,000.( | 5.0 - 50.0 | 2001 |
| Syrian Arab Republic | 6.0 | 4.5 - 7.5 | 30.0 - 70.0 | 2002 | 4,000.0 | 3,000.0 - 5,000.0 | 30.0 - 70.0 | 2002 |
| South Asia | | | | | | | | |
| Bangladesh | 0.8 | 0.7 - 1.0 | 2.0 - 7.0 | 2002 | 500.0 | 400.0 - 700.0 | 3.0 - 6.0 | 2002 |
| India | 0.3 | 0.3 - 0.4 | - | 1999 | 160.0 | 40.0 - 310.0 | - | 2002 |
| Sri Lanka | 6.6 | 4.8 - 8.5 | - | 2002 | | | | |

## OPIUM
### Retail and wholesale prices and purity levels:
### breakdown by drug, region and country or territory
(prices expressed in US$ or converted equivalent, and purity levels in percentage)

| Region / country or territory | RETAIL PRICE (per gram) | | | | WHOLESALE PRICE (per kilogram) | | | |
|---|---|---|---|---|---|---|---|---|
| | Typical | Range | Purity | Year | Typical | Range | Purity | Year |
| **Europe** | | | | | | | | |
| Eastern Europe | | | | | | | | |
| Estonia | 45.6 | | - | 2001 | | | | |
| Republic of Moldova | 0.8 | | 80.0 | 2001 | 800.0 | | 90.0 | 2001 |
| Romania | 3.0 | 2.0 - 4.0 | - | 2001 | 3,000.0 | 2,000.0 - 4,000.0 | - | 2001 |
| Russian Federation | 40.0 | | - | 1999 | 3,350.0 | 2,700.0 - 4,000.0 | - | 2001 |
| The former Yug.Rep of Macedonia | | | | | 570.0 | 470.0 - 660.0 | | 2002 |
| Ukraine | 1.0 | 0.8 - 1.2 | - | 2002 | 500.0 | 400.0 - 600.0 | - | 2002 |
| Western Europe | | | | | | | | |
| Cyprus | 43.0 | | - | 1996 | 12,903.0 | | - | 1996 |
| France | 13.5 | | - | 2001 | | | | |
| Greece | 7.3 | | 70.0 - 80.0 | 1997 | 5,474.0 | | 80.0 - 90.0 | 1997 |
| Norway | 28.6 | | - | 2002 | 10,360.0 | 8,480.0 - 12,240.0 | - | 2002 |
| Sweden | 37.2 | 24.8 - 49.6 | - | 2001 | 5,500.0 | 5,000.0 - 5,900.0 | - | 2001 |
| Turkey | 18.6 | 17.5 - 19.7 | | 1999 | 1,880.0 | 1,410.0 - 2,350.0 | - | 2002 |
| United Kingdom | 14.9 | 12.0 - 14.9 | - | 2002 | | | | |

365

## HEROIN
### Retail and wholesale prices and purity levels:
### breakdown by drug, region and country or territory
(prices expressed in US$ or converted equivalent, and purity levels in percentage)

| Region / country or territory | RETAIL PRICE (per gram) | | | | WHOLESALE PRICE (per kilogram) | | | |
|---|---|---|---|---|---|---|---|---|
| | Typical | Range | Purity | Year | Typical | Range | Purity | Year |
| **Africa** | | | | | | | | |
| East Africa | | | | | | | | |
| Kenya (Heroin no.3) | 10.2 | 10.2 - 12.7 | - | 2002 | 13,000.0 | | - | 1999 |
| (Heroin no.4) | 12.7 | 12.7 - 19.1 | | 2002 | | | | |
| Mauritius | 337.8 | | 2.0 - 5.0 | 2002 | 16,890.0 | | - | 2002 |
| | | | | | 20,000.0 | | - | 2002 |
| Uganda (Heroin no.3) | 9.0 | 8.0 - 10.0 | 15.0 - 25.0 | 2001 | 15,000.0 | 10,000.0 - 20,000.0 | 25.0 - 40.0 | 2001 |
| (Heroin no.4) | 15.0 | 10.0 - 20.0 | 40.0 - 60.0 | 2001 | 30,000.0 | 20,000.0 - 40,000.0 | 60.0 - 95.0 | 2001 |
| United Republic of Tanzania | 25.0 | | - | 1999 | 18,800.0 | | - | 1999 |
| North Africa | | | | | | | | |
| Algeria | | | | | 189,193.9 | | - | 1999 |
| Egypt | 108.5 | 86.8 - 130.3 | - | 2002 | 23,880.0 | 17,370.0 - 30,390.0 | - | 2002 |
| Southern Africa | | | | | | | | |
| Namibia (Heroin no.3 & 4) | 32.9 | 32.9 - 42.3 | - | 2002 | 4,758.9 | 4,441.6 - 5,076.1 | - | 2001 |
| South Africa | 23.5 | 19.3 - 26.3 | - | 2002 | 14,110.0 | 16,931.0 - 20,698.0 | - | 2002 |
| Swaziland | 75.0 | | - | 1998 | 50,000.0 | | - | 1998 |
| Zambia | 31.8 | | - | 2002 | | | | |
| Zimbabwe | 71.4 | 57.1 - 85.7 | - | 2002 | 320.0 | 270.0 - 360.0 | - | 2001 |
| West and Central Africa | | | | | | | | |
| Congo | | | | | 10,700.0 | 7,140.0 - 14,270.0 | - | 2002 |
| Benin | 20.2 | | - | 1998 | 18,500.0 | | - | 1998 |
| Côte d'Ivoire (Heroin no.4) | 3.6 | 1.4 - 7.1 | - | 2002 | 9,280.0 | 19.0 - 18,553.0 | - | 2002 |
| Ghana (Heroin no.3 & No.4) | 1.8 | 1.7 - 1.9 | - | 2002 | 18,250.0 | 17,000.0 - 19,500.0 | - | 2002 |
| Nigeria (Heroin no.3) | 21.0 | 16.8 - 21.0 | - | 2002 | 21,040.0 | 16,834.0 - 21,043.0 | - | 2002 |
| **Americas** | | | | | | | | |
| Central America | | | | | | | | |
| Costa Rica | | | | | 88,401.5 | 65,137.9 - 111,665.0 | 60.0 | 2001 |
| El Salvador | 75.0 | 69.9 - 80.0 | 60.0 - 100.0 | 2001 | 75,000.0 | 70,000.0 - 80.000.0 | - | 2002 |
| Guatemala | 63.6 | 50.9 - 76.3 | 75.0 - 90.0 | 2002 | 50,870.0 | 47,690.0 - 57,230.0 | 80.0 - 93.0 | 2002 |
| Nicaragua | 75.0 | | 90.0 | 2002 | 75,000.0 | | 90.0 | 2002 |
| Panama (Heroin no.3) | 12.5 | 10.0 - 15.0 | 80.0 - 90.0 | 2001 | 12,500.0 | 10,000.0 - 15,000.0 | 80.0 - 90.0 | 2001 |
| (Heroin no.4) | 12.5 | 10.0 - 15.0 | 80.0 - 90.0 | 2001 | 12,500.0 | 10,000.0 - 15,000.0 | 80.0 - 90.0 | 2001 |
| North America | | | | | | | | |
| Canada | 191.3 | 114.8 - 478.3 | 60.0 - 90.0 | 2002 | 51,020.0 | 51,020 - 89,290.0 | 50.0 - 90.0 | 2002 |
| Mexico | | | | | 32,850.0 | | - | 2002 |
| United States (Heroin no.3) | 70.0 | 60.0 - 80.0 | 40.0 - 75.0 | 2002 | 21,500.0 | 18,000.0 - 25,000.0 | 36.0 | 2002 |
| (Heroin no.4) | 95.0 | 90.0 - 100.0 | 20.0 - 25.0 | 2002 | 80,000.0 | 60,000.0 - 100,000.0 | 72.0 - 79.0 | 2002 |
| (black tar heroin) | 211.5 | 80.0 - 600.0 | | 2000 | 70,500.0 | 24,000.0 - 175,000.0 | | 2000 |
| South America | | | | | | | | |
| Argentina | | | | | 5,330.0 | 5,150.0 - 5,500.0 | - | 2002 |
| Colombia | 20.0 | 10.0 - 30.0 | - | 2002 | 8,520.0 | | - | 2002 |
| Ecuador | | | | | 5,000.0 | | 96.0 | 1999 |
| Uruguay | | | | | 115,000.0 | 100,000.0 - 130,000.0 | - | 2002 |
| Venezuela (Heroin no.4) | 9.2 | 8.4 - 10.1 | 10.0 - 20.0 | 2002 | 11,320.0 | 10,060 - 12,580.0 | 85.0 - 90.0 | 2002 |
| Caribbean | | | | | | | | |
| Bermuda | 20.0 | | - | 2002 | | | | |
| Dominican Republic | 30.0 | | - | 2001 | 30,000.0 | | - | 2001 |
| Saint Lucia | 30.0 | | - | 2000 | 25,000.0 | | - | 2000 |

## HEROIN
### Retail and wholesale prices and purity levels:
### breakdown by drug, region and country or territory
(prices expressed in US$ or converted equivalent, and purity levels in percentage)

| Region / country or territory | RETAIL PRICE (per gram) | | | | WHOLESALE PRICE (per kilogram) | | | |
|---|---|---|---|---|---|---|---|---|
| | Typical | Range | Purity | Year | Typical | Range | Purity | Year |
| **Asia** | | | | | | | | |
| Central Asia and Transcaucasia | | | | | | | | |
| Armenia | 135.0 | 120.0 - 150.0 | - | 2000 | | | | |
| Azerbaijan | 75.0 | 50.0 - 100.0 | - | 1999 | 36,000.0 | 35,000.0 - 37,000.0 | - | 2001 |
| Kazakhstan | | | | | 14,500.0 | | - | 2002 |
| Kyrgyzstan | | | | | 6,830.0 | | - | 2002 |
| (Heroin no.4) | 21.0 | 20.0 - 22.0 | 40.0 - 60.0 | 2002 | 8,000.0 | 6,000.0 - 10,000.0 | 50.0 - 90.0 | 2002 |
| Tajikistan | | | | | 6,830.0 | | - | 2002 |
| (Heroin no.4) | 6.0 | 4.0 - 8.0 | 10.0 | 2002 | 4,750.0 | 1,500.0 - 8,000.0 | 10.0 - 80.0 | 2002 |
| Turkmenistan | 13.3 | 9.0 - 17.6 | - | 2001 | 35,670.0 | | - | 2002 |
| Uzbekistan | 25.0 | 15.0 - 35.0 | - | 2002 | 22,070.0 | | - | 2002 |
| East and South-East Asia | | | | | | | | |
| Brunei Darussalam (Heroin no.4 | 112.0 | | - | 2001 | 239,521.0 | | - | 1998 |
| China | 50.0 | 13.0 - 185.0 | - | 2002 | 25,000.0 | 10,000.0 - 50,000.0 | - | 2002 |
| Hong Kong SAR, China (Heroin | 53.2 | 41.3 - 67.4 | 22.0 - 57.0 | 2002 | 28,570.0 | 22,910.0 - 33,000.0 | - | 2002 |
| Indonesia | 38.6 | 33.1 - 44.1 | - | 2002 | 22,070.0 | 27,590.0 - 33,100.0 | - | 2002 |
| Japan | 159.8 | | - | 2002 | 21,570.0 | | - | 2002 |
| Macau | 50.0 | 37.0 - 62.0 | - | 2002 | | | | |
| Malaysia | 355.7 | 81.3 - 609.8 | 32.5 | 1997 | 1,340.0 | | - | 1998 |
| Myanmar (Heroin no.4) | 9.3 | 4.6 - 11.1 | - | 2002 | 3,619.9 | | - | 1999 |
| Philippines | 109.4 | 90.1 - 128.7 | 90 | 1999 | | | | |
| Republic of Korea | 142.2 | 94.8 - 189.6 | - | 2001 | 27,640.0 | | - | 2001 |
| Singapore (Heroin no.3) | 62.7 | 55.7 - 69.7 | - | 2002 | 3,230.0 | 2,560.0 - 3,900.0 | - | 2002 |
| Thailand | 47.0 | 14.7 - 79.4 | - | 2001 | 8,507.5 | 7,292.2 - 9,722.9 | 70.0 - 90.0 | 1998 |
| Vietnam | 45.1 | 20.6 - 68.5 | - | 2002 | 20,750.0 | 16,000.0 - 25,700.0 | - | 2002 |
| Near and Middle East/ South- West Asia | | | | | | | | |
| Afghanistan | 2.7 | 2.0 - 3.4 | 85.0 - 95.0 | 2002 | 2,700.0 | 2,060.0 - 3,400.0 | 80.0 - 95.0 | 2002 |
| Iran ( Islamic Republic of) | 1.1 | 0.8 - 1.5 | 4.0 - 20.0 | 2001 | 3,410.0 | | | 2002 |
| Israel | 27.9 | 22.3 - 33.4 | - | 2002 | 17,780.0 | 13,330.0 - 22,220.0 | - | 2002 |
| Jordan | 49.4 | 42.4 - 56.5 | - | 2002 | 19,774.0 | 18,361.6 - 21,186.4 | - | 2002 |
| Kuwait | | | | | 98,684.2 | | - | 1998 |
| Lebanon (Heroin no.3) | 35.0 | 30.0 - 40.0 | 40.0 - 60.0 | 2002 | 20,000.0 | 15,000.0 - 25,000.0 | 30.0 - 50.0 | 2002 |
| (Heroin no.4) | 40.0 | 35.0 - 45.0 | - | 2002 | 40,000.0 | 35,000.0 - 45,000.0 | 70.0 - 80.0 | 2002 |
| Oman | 116.6 | | - | 2002 | 123,697.9 | 117,187.5 - 130,208.3 | - | 2001 |
| Pakistan | | | | | 4,510.0 | 4,060.0 - 4,740.0 | - | 2002 |
| (Heroin no.3) | 1.0 | 1.0 - 1.4 | - | 2002 | 1,009.2 | 934.1 - 1,084.2 | - | 2001 |
| (Heroin no.4) | 1.9 | 1.5 - 2.0 | - | 2002 | 4,295.1 | 3,919.8 - 4,670.4 | - | 2001 |
| Qatar | 137.0 | 137.0 - 164.0 | - | 2002 | 68,682.5 | 54,945.0 - 82,420.0 | - | 1996 |
| Saudi Arabia | 240.0 | 213.3 - 266.7 | - | 2001 | 266,666.0 | | 25.0 | 1998 |
| Syrian Arab Republic | 20.0 | 17.0 - 23.0 | 15.0 - 35.0 | 2002 | 17,000.0 | 15,000.0 - 19,000.0 | 25.0 - 50.0 | 2002 |
| South Asia | | | | | | | | |
| Bangladesh (Heroin no.3) | 5.0 | 4.0 - 6.0 | 2.0 - 4.0 | 2002 | 5,000.0 | 4,000.0 - 6,000.0 | 2.0 - 6.0 | 2002 |
| (Heroin no.4) | 6.0 | 5.0 - 8.0 | 3.0 - 7.0 | 2002 | 7,000.0 | 6,000.0 - 8,000.0 | 2.0 - 7.0 | 2002 |
| India | 5.0 | 2.7 - 7.3 | - | 2000 | 5,389.5 | 2,155.8 - 8,623.1 | - | 2001 |
| Maldives | | | | | 85,324.2 | | - | 1999 |
| Nepal | 20.6 | 14.3 - 26.9 | - | 1996 | 20,000.0 | 15,000.0 - 25,000.0 | - | 1998 |
| Sri Lanka | 24.8 | 11.6 - 38.0 | - | 2002 | 12,883.6 | 11,452.1 - 14,315.2 | - | 1999 |

367

## HEROIN
### Retail and wholesale prices and purity levels:
### breakdown by drug, region and country or territory
(prices expressed in US$ or converted equivalent, and purity levels in percentage)

| Region / country or territory | RETAIL PRICE (per gram) | | | | WHOLESALE PRICE (per kilogram) | | | |
|---|---|---|---|---|---|---|---|---|
| | Typical | Range | Purity | Year | Typical | Range | Purity | Year |
| **Europe** | | | | | | | | |
| Eastern Europe | | | | | | | | |
| Albania | 2.9 | 2.2 - 3.6 | - | 2002 | 14,500.0 | 12,000.0 - 17,000.0 | - | 2002 |
| Belarus (Heroin no.2) | 35.0 | 30.0 - 40.0 | - | 2002 | 20,000.0 | 15,000.0 - 30,000.0 | - | 2002 |
| Bulgaria | 2.9 | 2.4 - 3.4 | 8.0 | 2002 | 6,211.8 | 5,521.6 - 6,902.0 | 55.0 - 72.0 | 2001 |
| Croatia | 31.9 | 25.5 - 57.3 | 10.0 - 20.0 | 2002 | 25,480.0 | 12,740.0 - 38,220.0 | 60.0 - 80.0 | 2002 |
| Czech Republic | 42.4 | 21.7 - 63.1 | 5.0 - 41.0 | 2002 | 25,100.0 | 12,530.0 - 37,680.0 | 20.0 - 41.0 | 2002 |
| Estonia (Heroin no.4) | 45.3 | 36.3 - 54.4 | 10.0 | 2002 | 41,880.0 | 29,920.0 - 53.580.0 | 30.0 | 2002 |
| Hungary | 27.3 | 22.6 - 30.1 | 15.0 - 55.0 | 2002 | 12,240.0 | 11,300.0 - 13,190.0 | 10.0 - 55.0 | 2002 |
| Latvia (Heroin no.4) | 56.2 | 32.1 - 80.3 | - | 2001 | 5,624.4 | 3,214.0 - 8,034.9 | - | 2001 |
| Lithuania | 51.3 | 21.6 - 81.1 | 5.0 - 20.0 | 2002 | 25,670.0 | 13,510.0 - 37,830.0 | 30.0 - 60.0 | 2002 |
| Poland | 55.4 | 50.3 - 75.5 | 20.0 - 30.0 | 2002 | 27,670.0 | 25,160.0 - 30,190.0 | - | 2002 |
| Republic of Moldova | 63.0 | 50.4 - 75.6 | - | 2001 | 27,727.8 | 25,207.1 - 30,248.5 | - | 2001 |
| (Heroin no.3) | 30.0 | | - | 2001 | | | | |
| Romania | | | | | 30,000.0 | | 80.0 | 2001 |
| Russian Federation | 31.1 | 29.2 - 33.0 | - | 2002 | 15,540.0 | 14,130.0 - 16,950.0 | - | 2002 |
| Serbia and Montenegro | 27.5 | 25.0 - 30.0 | 6.0 - 12.0 | 2001 | 22,500.0 | 20,000.0 - 25,000.0 | - | 2001 |
| Slovakia | 23.6 | 18.8 - 28.3 | - | 2002 | 15,070.0 | 14,130.0 - 16,480.0 | - | 2002 |
| Slovenia | 22.1 | 17.7 - 26.6 | - | 2002 | 11,070.0 | | - | 2002 |
| The form.Yug.Rep of Macedoni | 37.2 | 33.0 - 41.4 | - | 2002 | 16,480.0 | 14,130.0 - 18,840.0 | - | 2002 |
| Ukraine | 16.5 | 14.1 - 18.8 | - | 2002 | 10,130.0 | 9,420.0 - 10,830.0 | - | 2002 |
| | 60.0 | 50.0 - 65.0 | - | 2002 | 48,000.0 | 45,000.0 - 50,000.0 | - | 2002 |
| Western Europe | | | | | | | | |
| Andorra | 128.5 | | - | 1999 | | | | |
| Austria (Heroin no.3) | 91.8 | 42.4 - 141.3 | 25.0 | 2002 | 23,550.0 | 18,840.0 - 28,260.0 | 2.0 - 51.0 | 2002 |
| Belgium (Heroin no.3) | 28.7 | 19.8 - 37.7 | - | 2002 | 22,230.0 | 17,570.0 - 26,940.0 | 6.0 - 90.0 | 2002 |
| Cyprus | 100.0 | 80.0 - 120.0 | - | 2002 | 22,500.0 | 20,000.0 - 25,000.0 | - | 2002 |
| Denmark (Heroin no.3) | 126.1 | 63.0 - 189.1 | - | 2002 | 20,800.0 | 18,910.0 - 22,690.0 | 18.0 - 78.0 | 2002 |
| (Heroin no.4) | 163.9 | 75.7 - 252.2 | - | 2002 | 69,340.0 | 63,040.0 - 75,650.0 | - | 2002 |
| Finland | 188.4 | 141.3 - 235.5 | 7.0 | 2002 | 51,800.0 | 47,090.0 - 56,510.0 | 7.0 | 2002 |
| France (Heroin no.3) | 47.1 | 42.4 - 65.9 | 2.0 - 10.0 | 2002 | 23,550.0 | | 10.0 - 40.0 | 2002 |
| (Heroin no.4) | 75.4 | 56.5 - 113.0 | 2.0 - 10.0 | 2002 | 37,680.0 | | 10.0 - 40.0 | 2002 |
| Germany | 38.3 | 17.0 - 59.3 | - | 2002 | 20,330.0 | 13,300.0 - 27,310.0 | - | 2002 |
| Greece (Heroin no.3) | 44.7 | 18.8 - 70.6 | - | 2002 | 15,540.0 | 11,300.0 - 19,780.0 | - | 2002 |
| (Heroin no.4) | 44.7 | 18.8 - 70.6 | - | 2002 | 19,310.0 | 14,130.0 - 24,490.0 | 2.0 - 80.0 | 2002 |
| Iceland | 372.0 | | - | 1998 | | | | |
| Ireland (Heroin no.3) | 179.0 | 169.5 - 188.4 | 25.0 - 35.0 | 2002 | 43,478.3 | | 60.0 - 70.0 | 1999 |
| Italy (Heroin no. 3) | 58.7 | 53.3 - 64.1 | - | 2002 | 27,000.0 | 24,560.0 - 29,450.0 | 3.0 - 30.0 | 2002 |
| (Heroin no. 4) | 77.7 | 72.3 - 83.2 | - | 2002 | 40,330.0 | 37,440.0 - 42,230.0 | - | 2002 |
| Liechtenstein | 48.5 | 34.7 - 62.4 | - | 1997 | 27,760.0 | | - | 1997 |
| Luxembourg | 138.5 | 108.0 - 170.5 | - | 1998 | 50,368.5 | 47,717.5 - 53,019.5 | - | 1999 |
| Malta (Heroin no.3) | 70.0 | | 20.0 | 2001 | 45,200.0 | | 60.0 | 2001 |
| Monaco | 86.5 | | 65.0 | 1997 | 87,100.0 | | 65.0 | 1997 |
| Netherlands | 34.9 | 22.6 - 47.1 | - | 2002 | 29,200.0 | 20,720.0 - 37,680.0 | - | 2002 |
| Norway | 164.8 | 94.2 - 235.5 | 10.0 - 75.0 | 2002 | 37,680.0 | 28,260.0 - 47,090.0 | 10.0 - 75.0 | 2002 |
| Portugal (Heroin no.3) | 41.2 | | 20.0 | 2002 | 25,840.0 | 23,490.0 - 28,190.0 | - | 2002 |
| Spain | 60.8 | | 34.0 | 2002 | 41,200.0 | | 51.0 | 2002 |
| Sweden (Heroin no.3) | 127.7 | 102.2 - 153.3 | - | 2002 | 25,540.0 | 20,440.0 - 30,650.0 | - | 2002 |
| (Heroin no.4) | 153.3 | 102.2 - 204.4 | - | 2002 | 71,530.0 | 61,310.0 - 81,740.0 | - | 2002 |
| Switzerland | 38.5 | 25.5 - 51.1 | - | 2002 | 19,150.0 | 12,770.0 - 19,150.0 | 8.0 - 21.0 | 2002 |
| Turkey | 17.5 | 15.0 - 20.0 | - | 2001 | 7,540.0 | 5,650.0 - 9,420.0 | - | 2002 |
| United Kingdom | 91.1 | 44.8 - 149.4 | - | 2002 | 30,620.0 | 23,900.0 - 37,340.0 | - | 2002 |
| **Oceania** | | | | | | | | |
| Australia | 201.9 | 114.3 - 539.8 | - | 2002 | 75,580.0 | 53,980.0 - 97,710.0 | - | 2002 |
| New Zealand | 387.2 | 318.9 - 455.5 | - | 2002 | | | | |

## 5.2. Cocaine: Wholesale and street prices and Purity Levels

### Prices in Europe and in USA, 1990-2003

**Retail price (street price), US$/gram**

| EUROPE | 1990 | 1991 | 1992 | 1993 | 1994 | 1995 | 1996 | 1997 | 1998 | 1999 | 2000 | 2001 | 2002 | 2003 |
|---|---|---|---|---|---|---|---|---|---|---|---|---|---|---|
| Austria | 198 | 180 | 167 | 120 | 126 | 156 | 138 | 118 | 113 | 93 | 94 | 78 | 71 | 91 |
| Belgium | 80 | 90 | 68 | 95 | 82 | 93 | 90 | 57 | 55 | 60 | 55 | 51 | 50 | 53 |
| Denmark | 144 | 135 | 111 | 90 | 150 | 176 | 169 | 108 | 119 | 165 | 106 | 120 | 91 | 105 |
| Finland | 159 | 150 | 126 | 105 | 165 | 191 | 184 | 123 | 179 | 157 | 138 | 121 | 111 | 152 |
| France | 99 | 119 | 140 | 153 | 151 | 174 | 125 | 87 | 84 | 82 | 50 | 87 | 75 | 91 |
| Germany | 120 | 103 | 111 | 95 | 109 | 103 | 90 | 77 | 72 | 68 | 57 | 58 | 57 | 68 |
| Greece | 150 | 120 | 105 | 54 | 116 | 111 | 144 | 91 | 54 | 82 | 69 | 72 | 75 | 96 |
| Iceland | 167 | 203 | 207 | 200 | 211 | 228 | 226 | 238 | 149 | 134 | 121 | 109 | 150 | 207 |
| Italy | 108 | 120 | 164 | 90 | 104 | 113 | 129 | 109 | 129 | 135 | 100 | 89 | 90 | 103 |
| Luxembourg | 150 | 150 | 150 | 150 | 172 | 194 | 127 | 115 | 110 | 119 | 119 | 119 | 107 | 96 |
| Netherlands | 66 | 70 | 74 | 66 | 60 | 79 | 52 | 64 | 38 | 33 | 33 | 33 | 33 | 50 |
| Norway | 176 | 170 | 255 | 156 | 145 | 150 | 153 | 177 | 133 | 128 | 114 | 157 | 165 | 201 |
| Portugal | 63 | 57 | 60 | 57 | 59 | 66 | 64 | 57 | 51 | 43 | 56 | 48 | 36 | 52 |
| Spain | 110 | 100 | 100 | 63 | 78 | 91 | 72 | 68 | 68 | 63 | 52 | 52 | 56 | 70 |
| Sweden | 160 | 152 | 183 | 123 | 148 | 118 | 118 | 98 | 88 | 97 | 77 | 79 | 87 | 96 |
| Switzerland | 178 | 144 | 188 | 136 | 146 | 148 | 127 | 117 | 110 | 109 | 77 | 69 | 74 | 74 |
| United Kingdom | 131 | 127 | 69 | 123 | 113 | 111 | 102 | 124 | 128 | 104 | 94 | 94 | 84 | 87 |
| Ireland | 141 | 137 | 120 | 110 | 100 | 119 | 32 | 34 | 32 | 30 | 28 | 28 | 94 | 115 |
| Average unweighted | 133 | 129 | 133 | 110 | 124 | 134 | 119 | 103 | 95 | 95 | 80 | 81 | 84 | 100 |
| **infl.adj.** | **188** | **175** | **174** | **141** | **154** | **162** | **139** | **119** | **107** | **104** | **85** | **84** | **86** | **100** |
| Weighted average | 117 | 115 | 118 | 104 | 112 | 118 | 105 | 92 | 92 | 88 | 70 | 74 | 72 | 84 |
| **Adjusted for inflation** | **165** | **155** | **154** | **132** | **139** | **143** | **123** | **106** | **103** | **97** | **75** | **77** | **73** | **84** |

Sources: ARQ or EUROPOL, except 2003 EUROPOL, and in italic UNODC

| | 1990 | 1991 | 1992 | 1993 | 1994 | 1995 | 1996 | 1997 | 1998 | 1999 | 2000 | 2001 | 2002 | 2003 |
|---|---|---|---|---|---|---|---|---|---|---|---|---|---|---|
| USA | 184 | 177 | 170 | 147 | 137 | 131 | 126 | 127 | 124 | 118 | 129 | 70 | 90 | |
| **Adjusted for inflation** | **260** | **239** | **223** | **188** | **169** | **159** | **148** | **145** | **140** | **130** | **138** | **73** | **92** | |

Sources: ONDCP 1990-2000 (prices for 1 gram or less, at street purity), ARQ 2001 - 2002 (mid-point of min/max prices)

**Wholesale price, US$/kg**

| EUROPE | 1990 | 1991 | 1992 | 1993 | 1994 | 1995 | 1996 | 1997 | 1998 | 1999 | 2000 | 2001 | 2002 | 2003 |
|---|---|---|---|---|---|---|---|---|---|---|---|---|---|---|
| Austria | 66,000 | 60,000 | 54,000 | 40,000 | 41,946 | 52,084 | 45,875 | 56,723 | 54,440 | 38,859 | 47,094 | 43,995 | 42,385 | 59,434 |
| Belgium | 25,000 | 24,000 | 38,250 | 28,000 | 26,920 | 30,560 | 21,927 | 17,025 | 19,167 | 23,859 | 22,376 | 26,771 | 28,111 | 20,717 |
| Denmark | 80,000 | 85,000 | 85,000 | 82,500 | 58,516 | 60,034 | 46,141 | 38,640 | 44,517 | 78,900 | 43,462 | 47,839 | 37,823 | 52,325 |
| Finland | 79,500 | 75,000 | 62,750 | 52,500 | 82,500 | 95,450 | 91,750 | 61,550 | 89,350 | 78,460 | 68,321 | 59,492 | 51,804 | 62,264 |
| France | 117,000 | 38,250 | 45,000 | 38,250 | 40,000 | 39,877 | 48,077 | 43,554 | 42,159 | 27,714 | 27,000 | 34,978 | 37,676 | 45,283 |
| Germany | 69,000 | 53,100 | 60,300 | 54,142 | 57,692 | 54,676 | 53,925 | 45,294 | 41,210 | 39,639 | 33,752 | 33,235 | 34,476 | 40,893 |
| Greece | 75,000 | 60,000 | 95,000 | 36,000 | 46,413 | 53,098 | 72,015 | 43,795 | 49,180 | 49,320 | 41,237 | 40,359 | 42,385 | 53,774 |
| Italy | 54,000 | 48,000 | 94,000 | 41,935 | 51,097 | 51,455 | 55,633 | 50,629 | 49,091 | 47,250 | 46,000 | 40,529 | 41,412 | 48,464 |
| Luxembourg | 93,919 | 95,939 | 113,521 | 50,847 | 157,593 | 141,343 | 47,625 | 43,103 | 41,072 | 47,718 | 47,718 | 47,718 | 47,718 | 47,718 |
| Netherlands | 26,500 | 27,000 | 29,500 | 26,500 | 24,680 | 33,232 | 23,894 | 29,698 | 22,355 | 27,500 | 27,500 | 27,500 | 27,500 | 27,453 |
| Norway | 120,000 | 120,000 | 127,500 | 110,000 | 39,971 | 50,000 | 41,670 | 60,028 | 81,699 | 57,545 | 51,417 | 51,569 | 54,159 | 64,953 |
| Portugal | 39,500 | 39,285 | 33,000 | 27,000 | 27,950 | 34,483 | 42,591 | 37,908 | 33,447 | 30,000 | 28,000 | 29,080 | 31,046 | 32,469 |
| Spain | 65,000 | 60,000 | 55,000 | 35,000 | 36,434 | 41,322 | 38,760 | 38,924 | 38,924 | 38,898 | 30,882 | 38,898 | 31,511 | 38,903 |
| Sweden | 80,000 | 76,200 | 91,375 | 61,450 | 73,825 | 55,556 | 59,255 | 45,573 | 50,484 | 48,508 | 38,394 | 34,693 | 35,763 | 41,991 |
| Switzerland | 63,900 | 94,250 | 116,250 | 50,847 | 72,012 | 75,949 | 51,587 | 40,780 | 41,152 | 41,000 | 35,482 | 23,392 | 19,274 | 19,274 |
| United Kingdom | 47,850 | 46,475 | 20,625 | 43,210 | 45,000 | 46,774 | 40,625 | 47,500 | 47,500 | 33,981 | 38,168 | 36,008 | 35,848 | 39,539 |
| Ireland | 45,000 | 45,000 | 40,000 | 50,000 | 45,000 | 42,000 | 31,646 | 33,733 | 31,530 | 29,891 | 29,891 | 29,891 | 29,891 | 29,891 |
| Average unweighted | 67,481 | 61,618 | 68,298 | 48,717 | 54,562 | 56,347 | 47,823 | 43,079 | 45,722 | 43,473 | 38,629 | 37,997 | 36,987 | 42,667 |
| **infl.adj.** | **95,069** | **83,310** | **89,592** | **62,056** | **67,733** | **68,033** | **56,095** | **49,385** | **51,582** | **48,013** | **41,266** | **39,473** | **37,838** | **42,667** |
| Weighted average | 67,800 | 50,675 | 57,354 | 43,992 | 47,026 | 48,138 | 47,737 | 43,965 | 43,425 | 38,478 | 35,569 | 36,091 | 35,946 | 41,949 |
| **Adjusted for inflation (kg)** | **95,519** | **68,515** | **75,235** | **56,037** | **58,379** | **58,123** | **55,995** | **50,401** | **48,991** | **42,496** | **37,998** | **37,493** | **36,773** | **41,949** |
| **inflation adjusted (gram)** | **96** | **69** | **75** | **56** | **58** | **58** | **56** | **50** | **49** | **42** | **38** | **37** | **37** | **42** |

Sources: ARQ or EUROPOL, except 2003 EUROPOL, and in italic UNODC

| | 1990 | 1991 | 1992 | 1993 | 1994 | 1995 | 1996 | 1997 | 1998 | 1999 | 2000 | 2001 | 2002 | 2003 |
|---|---|---|---|---|---|---|---|---|---|---|---|---|---|---|
| USA | 45,430 | 48,300 | 48,100 | 44,730 | 42,180 | 38,640 | 35,700 | 34,320 | 31,960 | 30,870 | 29,580 | 21,500 | 23,000 | |
| **Adjusted for inflation (kg)** | **45,430** | **48,300** | **48,100** | **44,730** | **42,180** | **38,640** | **35,700** | **34,320** | **31,960** | **30,870** | **29,580** | **22,335** | **23,529** | |
| **Adjusted for inflation (gram)** | **45** | **48** | **48** | **45** | **42** | **39** | **36** | **34** | **32** | **31** | **30** | **22** | **24** | |

Sources: ONDCP 1990-2000 (prices for 10-100 gram, at street purity), ARQ 2001 - 2002 (mid-point of min/max prices)

369

## COCAINE
### Retail and wholesale prices and purity levels:
### breakdown by drug, region and country or territory
(prices expressed in US$ or converted equivalent, and purity levels in percentage)

| Region / country or territory | RETAIL PRICE (per gram) | | | | WHOLESALE PRICE (per kilogram) | | | |
|---|---|---|---|---|---|---|---|---|
| | Typical | Range | Purity | Year | Typical | Range | Purity | Year |
| **Africa** | | | | | | | | |
| East Africa | | | | | | | | |
| Kenya | 31.8 | 25.5 - 38.2 | - | 2002 | 44,580.0 | 38,210.0 - 50,950.0 | 40.0 - 50.0 | 2002 |
| Rwanda | | | | | 26,000.0 | | - | 2002 |
| Uganda | 100.0 | | - | 2000 | 200,000.0 | | 90.0 | 2000 |
| North Africa | | | | | | | | |
| Egypt | 184.5 | 152.0 - 217.1 | - | 2002 | 97,690.0 | 86,830.0 - 108,540.0 | - | 2002 |
| Southern Africa | | | | | | | | |
| Namibia | 47.6 | 44.4 - 50.8 | - | 2001 | 4,758.8 | 4,441.6 - 5,076.1 | - | 2001 |
| (Crack) | 9.4 | 9.4 - 11.3 | - | 2002 | | | | |
| South Africa | 21.6 | 23.5 - 26.3 | - | 2002 | 15,990.0 | 13,169.0 - 20,694.0 | - | 2002 |
| (Crack) | | | | | 5,080.0 | | - | 2001 |
| Swaziland (Coca Base) | 188.1 | 141.1 - 282.2 | - | 2002 | 7,600.0 | | - | 1999 |
| (Crack) | 0.3 | 0.3 - 0.4 | - | 2001 | | | | |
| Zambia | 47.0 | | 80.0 | 2002 | | | | |
| Zimbabwe | 89.3 | 71.1 - 128.6 | - | 2002 | 50,000.0 | 18,181.8 - 81,818.2 | - | 2001 |
| (Crack) | 44.6 | 35.7 - 53.6 | | | | | | |
| West and Central Africa | | | | | | | | |
| Congo | | | | | 5,710.0 | 4,280.0 - 7,140.0 | - | 2002 |
| Côte d'Ivoire | 4.3 | 2.1 - 9.9 | - | 2002 | 12,130.0 | 24.0 - 24,262.0 | - | 2002 |
| Ghana | 1.5 | 1.4 - 1.6 | - | 2002 | 15,000.0 | 14,000.0 - 16,000.0 | - | 2002 |
| Nigeria | 25.3 | 21.0 - 25.3 | - | 2002 | 25.250.0 | 21,043.0 - 25,252.0 | - | 2002 |
| **Americas** | | | | | | | | |
| Central America | | | | | | | | |
| Costa Rica | 19.6 | 16.8 - 22.4 | - | 2002 | 5,180.0 | 4,760.0 - 5,600.0 | 53.0 - 90.0 | 2002 |
| (Crack) | 14.7 | 9.8 - 19.6 | - | 2002 | 2,330.0 | 1,550.0 - 3,100.0 | - | 2001 |
| El Salvador | 24.0 | 23.0 - 25.0 | - | 2002 | 24,000.0 | 23,000.0 - 25,000.0 | - | 2002 |
| (Crack) | 24.0 | 23.0 - 25.0 | - | 2002 | 24,000.0 | 23,000.0 - 25,000.0 | - | 2002 |
| Guatemala (Coca Base) | 12.7 | 10.2 - 12.7 | 80.0 - 90.0 | 2002 | 12,720.0 | 11,450.0 - 12,720.0 | 80.0 - 93.0 | 2002 |
| (Crack) | 8.6 | 7.6 - 9.5 | 50.0 - 60.0 | 2002 | 7,630.0 | 6,360.0 - 7,630.0 | 50.0 - 70.0 | 2002 |
| Honduras (Coca Base) | 15.3 | 12.2 - 18.3 | - | 2002 | 5,190.0 | 4,880.0 - 5,490.0 | - | 2002 |
| (Crack) | 6.7 | 6.1 - 7.3 | - | 2002 | 3,110.0 | 2,930.0 - 3,300.0 | - | 2002 |
| Nicaragua | 5.0 | | - | 2002 | 5,000.0 | | - | 2002 |
| (Crack) | 1.0 | | - | 2002 | 1,000.0 | | - | 2002 |
| Panama | 1.5 | 1.0 - 2.0 | 40.0 - 80.0 | 2001 | 1,600.0 | 1,200.0 - 2,000.0 | - | 2001 |
| (Coca Base) | 1.5 | 1.0 - 2.0 | 40.0 - 80.0 | 2001 | 1,600.0 | 1,200.0 - 2,000.0 | - | 2001 |
| (Crack) | 1.5 | 1.0 - 2.0 | 40.0 - 80.0 | 2001 | 1,600.0 | 1,200.0 - 2,000.0 | - | 2001 |
| North America | | | | | | | | |
| Canada | 51.0 | 31.9 - 127.6 | 68.0 | 2002 | 28,700.0 | 20,410.0 - 38,270.0 | 85.0 - 95.0 | 2002 |
| (Crack) | 95.7 | 63.0 - 127.6 | 72.0 | 2002 | | | | |
| Mexico | | | | | 7,880.0 | | - | 2002 |
| United States | 90.0 | 80.0 - 100.0 | 56.0 | 2002 | 23,000.0 | 10,000.0 - 36,000.0 | 69.0 | 2002 |
| (Crack) | 65.0 | 30.0 - 100.0 | - | 2002 | | | | |

## COCAINE
### Retail and wholesale prices and purity levels:
### breakdown by drug, region and country or territory
(prices expressed in US$ or converted equivalent, and purity levels in percentage)

| Region / country or territory | RETAIL PRICE (per gram) | | | | WHOLESALE PRICE (per kilogram) | | | |
|---|---|---|---|---|---|---|---|---|
| | Typical | Range | Purity | Year | Typical | Range | Purity | Year |
| **South America** | | | | | | | | |
| Argentina | 20.0 | 18.0 - 22.0 | 4.0 - 20.0 | 2001 | 3,870.0 | 2.580.0 - 5,150.0 | - | 2002 |
| (Coca Base) | 10.0 | 8.0 - 12.0 | - | 2001 | 2,060.0 | 1,720.0 - 2,410.0 | - | 2002 |
| (Crack) | 15.0 | 13.0 - 17.0 | - | 2001 | 1,460.0 | 1,370.0 - 1,550.0 | - | 2002 |
| Bolivia | 5.0 | | 80.0 | 2002 | 1,500.0 | | - | 2002 |
| (Coca Base) | 3.0 | | 70.0 | 2002 | 1,200.0 | | - | 2002 |
| Brazil | 4.9 | | - | 1997 | 2,500.0 | | - | 1996 |
| Chile | 2.4 | | - | 1997 | 6,000.0 | | 95.0 | 1998 |
| Colombia | 2.5 | 2.0 - 3.0 | - | 2002 | 1,750.0 | | - | 2002 |
| Ecuador | 1.0 | | 70.0 | 1999 | 2,000.0 | | 96.0 | 1999 |
| Guyana | 8.0 | 6.0 - 10.0 | - | 1996 | 5,360.0 | 4,500.0 - 6,210.0 | - | 1996 |
| Paraguay | 6.5 | | - | 1999 | 3,500.0 | | - | 1999 |
| Peru | 5.0 | 4.0 - 6.0 | 80.0 | 2001 | 870.0 | 850.0 - 880.0 | - | 2002 |
| (Coca Base) | 2.0 | 1.5 - 2.5 | 75.0 | 2001 | 350.0 | 300.0 - 400.0 | 70.0 | 2001 |
| Suriname (Coca Base) | 3.8 | 3.0 - 4.5 | - | 2001 | 4,000.0 | 3,000.0 - 5,000.0 | - | 2002 |
| (crack) | 1.7 | 1.2 - 2.3 | - | 2002 | | | | |
| Uruguay | 6.0 | 5.0 - 7.0 | 20.0 - 40.0 | 2002 | 5,750.0 | 5,000.0 - 6,500.0 | 20.0 - 40.0 | 2002 |
| Venezuela | 4.6 | 4.2 - 5.0 | 10.0 - 20.0 | 2002 | 3,150.0 | 2,940.0 - 3,350.0 | 85.0 - 90.0 | 2002 |
| (crack) | 1.5 | 1.3 - 1.7 | - | 2002 | 150.0 | 130.0 - 170.0 | - | 2002 |
| **Caribbean** | | | | | | | | |
| Bahamas (Coca Base) | | | | | 15,000.0 | 13,000.0 - 20,000.0 | - | 2002 |
| (crack) | 60.0 | 50.0 - 70.0 | - | 2002 | | | | |
| Bermuda | 125.0 | | - | 2002 | 65,000.0 | 60,000.0 - 70,000.0 | 50.0 - 80.0 | 2002 |
| (crack) | 50.0 | | - | 2002 | 65,000.0 | 60,000.0 - 70,000.0 | 50.0 - 70.0 | 2002 |
| Cayman Islands | 25.0 | 20.0 - 30.0 | 85.0 - 95.0 | 2002 | 11,000.0 | 10,000.0 - 12,000.0 | 85.0 - 95.0 | 2002 |
| (Coca Base) | 200.0 | 180.0 - 220.0 | 85.0 - 95.0 | 2002 | | | | |
| Cuba | 100.0 | | - | 1996 | 7,500.0 | 5,000.0 - 10,000.0 | 70.0 - 90.0 | 1996 |
| Dominican Republic | 10.0 | | - | 2001 | 10,000.0 | | - | 2001 |
| Grenada (Coca Base) | 19.4 | 16.7 - 22.2 | - | 2001 | 7,037.0 | 6,666.7 - 7,407.4 | - | 2001 |
| Haiti (Coca Base) | 6.5 | 6.0 - 7.0 | - | 2001 | 5,500.0 | 5,000.0 - 6,000.0 | - | 2001 |
| Jamaica | 7.0 | 6.0 - 8.0 | 90.0 | 2001 | 5,500.0 | 5,000.0 - 6,000.0 | 90.0 | 2001 |
| (crack) | 1.4 | 1.2 - 1.5 | - | 2001 | 215.0 | 210.0 - 220.0 | - | 2001 |
| Saint Lucia | 10.0 | | - | 2000 | 8,000.0 | | - | 2000 |
| Trinidad Tobago | 50.0 | | 5.1 | 2001 | 27,000.0 | | 75.0 | 2001 |
| Turks and Caicos Islands | 10.0 | 10.0 - 20.0 | 90.0 | 2002 | 8,000.0 | 6,000.0 - 8,000.0 | 95.0 | 2002 |
| **Asia** | | | | | | | | |
| **Central Asia and Transcaucasia** | | | | | | | | |
| Azerbaijan | 125.0 | | - | 1999 | | | | |
| **East and South-East Asia** | | | | | | | | |
| Hong Kong SAR, China | 161.9 | 128.4 - 182.9 | - | 2002 | 40.060.0 | 26,320.0 - 44,930.0 | - | 2002 |
| Republic of Korea | 720.1 | 593.0 - 847.1 | 85.0 | 1999 | 58,840.0 | 55,290.0 - 62,390.0 | - | 2001 |
| Indonesia | 49.7 | 44.1 - 55.2 | - | 2002 | 11,030.00 | 9,380.0 - 13,240.0 | - | 2002 |
| Japan | 103.9 | 47.9 - 195.8 | - | 2002 | | | | |
| (Coca Base) | 373.3 | | - | 2002 | | | | |
| Mongolia (Coca Base) | | | | | 27,390.0 | | - | 2001 |
| Philippines | 109.4 | 90.1 - 128.7 | - | 1999 | | | | |

371

## COCAINE
### Retail and wholesale prices and purity levels:
### breakdown by drug, region and country or territory
(prices expressed in US$ or converted equivalent, and purity levels in percentage)

| Region / country or territory | RETAIL PRICE (per gram) | | | | WHOLESALE PRICE (per kilogram) | | | |
|---|---|---|---|---|---|---|---|---|
| | Typical | Range | Purity | Year | Typical | Range | Purity | Year |
| **Near and Middle East /South-West Asia** | | | | | | | . | |
| Israel (Coca Base) | 67.5 | 45.0 - 90.0 | - | 2002 | 45,000.0 | 40,000.0 - 50,000.0 | - | 2002 |
| Jordan (Coca Base) | 141.2 | | - | 1998 | 70,621.5 | 63,559.3 - 77,683.6 | - | 2002 |
| Lebanon | 70.0 | 50.0 - 90.0 | 50.0 - 90.0 | 2001 | 65,000.0 | 50,000.0 - 80,000.0 | 80.0 - 90.0 | 2002 |
| (Coca Base) | 50.0 | 40.0 - 60.0 | 60.0 - 90.0 | 2001 | 50,000.0 | 30,000.0 - 70,000.0 | 70.0 - 90.0 | 2001 |
| Saudi Arabia | | | | | 9,070.0 | | 0.2 | 1998 |
| Syrian Arab Republic | 100.0 | 80.0 - 120.0 | 40.0 - 60.0 | 2002 | 60,000.0 | 50,000.0 - 70,000.0 | 50.0 - 70.0 | 2002 |
| **South Asia** | | | | | | | | |
| India (Coca Base) | | | | | 50,660.6 | 25,869.2 - 75,451.9 | - | 2001 |
| **Europe** | | | | | | | | |
| **Eastern Europe** | | | | | | | | |
| Albania | 54.2 | 50.6 - 57.8 | - | 2002 | 45,000.0 | 40,000.0 - 50,000.0 | - | 2002 |
| Bulgaria | 48.1 | 38.5 - 58.7 | - | 2002 | 32,209.3 | 27,608.0 - 36,810.6 | 90.0 - 92.0 | 2001 |
| Croatia | 63.7 | 51.0 - 76.4 | 20.0 - 50.0 | 2002 | 31,850.0 | 28,030.0 - 38,220.0 | 60.0 - 80.0 | 2002 |
| Czech Republic | 70.6 | 49.0 - 94.2 | 50.0 - 86.0 | 2002 | 43,940.0 | 31,080.0 - 56,510.0 | 75.0 - 86.0 | 2002 |
| Estonia | 48.3 | 36.3 - 60.4 | - | 2002 | 62,820.0 | 53,850.0 - 71,800.0 | - | 2002 |
| Hungary | 61.2 | 56.5 - 65.9 | 30.0 - 80.0 | 2002 | 32,020.0 | 30,140.0 - 33,910.0 | 30.0 - 80.0 | 2002 |
| Latvia | 68.3 | 56.2 - 80.3 | - | 2001 | | | | |
| Lithuania | 70.3 | 32.4 - 108.1 | 20.0 - 40.0 | 2002 | 27,020.0 | 21,610.0 - 32,420.0 | 40.0 - 60.0 | 2002 |
| (Coca Base) | 62.5 | 50.0 - 75.0 | 30.0 - 50.0 | 2001 | | | | |
| Poland (Coca Base) | 50.3 | 40.3 - 75.5 | 14.0 - 21.0 | 2002 | 27,670.0 | 25,160.0 - 30,190.0 | 40.0 - 84.0 | 2002 |
| Republic of Moldova (Coca E | 60.0 | | 90.0 | 2001 | 30,000.0 | | 90.0 | 2001 |
| Romania | 54.2 | 42.4 - 65.9 | - | 2002 | 23,550.0 | 18,840.0 - 28,260.0 | - | 2002 |
| Russian Federation | 110.0 | 100.0 - 120.0 | - | 2001 | 80,000.0 | 60,000.0 - 100,000.0 | 70.0 - 90.0 | 2001 |
| Serbia and Montenegro | 35.9 | 26.9 - 44.8 | - | 2001 | 38,100.0 | 31,400.0 - 44,800.0 | - | 2001 |
| (Coca Base) | 47.1 | 42.4 - 47.1 | - | 2002 | 37,680.0 | 28,260.0 - 51,800.0 | - | 2002 |
| Slovakia | | | | | 22,140.0 | | | 2002 |
| (crack) | 60.9 | 55.3 - 66.4 | - | 2002 | 104,000.8 | 41,600.3 - 166,401.2 | 60.0 - 95.0 | 2001 |
| Slovenia | 63.6 | 61.2 - 65.9 | - | 2002 | 63,580.0 | 61,220.0 - 65,930.0 | - | 2002 |
| The former Yug.Rep of Mac | 37.7 | 28.3 - 47.1 | - | 2002 | 30,610.0 | 23,550.0 - 37.680.0 | - | 2002 |
| Ukraine | 130.0 | 110.0 - 150.0 | - | 2002 | 100,000.0 | 90,000.0 - 110,000.0 | - | 2002 |
| **Western Europe** | | | | | | | | |
| Andorra | 59.0 | 53.6 - 64.4 | - | 2001 | | | | |
| Austria | 70.6 | 61.2 - 80.1 | 50.0 | 2002 | 42,390.0 | 37,680.0 - 47,090.0 | 1.0 - 92.0 | 2002 |
| Belgium | 50.4 | 39.6 - 60.8 | - | 2002 | 28,110.0 | 23,420.0 - 32,800.0 | 9.0 - 100.0 | 2002 |
| Cyprus (Coca Base) | 100.0 | 80.0 - 120.0 | - | 2002 | 28,500.0 | 27,000.0 - 30,000.0 | - | 2002 |
| Denmark | 91.4 | 56.7 - 126.1 | - | 2002 | 37,820.0 | 25,220.0 - 50,430.0 | 10.0 - 86.0 | 2002 |
| Finland | 110.7 | 63.1 - 158.2 | - | 2002 | 51,800.0 | 47,090.0 - 56,510.0 | - | 2002 |
| France | 75.4 | 47.1 - 84.8 | - | 2002 | 37,680.0 | 28,260.0 - 45,210.0 | 60.0 - 90.0 | 2002 |
| (Crack) | 6.7 | 4.5 - 9.0 | - | 2001 | | | | |
| Germany | 57.1 | 33.0 - 87.6 | - | 2002 | 34,480.0 | 25,350.0 - 44,740.0 | - | 2002 |
| Greece | 75.4 | 56.5 - 94.2 | - | 2002 | 42,390.0 | 32,970.0 - 51,810.0 | 4.0 - 87.0 | 2002 |
| Iceland | 150.0 | 100.0 - 200.0 | - | 2002 | | | | |
| Ireland | 89.7 | 80.7 - 98.7 | 60.0 - 70.0 | 2001 | 29,891.3 | | 60.0 - 70.0 | 1999 |
| Italy | 90.3 | 81.6 - 99.0 | - | 2002 | 41,410.0 | 37,440.0 - 45,670.0 | 18.0 - 87.0 | 2002 |
| Liechtenstein | 84.5 | 67.6 - 101.4 | 40.0 - 50.0 | 1998 | 40,540.0 | 33,780.0 - 47,300.0 | 70.0 - 80.0 | 1998 |
| Luxembourg | 119.3 | 79.5 - 159.1 | 15.0 - 35.0 | 1999 | 47,717.5 | 42,415.6 - 53,019.5 | 85.0 - 90.0 | 1999 |
| Malta | 79.1 | | 40.0 | 2001 | 67,810.0 | | 60.0 | 2001 |
| Monaco | 203.0 | | - | 1997 | | | | |
| Netherlands | 60.7 | 48.5 - 72.8 | - | 1999 | 27,500.0 | 25,000.0 - 30,000.0 | - | 1999 |
| Norway | 165.0 | 94.2 - 235.5 | 15.0 - 90.0 | 2002 | 54,160.0 | 37,680.0 - 70,640.0 | 15.0 - 90.0 | 2002 |
| Portugal | 36.3 | | - | 2002 | 28,190.0 | 25,840.0 - 30,540.0 | - | 2002 |
| Spain | 55.6 | | 50.0 | 2002 | 31,510.0 | | 71.0 | 2002 |
| Sweden | 86.9 | 71.5 - 102.2 | - | 2002 | 35,760.0 | 30,650.0 - 40,870.0 | - | 2002 |
| Switzerland | 73.1 | 51.1 - 95.7 | - | 2002 | 35,040.0 | 25,530.0 - 51,060.0 | 38.0 - 58.0 | 2002 |
| Turkey (Coca Base) | 80.0 | 70.0 - 90.0 | - | 2001 | 84,770.0 | 75,350.0 - 94,190.0 | - | 2002 |
| United Kingdom | 83.6 | 52.3 - 149.4 | 45.0 | 2002 | 35,850.0 | 26,890.0 - 44,810.0 | 1.0 - 89.0 | 2002 |
| (Crack) | 132.9 | 44.2 - 298.7 | 20.0 - 100.( | 2002 | 35,850.0 | 26,890.0 - 44,810.0 | 21.0 - 93.0 | 2002 |
| **OCEANIA** | | | | | | | | |
| Australia (Coca Base) | 146.8 | 99.0 - 269.9 | 39.0 | 2002 | 98,190.0 | 95,210.0 - 107,110.0 | - | 2002 |
| New Zealand | 170.8 | 136.7 - 205.0 | - | 2002 | | | | |

# 5.3. Cannabis: Wholesale and Street Prices and Purity Levels

**HERBAL CANNABIS**
**Retail and wholesale prices and purity levels:**
**breakdown by drug, region and country or territory**
(prices expressed in US$ or converted equivalent, and purity levels in percentage)

| Region / country or territory | RETAIL PRICE (per gram) | | | | WHOLESALE PRICE (per kilogram) | | | |
|---|---|---|---|---|---|---|---|---|
| | Typical | Range | Purity | Year | Typical | Range | Purity | Year |
| **Africa** | | | | | | | | |
| East Africa | | | | | | | | |
| Ghana | | | | | 51.0 | 39.2 - 62.7 | | 1999 |
| Kenya | 0.2 | 0.1 - 0.3 | - | 2002 | 119.8 | | - | 1996 |
| Madagascar | 1.3 | 1.1 - 1.4 | 100.0 | 2002 | 10.0 | | 100.0 | 2002 |
| Mauritius | 10.1 | | 80.0 - 100.0 | 2002 | 4,300.0 | 3,600.0 - 5,000.0 | | 2001 |
| Seychelles | 6.0 | | - | 1998 | 4,100.0 | 3,680.0 - 4,600.0 | - | 2002 |
| Uganda | 40.0 | 30.0 - 50.0 | - | 2001 | 75.0 | 50.0 - 100.0 | | 2001 |
| North Africa | | | | | | | | |
| Egypt | 0.3 | | - | 2001 | 120.0 | | 50.0 | 2001 |
| Morocco | | | | | 426.0 | | - | 1997 |
| Southern Africa | | | | | | | | |
| Malawi | 0.1 | | - | 2002 | 5.0 | 4.0 - 6.0 | | 2002 |
| Namibia | 0.3 | 0.3 - 2.4 | - | 2002 | 450.0 | 400.0 - 500.0 | - | 2001 |
| South Africa | 0.1 | | - | 2002 | 10.0 | 10.0 - 20.0 | - | 2002 |
| Swaziland | 0.1 | | - | 2001 | 50.0 | | - | 1998 |
| Zambia | 0.1 | 0.1 - 0.6 | 100.0 | 2002 | | | | |
| Zimbabwe | 0.1 | | - | 2002 | 40.0 | 30.0 - 40.0 | - | 2002 |
| West and Central Africa | | | | | | | | |
| Benin | | | | | 8.4 | | - | 1998 |
| Burkina Faso | | | | | 20.0 | | - | 2001 |
| Congo | | | | | 25.0 | 20.0 - 30.0 | - | 2001 |
| Côte d'Ivoire | 0.7 | 0.1 - 1.4 | - | 2002 | 7.0 | 1.0 - 36.0 | | 2002 |
| Ghana | 4.0 | 3.0 - 5.0 | - | 2002 | 300.0 | 230.0 - 350.0 | - | 2002 |
| Nigeria | 0.3 | 0.3 - 0.4 | - | 2002 | 13.0 | | - | 2002 |
| **Americas** | | | | | | | | |
| Central America | | | | | | | | |
| Costa Rica | 2.2 | 1.7 - 2.8 | - | 2002 | 840.0 | | | 2002 |
| El Salvador | 1.0 | 1.0 - 1.1 | - | 2002 | 1,070.0 | 1,000.0 - 1,140 | | 2002 |
| Guatemala | 1.9 | 1.3 - 2.5 | 100.0 | 2002 | 100.0 | | 100.0 | 2002 |
| Honduras | 0.5 | 0.3 - 0.6 | - | 2002 | 70.0 | 40.0 - 100.0 | - | 2002 |
| Nicaragua | 0.1 | | - | 2002 | 140.0 | 100.0 - 140.0 | - | 2002 |
| Panama | 0.8 | 0.5 - 1.0 | 60.0 - 80.0 | 2001 | 225.0 | 150.0 - 300.0 | - | 2001 |
| North America | | | | | | | | |
| Canada | 6.4 | 6.34 - 19.1 | - | 2002 | 4,465.0 | 3,830.0 - 5,100.0 | 3.0 - 18.0 | 2002 |
| Mexico | | | | | 80.0 | | - | 2002 |
| United States | 10.0 | 2.0 - 130.0 | 2.0 - 13.0 | 2002 | 2,300.0 | 600.0 - 4,000.0 | 4.0 - 13.0 | 2002 |
| South America | | | | | | | | |
| Argentina | 1.5 | 1.3 - 1.7 | 0.5 - 6.0 | 2001 | 300.0 | 170.0 - 450.0 | - | 2002 |
| Bolivia | 0.8 | | - | 2002 | 100.0 | | - | 2002 |
| Brazil | 0.9 | | - | 1997 | | | | |
| Colombia | 0.02 | | - | 2001 | 20.0 | | - | 2002 |
| Chile | 1.0 | | - | 1996 | 800.0 | | - | 1998 |
| Ecuador | | | | | 600.0 | | - | 1999 |
| Guyana | 0.2 | | - | 1996 | 65.0 | 50.0 - 80.0 | - | 1996 |
| Paraguay | 0.9 | 0.7 - 1.1 | - | 2002 | 10.0 | | - | 2002 |
| Peru | 1.5 | 1.0 - 2.0 | 95.0 | 2001 | 60.0 | 50.0 - 70.0 | 95.0 | 2001 |
| Suriname | 0.9 | 0.5 - 1.4 | - | 2002 | 7.5 | 5.0 - 10.0 | - | 2001 |
| Uruguay | 0.2 | 0.1 - 0.2 | 90.0 - 100.0 | 2002 | 160.0 | 120.0 -180.0 | 90.0 - 100.0 | 2002 |
| Venezuela | 1.9 | 1.7 - 2.1 | - | 2002 | 110.0 | 100.0 - 130.0 | | 2002 |

## HERBAL CANNABIS
### Retail and wholesale prices and purity levels:
### breakdown by drug, region and country or territory
(prices expressed in US$ or converted equivalent, and purity levels in percentage)

| Region / country or territory | RETAIL PRICE (per gram) | | | | WHOLESALE PRICE (per kilogram) | | | |
|---|---|---|---|---|---|---|---|---|
| | Typical | Range | Purity | Year | Typical | Range | Purity | Year |
| **Caribbean** | | | | | | | | |
| Bahamas | 5.0 | 5.0 - 10.0 | - | 2002 | 1,000.0 | 800.0 - 1,600.0 | - | 2002 |
| Bermuda | 50.0 | | | 2002 | 13,000.0 | 11,000.0 - 15,000.0 | - | 2002 |
| Cayman Islands | 8.0 | 6.0 - 10.0 | - | 2002 | 2,000.0 | 1,500.0 - 2,500.0 | - | 2002 |
| Dominican Republic | 0.6 | | - | 2001 | 450.0 | 400.0 - 500.0 | - | 1998 |
| Grenada | 1.3 | 1.1 - 1.4 | - | 2001 | 500.0 | 400.0 - 600.0 | - | 2001 |
| Jamaica | | | | | 61.0 | 57.0 - 65.0 | - | 2001 |
| Saint Lucia | 0.8 | | - | 2000 | 630.0 | 600.0 - 660.0 | - | 2000 |
| Trinidad Tobago | 5.0 | | - | 2001 | 3,000.0 | | - | 2001 |
| Turks and Caicos Islands | 10.0 | 10.0 - 20.0 | 100.0 | 2002 | 600.0 | 500,0 - 600.0 | 100.0 | 2002 |
| **Asia** | | | | | | | | |
| Central Asia and Transcaucasia | | | | | | | | |
| Armenia | | | | | 1,000.0 | | - | 1996 |
| Azerbaijan | 0.8 | 0.8 - 1.0 | - | 2002 | 700.0 | 650.0 - 800.0 | - | 2002 |
| Kyrgyzstan | 0.7 | 0.5 - 1.0 | 8.0 - 10.0 | 2002 | 10.0 | | 8.0 - 10.0 | 2002 |
| Tajikistan | 0.3 | 0.1 - 0.4 | - | 2001 | 125.0 | 50.0 - 200.0 | - | 2001 |
| Turkmenistan | 0.8 | 0.2 - 1.4 | - | 2001 | 356.5 | 38.0 - 675.0 | - | 2001 |
| Uzbekistan | | | | | 200.0 | 100.0 - 300.0 | - | 1998 |
| East and South-East Asia | | | | | | | | |
| Brunei Darussalam | 0.1 | | - | 2002 | 5,297.2 | | - | 1998 |
| Hong Kong SAR, China | 8.6 | 6.2 - 12.9 | - | 2002 | 2,105.0 | 1,440.0 - 3,850.0 | - | 2002 |
| Indonesia | 1.1 | | 100.0 | 2002 | 100.0 | 110.0 - 170.0 | 100.0 | 2002 |
| Japan | 52.2 | 4.0 - 100.3 | - | 2002 | 4,973.0 | 2,630.0 - 7,320.0 | - | 2002 |
| Malaysia | 0.5 | 0.5 - 0.6 | - | 1997 | 331.5 | 265.2 - 397.8 | - | 1999 |
| Macau | 12.0 | 10.0 - 15.0 | - | 2002 | 2,350.0 | 2,200.0 - 2,500.0 | - | 2002 |
| Myanmar | 0.1 | 0.1 - 0.2 | - | 2002 | 30.2 | | - | 1999 |
| Philippines | 0.1 | 0.1 - 0.2 | - | 2001 | 61.0 | 41.0 - 81.0 | - | 2001 |
| Republic of Korea | 0.8 | | - | 2001 | 100.0 | | - | 2001 |
| Singapore | 3.7 | | - | 2002 | 1,282.0 | 890.0 - 1,670.0 | - | 2002 |
| Thailand | 1.8 | 1.2 - 2.4 | - | 1999 | 90.0 | 30.0 -150.0 | - | 2001 |
| Near and Middle East /South-West Asia | | | | | | | | |
| Israel | 2.2 | | - | 2002 | 135.0 | 90.0 - 180.0 | - | 2002 |
| Jordan | 4.9 | 2.8 - 7.1 | - | 2002 | 565.0 | 490.0 - 640.0 | - | 2002 |
| Lebanon | | | | | 1,200.0 | | - | 2000 |
| Syrian Arab Republic | 1.1 | | - | 1999 | 652.2 | | - | 1999 |
| South Asia | | | | | | | | |
| Bangladesh | 0.3 | 0.2 - 0.3 | 3.0 - 6.0 | 2002 | 130.0 | 100.0 - 150.0 | 5.0 - 7.0 | 2002 |
| India | | | | | 40.0 | | - | 2001 |
| Maldives | 122.6 | 81.7 - 163.5 | - | 2001 | | | | |
| Nepal | | | | | 11.0 | 7.4 - 14.7 | - | 1999 |
| Sri Lanka | 18.5 | 15.8 - 21.1 | 7.0 - 75.0 | 2002 | | | | |

## HERBAL CANNABIS
### Retail and wholesale prices and purity levels:
### breakdown by drug, region and country or territory
(prices expressed in US$ or converted equivalent, and purity levels in percentage)

| Region / country or territory | RETAIL PRICE (per gram) | | | | WHOLESALE PRICE (per kilogram) | | | |
|---|---|---|---|---|---|---|---|---|
| | Typical | Range | Purity | Year | Typical | Range | Purity | Year |
| **Europe** | | | | | | | | |
| Eastern Europe | | | | | | | | |
| Albania | 1.3 | 1.1 - 1.5 | - | 2002 | 350.0 | | - | 2002 |
| Belarus | 4.0 | 3.0 - 5.0 | - | 2002 | 3,000.0 | 700.0 - 5,000.0 | - | 2002 |
| Bulgaria | 0.6 | 0.5 - 0.7 | - | 2002 | 45.0 | 40.0 - 50.0 | - | 2001 |
| Croatia | 2.5 | 1.9 - 4.5 | - | 2002 | 510.0 | 380.0 - 640.0 | - | 2002 |
| Czech Republic | 3.2 | 1.6 - 4.7 | 3.0 | 2002 | 4,239.0 | 1,600.0 - 6,900.0 | 21.0 | 2002 |
| Estonia | 7.0 | 6.0 - 7.8 | - | 2002 | 6,880.0 | 5,980.0 - 7,780.0 | - | 2002 |
| Hungary | 3.0 | 6.6 - 9.4 | 3.0 | 2002 | 1,319.0 | 1,130.0 - 1,510.0 | 3.0 | 2002 |
| Latvia | 7.6 | 2.4 - 12.9 | - | 2001 | 900.0 | 300.0 - 1,400.0 | - | 2001 |
| Lithuania | 14.9 | 2.7 - 27.02 | - | 2002 | 12,158.0 | 2,700.0 - 21,610.0 | - | 2002 |
| Poland | 6.3 | 5.0 - 8.8 | - | 2002 | 2,390.0 | 2,010.0 - 2,770.0 | - | 2002 |
| Republic of Moldova | 0.05 | | - | 1997 | 100.0 | | - | 1997 |
| Romania | 8.5 | 7.5 - 9.4 | - | 2002 | 4,709.0 | 3,770.0 - 5,650.0 | - | 2002 |
| Russian Federation | 1.0 | | - | 1999 | 300.0 | 100.0 - 500.0 | - | 2001 |
| Serbia and Montenegro | 2.8 | 2.8 - 4.7 | - | 2002 | 471.0 | 90.0 - 940.0 | | 2002 |
| Slovakia | 4.4 | 0.2 - 6.6 | - | 2002 | 2,200.0 | 200.0 - 4,200.0 | 1.0 - 15.0 | 2001 |
| Slovenia | 8.0 | 7.5 - 8.5 | - | 2002 | 2,826.0 | 1,880.0 - 3,770.0 | - | 2002 |
| The former Yug.Rep of Maced | 1.2 | 0.9 - 1.4 | - | 2002 | 212.0 | 190.0 - 240.0 | - | 2002 |
| Ukraine | 1.7 | 1.5 - 2.0 | - | 2002 | 1,300.0 | 1,000.0 - 1,500.0 | - | 2002 |
| Western Europe | | | | | | | | |
| Andorra | 2.7 | | - | 2001 | | | | |
| Austria | 6.1 | 3.8 - 8.5 | 11.0 | 2002 | 2,684.0 | 2,350.0 - 3,010.0 | 10.0 | 2002 |
| Belgium | 5.0 | 3.8 - 6.3 | - | 2002 | 2,072.0 | 1,660.0 - 2,480.0 | 2.0 - 18.0 | 2002 |
| Cyprus | 6.0 | 4.0 - 8.0 | - | 2002 | 2,000.0 | 1,500.0 - 2,500.0 | - | 2002 |
| Denmark | 9.0 | 8.8 - 9.2 | - | 1999 | | | | |
| Finland | 6.6 | 5.7 - 7.6 | - | 2002 | | | | |
| France | 4.7 | 1.9 - 6.6 | - | 2002 | 942.0 | 420.0 - 1,320.0 | - | 2002 |
| Germany | 6.8 | 3.8 - 10.4 | - | 2002 | 1,969.0 | 1,970.0 - 3,780.0 | - | 2002 |
| Greece | 2.1 | 1.4 - 2.8 | - | 2002 | 494.0 | 280.0 - 710.0 | - | 2002 |
| Iceland | 21.0 | 19.0 - 31.0 | - | 2002 | - | - | - | - |
| Ireland | 2.8 | 1.9 - 3.8 | - | 2002 | 2,691.2 | 2,549.6 - 2,832.9 | - | 1998 |
| Italy | 5.6 | 5.1 - 6.1 | - | 2002 | 1,036.0 | 820.0 - 1,260.0 | 2.0 - 17.0 | 2002 |
| Liechtenstein | 8.2 | | - | 1996 | 3,679.5 | | - | 1996 |
| Luxembourg | 2.5 | | - | 1998 | 1,916.7 | 1,642.9 - 2,190.5 | - | 1998 |
| Malta | 2.8 | | 17.0 | 2001 | 1,700.0 | | 17.0 | 2001 |
| Netherlands | 4.9 | 3.6 - 6.1 | - | 1999 | . | 1,005.0 - 1,538.5 | - | 1997 |
| Norway | 14.1 | 9.4 - 18.9 | - | 2002 | 4,500.0 | 3,600.0 - 5,400.0 | 0.2 - 38.5 | 2001 |
| Portugal | 2.5 | | 3.0 | 2002 | 704.0 | 470.0 - 940.0 | - | 2002 |
| Spain | 2.7 | | - | 2002 | 1,020.0 | | - | 2002 |
| Sweden | 5.0 | | - | 2001 | | | | |
| Switzerland | 4.8 | 3.2 - 6.4 | - | 2002 | 3,089.0 | 2,550.0 - 5,110.0 | 5.0 - 28.0 | 2002 |
| Turkey | 10.0 | 8.0 - 12.0 | - | 2001 | 500.0 | 400.0 - 600.0 | - | 2001 |
| United Kingdom | 7.5 | 4.2 - 15.0 | - | 2002 | 1,344.0 | 1,190.0 - 1,490.0 | - | 2002 |
| **Oceania** | | | | | | | | |
| Australia | 19.2 | | - | 1999 | 3,050.0 | | - | 1999 |
| New Zealand | 4.6 | | - | 2002 | 3,872.0 | 2,280.0 - 5,470.0 | 1.0 - 10.0 | 2002 |

## CANNABIS OIL
### Retail and wholesale prices and purity levels:
### breakdown by drug, region and country or territory
(prices expressed in US$ or converted equivalent, and purity levels in percentage)

| Region / country or territory | RETAIL PRICE (per gram) | | | | WHOLESALE PRICE (per kilogram) | | | |
|---|---|---|---|---|---|---|---|---|
| | Typical | Range | Purity | Year | Typical | Range | Purity | Year |
| **Africa** | | | | | | | | |
| Southern Africa | | | | | | | | |
| Zambia | 0.8 | | - | 2002 | - | - | - | - |
| | | | | | | | | |
| **Americas** | | | | | | | | |
| North America | | | | | | | | |
| Canada | 12.8 | 9.6 - 31.9 | - | 2002 | 5,102.0 | 3,190.0 - 9,570.0 | 3.0 - 28.0 | 2002 |
| United States | 45.0 | 35.0 - 55.0 | - | 1996 | 6,165.0 | 3,510.0 - 8,820.0 | - | 1996 |
| South America | | | | | | | | |
| Chile | 24.7 | | - | 1996 | - | - | - | - |
| Caribbean | | | | | | | | |
| Jamaica | | | | | 510.0 | 500.0 - 520.0 | - | 2001 |
| | | | | | | | | |
| **Asia** | | | | | | | | |
| Near and Middle East /South-West Asia | | | | | | | | |
| Israel | 10.0 | | - | 1998 | - | - | - | - |
| | | | | | | | | |
| **Europe** | | | | | | | | |
| Eastern Europe | | | | | | | | |
| Albania | 3.3 | 2.9 - 3.6 | - | 2002 | 600.0 | | - | 2002 |
| Bulgaria | | | | | 2,300.0 | | - | 2001 |
| Western Europe | | | | | | | | |
| Austria | | | | | 4,239.0 | 3,300.0 - 5,180.0 | - | 2002 |
| Cyprus | | | | | 9,000.0 | 8,000.0 - 10,000.0 | - | 1999 |
| France | 14.1 | 14.1 - 37.7 | - | 2002 | | | | |
| Iceland | 89.3 | | - | 1998 | - | - | - | - |
| Spain | 11.4 | | - | 2001 | 2,330.0 | | - | 2002 |
| Switzerland | 19.0 | 8.8 - 29.2 | - | 2001 | - | - | - | - |
| United Kingdom | 22.4 | 17.9 - 29.9 | - | 2002 | 2,481.00 | 1,145.0 - 3,817.0 | - | 2000 |
| | | | | | | | | |
| **Oceania** | | | | | | | | |
| Australia | 27.0 | | - | 2002 | 8,000.0 | 6,666.7 - 9,333.3 | - | 1998 |
| New Zealand | 18.2 | 9.1 - 22.8 | - | 2002 | 14,461.0 | 9,640.0 - 19,280.0 | 10.0 - 23.0 | 2002 |

## CANNABIS RESIN
### Retail and wholesale prices and purity levels:
### breakdown by drug, region and country or territory
(prices expressed in US$ or converted equivalent, and purity levels in percentage)

| Region / country or territory | RETAIL PRICE (per gram) | | | | WHOLESALE PRICE (per kilogram) | | | |
|---|---|---|---|---|---|---|---|---|
| | Typical | Range | Purity | Year | Typical | Range | Purity | Year |
| **Africa** | | | | | | | | |
| East Africa | | | | | | | | |
| Kenya | 0.9 | 0.8 - 1.0 | - | 2002 | | | | |
| Seychelles | | | | | 8,560.0 | 8,110.0 - 9,010.0 | - | 2000 |
| Uganda | | | | | 2,250.0 | 2,250.0 | - | 1998 |
| North Africa | | | | | | | | |
| Algeria | 2.2 | | - | 2002 | 2,207.3 | 2,207.3 | - | 1999 |
| Egypt | 1.2 | 0.1 - 2.3 | - | 2001 | 2,279.0 | 1,740.0 - 2,820.0 | - | 2002 |
| Tunisia | 1.5 | | - | 2002 | 1,121.7 | 1,035.4 - 1,207.9 | - | 1999 |
| Southern Africa | | | | | | | | |
| South Africa | 8.38 | | - | 2001 | 5,710.0 | | - | 2001 |
| Swaziland | 0.2 | | - | 2001 | | | | |
| Zambia | 0.5 | | - | 2002 | | | | |
| **Americas** | | | | | | | | |
| North America | | | | | | | | |
| Canada | 12.8 | 12.8 - 38.3 | - | 2002 | 6,059.0 | 3,830.0 - 7,650.0 | 7.0 - 10.0 | 2002 |
| United States | | | | | 4,962.5 | 2,205.0 - 7,720.0 | - | 1996 |
| South America | | | | | | | | |
| Argentina | 2.0 | 1.8 - 2.2 | - | 2001 | 600.0 | 500.0 - 700.0 | - | 2001 |
| Caribbean | | | | | | | | |
| Bermuda | 100.0 | | - | 2002 | | | | |
| Jamaica | | | | | 260.0 | 250.0 - 270.0 | - | 2001 |
| **Asia** | | | | | | | | |
| Central Asia and Transcaucasia | | | | | | | | |
| Armenia | 5.0 | 5.0 | - | 2000 | 5,000.0 | 5,000.0 | - | 1999 |
| Azerbaijan | 2.0 | 1.8 - 2.2 | - | 2002 | 1,800.0 | 1,700.0 - 2,000.0 | - | 2002 |
| Kyrgyzstan | 0.9 | 0.5 - 1.5 | 2.0 - 3.0 | 2002 | 63.0 | 50.0 - 70.0 | 2.0 - 3.0 | 2002 |
| Tajikistan | 2.0 | 1.0 - 3.0 | - | 2002 | 200.0 | 100.0 - 300.0 | - | 2002 |
| Uzbekistan | 1.1 | 0.7 - 1.5 | - | 1999 | 700.0 | 400.0 - 1,000.0 | - | 1999 |
| East and South-East Asia | | | | | | | | |
| Hong Kong SAR, China | 9.0 | 9.0 | - | 1999 | 21,882.3 | 21,882.3 | - | 1999 |
| Indonesia | 1.7 | | - | 2002 | 1,660.0 | | - | 2002 |
| Japan | 52.1 | 24.4 - 80.0 | - | 2002 | 2,696.0 | 1,400.0 - 3,990.0 | - | 2002 |
| Republic of Korea | 10.3 | 9.5 - 11.1 | - | 2001 | 7,900.0 | | - | 2001 |
| Macau SAR, China | 12.5 | 10.0 - 15.0 | - | 2002 | 2,350.0 | 2,200.0 - 2,500.0 | - | 2002 |
| Philippines | 3.4 | 3.2 - 3.7 | - | 2001 | 3,400.0 | 3,100.0 - 3,700.0 | - | 2001 |
| Near and Middle East /South-West Asia | | | | | | | | |
| Afghanistan | 0.2 | 0.1 - 0.3 | 70.0 - 90.0 | 2002 | 189.0 | 140.0 - 250.0 | 70.0 - 90.0 | 2002 |
| Iran ( Islamic Republic of) | | | | | 360.0 | | - | 2002 |
| Israel | 5.6 | 2.2 - 9.0 | - | 2002 | 1,565.0 | 900.0 - 2,230.0 | - | 2002 |
| Jordan | 5.7 | 3.5 - 7.8 | - | 2002 | 706.0 | 560.0 - 850.0 | - | 2002 |
| Kuwait | | | | | 4,934.2 | 4,934.2 | - | 1998 |
| Lebanon | 9.0 | 8.0 - 10.0 | 70.0 - 90.0 | 2002 | 300.0 | 200.0 - 400.0 | 90.0 | 2002 |
| Oman | 2.0 | | - | 2002 | 2,900.0 | 2,600.0 - 3,100.0 | - | 2001 |
| Pakistan | 0.3 | 0.1 - 0.4 | - | 2002 | 90.0 | 50.0 - 200.0 | - | 2002 |
| Qatar | 8.8 | 8.8 - 9.6 | - | 2002 | 6,850.0 | 5,550.0 - 7,240.0 | - | 2002 |
| Saudia Arabia | 8.0 | 6.7 - 9.3 | - | 2001 | 1,250.0 | 1,200.0 - 1,300.0 | 60.0 - 80.0 | 2001 |
| Syrian Arab Republic | 1.0 | 0.8 - 1.2 | 70.0 - 90.0 | 2002 | 800.0 | 600.0 - 1,000.0 | 70.0 - 90.0 | 2002 |
| Yeman | 0.2 | 0.2 - 0.3 | - | 2002 | 125.0 | 100.0 - 150.0 | - | 2002 |

## CANNABIS RESIN
### Retail and wholesale prices and purity levels:
### breakdown by drug, region and country or territory
(prices expressed in US$ or converted equivalent, and purity levels in percentage)

| Region / country or territory | RETAIL PRICE (per gram) | | | | WHOLESALE PRICE (per kilogram) | | | |
|---|---|---|---|---|---|---|---|---|
| | Typical | Range | Purity | Year | Typical | Range | Purity | Year |
| **South Asia** | | | | | | | | |
| Bangladesh | 0.8 | 0.6 - 1.0 | 2.0 - 5.0 | 2002 | 500.0 | 450.0 - 700.0 | 3.0 - 6.0 | 2002 |
| India | 0.3 | 0.2 - 0.4 | - | 1999 | 430.0 | 220.0 - 650.0 | - | 2001 |
| Nepal | 0.1 | 0.1 - 0.2 | - | 1999 | 40.5 | 36.8 - 44.2 | - | 1998 |
| Sri Lanka | 0.3 | 0.3 | - | 1997 | 244.0 | 244.0 | - | 1997 |
| **Europe** | | | | | | | | |
| Eastern Europe | | | | | | | | |
| Albania | | | | | 500.0 | | - | 2002 |
| Belarus | 15.0 | | - | 2002 | 5,000.0 | 4,000.0 - 6,000.0 | - | 2002 |
| Bulgaria | 1.8 | | - | 2001 | 1,380.0 | | - | 2001 |
| Croatia | 4.5 | 1.9 - 5.1 | - | 2002 | 892.0 | 760.0 - 1,020.0 | - | 2002 |
| Czech Republic | 6.2 | 4.7 - 7.8 | 3.0 - 10.0 | 2002 | 3,000.0 | 3,110.0 - 7,850.0 | 3.0 - 10.0 | 2002 |
| Estonia | 13.6 | 12.1 - 15.1 | - | 2002 | 2,000.0 | | - | 2001 |
| Hungary | 6.6 | 3.8 - 9.4 | 5.0 | 2002 | 1,319.0 | 1,130.0 - 1,510.0 | 5.0 | 2002 |
| Latvia | 13.7 | 9.6 - 17.7 | - | 2001 | 1,200.0 | 800.0 - 1,600.0 | - | 2001 |
| Lithuania | 13.0 | 4.1 - 21.6 | - | 2002 | 8,916.0 | 1,620.0 - 16,210 | - | 2002 |
| Poland | 7.6 | 5.0 - 10.1 | - | 2002 | 2,440.0 | 2,010.0 - 3,020.0 | - | 2002 |
| Republic of Moldova | 0.4 | | 60.0 | 2001 | 400.0 | | 70.0 | 2001 |
| Romania | 1.5 | 1.3 - 1.7 | - | 2002 | 7,535.0 | 6,590.0 - 8,480.0 | - | 2002 |
| Russian Federation | 4.5 | 3.0 - 6.0 | - | 2001 | 4,600.0 | 2,700.0 - 6,500.0 | - | 2001 |
| Serbia and Montenegro | 4.7 | 4.7 - 6.6 | - | 2002 | 4,100.0 | 3,400.0 - 4,800.0 | 40.0 - 50.0 | 2001 |
| Slovakia | 2.6 | 1.0 - 4.2 | 2.0 - 20.0 | 2001 | 2,210.0 | | - | 2002 |
| Slovenia | 8.0 | 7.5 - 8.5 | - | 2002 | 8,006.0 | 7,540.0 - 8,480.0 | - | 2002 |
| The former Yug.Rep of Macedonia | 2.1 | 1.4 - 2.8 | - | 2002 | 518.0 | 380.0 - 660.0 | | 2002 |
| Ukraine | 4.0 | 3.0 - 5.0 | - | 2001 | 1,250.0 | 1,000.0 - 1,500.0 | | 2001 |
| Western Europe | | | | | | | | |
| Andorra | 2.2 | | - | 2001 | | | | |
| Austria | 5.7 | 4.7 - 6.6 | 1.0 - 44.0 | 2002 | 2,590.0 | 2,350.0 - 2,830.0 | 2.0 - 15.0 | 2002 |
| Belgium | 5.7 | 4.2 - 7.1 | - | 2002 | 2,000.0 | 1,600.0 - 2,400.0 | - | 2001 |
| Cyprus | 8.0 | 7.0 - 10.0 | - | 2002 | 3,000.0 | 2,500.0 - 3,500.0 | - | 2002 |
| Denmark | 8.5 | 3.2 - 13.9 | - | 2002 | 2,837.0 | 1,260.0 - 4,410.0 | 39.0 | 2002 |
| Finland | 9.4 | 7.5 - 11.3 | - | 2002 | 3,110.0 | | - | 2002 |
| France | 10.4 | 6.6 - 14.1 | - | 2002 | 1,884.0 | 940.0 - 2,830.0 | 5.0 - 10.0 | 2002 |
| Germany | 5.8 | 2.8 - 8.5 | - | 2002 | 2,273.0 | 1,340.0 - 3,380.0 | - | 2002 |
| Greece | 4.2 | 2.8 - 5.7 | - | 2002 | 850.0 | 850.0 - 2,070.0 | - | 2002 |
| Iceland | 32.0 | 25.0 - 50.0 | - | 2002 | | | | |
| Ireland | 11.8 | 9.4 - 14.1 | - | 2002 | 3,060.0 | | - | 2002 |
| Italy | 7.2 | 6.5 - 8.0 | - | 2002 | 1,968.0 | 1,570.0 -2,360.0 | 2.0 - 25.0 | 2002 |
| Luxembourg | 5.3 | 5.3 | - | 1999 | 3,313.7 | 2,651.0 - 3,976.5 | - | 1999 |
| Monaco | | | | | 5,807.0 | 5,807.0 | - | 1997 |
| Netherlands | 8.5 | 4.9 - 12.1 | - | 1999 | 1,671.7 | 1,237.6 - 2,475.2 | - | 1998 |
| Norway | 16.5 | 9.4 - 23.6 | - | 2002 | 4,709.0 | 3,770.0 - 5,650.0 | - | 2002 |
| Portugal | 2.3 | | 4.0 | 2002 | 1,409.0 | 940.0 - 1,880 | - | 2002 |
| Spain | 3.5 | | - | 2001 | 1,310.0 | | - | 2002 |
| Sweden | 9.2 | 8.2 - 10.2 | - | 2002 | 3,270.0 | 2,550.0 - 4,090.0 | - | 2002 |
| Switzerland | 8.0 | 6.4 - 9.6 | - | 2002 | 3,670.0 | 5,110.0 - 6,380.0 | 7.0 - 28.0 | 2002 |
| Turkey | | | | | 1,107.0 | 800.0 - 1,410.0 | - | 2002 |
| United Kingdom | 6.9 | 3.9 - 7.5 | - | 2002 | 1,344.0 | 1,190.0 - 1,490.0 | - | 2002 |
| **Oceania** | | | | | | | | |
| Australia | 24.3 | 16.2 - 27.0 | - | 2002 | 6,550.0 | 6,550.0 | - | 1999 |

## 5.4. Amphetamine-type stimulants (ATS): Wholesale and Street Prices and Purity Levels

**AMPHETAMINE**
**Retail and wholesale prices and purity levels:**
**breakdown by drug, region and country or territory**
(prices expressed in US$ or converted equivalent, and purity levels in percentage)

| Region / country or territory | RETAIL PRICE (*) | | | | | WHOLESALE PRICE (**) | | | | |
| --- | --- | --- | --- | --- | --- | --- | --- | --- | --- | --- |
| | Typical | Range | Purity | Year | Unit | Typical | Range | Purity | Year | Unit |
| **Africa** | | | | | | | | | | |
| East Africa | | | | | | | | | | |
| Seychelles | | | | | | 4,055.0 | 3,600.0 - 4,510.0 | | 2000 | |
| Uganda | | | | | | 125.0 | 100.0 - 150.0 | | 2000 | |
| Southern Africa | | | | | | | | | | |
| South Africa | 5.7 | 4.9 - 6.5 | - | 1999 | T | | | | | |
| West and Central Africa | | | | | | | | | | |
| Burkina Faso | 0.1 | 0.1 - 0.1 | - | 2001 | | 22.4 | 20.4 - 24.5 | - | 2001 | |
| Côte d'Ivoire | 1.4 | 0.1 - 2.7 | 100.0 | 2001 | | 4.1 | 2.7 - 5.4 | 100.0 | 2001 | |
| Nigeria | 0.6 | 0.4 - 0.8 | - | 2001 | | 436.5 | 392.9 - 480.2 | - | 2001 | |
| **Americas** | | | | | | | | | | |
| Caribbean | | | | | | | | | | |
| Saint Lucia | 0.7 | 0.7 - 0.8 | | 2000 | | 630.0 | 600.0 - 660.0 | | 2000 | |
| North America | | | | | | | | | | |
| United States | 240.0 | 80.0 - 600.0 | | 2000 | | 70,500.0 | 24,000.0 - 175,000.0 | | 2000 | |
| South America | | | | | | | | | | |
| Argentina | 4.0 | 3.0 - 5.0 | - | 2001 | | 300.0 | 250.0 - 350.0 | | 2000 | |
| Venezuela | 2.6 | 2.2 - 3.0 | | 2000 | | 260.0 | 222.0 - 295.7 | | 2000 | |
| **Asia** | | | | | | | | | | |
| Central Asia and Transcaucasian countries | | | | | | | | | | |
| Kyrgyzstan | 0.3 | 0.1 - 0.4 | | 2000 | | 190.0 | 80.0 - 300.0 | | 2000 | |
| East and South-East Asia | | | | | | | | | | |
| Brunei Darussalam | 12.2 | 9.2 - 15.3 | | 2000 | | | | | | |
| Indonesia | | | | | | 500.0 | | - | 2001 | |
| Macau | 8.0 | 7.0 - 9.0 | | 2000 | | | | | | |
| Myanmar | 0.3 | 0.2 - 0.5 | - | 2001 | T | 156.6 | 100.0 - 213.1 | - | 2001 | TT |
| Vietnam | 5.1 | 4.0 - 7.7 | - | 2002 | | | | | | |
| Near and Middle East/South | | | | | | | | | | |
| Jordan | 2.8 | 2.8 - 4.2 | - | 2002 | T | 2,820.0 | 2,820.0 - 3,670.0 | - | 2002 | TT |
| Israel | | | | | | 288.0 | 200.0 - 375.0 | | 2000 | |
| Qatar | 2.7 | | - | 2002 | | | | | | |
| Saudi Arabia | 6.8 | 6.7 - 6.9 | - | 2001 | T | 6,800.0 | 6,666.7 - 6,933.3 | 40.0 - 90.0 | 2001 | TT |
| Syrian Arab Republic | 12.0 | 10.0 - 14.0 | 10.0 - 14.0 | 2002 | | 8,000.0 | 6,000.0 - 12,000.0 | - | 2002 | |

## AMPHETAMINE
### Retail and wholesale prices and purity levels:
### breakdown by drug, region and country or territory
(prices expressed in US$ or converted equivalent, and purity levels in percentage)

| Region / country or territory | RETAIL PRICE (*) | | | | | WHOLESALE PRICE (**) | | | | |
| --- | --- | --- | --- | --- | --- | --- | --- | --- | --- | --- |
| | Typical | Range | Purity | Year | Unit | Typical | Range | Purity | Year | Unit |
| **Europe** | | | | | | | | | | |
| _Eastern Europe_ | | | | | | | | | | |
| Belarus | 25.0 | 20.0 - 30.0 | - | 2002 | | 15,000.0 | | - | 2002 | |
| Bulgaria | 8.2 | 7.2 - 9.6 | - | 2002 | | 3,220.0 | | 30.0 - 60.0 | 2001 | |
| Croatia | 10.2 | 8.9 - 15.3 | - | 2002 | | 5,100.0 | 3,820.0 - 6,370.0 | - | 2002 | |
| Czech Republic | 16.8 | 15.5 - 18.1 | - | 2001 | | 18,790.0 | 12,530.0 - 25,050.0 | 10.0 - 34.0 | 2002 | |
| Estonia | 10.6 | 6.0 - 15.1 | 50.0 | 2002 | | 2,990.0 | | 50.0 - 98.0 | 2002 | |
| Hungary | 10.4 | 9.4 - 11.3 | 4.0 - 50.0 | 2002 | | 2,830.0 | 1,980.0 - 3,770.0 | 4.0 - 50.0 | 2002 | |
| Latvia | 22.5 | 16.1 - 28.9 | - | 2001 | | 2,089.1 | 1,446.3 - 2,731.9 | - | 2001 | |
| Lithuania | 13.0 | 4.1 - 21.6 | 15.0 - 60.0 | 2002 | | 8,920.0 | 1,620.0 - 16,210.0 | 20.0 - 80.0 | 2002 | |
| Poland | 12.6 | 5.0 - 22.7 | 20.0 - 35.0 | 2002 | | 3,770.0 | 2,520.0 - 5,030.0 | 60.0 - 90.0 | 2002 | |
| Romania | 4.0 | 3.0 - 5.0 | - | 2001 | T | 4,000.0 | 3,000.0 - 5,000.0 | - | 2001 | TT |
| Slovakia | 8.9 | 4.4 - 13.3 | - | 2002 | | | | | | |
| Slovenia | 8.8 | 6.5 - 11.1 | 20.0 - 25.0 | 2000 | | 3,705.0 | 2,780.0 - 4,630.0 | 20.0 - 25.0 | 2000 | |
| Ukraine | 28.0 | 25.0 - 30.0 | - | 2002 | | | | | | |
| _Western Europe_ | | | | | | | | | | |
| Andorra | 12.1 | 8.0 - 16.1 | - | 2001 | T | | | | | |
| Austria | 16.5 | 14.1 - 18.8 | 50.0 | 2002 | | 12,720.0 | 11,300.0 - 14,130.0 | 2.0 - 92.0 | 2002 | |
| Belgium | 11.3 | 9.0 - 13.7 | - | 2002 | | 2,170.0 | 2,060.0 - 3,390.0 | 49.0 | 2002 | |
| Denmark | 31.5 | 12.6 - 50.4 | - | 2002 | | 7.560.0 | 2,520.0 - 12,610.0 | 1.0 - 70.0 | 2002 | |
| Finland | 23.6 | 14.1 - 33.0 | - | 2002 | | 5,650.0 | 5,000.0 - 6,310.0 | 54.0 - 71.0 | 2002 | |
| France | 12.7 | 6.6 - 18.8 | - | 2002 | T | 1,880.0 | 940.0 - 2,830.0 | - | 2002 | TT |
| Germany | 13.0 | 5.7 - 18.8 | - | 2002 | | 4,490.0 | 2,280.0 - 7,120.0 | - | 2002 | TT |
| Greece | 3.8 | 2.8 - 4.7 | - | 2002 | | 2,540.0 | 2,260.0 - 2,830.0 | - | 2002 | |
| Iceland | 62.0 | 50.0 - 75.0 | - | 2002 | | | | | | |
| Ireland | 5.7 | | - | 2002 | D | 1,880.0 | | - | 2002 | TD |
| Italy | 18.1 | 16.9 - 19.2 | - | 2001 | | 6,950.0 | 6,830.0 - 7,060.0 | - | 2002 | |
| Luxembourg | 19.9 | 13.3 - 26.5 | - | 1999 | | | | | | |
| Netherlands | 5.1 | 2.5 - 7.8 | - | 1998 | | 3,013.3 | 2,604.2 - 3,465.3 | - | 1998 | |
| Norway | 58.9 | 23.6 - 94.2 | 10.0 - 90.0 | 2002 | | 11,770.0 | 9,420.0 - 14,130.0 | 10.0 - 80.0 | 2002 | |
| Portugal | 10.0 | 5.7 - 14.3 | - | 1998 | | | | | | |
| Spain | 23.0 | | - | 2001 | | 15,810.0 | | - | 2001 | |
| Sweden | 20.4 | 10.2 - 30.7 | - | 2002 | | 7,660.0 | 5,110.0 - 10,220.0 | - | 2002 | |
| Switzerland | 19.20 | 12.8 - 25.5 | - | 2002 | | 20,520.0 | 9,570.0 - 31,910.0 | - | 2002 | |
| United Kingdom | 13.4 | 4.5 - 22.4 | 40.0 | 2002 | | 2,240.0 | 1,490.0 - 2,990.0 | 1.0 - 73.0 | 2002 | |
| **Oceania** | | | | | | | | | | |
| Australia | 95.8 | 21.0 - 215.9 | - | 2002 | | 49,480.0 | 10,800.0 - 86,370.0 | | 2002 | |
| New Zealand | 41.1 | 15.3 - 51.6 | | 2000 | T | 22,840.0 | 18,270.0 - 27,410.0 | | 2000 | TT |

(*) in Gram or otherwise as indicated
(**) in Kilogram or otherwise as indicated
D : Doses unit
T : Tablets unit
TD: Thousand of doses
TT: Thousand of tablets

## METHAMPHETAMINE
### Retail and wholesale prices and purity levels:
### breakdown by drug, region and country or territory
(prices expressed in US$ or converted equivalent, and purity levels in percentage)

| Region / country or territory | RETAIL PRICE (per gram) | | | | WHOLESALE PRICE (per kilogram) | | | | |
|---|---|---|---|---|---|---|---|---|---|
| | Typical | Range | Purity | Year | | Typical | Range | Purity | Year |
| **Africa** | | | | | | | | | |
| Southern Africa | | | | | | | | | |
| Malawi | 5.0 | | - | 1997 | | 2,000.0 | | - | 1997 |
| Namibia | 10.0 | | - | 1996 | | 2,000.0 | | - | 1996 |
| South Africa | 6.2 | 3.4 - 8.9 | - | 1997 | | 2,250.0 | 1,800.0 - 2,700.0 | - | 1997 |
| West and Central Africa | | | | | | | | | |
| Burkina Faso | 0.1 | 0.1 - 0.1 | - | 2001 | | 22.4 | 20.4 - 24.5 | - | 2001 |
| **Americas** | | | | | | | | | |
| North America | | | | | | | | | |
| Canada | 51.0 | 51.0 - 127.6 | - | 2002 | | 22,497.0 | 19,690.0 - 25,310.0 | - | 2002 |
| United States | 210.0 | 20.0 - 400.0 | 38.0 | 2001 | | 25,500.0 | 6,000.0 - 45,000.0 | - | 2001 |
| **Asia** | | | | | | | | | |
| East and South-East Asia | | | | | | | | | |
| Brunei Darussalam | 0.4 | | - | 2002 | | 64,744.0 | 58,858.2 - 70,629.8 | - | 1999 |
| China | | | | | | 4,500.0 | 3,100.0 - 6,100.0 | 60.0 - 90.0 | 2002 |
| China (Hong Kong SAR) | 48.0 | 36.5 - 65.9 | - | 2002 | | 5,194.0 | 4,620.0 - 5,460.0 | - | 2002 |
| Indonesia | 38.6 | 33.1 - 44.1 | - | 2002 | | 16,552.0 | 11,030.0 - 22,070.0 | - | 2002 |
| Japan | 419.4 | 40.0 - 799.0 | 95.0 | 2002 | TT | 30,763.0 | 19,980.0 - 41,540.0 | 95.0 | 2002 |
| Macau | 18.0 | 12.0 - 25.0 | - | 2002 | | | | | |
| Myanmar | 1.3 | 0.7 - 1.9 | - | 2002 | | | | | |
| Philippines | 36.5 | 32.4 - 40.6 | - | 2001 | | 40,556.2 | 36,500.6 - 44,611.8 | - | 2001 |
| Republic of Korea | 327.8 | 213.2 - 442.3 | 98.0 | 2001 | | 39,490.0 | 31,592.0 - 47,388.0 | - | 2001 |
| Singapore | 31.8 | 4.5 - 72.5 | 16.0 - 77.0 | 2002 | | 27,866.0 | 22,290.0 - 33,440.0 | - | 2002 |
| Thailand | 3.0 | 2.4 - 3.6 | - | 1998 | | | | | |
| **Europe** | | | | | | | | | |
| Eastern Europe | | | | | | | | | |
| Czech Republic | 25.9 | | 40.0 - 80.0 | 2001 | | 25,101.0 | 12,530.0 - 37,680.0 | 60.0 - 75.0 | 2002 |
| Estonia | | | | | | 2,990.0 | | 50.0 - 98.0 | 2002 |
| Lithuania | 17.6 | 13.5 - 21.6 | 17.0 - 65.0 | 2002 | | 6,214.0 | 4,050.0 - 8,111.0 | 20.0 - 80.0 | 2002 |
| Russian Federation | 17.5 | 15.0 - 20.0 | - | 2001 | | | | | |
| Slovakia | | | | | | 16,600.0 | | - | 2002 |
| Ukraine | 20.0 | 10.0 - 30.0 | - | 2001 | | 2,000.0 | 1,000.0 - 3,000.0 | - | 2001 |
| Western Europe | | | | | | | | | |
| Finland | 27.0 | 18.0 - 36.0 | - | 1999 | | 11,241.0 | 9,892.1 - 12,589.9 | 31.0 | 1999 |
| France | | | | | TD | 1,884.0 | 940.0 - 2,830.0 | - | 2002 |
| Germany | 16.8 | 7.1 - 26.5 | - | 2000 | | 5,595.0 | 3,200.0 - 7,990.0 | - | 2000 |
| Netherlands | 9.7 | 7.3 - 12.1 | - | 1999 | | - | - | - | - |
| Norway | 42.4 | 9.4 - 75.3 | 10.0 - 80.0 | 2002 | | 11,774.0 | 9,420.0 - 14,130.0 | 10.0 - 80.0 | 2002 |
| Spain | 25.1 | 24.3 - 25.8 | - | 1997 | | 23,058.8 | 21,812.1 - 24,305.6 | - | 1997 |
| Sweden | 19.8 | 14.9 - 24.8 | - | 2001 | | 7,663.0 | 5,110.0 - 10,220.0 | - | 2002 |
| Switzerland | 23.4 | 8.8 - 38.0 | - | 2001 | | | | | |
| **Oceania** | | | | | | | | | |
| New Zealand | 432.7 | 318.9 - 546.6 | 70.0 - 80.0 | 2002 | | 176,741.0 | 160,670.0 - 192,810.0 | 80.0 | 2002 |

TD: Thousand of doses

TT: Thousand of tablets

## L.S.D
### Retail and wholesale prices and purity levels:
### breakdown by drug, region and country or territory
(prices expressed in US$ or converted equivalent, and purity levels in percentage)

| Region / country or territory | RETAIL PRICE (per dose) | | | | WHOLESALE PRICE (per thousand dose) | | | |
|---|---|---|---|---|---|---|---|---|
| | Typical | Range | Purity | Year | Typical | Range | Purity | Year |
| **Africa** | | | | | | | | |
| Southern Africa | | | | | | | | |
| Namibia | 11.3 | 11.3 - 14.1 | - | 2002 | | | | |
| South Africa | 7.5 | | - | 2002 | 6,302.0 | | - | 2002 |
| Zambia | 42.8 | | - | 1998 | | | | |
| Zimbabwe | 4.6 | 4.3 - 5.0 | - | 2002 | | | | |
| West and Central Africa | | | | | | | | |
| Ghana | 12.0 | 10.0 - 14.0 | - | 2002 | | | | |
| | | | | | | | | |
| **Americas** | | | | | | | | |
| Central America | | | | | | | | |
| Costa Rica | 16.8 | | - | 2002 | 15,500.0 | | - | 2001 |
| North America | | | | | | | | |
| Canada | 3.2 | 1.9 - 9.6 | - | 2002 | 1,590.0 | 640.0 - 2,550.0 | - | 2002 |
| United States | 5.5 | 1.0 - 10.0 | - | 1996 | 375.0 | 250.0 - 500.0 | 20.0 - 80.0 | 1996 |
| South America | | | | | | | | |
| Argentina | 25.1 | 20.0 - 30.1 | - | 2001 | 100.0 | 20.0 - 150.0 | - | 2002 |
| | | | | | | | | |
| **Asia** | | | | | | | | |
| East and South-East Asia | | | | | | | | |
| Japan | 32.0 | 24.0 - 40.0 | - | 2002 | | | | |
| Republic of Korea | 15.8 | | - | 2001 | | | | |
| Singapore | 30.7 | 27.9 - 33.4 | - | 2002 | 3,900.0 | | - | 2002 |
| Near and Middle East /South-West Asia | | | | | | | | |
| Israel | 5.6 | 4.5 - 6.7 | - | 2002 | 5,600.0 | 4,500.0 - 6,700.0 | - | 2002 |
| | | | | | | | | |
| **Europe** | | | | | | | | |
| Eastern Europe | | | | | | | | |
| Bulgaria | 13.8 | | - | 2001 | | | | |
| Croatia | 14.0 | 12.7 - 15.3 | - | 2002 | 6,370.0 | 5,100.0 - 7,640.0 | - | 2002 |
| Czech Republic | 7.1 | 7.1 - 9.4 | - | 2002 | 5,180.0 | 4,710.0 - 5,650.0 | - | 2002 |
| Estonia | 9.4 | | - | 2002 | | | | |
| Hungary | 10.2 | 8.5 - 11.9 | - | 2001 | 6,475.2 | 6,134.4 - 6,816.0 | 60.0 - 70.0 | 2001 |
| Latvia | 9.6 | | - | 2001 | 800.0 | | | 2001 |
| Lithuania | 9.5 | 5.4 - 13.5 | - | 2002 | 5,400.0 | 2,700.0 - 8,110.0 | - | 2002 |
| Poland | 8.8 | 7.6 - 11.3 | - | 2002 | 3,770.0 | 2,520.0 - 5,030.0 | - | 2002 |
| Romania | 22.1 | 20.7 - 23.6 | - | 2002 | 10,830.0 | 9,420.0 - 12,240.0 | - | 2002 |
| Serbia and Montenegro | 4.7 | 4.7 - 6.6 | - | 2002 | | | | |
| Slovakia | 7.8 | 2.2 - 13.3 | - | 2002 | | | | |
| Slovenia | 10.7 | | - | 2001 | | | | |
| Ukraine | 18.0 | 15.0 - 20.0 | - | 2002 | 12,000.0 | 10,000.0 - 15,000.0 | - | 2002 |

## L.S.D
### Retail and wholesale prices and purity levels:
### breakdown by drug, region and country or territory
(prices expressed in US$ or converted equivalent, and purity levels in percentage)

| Region / country or territory | RETAIL PRICE (per dose) | | | | WHOLESALE PRICE (per thousand dose) | | | |
|---|---|---|---|---|---|---|---|---|
| | Typical | Range | Purity | Year | Typical | Range | Purity | Year |
| Western Europe | | | | | | | | |
| Austria | 10.8 | 7.5 - 14.1 | 10.0 | 2002 | 3,300.0 | 2,830.0 - 3,770.0 | - | 2002 |
| Belgium | 8.2 | 7.1 - 9.4 | - | 2002 | 2,017.9 | 1,793.7 - 2,242.2 | - | 2001 |
| Denmark | 6.3 | | - | 2002 | 4,622.5 | | - | 1999 |
| Finland | 14.1 | 9.2 - 19.3 | - | 1998 | 9,404.1 | 9,174.3 - 9,633.9 | - | 1998 |
| France | 9.4 | 4.7 - 14.1 | - | 2002 | | | | |
| Germany | 8.1 | 3.7 - 13.2 | - | 2002 | 2,509.3 | 456.2 - 4,562.4 | - | 2001 |
| Greece | 7.1 | 5.7 - 8.5 | - | 2002 | 3,770.0 | 2,830.0 - 4,710.0 | - | 2002 |
| Iceland | 17.9 | | - | 1998 | - | - | - | - |
| Ireland | 14.3 | 14.1 - 14.6 | - | 1998 | 1,790.0 | | - | 2001 |
| Italy | 25.8 | 25.2 - 26.4 | - | 2002 | 8,240.0 | | - | 2002 |
| Luxembourg | 12.3 | | - | 1998 | 9,943.2 | | - | 1998 |
| Netherlands | 5.7 | 1.9 - 9.4 | - | 2002 | | | | |
| Norway | 8.5 | 5.7 - 11.3 | - | 2002 | | | | |
| Portugal | 6.5 | | - | 2002 | | | | |
| Spain | 8.0 | | - | 2002 | 8,965.5 | | - | 1998 |
| Sweden | 7.7 | 5.1 - 10.2 | - | 2002 | | | | |
| Switzerland | 10.2 | 8.8 - 11.7 | - | 2001 | 13,240.0 | 7,660.0 - 19,150.0 | - | 2002 |
| United Kingdom | 4.8 | 1.5 - 7.5 | - | 2002 | 2,880.7 | 1,440.3 - 4,321.0 | - | 2001 |
| | | | | | | | | |
| Oceania | | | | | | | | |
| Australia | 16.5 | 12.4 - 26.7 | - | 1998 | | | | |
| New Zealand | 15.9 | 13.7 - 18.2 | - | 2002 | 9,110.0 | | - | 2002 |

## ECSTASY
### Retail and wholesale prices and purity levels:
### breakdown by drug, region and country or territory
(prices expressed in US$ or converted equivalent, and purity levels in percentage)

| Region / country or territory | RETAIL PRICE ( per tablet ) | | | | WHOLESALE PRICE ( per thousand tablets ) | | | |
|---|---|---|---|---|---|---|---|---|
| | Typical | Range | Purity | Year | Typical | Range | Purity | Year |
| **Africa** | | | | | | | | |
| North Africa | | | | | | | | |
| Egypt | 26.1 | 19.5- 32.6 | - | 2002 | 10,850.0 | | - | 2002 |
| Southern Africa | | | | | | | | |
| Namibia | 7.5 | 7.5 - 11.3 | - | 2002 | 12,055.8 | 11,421.3 - 12,690.4 | - | 2001 |
| South Africa | 8.5 | | - | 2002 | 6,960.6 | | - | 2002 |
| Zambia | 1.6 | | 10.0 | 2002 | | | | |
| Zimbabwe | 6.4 | 5.7 - 7.1 | - | 2002 | 50,000.0 | 45,454.5 - 54,545.4 | - | 2001 |
| West and Central Africa | | | | | | | | |
| Ghana | 6.0 | 5.0 - 7.0 | - | 2002 | | | | |
| **Americas** | | | | | | | | |
| Caribbean | | | | | | | | |
| Bahamas | 30.0 | 30.0 - 40.0 | - | 2002 | 30,000.0 | 25,000.0 - 40,000.0 | - | 2002 |
| Bermuda | 40.0 | 30.0 - 50.0 | - | 2002 | | | | |
| Cayman Islands | 25.0 | | - | 2002 | 25,000.0 | | - | 2002 |
| Jamaica | 22.5 | 20.0 - 25.0 | - | 2001 | | | | |
| Central America | | | | | | | | |
| Costa Rica | 11.9 | 9.8 - 14.0 | - | 2002 | 13,182.7 | 10,856.3 - 15,509.0 | - | 2001 |
| Nicaragua | 25.0 | | 90.0 | 2002 | 25,000.0 | | - | 2002 |
| Panama | 8.5 | 5.0 - 12.0 | 35.0 - 60.0 | 2001 | 8,000.0 | 6,000.0 - 10,000.0 | - | 2001 |
| North America | | | | | | | | |
| Canada | 22.3 | 12.8 - 31.9 | 37.0 | 2002 | 7,650.0 | 6,380.0 - 9,570.0 | - | 2002 |
| United States | 27.5 | 10,0 - 45.0 | - | 2000 | 11,000.0 | 2,000.0 - 20,000.0 | - | 2000 |
| South America | | | | | | | | |
| Argentina | 30.1 | 25.1 - 35.1 | - | 2001 | 34,360.0 | 27,490.0 - 41,230.0 | - | 2002 |
| Peru | 45.0 | 40.0 - 50.0 | 95.0 | 2001 | 20,000.0 | 15,000.0 - 25,000.0 | 95.0 | 2001 |
| Suriname | 3.5 | 2.3 - 4.6 | - | 2002 | | | | |
| Uruguay | 22.0 | 18.0 - 25.0 | - | 2002 | 21,500.00 | 18,000.0 - 25,000.0 | - | 2002 |
| Venezuela | 14.7 | 12.6 - 16.8 | - | 2002 | | | | |
| **Asia** | | | | | | | | |
| East and South-East Asia | | | | | | | | |
| China | 34.3 | | - | 1999 | 7,258.7 | 4,839.1 - 9,678.2 | - | 2001 |
| China (Hong Kong SAR) | 11.2 | 9.1 - 13.2 | - | 2002 | 4,970.0 | 4,490.0 - 7,060.0 | - | 2002 |
| Indonesia | 7.7 | 6.6 - 8.3 | - | 2002 | 7,720.0 | 6,620.0 - 8,830.0 | - | 2002 |
| Japan | 54.7 | 13.6 - 95.9 | - | 2002 | | | | |
| Republic of Korea | 59.2 | 39.5 - 79.0 | - | 2001 | 35,541.0 | 31,592.0 - 39,490.0 | - | 2001 |
| Macau | 22.0 | 18.0 - 31.0 | - | 2002 | | | | |
| Philippines | 34.5 | 32.4 - 36.5 | - | 2001 | | | | |
| Singapore | 12.6 | 11.2 - 13.9 | 39.0 | 2002 | 6,130.0 | 3,900.0 - 8,360.0 | - | 2002 |
| Thailand | 10.6 | 10.6 | - | 1999 | | | | |
| Vietnam | 18.4 | 16.7 - 20.0 | - | 2002 | | | | |
| Near and Middle East /South-West Asia | | | | | | | | |
| Israel | 12.5 | 7.0 - 18.0 | - | 2002 | 7,670.0 | 6,670.0 - 8,670.0 | - | 2002 |

## ECSTASY
### Retail and wholesale prices and purity levels:
### breakdown by drug, region and country or territory
(prices expressed in US$ or converted equivalent, and purity levels in percentage)

| Region / country or territory | RETAIL PRICE ( per tablet ) | | | | WHOLESALE PRICE ( per thousand tablets ) | | | |
|---|---|---|---|---|---|---|---|---|
| | Typical | Range | Purity | Year | Typical | Range | Purity | Year |
| **Europe** | | | | | | | | |
| Eastern Europe | | | | | | | | |
| Belarus | 17.0 | 15.0 - 20.0 | - | 2002 | | | | |
| Bulgaria | 9.6 | 7.2 - 12.0 | - | 2002 | 8,972.6 | 4,141.2 - 13,804.0 | - | 2001 |
| Croatia | 3.8 | 2.6 - 6.4 | - | 2002 | 1,910.0 | 1,270.0 - 2,550.0 | - | 2002 |
| Czech Republic | 5.7 | 3.8 - 7.5 | 10.0 - 20.0 | 2002 | 3,300.0 | 1,880.0 - 4,710.0 | 10.0 - 20.0 | 2002 |
| Estonia | 6.3 | 5.4 - 7.3 | 40.0 | 2002 | 1,560.0 | 1,320.0 - 1,790.0 | 50.0 - 98.0 | 2002 |
| Hungary | 9.4 | | 8.0 - 50.0 | 2002 | 3,770.0 | 1,880.0 - 5,650.0 | 8.0 - 50.0 | 2002 |
| Latvia | | | | | 803.5 | 401.7 - 1,205.2 | - | 2001 |
| Lithuania | 6.8 | 2.7 - 10.8 | 10.0 - 30.0 | 2002 | 3,510.0 | 1,350.0 - 5,400.0 | 10.0 - 30.0 | 2002 |
| Poland | 5.0 | 2.5 - 7.6 | - | 2002 | 1,764.5 | 1,512.4 - 2,016.6 | - | 2002 |
| Romania | 8.5 | 7.5 - 9.4 | - | 2002 | 3,770.0 | 2,830.0 - 4,710.0 | - | 2002 |
| Russian Federation | 17.5 | 15.0 - 20.0 | - | 2001 | | | | |
| Serbia and Montenegro | 4.7 | 4.7 - 6.6 | - | 2002 | 3,300.0 | 1,880.0 - 4,710.0 | - | 2002 |
| Slovakia | 7.3 | 4.2 - 10.4 | - | 2001 | | | | |
| Slovenia | 7.3 | 6.2 - 8.3 | - | 2002 | 6,590.0 | 5,650.0 - 7,540.0 | - | 2002 |
| The former Yug.Rep of M | 7.1 | 4.7 - 9.4 | - | 2002 | | | | |
| Western Europe | | | | | | | | |
| Andorra | 9.4 | 8.0 - 10.7 | - | 2001 | | | | |
| Austria | 8.5 | 3.8 - 13.2 | 1.0 - 80.0 | 2002 | 3,300.0 | 2,830.0 - 3,770.0 | - | 2002 |
| Belgium | 6.4 | 4.7 - 8.2 | 28.0 - 33.0 | 2002 | 710.0 | | - | 2002 |
| Cyprus | 10.0 | 7.0 - 15.0 | - | 2002 | | | | |
| Denmark | 17.8 | 4.4 - 31.5 | - | 2002 | 3,150.0 | 2,520.0 - 3,780.0 | - | 2002 |
| Finland | 15.1 | 11.3 - 18.8 | - | 2002 | 28,260.0 | 9,420.0 - 47,090.0 | - | 2002 |
| France | 9.4 | 6.6 - 14.1 | - | 2002 | 1,650.0 | 940.0 - 2,350.0 | - | 2002 |
| Germany | 8.2 | 3.8 - 13.2 | - | 2002 | 2,690.0 | 1,340.0 - 3,960.0 | - | 2002 |
| Greece | 18.8 | | - | 2002 | 9,890.0 | 5,650.0 - 14,130.0 | - | 2002 |
| Iceland | 37.0 | 25.0 - 50.0 | - | 2002 | | | | |
| Ireland | 11.8 | 9.4 - 14.1 | - | 2002 | 1,880.0 | | - | 2002 |
| Italy | 20.7 | 18.5 - 22.9 | - | 2002 | 4,890.0 | 4,690.0 - 5,090.0 | 1.0 - 35.0 | 2002 |
| Luxembourg | 13.3 | | - | 1999 | 6,925.0 | 6,747.6 - 7,102.3 | - | 1998 |
| Malta | 24.9 | 22.6 - 27.1 | - | 2001 | 15,821.8 | 13,561.5 - 18,082.0 | - | 2001 |
| Netherlands | 3.8 | | - | 2002 | 2,848.3 | 2,475.5 - 3,465.3 | - | 1998 |
| Norway | 17.4 | 11.3 - 23.6 | 20.0 - 50.0 | 2002 | 37,680.0 | 28,260.0 - 47,090.0 | 20.0 - 50.0 | 2002 |
| Portugal | 5.6 | | - | 2002 | 1,410.0 | 940.0 - 1,880.0 | - | 2002 |
| Spain | 10.3 | | - | 2002 | 15,689.7 | | - | 1998 |
| Sweden | 12.8 | 10.2 - 15.3 | - | 2002 | 4,090.0 | 2,040.0 - 6,130.0 | - | 2002 |
| Switzerland | 14.4 | 9.6 - 19.2 | - | 2002 | 13,500.0 | 6,380.0 - 25,530.0 | - | 2002 |
| Turkey | 17.5 | 15.0 - 20.0 | - | 2001 | 12,720.0 | 6,590.0 - 18,840.0 | - | 2002 |
| United Kingdom | 9.0 | 1.5 - 22.4 | - | 2002 | 2,610.0 | 2,240.0 - 2,990.0 | - | 2002 |
| **Oceania** | | | | | | | | |
| Australia | 28.6 | 15.6 - 41.7 | - | 2001 | 12,785.0 | 9,590.0 - 15,980.0 | - | 1999 |
| New Zealand | 38.7 | 31.9 - 45.6 | - | 2002 | 25,050.0 | 18,220.0 - 31,880.0 | - | 2002 |

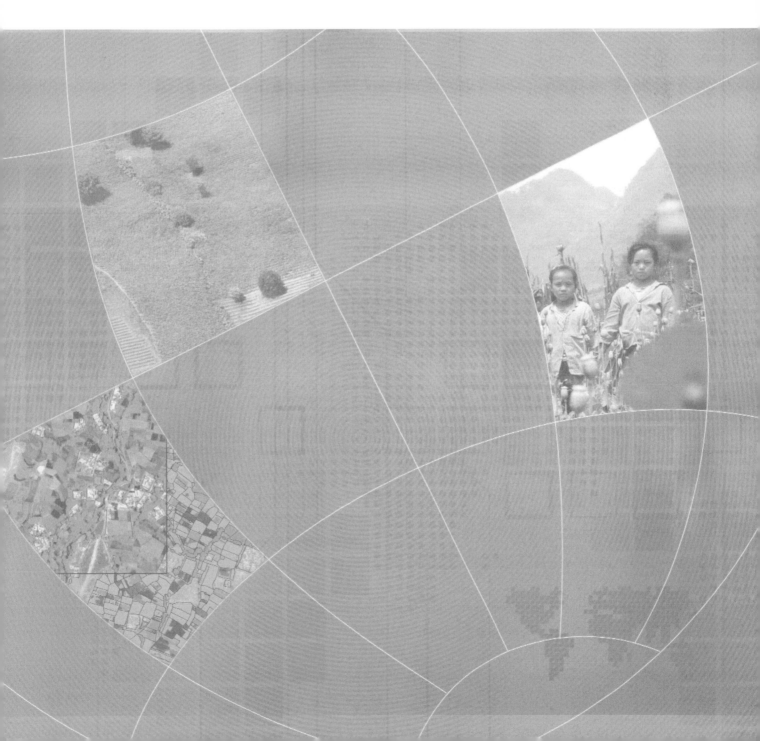

# 6. CONSUMPTION

# 6.1. Annual prevalence of drug abuse

## 6.1.1. Opiates

**OPIATES**

Annual prevalence of abuse as percentage of the population
aged 15-64 (unless otherwise indicated)

**AFRICA & AMERICAS**

**AFRICA**

**North and Eastern Africa**

| | |
|---|---|
| Mauritius, 1998 | 0.8 |
| Morocco** | 0.2 |
| Kenya** | 0.1 |
| Uganda** | 0.04 |
| Rwanda** | 0.04 |
| Ethiopia** | 0.04 |
| Tanzania, United Rep 1998 | 0.02 |

**West and Central Africa**

| | |
|---|---|
| Ghana, 1998 | 0.7 |
| Nigeria, (10+), 1999 * | 0.6 |
| Chad, 1995 | 0.2 |
| Senegal ** | 0.03 |
| Sierra Leone, 1997 | 0.01 |

**Southern Africa**

| | |
|---|---|
| South Africa | 0.2 |
| Namibia, 2000 | 0.03 |
| Zimbabwe ** | 001 |

**AMERICAS**

**Central America**

| | |
|---|---|
| Costa Rica * | 0.1 |
| Honduras, 1995 | 0.1 |
| Panama ** | 0.1 |
| El Salvador ** | 0.1 |

**North America**

| | |
|---|---|
| USA, (12+), 2000 | 0.6 |
| Canada, (Ontario,18+), 2000 | 0.4 |
| Mexico, (12-65), 2001 | 0.4 |

**South America**

| | |
|---|---|
| Brazil, (12-65), 2001 | 0.6 |
| Venezuela, 2002 | 0.3 |
| Chile, (15-64), 2002 | 0.3 |
| Colombia, (15-64), 1998 | 0.2 |
| Argentina (16-64), 1999 | 0.1 |
| Ecuador* (15-64), 1999 | 0.1 |
| Bolivia ** | 0.04 |
| Suriname, 1998 | 0.02 |
| Uruguay, 2001 | 0.01 |

**The Caribbean**

| | |
|---|---|
| Dominican Rep,*(12-70), 2001 | 0.09 |
| Antigua Barbuda, 2000 | 0.05 |
| Barbados,** | 0.01 |

*UNODC estimates based on local studies, special population group studies, and/or law enforcement agency assessments.
** Tentative estimate for the late 1990s.

Sources: Annual Report Questionnaires, Government Reports, US Department of State, European Monitoring Center for Drugs and Drug Abuse (EMCDDA)

0%   0.5%   1.0%   1.5%   2.0%   2.5%   3%

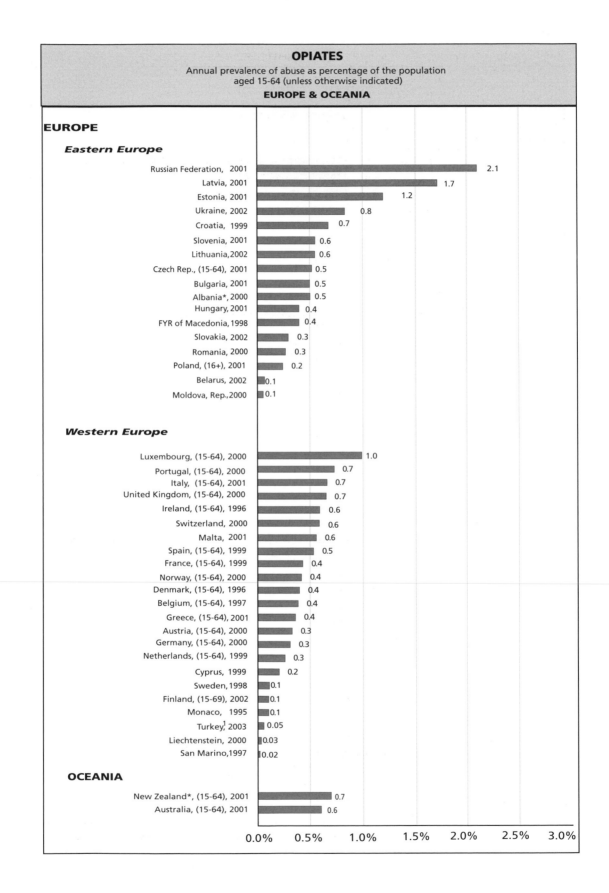

**OPIATES**

Annual prevalence of abuse as percentage of the population
aged 15-64 (unless otherwise indicated)

**EUROPE & OCEANIA**

**EUROPE**

*Eastern Europe*

| | |
|---|---|
| Russian Federation, 2001 | 2.1 |
| Latvia, 2001 | 1.7 |
| Estonia, 2001 | 1.2 |
| Ukraine, 2002 | 0.8 |
| Croatia, 1999 | 0.7 |
| Slovenia, 2001 | 0.6 |
| Lithuania,2002 | 0.6 |
| Czech Rep., (15-64), 2001 | 0.5 |
| Bulgaria, 2001 | 0.5 |
| Albania*, 2000 | 0.5 |
| Hungary, 2001 | 0.4 |
| FYR of Macedonia, 1998 | 0.4 |
| Slovakia, 2002 | 0.3 |
| Romania, 2000 | 0.3 |
| Poland, (16+), 2001 | 0.2 |
| Belarus, 2002 | 0.1 |
| Moldova, Rep.,2000 | 0.1 |

*Western Europe*

| | |
|---|---|
| Luxembourg, (15-64), 2000 | 1.0 |
| Portugal, (15-64), 2000 | 0.7 |
| Italy, (15-64), 2001 | 0.7 |
| United Kingdom, (15-64), 2000 | 0.7 |
| Ireland, (15-64), 1996 | 0.6 |
| Switzerland, 2000 | 0.6 |
| Malta, 2001 | 0.6 |
| Spain, (15-64), 1999 | 0.5 |
| France, (15-64), 1999 | 0.4 |
| Norway, (15-64), 2000 | 0.4 |
| Denmark, (15-64), 1996 | 0.4 |
| Belgium, (15-64), 1997 | 0.4 |
| Greece, (15-64), 2001 | 0.4 |
| Austria, (15-64), 2000 | 0.3 |
| Germany, (15-64), 2000 | 0.3 |
| Netherlands, (15-64), 1999 | 0.3 |
| Cyprus, 1999 | 0.2 |
| Sweden,1998 | 0.1 |
| Finland, (15-69), 2002 | 0.1 |
| Monaco, 1995 | 0.1 |
| Turkey[1] 2003 | 0.05 |
| Liechtenstein, 2000 | 0.03 |
| San Marino,1997 | 0.02 |

**OCEANIA**

| | |
|---|---|
| New Zealand*, (15-64), 2001 | 0.7 |
| Australia, (15-64), 2001 | 0.6 |

0.0%    0.5%    1.0%    1.5%    2.0%    2.5%    3.0%

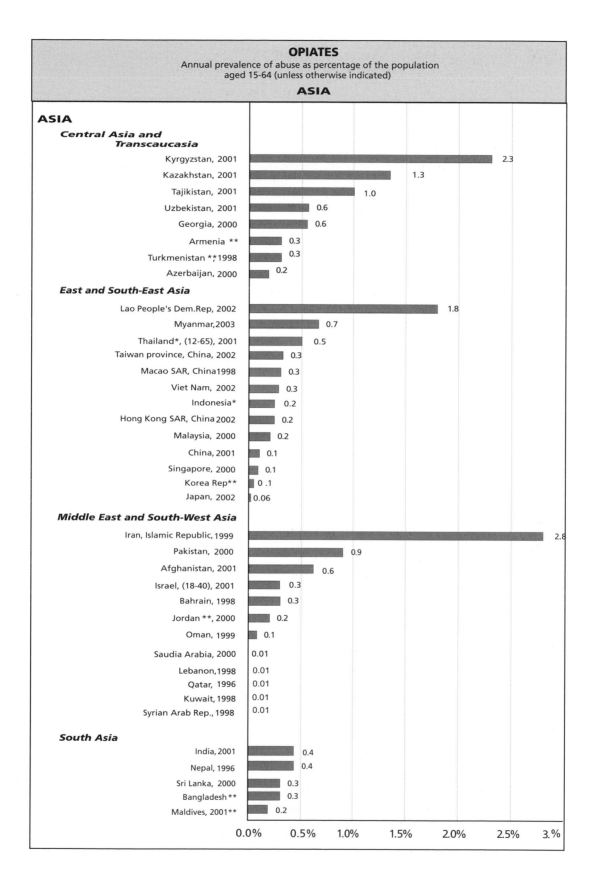

**OPIATES**
Annual prevalence of abuse as percentage of the population
aged 15-64 (unless otherwise indicated)
**ASIA**

**ASIA**

**Central Asia and Transcaucasia**

| | |
|---|---|
| Kyrgyzstan, 2001 | 2.3 |
| Kazakhstan, 2001 | 1.3 |
| Tajikistan, 2001 | 1.0 |
| Uzbekistan, 2001 | 0.6 |
| Georgia, 2000 | 0.6 |
| Armenia ** | 0.3 |
| Turkmenistan **,1998 | 0.3 |
| Azerbaijan, 2000 | 0.2 |

**East and South-East Asia**

| | |
|---|---|
| Lao People's Dem.Rep, 2002 | 1.8 |
| Myanmar,2003 | 0.7 |
| Thailand*, (12-65), 2001 | 0.5 |
| Taiwan province, China, 2002 | 0.3 |
| Macao SAR, China1998 | 0.3 |
| Viet Nam, 2002 | 0.3 |
| Indonesia* | 0.2 |
| Hong Kong SAR, China 2002 | 0.2 |
| Malaysia, 2000 | 0.2 |
| China, 2001 | 0.1 |
| Singapore, 2000 | 0.1 |
| Korea Rep** | 0 .1 |
| Japan, 2002 | 0.06 |

**Middle East and South-West Asia**

| | |
|---|---|
| Iran, Islamic Republic, 1999 | 2.8 |
| Pakistan, 2000 | 0.9 |
| Afghanistan, 2001 | 0.6 |
| Israel, (18-40), 2001 | 0.3 |
| Bahrain, 1998 | 0.3 |
| Jordan **, 2000 | 0.2 |
| Oman, 1999 | 0.1 |
| Saudia Arabia, 2000 | 0.01 |
| Lebanon,1998 | 0.01 |
| Qatar, 1996 | 0.01 |
| Kuwait, 1998 | 0.01 |
| Syrian Arab Rep., 1998 | 0.01 |

**South Asia**

| | |
|---|---|
| India, 2001 | 0.4 |
| Nepal, 1996 | 0.4 |
| Sri Lanka, 2000 | 0.3 |
| Bangladesh ** | 0.3 |
| Maldives, 2001** | 0.2 |

0.0%  0.5%  1.0%  1.5%  2.0%  2.5%  3.%

## 6.1.2. Cocaine

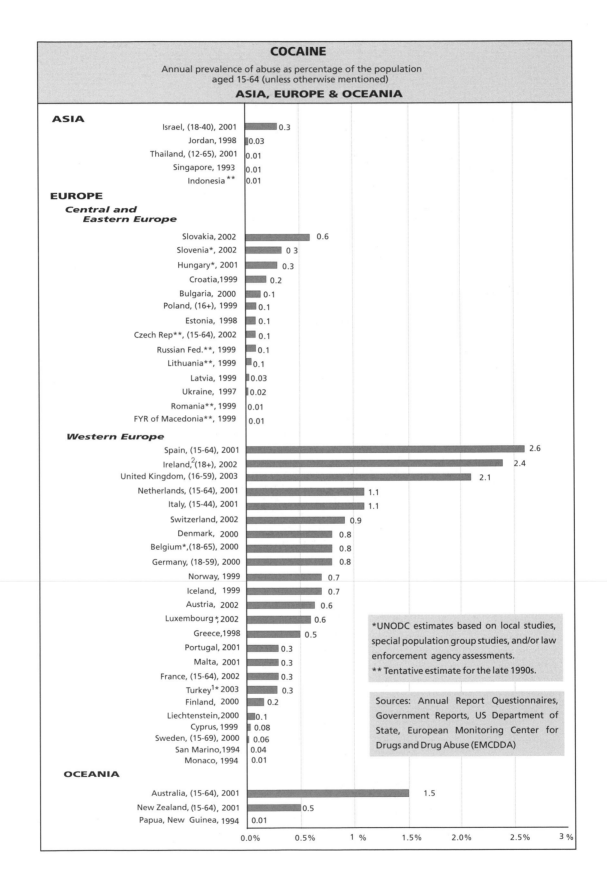

**COCAINE**

Annual prevalence of abuse as percentage of the population
aged 15-64 (unless otherwise mentioned)

**ASIA, EUROPE & OCEANIA**

**ASIA**

| | |
|---|---|
| Israel, (18-40), 2001 | 0.3 |
| Jordan, 1998 | 0.03 |
| Thailand, (12-65), 2001 | 0.01 |
| Singapore, 1993 | 0.01 |
| Indonesia** | 0.01 |

**EUROPE**

*Central and Eastern Europe*

| | |
|---|---|
| Slovakia, 2002 | 0.6 |
| Slovenia*, 2002 | 0 3 |
| Hungary*, 2001 | 0.3 |
| Croatia,1999 | 0.2 |
| Bulgaria, 2000 | 0·1 |
| Poland, (16+), 1999 | 0.1 |
| Estonia, 1998 | 0.1 |
| Czech Rep**, (15-64), 2002 | 0.1 |
| Russian Fed.**, 1999 | 0.1 |
| Lithuania**, 1999 | 0.1 |
| Latvia, 1999 | 0.03 |
| Ukraine, 1997 | 0.02 |
| Romania**, 1999 | 0.01 |
| FYR of Macedonia**, 1999 | 0.01 |

*Western Europe*

| | |
|---|---|
| Spain, (15-64), 2001 | 2.6 |
| Ireland,[2](18+), 2002 | 2.4 |
| United Kingdom, (16-59), 2003 | 2.1 |
| Netherlands, (15-64), 2001 | 1.1 |
| Italy, (15-44), 2001 | 1.1 |
| Switzerland, 2002 | 0.9 |
| Denmark, 2000 | 0.8 |
| Belgium*,(18-65), 2000 | 0.8 |
| Germany, (18-59), 2000 | 0.8 |
| Norway, 1999 | 0.7 |
| Iceland, 1999 | 0.7 |
| Austria, 2002 | 0.6 |
| Luxembourg *, 2002 | 0.6 |
| Greece,1998 | 0.5 |
| Portugal, 2001 | 0.3 |
| Malta, 2001 | 0.3 |
| France, (15-64), 2002 | 0.3 |
| Turkey[1]* 2003 | 0.3 |
| Finland, 2000 | 0.2 |
| Liechtenstein,2000 | 0.1 |
| Cyprus, 1999 | 0.08 |
| Sweden, (15-69), 2000 | 0.06 |
| San Marino,1994 | 0.04 |
| Monaco, 1994 | 0.01 |

*UNODC estimates based on local studies, special population group studies, and/or law enforcement agency assessments.
** Tentative estimate for the late 1990s.

Sources: Annual Report Questionnaires, Government Reports, US Department of State, European Monitoring Center for Drugs and Drug Abuse (EMCDDA)

**OCEANIA**

| | |
|---|---|
| Australia, (15-64), 2001 | 1.5 |
| New Zealand, (15-64), 2001 | 0.5 |
| Papua, New Guinea, 1994 | 0.01 |

0.0%   0.5%   1 %   1.5%   2.0%   2.5%   3 %

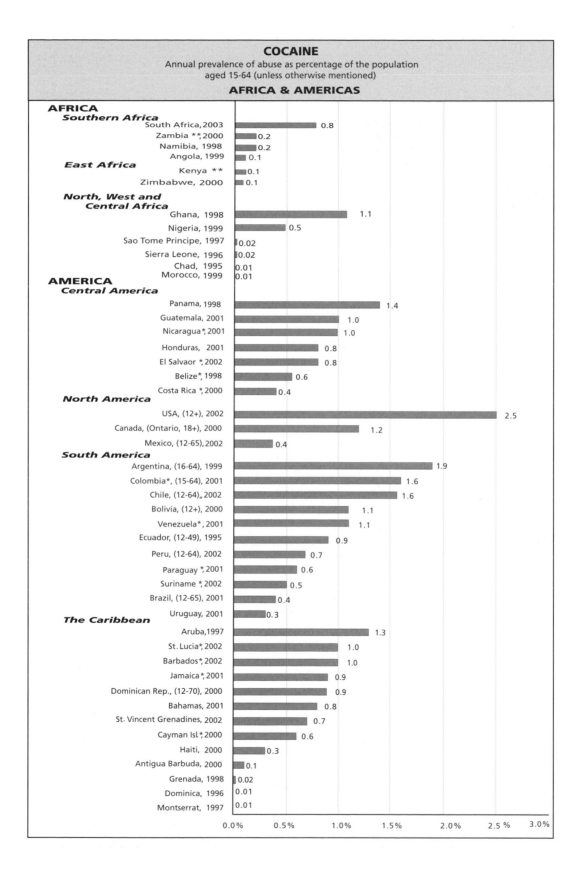

**COCAINE**

Annual prevalence of abuse as percentage of the population aged 15-64 (unless otherwise mentioned)

**AFRICA & AMERICAS**

**AFRICA**
**Southern Africa**
- South Africa, 2003 — 0.8
- Zambia **, 2000 — 0.2
- Namibia, 1998 — 0.2
- Angola, 1999 — 0.1

**East Africa**
- Kenya ** — 0.1
- Zimbabwe, 2000 — 0.1

**North, West and Central Africa**
- Ghana, 1998 — 1.1
- Nigeria, 1999 — 0.5
- Sao Tome Principe, 1997 — 0.02
- Sierra Leone, 1996 — 0.02
- Chad, 1995 — 0.01
- Morocco, 1999 — 0.01

**AMERICA**
**Central America**
- Panama, 1998 — 1.4
- Guatemala, 2001 — 1.0
- Nicaragua *, 2001 — 1.0
- Honduras, 2001 — 0.8
- El Salvaor *, 2002 — 0.8
- Belize*, 1998 — 0.6
- Costa Rica *, 2000 — 0.4

**North America**
- USA, (12+), 2002 — 2.5
- Canada, (Ontario, 18+), 2000 — 1.2
- Mexico, (12-65), 2002 — 0.4

**South America**
- Argentina, (16-64), 1999 — 1.9
- Colombia*, (15-64), 2001 — 1.6
- Chile, (12-64),, 2002 — 1.6
- Bolivia, (12+), 2000 — 1.1
- Venezuela*, 2001 — 1.1
- Ecuador, (12-49), 1995 — 0.9
- Peru, (12-64), 2002 — 0.7
- Paraguay *, 2001 — 0.6
- Suriname *, 2002 — 0.5
- Brazil, (12-65), 2001 — 0.4
- Uruguay, 2001 — 0.3

**The Caribbean**
- Aruba, 1997 — 1.3
- St. Lucia*, 2002 — 1.0
- Barbados*, 2002 — 1.0
- Jamaica*, 2001 — 0.9
- Dominican Rep., (12-70), 2000 — 0.9
- Bahamas, 2001 — 0.8
- St. Vincent Grenadines, 2002 — 0.7
- Cayman Isl.*, 2000 — 0.6
- Haiti, 2000 — 0.3
- Antigua Barbuda, 2000 — 0.1
- Grenada, 1998 — 0.02
- Dominica, 1996 — 0.01
- Montserrat, 1997 — 0.01

0.0%   0.5%   1.0%   1.5%   2.0%   2.5%   3.0%

## 6.1.3. Cannabis

**CANNABIS**

Annual prevalence of abuse as percentage of the population aged
15-64 (unless otherwise indicated)

**AFRICA & AMERICAS**

**AFRICA**

*Eastern Africa*

| | |
|---|---|
| Mauritius, 2000 | 7.0 |
| Kenya*, 1994 | 4.0 |
| Ethiopia, 1998 | 2.6 |
| Somalia, 2002 | 2.5 |
| Uganda ** | 1.4 |
| Tanzania, United Rep., 1999 | 0.2 |

*North Africa*

| | |
|---|---|
| Morocco ** | 7.4 |
| Egypt**, 1997 | 5.2 |
| Libyan Arab Jamahiriya, 1998 | 0.1 |

*West and Central Africa*

| | |
|---|---|
| Ghana, 1998 | 21.5 |
| Sierra Leone, 1996 | 16.1 |
| Nigeria, 1999 | 13.8 |
| Mali*, 1999 | 7.8 |
| Angola, 1999 | 2.1 |
| Chad, 1995 | 0.9 |
| Sao Tom & Prin., 1997 | 0.01 |
| Cote d'Ivoire, 1999 | 0.01 |

*Southern Africa*

| | |
|---|---|
| Zambia, 2000 | 15.0 |
| South Africa*, 2002 | 8.4 |
| Zimbabwe, 2000 | 6.9 |
| Namibia, 2000 | 3.9 |

**AMERICAS**

*Central America*

| | |
|---|---|
| Belize* | 6.8 |
| Guatemala*, 2002 | 3.8 |
| Nicaragua ** | 2.6 |
| Panama, 1999 | 2.5 |
| El Salvador ** | 2.0 |
| Honduras * | 1.6 |
| Costa Rica, 2001 | 1.3 |

*North America*

| | |
|---|---|
| USA, (12+), 2002 | 11.0 |
| Canada, (Ontario, 18+), 2000 | 10.8 |
| Mexico, (12-65), 2002 | 0.6 |

*South America*

| | |
|---|---|
| Chile, (12-64), 2002 | 5.2 |
| Colombia, (15-64), 2001 | 4.3 |
| Argentina, (16-64), 1999 | 3.7 |
| Venezuela*, 2002 | 3.0 |
| Ecuador (12-49), 1995 | 3.0 |
| Guyana*, 2002 | 2.6 |
| Bolivia, (12-50), 2000 | 2.5 |
| Suriname*, 2002 | 2.3 |
| Paraguay, 2002 | 1.8 |
| Peru, (12-64), 2002 | 1.8 |
| Uruguay, 2001 | 1.5 |
| Brazil, (12-65), 2001 | 1.0 |

*The Caribbean*

| | |
|---|---|
| Jamaica*, 2002 | 8.0 |
| Barbados*, 2002 | 7.7 |
| St. Vincent Grenadines** | 6.8 |
| Bahamas* | 5.0 |
| Dominican Rep.* (12-70), 2001 | 2.1 |
| Montserrat, 1997 | 0.8 |
| Dominica, 1997 | 0.1 |
| Grenada, 1998 | 0.01 |

*UNODC estimates based on local studies, special population group studies, and/or law enforcement agency assessments.
** Tentative estimate for the late 1990s.

Sources: Annual Report Questionnaires, Government Reports, US Department of State, European Monitoring Center for Drugs and Drug Abuse (EMCDDA)

0%   5%   10%   15%   20%   25%

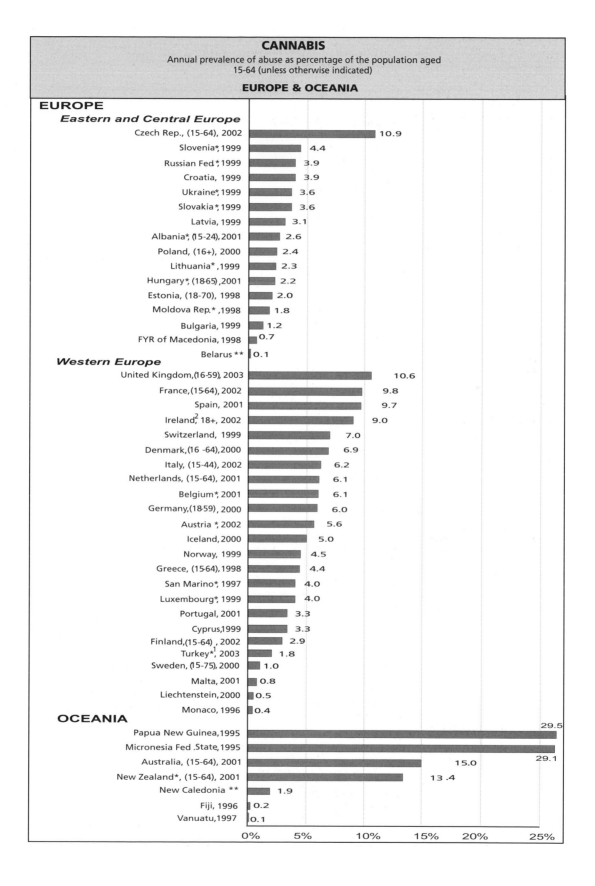

**CANNABIS**

Annual prevalence of abuse as percentage of the population aged
15-64 (unless otherwise indicated)

**EUROPE & OCEANIA**

**EUROPE**

*Eastern and Central Europe*

| | |
|---|---|
| Czech Rep., (15-64), 2002 | 10.9 |
| Slovenia*, 1999 | 4.4 |
| Russian Fed.*, 1999 | 3.9 |
| Croatia, 1999 | 3.9 |
| Ukraine*, 1999 | 3.6 |
| Slovakia*, 1999 | 3.6 |
| Latvia, 1999 | 3.1 |
| Albania*, (15-24), 2001 | 2.6 |
| Poland, (16+), 2000 | 2.4 |
| Lithuania*, 1999 | 2.3 |
| Hungary*, (18-65), 2001 | 2.2 |
| Estonia, (18-70), 1998 | 2.0 |
| Moldova Rep.*, 1998 | 1.8 |
| Bulgaria, 1999 | 1.2 |
| FYR of Macedonia, 1998 | 0.7 |
| Belarus ** | 0.1 |

*Western Europe*

| | |
|---|---|
| United Kingdom, (16-59), 2003 | 10.6 |
| France, (15-64), 2002 | 9.8 |
| Spain, 2001 | 9.7 |
| Ireland,[2] 18+, 2002 | 9.0 |
| Switzerland, 1999 | 7.0 |
| Denmark, (16-64), 2000 | 6.9 |
| Italy, (15-44), 2002 | 6.2 |
| Netherlands, (15-64), 2001 | 6.1 |
| Belgium*, 2001 | 6.1 |
| Germany, (18-59), 2000 | 6.0 |
| Austria *, 2002 | 5.6 |
| Iceland, 2000 | 5.0 |
| Norway, 1999 | 4.5 |
| Greece, (15-64), 1998 | 4.4 |
| San Marino*, 1997 | 4.0 |
| Luxembourg*, 1999 | 4.0 |
| Portugal, 2001 | 3.3 |
| Cyprus, 1999 | 3.3 |
| Finland, (15-64), 2002 | 2.9 |
| Turkey*,[1] 2003 | 1.8 |
| Sweden, (15-75), 2000 | 1.0 |
| Malta, 2001 | 0.8 |
| Liechtenstein, 2000 | 0.5 |
| Monaco, 1996 | 0.4 |

**OCEANIA**

| | |
|---|---|
| Papua New Guinea, 1995 | 29.5 |
| Micronesia Fed .State, 1995 | 29.1 |
| Australia, (15-64), 2001 | 15.0 |
| New Zealand*, (15-64), 2001 | 13.4 |
| New Caledonia ** | 1.9 |
| Fiji, 1996 | 0.2 |
| Vanuatu, 1997 | 0.1 |

0%   5%   10%   15%   20%   25%

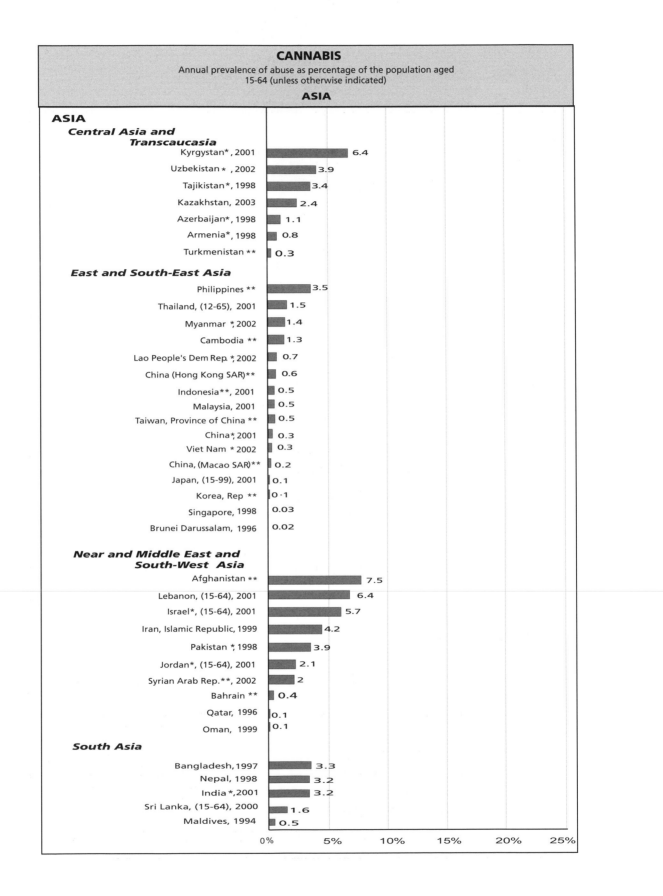

**CANNABIS**
Annual prevalence of abuse as percentage of the population aged
15-64 (unless otherwise indicated)

**ASIA**

**ASIA**
**Central Asia and Transcaucasia**

| | |
|---|---|
| Kyrgystan*, 2001 | 6.4 |
| Uzbekistan * , 2002 | 3.9 |
| Tajikistan*, 1998 | 3.4 |
| Kazakhstan, 2003 | 2.4 |
| Azerbaijan*, 1998 | 1.1 |
| Armenia*, 1998 | 0.8 |
| Turkmenistan ** | 0.3 |

**East and South-East Asia**

| | |
|---|---|
| Philippines ** | 3.5 |
| Thailand, (12-65), 2001 | 1.5 |
| Myanmar *, 2002 | 1.4 |
| Cambodia ** | 1.3 |
| Lao People's Dem Rep. *, 2002 | 0.7 |
| China (Hong Kong SAR)** | 0.6 |
| Indonesia**, 2001 | 0.5 |
| Malaysia, 2001 | 0.5 |
| Taiwan, Province of China ** | 0.5 |
| China*, 2001 | 0.3 |
| Viet Nam * 2002 | 0.3 |
| China, (Macao SAR)** | 0.2 |
| Japan, (15-99), 2001 | 0.1 |
| Korea, Rep ** | 0.1 |
| Singapore, 1998 | 0.03 |
| Brunei Darussalam, 1996 | 0.02 |

**Near and Middle East and South-West Asia**

| | |
|---|---|
| Afghanistan ** | 7.5 |
| Lebanon, (15-64), 2001 | 6.4 |
| Israel*, (15-64), 2001 | 5.7 |
| Iran, Islamic Republic, 1999 | 4.2 |
| Pakistan *, 1998 | 3.9 |
| Jordan*, (15-64), 2001 | 2.1 |
| Syrian Arab Rep.**, 2002 | 2 |
| Bahrain ** | 0.4 |
| Qatar, 1996 | 0.1 |
| Oman, 1999 | 0.1 |

**South Asia**

| | |
|---|---|
| Bangladesh,1997 | 3.3 |
| Nepal, 1998 | 3.2 |
| India *,2001 | 3.2 |
| Sri Lanka, (15-64), 2000 | 1.6 |
| Maldives, 1994 | 0.5 |

0%   5%   10%   15%   20%   25%

## 6.1.4. Amphetamines-type stimulants

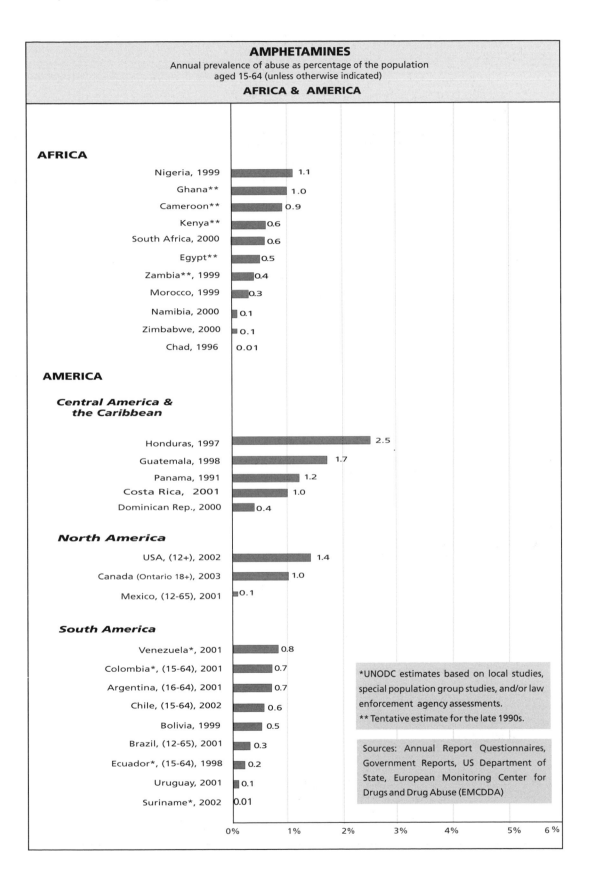

**AMPHETAMINES**
Annual prevalence of abuse as percentage of the population
aged 15-64 (unless otherwise indicated)
**AFRICA & AMERICA**

**AFRICA**

| | |
|---|---|
| Nigeria, 1999 | 1.1 |
| Ghana** | 1.0 |
| Cameroon** | 0.9 |
| Kenya** | 0.6 |
| South Africa, 2000 | 0.6 |
| Egypt** | 0.5 |
| Zambia**, 1999 | 0.4 |
| Morocco, 1999 | 0.3 |
| Namibia, 2000 | 0.1 |
| Zimbabwe, 2000 | 0.1 |
| Chad, 1996 | 0.01 |

**AMERICA**

*Central America & the Caribbean*

| | |
|---|---|
| Honduras, 1997 | 2.5 |
| Guatemala, 1998 | 1.7 |
| Panama, 1991 | 1.2 |
| Costa Rica, 2001 | 1.0 |
| Dominican Rep., 2000 | 0.4 |

*North America*

| | |
|---|---|
| USA, (12+), 2002 | 1.4 |
| Canada (Ontario 18+), 2003 | 1.0 |
| Mexico, (12-65), 2001 | 0.1 |

*South America*

| | |
|---|---|
| Venezuela*, 2001 | 0.8 |
| Colombia*, (15-64), 2001 | 0.7 |
| Argentina, (16-64), 2001 | 0.7 |
| Chile, (15-64), 2002 | 0.6 |
| Bolivia, 1999 | 0.5 |
| Brazil, (12-65), 2001 | 0.3 |
| Ecuador*, (15-64), 1998 | 0.2 |
| Uruguay, 2001 | 0.1 |
| Suriname*, 2002 | 0.01 |

*UNODC estimates based on local studies, special population group studies, and/or law enforcement agency assessments.
** Tentative estimate for the late 1990s.

Sources: Annual Report Questionnaires, Government Reports, US Department of State, European Monitoring Center for Drugs and Drug Abuse (EMCDDA)

0%   1%   2%   3%   4%   5%   6 %

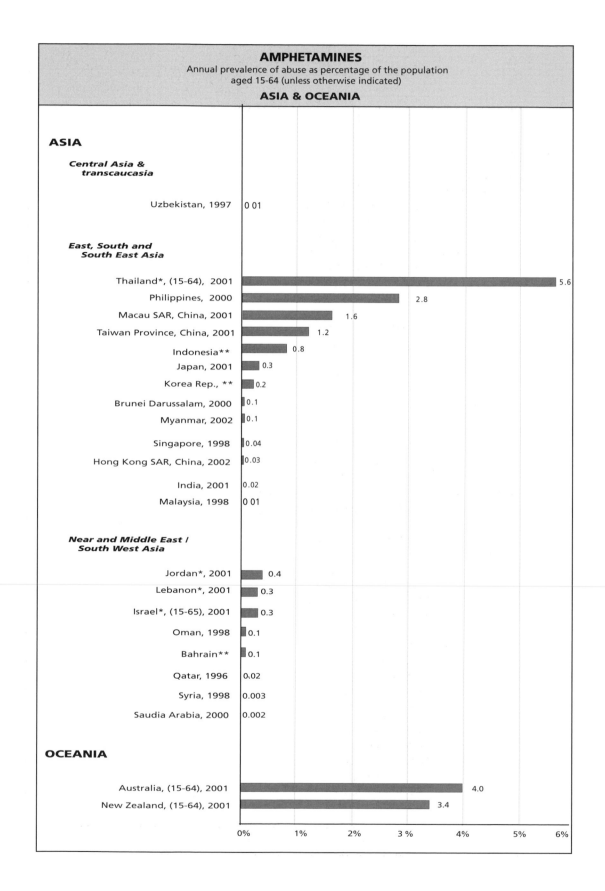

**AMPHETAMINES**
Annual prevalence of abuse as percentage of the population
aged 15-64 (unless otherwise indicated)

**ASIA & OCEANIA**

**ASIA**

*Central Asia &
transcaucasia*

Uzbekistan, 1997 — 0 01

*East, South and
South East Asia*

Thailand*, (15-64), 2001 — 5.6
Philippines, 2000 — 2.8
Macau SAR, China, 2001 — 1.6
Taiwan Province, China, 2001 — 1.2
Indonesia** — 0.8
Japan, 2001 — 0.3
Korea Rep., ** — 0.2
Brunei Darussalam, 2000 — 0.1
Myanmar, 2002 — 0.1
Singapore, 1998 — 0.04
Hong Kong SAR, China, 2002 — 0.03
India, 2001 — 0.02
Malaysia, 1998 — 0 01

*Near and Middle East /
South West Asia*

Jordan*, 2001 — 0.4
Lebanon*, 2001 — 0.3
Israel*, (15-65), 2001 — 0.3
Oman, 1998 — 0.1
Bahrain** — 0.1
Qatar, 1996 — 0.02
Syria, 1998 — 0.003
Saudia Arabia, 2000 — 0.002

**OCEANIA**

Australia, (15-64), 2001 — 4.0
New Zealand, (15-64), 2001 — 3.4

0%  1%  2%  3 %  4%  5%  6%

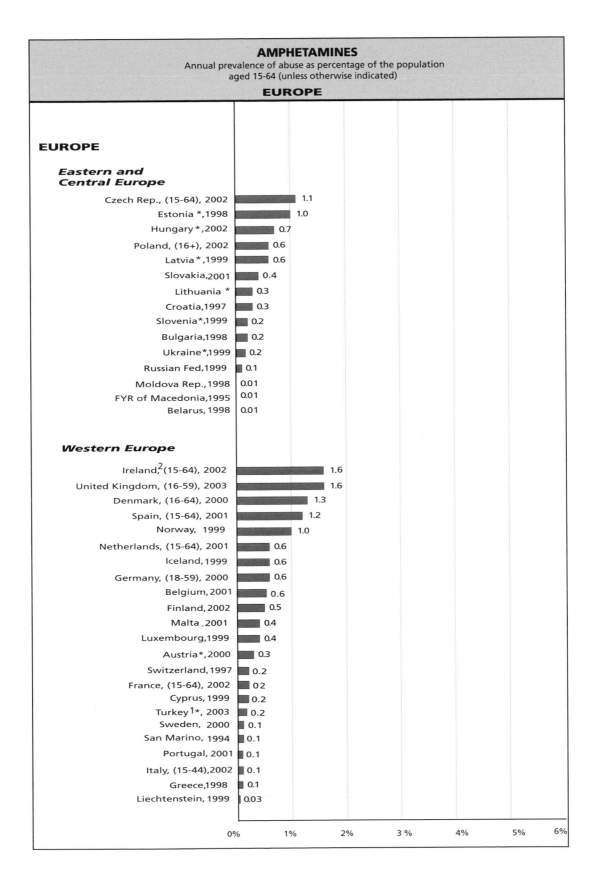

**AMPHETAMINES**
Annual prevalence of abuse as percentage of the population
aged 15-64 (unless otherwise indicated)

**EUROPE**

**EUROPE**

*Eastern and
Central Europe*

|  |  |
|---|---|
| Czech Rep., (15-64), 2002 | 1.1 |
| Estonia *,1998 | 1.0 |
| Hungary *,2002 | 0.7 |
| Poland, (16+), 2002 | 0.6 |
| Latvia *,1999 | 0.6 |
| Slovakia,2001 | 0.4 |
| Lithuania * | 0.3 |
| Croatia,1997 | 0.3 |
| Slovenia*,1999 | 0.2 |
| Bulgaria,1998 | 0.2 |
| Ukraine*,1999 | 0.2 |
| Russian Fed,1999 | 0.1 |
| Moldova Rep.,1998 | 0.01 |
| FYR of Macedonia,1995 | 0.01 |
| Belarus, 1998 | 0.01 |

*Western Europe*

|  |  |
|---|---|
| Ireland[2] (15-64), 2002 | 1.6 |
| United Kingdom, (16-59), 2003 | 1.6 |
| Denmark, (16-64), 2000 | 1.3 |
| Spain, (15-64), 2001 | 1.2 |
| Norway, 1999 | 1.0 |
| Netherlands, (15-64), 2001 | 0.6 |
| Iceland,1999 | 0.6 |
| Germany, (18-59), 2000 | 0.6 |
| Belgium,2001 | 0.6 |
| Finland,2002 | 0.5 |
| Malta .2001 | 0.4 |
| Luxembourg,1999 | 0.4 |
| Austria*,2000 | 0.3 |
| Switzerland,1997 | 0.2 |
| France, (15-64), 2002 | 0.2 |
| Cyprus,1999 | 0.2 |
| Turkey[1]*, 2003 | 0.2 |
| Sweden, 2000 | 0.1 |
| San Marino, 1994 | 0.1 |
| Portugal, 2001 | 0.1 |
| Italy, (15-44),2002 | 0.1 |
| Greece,1998 | 0.1 |
| Liechtenstein, 1999 | 0.03 |

0%   1%   2%   3 %   4%   5%   6%

## 6.1.5. Ecstasy

**ECSTASY**

Annual prevalence of abuse as percentage of the population aged 15-64

**EUROPE**

**EUROPE**
*Eastern and Central Europe*

|  |  |
|---------|-------|
| Czech Rep., (15-64), 2002 | 2.5 |
| Hungary *, 2001 | 1.0 |
| Slovakia*, 2002 | 0.8 |
| Latvia**, 1999 | 0.7 |
| Slovenia* | 0.5 |
| Lithuania**, 1999 | 0.3 |
| Estonia**, 1999 | 0.3 |
| Croatia, 1999 | 0.3 |
| Poland, (16+), 2002 | 0.2 |
| Bulgaria, 2000 | 0.2 |
| Ukraine**, 1999 | 0.1 |
| Russian Fed., 1999 | 0.1 |
| FYR of Macedonia **, 1999 | 0.1 |
| Belarus*, 1997 | 0.01 |

*Western Europe*

|  |  |
|---------|-------|
| Ireland,[2] (18+), 2002 | 3.4 |
| United Kingdom, (16-59), 2003 | 2.0 |
| Spain, 2001 | 1.8 |
| Netherlands, (15-64), 2001 | 1.5 |
| Belgium**, 1999 | 0.9 |
| Iceland, 2001 | 0.9 |
| Germany, (18-59), 2002 | 0.7 |
| Norway, 1999 | 0.6 |
| Austria**, 2000 | 0.6 |
| Denmark, 2000 | 0.5 |
| Finland, 2002 | 0.5 |
| Luxembourg*, 1998 | 0.4 |
| Monaco ** | 0.4 |
| Portugal**, 2001 | 0.4 |
| Switzerland, 1997 | 0.4 |
| France, (15-64), 2002 | 0.3 |
| San Marino** , 1999 | 0.3 |
| Turkey*,[1] 2003 | 0.3 |
| Italy, (15-44), 2002 | 0.2 |
| Malta, 2001 | 0.2 |
| Liechtenstein, 1998 | 0.2 |
| Sweden*, 2000 | 0.2 |
| Greece, 2000 | 0.1 |
| Cyprus, 1999 | 0.1 |

*UNODC estimates based on local studies, special population group studies, and/or law enforcement agency assessments.
** Tentative estimate for the late 1990s.

Sources: Annual Report Questionnaires, Government Reports, US Department of State, European Monitoring Center for Drugs and Drug Abuse (EMCDDA)

0% 0.5% 1.0% 1.5% 2.0% 2.5% 3.0%

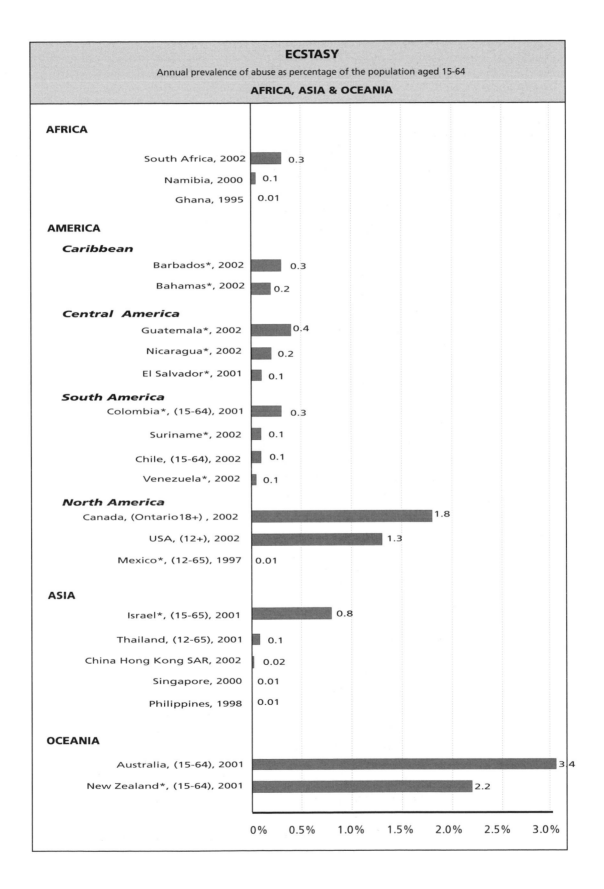

**ECSTASY**

Annual prevalence of abuse as percentage of the population aged 15-64

**AFRICA, ASIA & OCEANIA**

**AFRICA**

South Africa, 2002 — 0.3
Namibia, 2000 — 0.1
Ghana, 1995 — 0.01

**AMERICA**

*Caribbean*

Barbados*, 2002 — 0.3
Bahamas*, 2002 — 0.2

*Central America*

Guatemala*, 2002 — 0.4
Nicaragua*, 2002 — 0.2
El Salvador*, 2001 — 0.1

*South America*

Colombia*, (15-64), 2001 — 0.3
Suriname*, 2002 — 0.1
Chile, (15-64), 2002 — 0.1
Venezuela*, 2002 — 0.1

*North America*

Canada, (Ontario18+), 2002 — 1.8
USA, (12+), 2002 — 1.3
Mexico*, (12-65), 1997 — 0.01

**ASIA**

Israel*, (15-65), 2001 — 0.8
Thailand, (12-65), 2001 — 0.1
China Hong Kong SAR, 2002 — 0.02
Singapore, 2000 — 0.01
Philippines, 1998 — 0.01

**OCEANIA**

Australia, (15-64), 2001 — 3.4
New Zealand*, (15-64), 2001 — 2.2

0%  0.5%  1.0%  1.5%  2.0%  2.5%  3.0%

Notes:

1.  Estimates shown for Turkey for opiates are based on a study conducted by UNODC in cooperation with the Government of Turkey: *Drug Abuse in Turkey – Results from the Year 2003 National Assessment*. Estimates shown for Turkey for cannabis, cocaine, amphetamines and ecstasy were derived from school surveys among 15-16 year olds, conducted in Turkey in 2003, applying average transformation ratios found in neighbouring countries (other south-European countries). Using average transformation ratios of Western Europe as a whole, would have led to far higher estimates. These higher estimates were not used as a study conducted by the Turkish Psychological Association in 2002 suggested very low levels of drug abuse in Turkey. This study revealed an overall level of drug abuse of 0.3% in the country. The rate of cannabis dependence was found to amount to 0.15%. However, since data for other substances were not reported to UNODC at the time of preparation of the present report, results from this study could not be used.

2.  The source of the data for Ireland shown in the graphs is the Centre for Health Promotion Studies, *The National Health & Lifestyle Surveys* (SLAN), April 2003, which in comparison with data from previous years, enables a trend analysis. The National Advisory Committee on Drugs (NACD) and the Drug and Alcohol Information and Research Unit (DAIRU), conducted a national household survey in 2002/2003 which provides a new source of estimates (not directly comparable, however, with the SLAN estimates). It found an annual prevalence of cannabis use among the population age 15-64 of 5.1%, of cocaine-type substances of 1.1%, of ecstasy-type substances of 1.1% and of amphetamine of 0.4%.

# 6.2. Treatment demand (Primary drugs of abuse)

## PRIMARY DRUGS OF ABUSE AMONG PERSONS TREATED FOR DRUG PROBLEMS IN WEST EUROPEAN COUNTRIES, 2002 2002 (or latest year available)

| Country | Source | Year | Distribution of main drug in percentages | | | | | | | |
|---|---|---|---|---|---|---|---|---|---|---|
| | | | Opiates | Cocaine | Amphetamines | Ecstasy | Hallucinogens | Cannabis | Other Illegal Drugs |
| Austria | EMCDDA | 2001 | 100.0% | - | - | - | - | - | - |
| Belgium* | Focal Point | 2000 | 62.6% | 6.0% | 12.0% | 2.0% | 1.0% | 17.3% | |
| Denmark | EMCDDA | 2001 | 61.0% | 6.7% | 3% | 1.0% | 0% | 17.0% | 16.0% |
| Finland | EMCDDA | 2001 | 32.9% | 0.2% | 31.1% | 0.9% | 0.2% | 25.6% | 9.1% |
| France | UNODC | 2002 | 62.1% | 7.3% | 0.9% | 1.40% | 0.90% | 23.2% | 4.2% |
| Germany | EMCDDA | 2001 | 51.7% | 6.9% | 8.7% | - | 0.1% | 27.2% | 4.7% |
| Greece | EMCDDA | 2001 | 89.8% | 0.8% | 0% | 0.2% | 0.10% | 7.3% | 1.4% |
| Ireland | EMCDDA | 2000 | 67.9% | 1.2% | 0.6% | 5.9% | 0.2% | 21.4% | 2.8% |
| Italy | EMCDDA | 2001 | 82.4% | 5.8% | 0.2% | 0.8% | 0.1% | 8.2% | 2.5% |
| Luxembourg | EMCDDA | 2001 | 71.0% | 7.0% | 0% | 1.0% | 0% | 17.0% | 4.0% |
| Netherlands | EMCDDA | 2001 | 50.4% | 29.9% | 1.5% | 0.8% | 0.2% | 14.9% | 2.3% |
| Portugal | EMCDDA | 2000 | 38.7% | 1.5% | - | 0% | 0% | 2.3% | 0.1% |
| Spain | EMCDDA | 2001 | 70.7% | 19.0% | 0.5% | 0.7% | 0.2% | 7.4% | 1.5% |
| Sweden | EMCDDA | 2001 | 25.0% | 1% | 29% | 3% | 0% | 25.0% | 17.0% |
| Unied Kingdom | EMCDDA | 2001 | 77.5% | 6.1% | 2.7% | 1.3% | 0% | 8.7% | 3.6% |
| **Average** | | | **62.9%** | **7.1%** | **6.9%** | **1.5%** | **0.2%** | **15.9%** | **5.3%** |

- Austria : data refers to clients in substitution treatment only: data on opiates as main drug are consequently 100%.
- Belgium : data for opiates, cocaine and cannabis refer to treatment centres in the French community in 2000; data for amphetamine and ecstasy refer to outpatient treatment in Belgium in 1999.
- Denmark : data on opiates refer to heroin only,
- Germany : data only refer to outpatient treatment centres; data on opiates refer to heroin only and data on hallucinogens to LSD.
- France: data refer to the annual census on clients in treatment carried out in November 1999
- Italy : data only refer to outpatient treatment centres; opiates refer to heroin only.
- Netherlands : data only refer to outpatient treatment centres.
- Portugal : data on treatment demand refers to interventions (not people): opiates only refer to heroin.
- Sweden : data only refer to outpatient treatment centres.
- UK : data relate to the period from 1 Oct. 2000 to 31 March 2001.
Sources: EMCDDA, 2001 Annual Report on the State of the Drug Problem in the European Union; Govt. reports.

## PRIMARY DRUGS OF ABUSE AMONG PERSONS TREATED FOR DRUG PROBLEMS IN EUROPE, 2002 (or latest year available)

| City | Source | Year | Distribution of main drug in percentages | | | | | | | |
| | | | Opiates | Cocaine | Amphetamine-type stimulants | | Hallucinogens | Cannabis | Hypnotics and Sedatives | Inhalants/ solvents |
| | | | | | Amphetamines | Ecstasy | | | | |
| Austria, Vienna | UNODC | 1997 | 72.2 % | | | | | | | |
| Belgium | EMCDDA/Focal Point | 2000 | 62.6% | 6.0% | 12.0 % | 12.0 % | 12.0 % | 12.0 % | 12.0 % | 12.0 % |
| Bulgaria | UNODC | 1999 | 96.9% | 0.5% | - | - | - | 1.2 | 1.1 % | - |
| Croatia | UNODC | 2002 | 71.5% | 0.4% | - | 1.7 % | - | 24.2 | 1.9 % | 0.4 % |
| Cyprus* | UNODC | 1999 | 54.1% | 7.7% | - | - | - | 38.1 | - | - |
| Czech Republic | UNODC | 2002 | 25.0% | 0.1% | 51.9 % | 2.5 % | - | 16.8 | - | 3.7 % |
| Denmark | UNODC | 2002 | 37.1% | 3.0% | 4.1 % | 0.8 % | 0.2 % | 20.4 | - | 34.3 % |
| Finland | EMCDDA | 2001 | 32.9% | 0.2% | 31.1 % | 0.9 % | 0.2 % | 25.6 | - | - |
| France | UNODC | 2002 | 62.1% | 7.3% | 0.9 % | 1.4 % | 0.9 % | 23.2 | - | - |
| Germany | UNODC | 2002 | 34.1% | 11.9% | 8.9 % | 8.7 % | 4.6 % | 31.8 | - | - |
| Greece | UNODC | 2002 | 50.5% | 0.7% | - | 0.2 % | - | 47.3 % | 0.7 % | - |
| Hungary | UNODC | 2002 | 29.1% | 2.4% | 3.9 % | 2.3 % | - | 15.6 % | 46.7 % | - |
| Iceland | UNODC | 2001 | 0.1% | 7.1% | 65.6 % | 0.9 % | - | 26.3 % | - | - |
| Ireland | UNODC | 2002 | 76.7% | 1.1% | 0.4 % | 4.2 % | - | 15.4 % | 1.4 % | - |
| Italy | UNODC | 2002 | 80.5% | 7.0% | - | 1.0 % | - | 9.0 % | 0.6 % | - |
| Latvia | UNODC | 2002 | 82.5% | 0.3% | 3.5 % | - | - | 0.7 % | 3.9 % | - |
| Liechtenstein | UNODC | 2002 | 17.2% | 17.2% | 6.9 % | - | - | 58.3 % | - | - |
| Lithuania | UNODC | 2002 | 81.7% | 0.1% | 2.6 % | - | - | 0.8 % | - | 4.0 % |
| Luxembourg | UNODC | 2001 | 80.0% | 5.2% | 1.7 % | 1.7 % | - | 11.3 % | - | - |
| Malta | UNODC | 2001 | 100.0% | 0.0% | - | - | - | - | - | - |
| Poland | UNODC | 2002 | 65.2% | 0.3% | 9.6 % | - | 1.1 % | 4.7 % | 12.9 % | 6.0 % |
| Portugal | UNODC | 2000 | 90.8% | 3.5% | - | - | - | 5.4 % | 0.2 % | - |
| Romania | UNODC | 2002 | 81.7% | 0.2% | 1.7 % | 0.8 % | 1.3 % | 0.9 % | - | 13.5 % |
| Russian Fed. | UNODC | 2001 | 61.5% | 0.1% | 3.5 % | - | - | 13.5 % | - | - |
| Slovakia | UNODC | 2002 | 65.6% | 0.6% | 9.2 % | 0.4 % | - | 10.6 % | 5.7 % | 8.0 % |
| Slovenia | UNODC | 2002 | 90.8% | 0.6% | 0.4 % | 0.4 % | - | 7.7 % | - | - |
| Spain | UNODC | 2002 | 71.1% | 19.1% | 0.5 % | 0.7 % | 0.2 % | 7.5 % | - | - |
| Sweden | UNODC | 2002 | 40.4% | 2.0% | 34.3 % | 1.5 % | - | 13.5 % | 7.0 % | - |
| Switzerland, Geneva | UNODC | 1997 | 93.6% | 0.6% | 1.9 % | - | - | 1.9 % | 1.3 % | - |
| The Netherlands | UNODC | 2002 | 62.2% | 23.2% | 1.7 % | 0.8 % | - | 12.1 % | - | - |
| Turkey | UNODC | 2001 | 58.6% | 0.0% | - | - | - | 13.0 % | 8.0 % | 20.5 % |
| UK | UNODC | 2002 | 69.3% | 6.2% | 2.8 % | 1.3 % | - | 8.8 % | 2.3 % | - |
| Average | | | 61.4% | 4.3% | 8.4% | 1.4% | 0.7% | 15.4% | 3.4% | 3.3% |

This table does not include "other drugs", therefore the percentages may not add up to 100%.

* First Treatment Demand

Sources: UNODC, Annual Reports Questionnaire Data, EMCDDA, Data Library.

## PRIMARY DRUGS OF ABUSE AMONG PERSONS TREATED FOR DRUG PROBLEMS IN ASIA, 2002 (or latest year available)

| City | Source | Year | Distribution of main drug in percentages | | | | | | | |
|------|--------|------|---------|---------|--------------|---------|----------|----------|-----------|-----------|
| | | | Opiates | Cocaine | Amphetamine-type stimulants | | | Cannabis | Inhalants | Sedatives |
| | | | | | Amphetamines | Ecstasy | | | | |
| Azerbaijan | ARQ | 1999 | 100.0% | 0.0% | 0.0% | 0.0% | 0.0% | 0.0% | 0.0% |
| Bahrein | ARQ | 1998 | 100.0% | 0.0% | 0.0% | 0.0% | 0.0% | 0.0% | 0.0% |
| Bangladesh | ARQ | 2002 | 86.5% | 0.0% | 0.0% | 0.0% | 9.8% | 0.0% | 1.8% |
| Brunei Darussalam | ARQ | 1999 | 0.0% | 0.0% | 96.4% | 0.0% | 0.0% | 3.6% | 0.0% |
| China | Govt. Rep. | 2003 | 74.3% | 0.0% | 0.0% | 0.0% | 0.0% | 0.0% | 0.0% |
| Hongkong, SAR of China | Govt | 2000 | 91.0% | 0.0% | 0.0% | 0.0% | 0.0% | 0.0% | 0.0% |
| India | UNODC/Govt. Study | 2002 | 57.5% | 3.8% | 0.4% | 0.0% | 25.6% | 0.0% | 0.0% |
| Indonesia | ARQ | 2002 | 56.0% | 0.0% | 28.6% | 0.0% | 15.4% | 0.0% | 0.0% |
| Iran | ARQ | 1999 | 96.3% | 0.0% | 0.0% | 0.0% | 2.5% | 0.0% | 0.0% |
| Japan | Govt | 2000 | 0.4% | 0.0% | 60.5% | 0.0% | 0.5% | 18.8% | 0.0% |
| Jordan | ARQ | 1999 | 21.4% | 0.0% | 45.2% | 0.0% | 0.0% | 6% | 0.0% |
| Kazakhstan | ARQ | 2000 | 74.6% | 0.0% | 0.1% | 0.0% | 20% | 0.0% | 0.0% |
| Kuwait | ARQ | 2001 | 100.0% | 0.0% | 0.0% | 0.0% | 0.0% | 0.0% | 0.0% |
| Kyrgyzstan | ARQ | 2002 | 71.4% | 0.0% | 0.0% | 0.0% | 28.6% | 0.0% | 0.0% |
| Macao, SAR of China | ARQ | 2002 | 96.6% | 0.0% | 2.6% | 0.0% | 0.0% | 0.0% | 0.7% |
| Malaysia, Penang | AMCEWG | 2001 | 76.0% | 0.0% | 0.2% | 0.2% | 27.0% | 0.0% | 0.0% |
| Maldives | ARQ | 1998 | 50.0% | 0.0% | 0.0% | 0.0% | 50.0% | 0.0% | 0.0% |
| Mongolia | ARQ | 2001 | 71.4% | 0.0% | 0.0% | 0.0% | 28.6% | 0.0% | 0.0% |
| Myanmar | ARQ | 2002 | 91.8% | 0.0% | 5.9% | 0.0% | 1.5% | 0.0% | 0.0% |
| Nepal, Kathmandu | AMCEWG | 1994 | 87.2% | 0.0% | 0.0% | 0.0% | 5.4% | 0.0% | 0.0% |
| Oman | ARQ | 2002 | 100.0% | 0.0% | 0.0% | 0.0% | 0.0% | 0.0% | 0.0% |
| Pakistan | ARQ/UNODC Study | 2002 | 97.6% | 0.0% | 0.0% | 0.0% | 1.0% | 0.0% | 0.0% |
| Philippines | ARQ | 2001 | 0.0% | 0.0% | 75.5% | 0.0% | 24.5% | 0.0% | 0.0% |
| Qatar | ARQ | 1997 | 25.4% | 0.0% | 1.7% | 0.0% | 5.1% | 10.2% | 0.0% |
| Republic of Korea | ARQ | 2002 | 1.0% | 0.0% | 83.2% | 1.0% | 13.1% | 0.0% | 0.0% |
| Saudi Arabia | ARQ | 2001 | 15.1% | 0.0% | 41.3% | 0.0% | 15.9% | 27.8% | 0.0% |
| Singapore | ARQ | 2001 | 100.0% | 0.0% | 0.0% | 0.0% | 0.0% | 0.0% | 0.0% |
| Sri Lanka | ARQ | 2001 | 100.0% | 0.0% | 0.0% | 0.0% | 0.0% | 0.0% | 0.0% |
| Taiwan, Province of China | AMCEWG | 1999 | 37.5% | 0.0% | 44.8% | 0.0% | 0.0% | 8.2% | 7.2% |
| Tajikistan | ARQ | 2002 | 98.6% | 0.0% | 0.0% | 0.0% | 1.4% | 0.0% | 0.0% |
| Thailand | Govt. Rep. | 2001 | 40.8% | 0.0% | 56.2% | 0.0% | 1.4% | 1.5% | 0.0% |
| Uzbekistan | ARQ | 2002 | 79.4% | 0.0% | 0.0% | 0.0% | 16.3% | 0.6% | 0.6% |
| Viet Nam | AMCEWG | 2001 | 98.0% | 0.0% | 2.0% | 0.0% | 0.0% | 0.0% | 0.0% |
| Average | | | 66.5% | 0.1% | 16.5% | 0.0% | 8.6% | 2.2% | 0.3% |

This table does not include hallucinogens and "other drugs", therefore the percentages may not add up to 100% for all cities.

Sources: UNODC. Annual Reports Questionnaire Data; Asian Multicity Epidemiology work group (AMCEWG); Govt. reports

## PRIMARY DRUGS OF ABUSE AMONG PERSONS TREATED FOR DRUG PROBLEMS IN OCEANIA
### 2002 (or latest year available)

| Country and year | Source | Year | Opiates | Cocaine | Cannabis | Amphetamie-type stimulants | | | Inhalants | Sedatives |
| | | | | | | Amphetamines | Ecstasy | | | |
|---|---|---|---|---|---|---|---|---|---|---|
| Australia | Govt | 2001 | 62.4% | 1.0% | 14.8% | 13.2% | 0.8% | | | 3.8% |
| New Zealand* | Govt | 1998/2003 | 31.7% | 0.4% | 23.1% | 7.8% | | | 3.2% | 38.6% |
| Average | | | 47.1% | 0.7% | 19.0% | 10.5% | 0.8% | | 3.2% | 21.2% |

* Data for New Zealand refer to 1998; the latest year for which a breakdown of drug related treatment data has been published; the proportion shown for amphetamines refers to 2003. The proportion of methamphetamine related telephone helpline calls is used as a proxy for the importance of methamphetamine in overall treatment. In 1998 0.4% of treatment cases concerned amphetamines; telephone helplines reported a major increase with regard to methamphetamine from 0.5% in 2001 to 1.4% in 2002 and 7.8% in 2003, in parallel, to hospital reports of strong increases in methamphetamine related cases.

## PRIMARY DRUG OF ABUSE AMONG PERSONS TREATED FOR DRUG PROBLEMS IN AFRICA, 2002 (or latest year available)

| Country | Source | Year | Distribution of main drugs in percentages | | | | | | |
|---|---|---|---|---|---|---|---|---|---|
| | | | Cannabis | Opiates | Cocaine | Amphetamine-type stimulants | Methaqualone | Inhalants | Khat |
| Algeria | ARQ | 1999 | 81.3 % | 6.6 % | 0.2 % | | - | 2.1 % | - |
| Botswana | SENDU | 2002 | 87.8 % | - | 0.8 % | | 0.8 % | - | - |
| Cameroon* | RAS | 1995 | 48.5 % | 12.1 % | 13.6 % | | - | 36.4 % | - |
| Chad | ARQ | 1996 | 50.6 % | - | 0.2 % | 18.8 % | - | 6.3 % | - |
| Congo | ARQ | 1995 | 100.0 % | - | | | - | - | - |
| Cote d'Ivoire | ARQ | 1998 | 91.0 % | 4.1 % | 3.0 % | | - | - | - |
| Egypt | Field | 1999 | 22.1 % | 45.1 % | 0.4 % | | - | - | - |
| Ethiopia | ARQ | 1999 | 14.6 % | 9.6 % | | | - | - | 75.6 % |
| Ghana | ARQ | 2002 | 86.1 % | 1.0 % | 0.6 % | | - | - | - |
| Kenya** | RAS | 1995 | 33.8 % | 4.8 % | 2.9 % | 5.2 % | - | 20.5 % | 14.3 % |
| Lesotho | SENDU | 2002 | 100.0 % | - | | | - | - | |
| Madagascar | EADIS | 2002 | 87.3 % | - | | 0.4 % | - | - | |
| Malawi | SENDU | 2002 | 100.0 % | - | | | - | - | |
| Mauritius | ARQ | 2002 | 15.5 % | 79.6 % | 1.0 % | | - | 0.7 % | |
| Mozambique | SENDU | 2002 | 56.5 % | 41.3 % | 2.5 % | | - | - | |
| Namibia | SENDU | 2002 | 35.2 % | - | 16.5 % | 5.0 % | 42.8 % | - | |
| Nigeria | ARQ | 1997 | 63.9 % | 3.5 % | 9.7 % | 15.3 % | - | 7.6 % | - |
| Sao Tome & Principe | ARQ | 1997 | 22.2 % | 5.5 % | 72.2 % | | - | - | - |
| Seychelles | ARQ | 2001/02 | 71.4 % | 28.6 % | 7.8 % | 3.9 % | - | - | - |
| Sierra Leone | ARQ | 1997 | 96.8 % | - | 0.6 % | | - | - | - |
| South Africa | ARQ | 2002 | 48.2 % | 12.2 % | 13.3 % | 2.7 % | 23.7 % | - | - |
| Tanzania | ARQ | 1999 | 95.2 % | 4.8 % | | | - | - | - |
| Togo | ARQ | 2001 | 90.7 % | 0.1 % | 0.3 % | 0.3 % | - | - | - |
| Zambia | ARQ | 2002 | 69.8 % | 30.2 % | | | - | - | - |
| Average | | | 65.4 % | 12.0 % | 8.6 % | 6.5 % | 2.8 % | 3.1 % | 3.7 % |

\* Proxy: drugs locally consumed, based on key informants from social services (health affairs,), from traditional healers, and repression

\*\* Proxy: drugs consumed, based on health workers.

Source: UNODC Annual Reports Questionnaires

## PRIMARY DRUGS OF ABUSE AMONG PERSONS TREATED FOR DRUG PROBLEMS IN THE AMERICAS, 2002 (or latest year available)

| Country and year | Source | Year | Cocaine-type (cocaine, basuco & crack-cocaine) | Cocaine | Basuco | Crack | Cannabis | Amphetamine - type Amphetamines | Amphetamine - type Ecstasy | Inhalants | Tranquilizers | Opiates |
|---|---|---|---|---|---|---|---|---|---|---|---|---|
| Argentina | ARQ | 2002 | 51.7% | | | | 25.2% | | | | 13.6% | 2.0% |
| Bahamas | ARQ | 1998 | 93.0% | | | | 7.0% | | | | | |
| Barbados | SIDUC | 1998 | 72.3% | 5.6% | | 66.7% | 27.8% | | | | | |
| Bolivia | SIDUC | 1998 | 54.8% | 23.1% | 31.8% | | 14.7% | 1.4% | | 23.5% | | |
| Canada | CCENDU | 2001 | 28.3% | | | | 27.2% | 0.5% | | | 35.1% | 6.8% |
| Brazil | SIDUC | 1999 | 59.2% | 14.4% | | 44.8% | 27.2% | | | 2.0% | 2.4% | 0.4% |
| Chile | SIDUC | 1998 | 89% | 21.2% | 67.8% | | 4.1% | 4.1% | | | | |
| Colombia | SIDUC | 1998 | 56.3% | 28.1% | 28.2% | | 13.4% | 3.6% | | 4.8% | | |
| Costa Rica | ARQ | 2002 | 44.2% | | | 55.8% | | | | | | |
| Dominican Rep., | ARQ | 2001 | 76.4% | | | | 20.0% | | | | | 3.6% |
| Ecuador | SIDUC | 1998 | 66.1% | 13.5% | 52.5% | | 10.2% | | | 4.6% | | |
| El Salvador | ARQ | 1998 | 100.0% | | | | | | | | | |
| Grenada | ARQ | 2001 | 56.3% | | | | 43.8% | | | | | |
| Guatemala | ARQ | 2002 | 31.3% | 62.5% | | | | 6.3% | | | | |
| Haiti | ARQ | 2002 | 40.0% | 3.1% | | | 50.0% | | | 10.0% | | |
| Honduras | SIDUC | 1998 | 9.0% | | | 5.9% | 34.4% | | | 9.0% | | |
| Jamaica | SIDUC | 1998 | 58% | | | 58% | 28.9% | | | | | |
| Mexico | ARQ | 2002 | 35.1% | | | 62.8% | 31.2% | 6.8% | | 16.0% | 8.0% | 3.0% |
| Nicaragua | SIDUC | 1998 | 77.3% | 14.5% | | | 7.3% | | | 12.7% | | |
| Panama | SIDUC | 1998 | 49.4% | 48.9% | 0.5% | | 5.1% | | | 0.5% | | |
| Peru | SIDUC | 1998 | 90.8% | 20.4% | 70.4% | | 5.6% | | | | | |
| St. Vincent & Grenadines | ARQ | 2001 | 13.4% | | | | 86.6% | | | | | |
| Trinidad & Tobago, | ARQ | 2001 | 67.2% | | | | 32.8% | | | | | |
| Uruguay | SIDUC | 1998 | 46.4% | 46.4% | | | 12.2% | 0.6% | | 9.2% | | |
| USA | TEDS | 2002 | 22.5% | 6.1% | | 16.4% | 26.4% | 11.7% | 0.3% | 0.1% | 0.8% | 30.8% |
| Venezuela | ARQ | 2002 | 86.0% | | | | 12.8% | 0.2% | 0.2% | 0.3% | | 0.9% |
| Unweighted average | | | 56.7% | | | | 26.9% | 3.9% | 0.2% | 7.7% | 12.0% | 1.8% |
| Average North America | | | 28.6% | | | | 28.3% | 6.3% | 0.3% | 8.1% | 14.6% | 13.6% |
| Average South America | | | 60.4% | | | | 25.5% | 0.7% | 0.0% | 3.3% | 0.7% | 0.3% |

Note: These drugs represent the most common drugs of impact across countries, therefore the percentages may not add up to 100% for all countries.

Sources: SIDUC, Treatment Centres Data 1998, Drug of impact; SIDUC 1997 Report; Treatment episode data set TEDS, USA 1992.; Treatment episode data set TEDS, USA 1992-2002; Secretaria Nacional Antidrogas, Brazil (Data refer to one treatment centre in Minas Gerais (985 cases); Canadian Community Epidemiology Network on Drug Use (CCENDU).
Morbidity Statistics 2000/2001 (separations related to illicit drug use).

# Methodology

Considerable efforts have been made over the last few years to improve all available drug related estimates. The data must still be interpreted with caution because of the clandestine nature of drug production, trafficking and abuse. Apart from the 'hidden' nature of the phenomenon being measured, the main problems with regard to data relate to the irregularity and incompleteness in reporting. This affects the quantity, quality and comparability of information received. First, the irregular intervals at which some Governments report may result in absence of data in some years but availability in others. The lack of regular data, for which UNODC tries to compensate by reference to other sources, can influence trend patterns. Secondly, submitted questionnaires are not always complete or sufficiently comprehensive. All figures should thus be seen as likely orders of magnitude of the drug problem, but not as precise results. It should be also noted that all figures provided, particularly those of more recent years, are subject to updating.

## Sources and limitations of data on the supply side

### Cultivation, production and manufacture

Global estimates are, in general, more robust on the production side, notably data for plant based drugs, than on the demand side. In line with decisions of the Member States (1998 UNGASS and subsequent CND resolutions), UNODC launched an Illicit Crop Monitoring Programme (ICMP) in 1999. The objective of the programme is to assist Member States in establishing national systems to monitor the extent and evolution of the illicit cultivation of narcotics crops on their territories. The results are compiled by UNODC to present global estimates on an annual basis. Data on cultivation of opium poppy and coca bush and production of opium and coca leaf, presented in this report for the main producing countries (Afghanistan, Myanmar and the Lao PDR for opium and Colombia, Peru and Bolivia for coca) have been derived from these national monitoring systems operating in the countries of illicit production. UNODC also conducted in 2003, for the first time, a survey on cannabis resin production in Morocco, in close cooperation with the Government of Morocco. Estimates for other countries presented in this report have been drawn from various other sources including reports from Governments, UNODC field offices and the United States Department of State's Bureau for International Narcotics and Law Enforcement Affairs.

The key indicator for measuring progress made towards the supply reduction goals set out in the UNGASS Political Declaration of June 1998 is the area under cultivation of narcotic crops. Since 1999, UNODC has been supporting the establishment of national monitoring systems in the main narcotics production countries. These monitoring systems are tailored to national specificities. The direct participation of UNODC ensures the transparency of the survey activities. Through its network of monitoring experts at headquarters and in the field, the UNODC ensures the conformity of the national systems so that they meet international methodological standards and the information requirements of the international community. Most of these monitoring systems rely on remote sensing technology (i.e. analysis of satellite imagery) in combination with extensive field visits which is made possible through UNODC's field presence in all of the main narcotics producing countries. Satellite images, in combination with ground information, offer a reliable and objective way of estimating illicit crops. Depending on the local conditions, the surveys are conducted either on a census approach (coca cultivation in Colombia, Peru and Bolivia, cannabis cultivation in Morocco) or a sample approach (opium poppy cultivation in Afghanistan, Myanmar and Laos). In addition, the ground surveys made possible through UNODC's field presence in all of the main narcotics producing countries, assist UNODC to obtain information on yields, drug prices and various other socio-economic data that is useful for alternative development interventions. Detailed discussion of the methodological approaches can be found on www.unodc.org/unodc/en/crop_monitoring.

UNODC has also started to conduct yield surveys in some countries, measuring the yield of test fields, and to develop methodologies to extrapolate the yields from proxy variables such as the volume of poppy capsules. All of this is intended to further improve yield estimates, aiming at information that is independent from farmers' reports. In countries in which UNODC has not, as yet, undertaken yield surveys, results from other surveys conducted at the national level are used. This is currently still the case in all of the Andean countries. The disadvantage of having to take recourse to yield data from other sources is that year on year variations, due to weather conditions, or due to the introduction of improved seeds, fertilizers and pesticides, are not properly reflected in the end results.

More problematic, in general, are the transformation ratios used to calculate the potential cocaine production from coca leaf or the heroin production from opium. In order to be precise, these calculations would require detailed information at the local level on the morphine content in opium or the cocaine content in the coca leaf, as well as detailed information on the clandestine laboratory efficiency, which in turn is a function of know-how, equipment and precursor chemicals. This information is not available. However, a number of studies conducted by enforcement agencies in the main drug producing countries have provided some orders of magnitude for the transformation from the raw material to the end product. Nonetheless, potential margins of error in this rapidly changing environment, with new laboratories coming on stream while others are being dismantled, are still substantial. This also applies to the question of the psychoactive content of the narcotic plants. One recent study conducted by UNODC in Afghanistan indicated that the morphine content of Afghan opium could be significantly higher than was thought so far. This could mean higher levels of heroin production than those estimated earlier. However, little is known about laboratory efficiency in Afghanistan and neighbouring countries, or about the wastage in clandestine manufacturing or losses in Afghan heroin shipments. As a consequence, UNODC has not changed the traditional 10:1 ratio for converting opium into heroin.

'Potential' heroin or cocaine production, the indicator used throughout this report, shows the level of production of heroin or cocaine if all of the opium or coca leaf were transformed into the end products. In reality, however, part of the opium or the coca leaf is directly consumed in the producing countries or in neighbouring countries, prior to the transformation into heroin or cocaine. There are important illicit opium markets in Iran or Pakistan and coca leaf is used by the local population in Bolivia, Peru and northern Chile. In addition, significant quantities of the intermediate products, coca paste or morphine, are also consumed in the producing countries.

As the transformation ratios used are rather conservative, total 'potential' production, however, may well be close to 'actual' production of the end products if one takes the *de-facto* lower amounts available for starting the transformation process into account. There are thus two kinds of potential biases in the estimates which (at least partly) can be expected to offset each other.

The use of the concept of 'potential production' at the country level also means that actual heroin or cocaine production is under-estimated in some countries, and over-estimated in others while the estimate for the global level should not be affected by this. The calculation of 'potential' cocaine production estimates for Peru, for instance, exceeds actual local cocaine production as significant amounts of the coca paste or coca base produced in Peru are exported to neighbouring Colombia for further processing into cocaine. Based on the same reasoning, potential cocaine production estimates for Colombia under-estimate actual cocaine production in the country. Actual cocaine manufacture in Colombia takes place from locally produced coca leaf as well as from coca base imported from Peru.

In the case of cannabis, the globally most dispersed illegal drug, all available production estimates were aggregated. In most cases, however, these estimates were not based on scientific studies and often referred to different years (as only a few countries provided such estimates in the last Annual Reports Questionnaire submitted to UNODC in 2003). The cannabis production estimate is thus less robust than the opium or cocaine estimates which are based on detailed surveys. Nonetheless, cross-checks with existing seizure statistics suggest that the magnitude of the overall cannabis estimate is probably correct. Plausibility considerations based on seizure statistics suggest that any lower production of cannabis herb was very unlikely, as this would have meant very high interception rates for cannabis. At the same time, UNODC's first scientific study on the extent of cannabis resin cultivation, conducted in Morocco, in combination with Member States reports of the origin of cannabis resin seizures, also fit well with the global cannabis herb estimates. The cannabis resin production data from Morocco suggested that significantly higher cannabis herb production estimates were unlikely as this would have meant that law enforcement – worldwide – was only concentrating on cannabis resin and ignoring cannabis herb. The strong efforts undertaken by enforcement agencies in North America (notably in Mexico and the USA), resulting in the bulk of global cannabis herb seizures, do not provide evidence that this was the case at the global level. Thus plausibility consideration established both a lower limit and an upper limit at around the current cannabis production estimates. Though the resulting global cannabis herb and global cannabis resin estimates cannot be considered to be very precise, they show magnitudes that are in line with existing data from other sources, and they also enable the establishment of a trend, which is in line with trafficking and abuse estimates.

The potential margins of error for synthetic drugs, such as the ATS, are similar to those of the cannabis estimates, and thus significantly larger than the estimates for heroin or cocaine. The approach taken in this case was one of triangulation, estimating production based on reported seizures of the end products in combination with some assumptions of law enforcement effectiveness, seizure data of precursor chemicals and estimates based on the number of consumers and their likely levels of *per capita* consumption. While each individual calculation may well raise some questions, the overall results of the three approaches showed similar orders of magnitude, suggesting that actual production levels of ATS may not be too far-off from the resulting mid-point estimates.

This approach, however, does not enable year-on-year production estimates for the ATS. An indirect indicator for the evolution of clandestine manufacturing activities is the detection and dismantling of laboratories producing ATS. This indicator has shown a clear increase over the last decade, in line with observations of increased trafficking and abuse. The validity of this trend indicator is, however, limited. There is, first of all, a serious problem of irregular reporting by Member States. There are also problems of consistency in reporting. For example, some countries include "kitchen" laboratories in the total number of manufacturing sites detected while others only count fully equipped clandestine laboratories. By the same token, if a country changes its reporting practice to include "kitchen" laboratories, when it earlier excluded them, the picture can be potentially distorted.

## Trafficking

The information on trafficking, as presented in this report, is mainly drawn from the Annual Reports Questionnaires (ARQ), submitted by Governments to UNODC in 2003 and early 2004 and refers to the year 2002 (and previous years). Additional sources, such as other governmental reports, the International Criminal Police Organization (Interpol), the World Customs Organization (WCO) and UNODC's field offices, were used to supplement the information. Priority was, however, given to officially transmitted data in the Annual Reports Questionnaire. The analysis of quantities seized, shown in this report, was based on information provided by 165 countries & territories in 2000, 161 in 2001 and 152 in 2002. Seizures are thus the most comprehensive indicator of the drug situation and its evolution at the global level. Though they may not always reflect trafficking trends correctly at the national level, they tend to show good representations of trafficking trends at the regional and global levels.

There are some technical problems as – depending on the drugs - some countries report seizures in weight terms (kg), in volume terms (litres) while other countries report seizures in 'unit terms'. In Volume II, seizures are shown as reported. In the analytical sections of Volume I of the report, seizure data have been aggregated and transformed into a unique measurement: seizures in 'kilogram equivalents'. For the purposes of the calculations a 'typical consumption unit' (at street purity) was assumed to be: cannabis herb: 0.5 grams, cannabis resin: 0.135 grams; cocaine and ecstasy: 0.1 grams, heroin and amphetamines: 0.03 grams, LSD: 0.00005 grams (50 micrograms). A litre of seizures was assumed to be equivalent to a kilogram. For opiate seizures, it was assumed that 10 kg of opium were equivalent to 1 kg of morphine or heroin. Though all of these transformation ratios can be disputed, they at least provide a possibility of combining all the different seizure reports into one comprehensive measure. The transformation ratios have been derived from those used by law enforcement agencies, in the scientific literature, by the INCB, and were established in consultation with UNODC's Laboratory and Scientific Section.

Seizures are used as an indicator for trends and patterns in trafficking. In combination with changes in drug prices or drug purities, changes in seizures can indicate whether trafficking has increased or declined. Increases in seizures in combination with stable or falling drug prices is a strong indication of rising trafficking activities. Increasing seizures and rising drug prices, in contrast, may be a reflection of improved enforcement effectiveness. Changes in trafficking can also serve as an indirect indicator for global production and abuse of drugs. Seizures are, of course, only an indirect indicator for trafficking activities, influenced by a number of additional factors, such as variations in law enforcement practices and changes in reporting modalities. Thus, the extent to which seizure statistics from some countries constitute all reported national cases, regardless of the final destination of the illicit drug, can vary and makes it sometimes difficult to assess actual trafficking activities. The problem is exacerbated by increasing amounts of drugs being seized in countries along the main transit routes, the increasing use of 'controlled deliveries', in which countries forego the possibility of seizing drugs immediately in order to identify whole trafficking networks operating across countries, and 'upstream disruptions', making use of intelligence information to inform partner countries and enable them to seize such deliveries prior to entering the country of final destination. Some of the increase of cocaine seizures in the Andean countries and declines of such seizures in North America and Western Europe in 2002, for instance, may have been linked to such upstream market disruptions.

However, over longer periods of time and over larger geographical entities, seizures have proven to be a good indicator to reveal underlying trafficking trends. While seizures at the national level may be influenced by large quantities of drugs in transit or by shifts in law enforcement priorities, it is not very likely that the same is true at the regional or at the global level. If a large drug shipment, while in transit, is taken out of the market in one country, fewer drugs will be probably seized in the neighbouring countries. Similarly, if enforcement efforts and thus seizures decline in one country, the neighbouring countries are likely to suffer from intensified trafficking activities, resulting in rising levels of seizures. The net results, emerging from changes of enforcement priorities of an individual country, are thus, in general, not significant at the regional or at the global level. Actual changes in trafficking can thus be considered to be among the main reasons for changes in seizures at the regional level or the global level. Indeed, comparisons, on a time-series basis, of different indicators with statistical dependence have shown strong correlations (e.g. global opium production estimates and global seizures of opiates, or global coca leaf production and global cocaine seizures), supporting the statistical worth of seizure statistics at regional and global levels. At the same time, data also show that interception rates have gradually increased over the last decade, reflecting improved law enforcement effectiveness at the global level.

## Sources and limitations of data on consumption

### Extent of drug abuse

#### a. Overview

UNODC estimates of the extent of drug abuse in the world have been published periodically since 1997 (see *World Drug Reports 1997* and *2000,* and *Global Illicit Drug Trends 2002 and 2003).* The fifth round of estimates, presented in this report, is based on information received until April 2004.

Assessing the extent of drug abuse (the number of drug abusers) is a particularly difficult undertaking because it involves measuring the size of a hidden population. Margins of error are considerable, and tend to multiply as the scale of estimation is raised, from local to national, regional and global levels. Despite some improvements in recent years, estimates provided by member states to UNODC are still very heterogeneous in terms of quality and reliability. These estimates cannot simply be aggregated globally to arrive at the total number of drug users in the world. Yet it is both desirable and possible to establish basic orders of magnitude - which are obviously subject to revision as new and better information is generated.

A global estimate of the level of abuse of specific drugs involves the following steps:

1. Identification and analysis of appropriate sources.
2. Identification of key benchmark figures for the level of drug abuse in selected countries (annual prevalence of drug abuse among the general population age 15-64) which then serve as 'anchor points' for subsequent calculations.
3. ' Standardization' of existing data (e.g. from age group 12 and above to a standard age group of 15-64).
4. Extrapolation of existing results based on information from neighbouring countries with similar cultural, social and economic situations (e.g. life-time prevalence or current use to annual prevalence, or school survey results to annual prevalence among the general population).
5. Extrapolation of available results from countries in a region to the region as a whole, using all available quantitative and qualitative information.
6. Aggregation of regional results to arrive at global results.

Estimates of illicit consumption for a large number of countries have been received by UNODC over the years (in the form of Annual Reports Questionnaires (ARQ) submitted by Governments), and been identified from additional sources, such as other governmental reports and research results from scientific literature. Officially transmitted information in any specific year, however, would not suffice to establish global estimates. In 2002, for instance, only 59 countries provided UNODC with quantitative estimates of the drug situation in their country, including 44 countries providing estimates of the prevalence of drug consumption among the general population and 56 countries providing estimates of prevalence of drug use among their student populations. For countries that did not submit information, other sources, where available, were identified. Alternatively, information provided by Governments in previous years was used. In such cases, the prevalence rates were left unchanged and applied to new population estimates for the year 2002. In addition, a number of estimates needed to be 'adjusted' (see below). Using all of these sources, estimates were established for 135 countries and then aggregated into the global estimate.

Detailed information is available from countries in North America, a large number of countries in Europe, a number of countries in South America, a few countries in Oceania (though including the two largest countries) and a limited number of countries in Asia and in Africa. For other countries, available qualitative information on the drug abuse situation only allows for some 'guess estimates'. In the case of complete data gaps for individual countries, it was assumed that drug abuse was likely to be close to the respective sub-regional average, unless other available indicators suggested that they were likely to be above or below such an average.

One key problem in currently available prevalence estimates from countries is still the level of accuracy, which varies strongly from country to country. While a number of estimates are based on sound epidemiological surveys, some are obviously the result of guesswork. In other cases, the estimates simply reflect the aggregate number of drug addicts found in drug registries which probably cover only a small fraction of the total drug abusing population in a country.

Even in cases where detailed information is available, there is often considerable divergence in definitions used - registry data (people in contact with the treatment system or the judicial system) versus survey data (usually extrapolation of results obtained through interviews of a selected sample); general population versus specific surveys of groups in terms of age (e.g. school surveys), special settings (such as hospitals or prisons), life-time, annual, or monthly prevalence, etc.

In order to reduce the error from simply aggregating such diverse estimates, an attempt was made to standardize - as a far as possible - the very heterogeneous data set. Thus, all available estimates were transformed into one single indicator – annual prevalence among the general population age 15 to 64 and above - using transformation ratios derived from analysis of the situation in neighbouring countries, and if such data were not available, on estimates from the USA, the most studied country worldwide with regard to drug abuse.

The basic assumption is that the level of drug use differs between countries, but that there are general patterns (e.g. lifetime time prevalence is higher than annual prevalence; young people consume more drugs than older people) which apply universally. It also assumed that the ratio between lifetime prevalence and annual prevalence among the general population or between lifetime prevalence among young people and annual prevalence among the general population, do not vary too much among countries with similar social, cultural and economic situation. Various calculations of long-term data from a number of countries seem to confirm these assumptions.

In order to minimize the potential error from the use of different methodological approaches, all available estimates for the same country - after transformation - were taken into consideration and - unless methodological considerations suggested a clear superiority of one method over another - the mean of the various estimates was calculated and used as UNODC's country estimate.

## b. Indicators used

The most widely used indicator at the global level is the annual prevalence rate: the number of people who have consumed an illicit drug at least once in the last twelve months prior to the survey. As "annual prevalence" is the most commonly used indicator to measure prevalence, it has been adopted by UNODC as the key indicator to measure the extent of drug abuse. It is also part of the Lisbon Consensus[a] (20-21 January 2000) on

---

[a] The basic indicators to monitor drug abuse, agreed by all participating organizations that formed part of the Lisbon Consensus in 2000, are:
- Drug consumption among the general population (estimates of prevalence and   incidence);
- Drug consumption among the youth population (estimates of prevalence and incidence);
- High-risk drug abuse (estimates of the number of injecting drug users and the proportion engaged in high-risk behaviour, estimates of the number of daily drug users);
- Utilization of services for drug problems (number of individuals seeking help for drug problems);
- Drug-related morbidity (prevalence of HIV, hepatitis B virus and hepatitis C virus among illicit drug consumers);
- Drug-related mortality (deaths directly attributable to drug consumption).

core epidemiological demand indicators (CN.7/2000/CRP.3). The use of "annual prevalence" is a compromise between "life-time prevalence" data (drug use at least once in a life-time) and data on current use. Lifetime prevalence data are, in general, easier to generate but are not very illustrative. (The fact that a 50-year-old person smoked marijuana at the age of 20 does not provide much insight into the current drug abuse problem). Data on current use (e.g. monthly prevalence) are of more value. However, they often require larger samples in order to obtain meaningful results, and are thus more costly to generate.

The "annual prevalence" rate is usually shown as a percentage of the youth and adult population. The definitions of the age groups vary, however, from country to country. Given a highly skewed distribution of drug abuse among the different age cohorts in most countries (youth and young adults tend to have substantially higher prevalence rates than older adults or retired persons), differences in the age groups can lead to substantially diverging results. Typical age groups used are: 12+; 16-59; 12-60; 15+; 18+; 18-60; 15-45; 15-75; and increasingly age 15-64. In the past UNODC reported the prevalence rate in percent of the population age 15+. The new Annual Reports Questionnaire adopted by Member States stipulates the age group 15-64 as the key population group for which drug abuse it to be measured. Thus, prevalence data in this report are now reported for the age group 15-64. In case the age groups reported by Member States did not differ significantly from the 15-64 age group, they were presented as reported and the age group was explicitly added. In cases where studies were based on significantly different age groups (e.g. age 15-45) and there were reasons to believe that drug use would be different among those 15-64, results were adjusted to the age group of 15-64. (See below).

The methods used for collecting data on illicit activities vary from country to country. This reduces comparability. Possibilities to reduce differences – ex post – arising due to different methodological approaches are limited. UNODC thus welcomes efforts at the regional level to arrive at more comparable data (as is currently the case in Europe under the auspices of EMCDDA and in the Americas under the auspices of CICAD).

In a number of cases, diverging results are also obtained for the same country, applying differing methodological approaches. In such cases, the sources were analysed in-depth and priority was given to the methodological approaches that are usually also used in other countries. For example, it is generally accepted that household surveys are reasonably good instruments to estimate cannabis, ATS or cocaine abuse among the general population. Thus household survey results were usually given priority over other sources of prevalence estimates, such as reported registry data from the police or from treatment providers.

However, when it comes to heroin abuse (or drug injecting), there seems to be a general agreement that annual prevalence data derived from national household surveys tend to grossly under-estimate such abuse because severe heroin addicts often do not live in households[b] They are often homeless, in hospitals or in prisons. Moreover, heroin abuse is highly stigmatized in many countries so that the willingness to openly report a heroin abuse problem is limited. However, a number of indirect methods have been developed over the last two decades to provide estimates for this group of problem drug users. They include various multiplier methods (e.g. treatment multipliers, police data multipliers, HIV/AIDS multipliers or mortality multipliers), capture-recapture methods, and multivariate indicators.

Treatment multiplier: If a survey among heroin addicts reveals, for instance, that one quarter of them was in treatment in the last year, the multiplication of the registered treatment population with a multiplier of four provides an estimate of the likely total number of problem heroin users in a country. Police data multiplier: Similarly, if a survey among heroin addicts reveals that one out of five addicts was arrested in the previous year, a multiplication of the persons arrested for heroin possession by the multiplier (five) provides another estimate for the number of heroin users. Establishing various multipliers and applying them to the registered drug using population, provides a range of likely estimates of the heroin abuse population in a country. Either the mid-point of the range, the median or the mean of these estimates can be subsequently used to arrive at a national estimate.

---

While in the analysis of the drug abuse situation and drug abuse trends all these indicators were considered, when it came to provide a global comparison a choice was made to rely on the one key indicator that is most available and provides an idea of the magnitude for the drug abuse situation: annual prevalence among the population aged 15 to 64.

[b] The problem of under-estimation is more widespread for heroin, but it is not excluded for other drugs, especially drugs related to problem drug use such as cocaine or methamphetamine.

Capture-recapture models are another method based on probability considerations, which can be undertaken without additional field research[c]. If in one register (e.g. arrest register) 5000 persons are found (for possession of heroin) and in a second register (e.g. treatment register) 2000 persons are found (for treatment of heroin abuse), and there are 400 persons who appear in both registries, it can be assumed that 20% (400/2000) of the drug addicts have been arrested, so that the total heroin addict population could be around 25,000 (5000/20%), five times larger than the total number of arrested heroin users.[d] Results can usually be improved if data from more than two registers are analysed (e.g. data from arrest register, treatment register, ambulance register, mortality register, substitution treatment register, HIV register etc). More sophisticated capture-recapture models exist, and are used by some advanced countries, in order to make calculations based on more than two registries. However in order to arrive at reasonable orders of magnitude of the heroin problem in a particular country it is probably sufficient to calculate the various combinations shown above and subsequently report the mid-point, the median or the mean of the resulting estimates.

Another interesting approach is the use of multivariate indicators. For this approach, a number of local/regional studies are conducted, using various multiplier and/or capture-recapture methods. Such local studies are usually far cheaper than comprehensive national studies. They serve as anchor points for the subsequent estimation procedures. The subsequent assumption is that drug abuse at the local level correlates with other data that are readily available. For instance, heroin arrest data, heroin treatment data, IDU related HIV data, etc. are likely to be higher in communities where heroin abuse is high and lower in communities where heroin abuse is low. In addition, heroin abuse may correlate with some readily available social indicators (higher levels in deprived areas than in affluent areas; higher levels in urban than in rural areas etc). Taking all of this additional information into account, results from the local studies are then extrapolated to the national level.

Whenever such indirect estimates for problem drug use were available, they were given priority over household survey results. Most of the estimates for problem drug use were obtained from European countries. Unless there was evidence that a significant proportion of problem drug use was related to the use of other drugs, it was assumed that the problem drug use concerned opiates. In the case of some of the Nordic countries, where amphetamine use is known to account for a significant proportion of overall problem drug use, the data of reported problem drug users were corrected by applying the proportion of opiate consumers in treatment in order to arrive at estimates for opiate abuse.

For other drugs, priority was given to annual prevalence data found by means of household surveys. A number of countries, however, did not report annual prevalence data, but lifetime or current use of drug consumption, or they provided annual prevalence data but for a different age group. In order to arrive at basically comparable results, it was thus necessary to extrapolate from reported current use or lifetime prevalence data to annual prevalence rates and/or to adjust results for differences in age groups.

### c. Extrapolation methods used

The methods used for these adjustments and extrapolations are best explained by providing a number of concrete examples:

*Adjustment for differences in the age groups:*

New Zealand, for instance, undertook a household survey in 2001, covering the population age 15-45. According to this survey, annual prevalence of ecstasy use was found to affect 3.4% of the population 15-45, equivalent to about 56,000 people. Given the strong association between ecstasy use and younger age groups it can be assumed that there is little ecstasy use in the 45+ age group. Thus, simply dividing the ecstasy using population established above by the age group 15-64 gives an estimated prevalence rate of 2.25%.

---

[c] Such methods were originally developed to estimate the size of animal population. If, for instance, 200 fish are caught ('capture'), marked, and released back into the lake, and then the next day 100 fish are caught, of which 10 were already marked ('re-captured'), probability considerations suggest that the number of fish captured the first day were a 10% sample of the total population. Thus the total population of the lake can be estimated at around 2000 fish.

[d] The advantage of this method is that no additional field research is necessary. There are, however, problems as the two 'sampling processes' for the registries in practice are not independent from each other so that some of the underlying assumptions of the model may be violated (e.g. the ratio could be higher as some of the people arrested are likely to be transferred to a treatment facility; thus the ratio does not correspond any longer to the true proportion of people arrested among the addicts population, and may lead to an under-estimation of the total heroin addict population).

The situation is slightly more complex when it comes to cocaine. The same approach for New Zealand would lower the annual cocaine prevalence rate from 0.6% of the population age 15-45 to 0.4% of the population age 15-64. In this case, however, it must be assumed that there are still some people above the age of 45 consuming cocaine. A rate of 0.4% is thus a minimum estimate. An alternative estimation approach, however, is indicated. Thus, the relationship between cocaine consumption among the group of those age 15-45 and those age 15-64 in other countries was investigated. The finding was that the prevalence rate of cocaine use among those age 15-64 tends to be around 75% of the prevalence rate of those age 15-45. Instead of 0.4%, the cocaine prevalence rate in New Zealand has thus been estimated to affect 0.45% of the population age 15-64.

Similar considerations were also used for the age-group adjustment of data from other countries. A number of countries reported prevalence rates for the age groups 15+ or 18+. In these cases it was generally assumed that there was no substance abuse above the age of 65. The number of drug users based on the population age 15+ (or age 18+) was thus simply shown as a proportion of the population age 15-64.

*Extrapolation of results from lifetime prevalence to annual prevalence*

Some countries have conducted surveys in recent years, but did not ask the question whether drug consumption took place over the last year. In such cases, results can be still extrapolated to arrive at annual prevalence estimates and reasonably good estimates can be expected. Taking data for life-time and annual prevalence of cocaine use in countries of Western Europe, for instance, it can be shown that there is a rather strong positive correlation between the two measures (correlation coefficient R = 0.91); i.e. the higher the life-time prevalence, the higher is, in general, annual prevalence and *vice versa*. Based on the resulting regression curve (x = 0.448y - 0.206 with x = annual prevalence and y = life-time prevalence) it can be estimated that a West European country with a life-time prevalence of 2% is likely to have an annual prevalence of around 0.7% (0.448*2 - 0.206 = 0.7; also see figure).

**Annual and life-time prevalence rates of cocaine use in Western Europe**

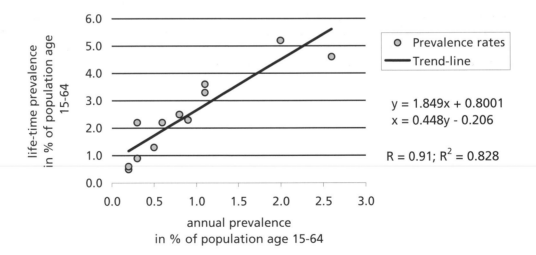

Sources: UNODC, Annual Reports Questionnaire Data / EMCDDA.

Almost the same result is obtained by calculating the ratio of the unweighted annual prevalence rates of the West European countries and the unweighted life-time prevalence rate (0.88/2.43 = 0.362) and multiplying this ratio with the life-time prevalence of the country concerned (0.362 * 2% = 0.7%).

A similar approach used was to calculate the overall ratio by averaging the annual/life-time ratios, calculated for each country[e]. Multiplying the resulting average ratio (0.347) with the lifetime prevalence of the country concerned provides the estimate for the annual prevalence (0.347 * 2% = 0.7%). This approach also enables the calculation of a confidence interval for the estimate. With a 95% probability the likely annual prevalence

---

[e] For each country the ratio between annual prevalence and lifetime prevalence is calculated. The results are than averaged: In our example: (0.4+0.33+0.14+0.33+0.38+0.27+0.32+0.39+0.33+0.31+0.38+0.57)/12 = 0.347.

estimate for the country concerned falls within a range of 0.6% to 0.8%[f]. Given this close relationship between life-time and annual prevalence (and an even stronger correlation between annual prevalence and monthly prevalence), extrapolations from life-time or current use data to annual prevalence data was usually given preference to other kinds of possible extrapolations.

However, data also show that good estimation results (showing only a small potential error) can only be expected from extrapolations done for a country located within the same region. If instead of using the West European average (0.35), the ratio found in the USA was used (0.17), the estimate for a country with a lifetime prevalence of cocaine use of 2% would decline to 0.3% (2% * 0.17). Such an estimate is likely to be correct for a country with a drug history similar to the United States, but it is probably not correct for a West European country where the dynamics of the drug markets showed a different pattern. The reason for the difference is that the USA has had a cocaine problem for more than two decades and is thus confronted with very high lifetime prevalence rates while it made considerable progress in reducing cocaine consumption as compared to the mid 1980s. All of this leads to a small proportion of annual prevalence to lifetime prevalence. In Western Europe, by contrast, the cocaine problem is largely a phenomenon of the last decade and still growing. The result, obviously, is a much larger ratio.

Against this background, data from countries in the same region were used, wherever possible, for extrapolation purposes. Thus, data from Eastern Europe were used to extrapolate results for countries which did not collect annual prevalence rates. All of the East European countries had very low drug abuse levels during the cold war, but they grew rapidly in the 1990s. UNODC received annual prevalence estimates from the Czech Republic, Slovakia, Poland and Estonia, and lifetime prevalence estimates from Hungary and Estonia. The following example shows how the extrapolations were done for cannabis. Based on available data, an average ratio of annual prevalence to lifetime prevalence of 0.38 was established for the region. Applying this ratio to the lifetime prevalence found in Hungary (5.7%) provided an estimate of 2.2% (range: 1.2%-3.2%). In the case of Slovenia, the lifetime prevalence had first to be adjusted from the population 18+ to the age group 15-64. The resulting lifetime prevalence (10%) was then multiplied with the ratio (10% * 0.38) to arrive at an estimate of annual prevalence of cannabis use in the country (3.8%; range: 2.1%-5.6%). The calculation of the confidence intervals was the same as discussed above. If the ratios found in the USA had been used instead, the estimate would have been 1.5% for Hungary and 2.7%for Slovenia. Such estimates are likely to underestimate annual prevalence of cannabis use in the two countries and were thus not used. Nonetheless, they are useful as they provide some idea of the likely magnitude of the lower limit for the country estimates.

---

[f] The calculation of the *confidence interval* can be done as follows:

1).Determination of alpha (usually 0.05);

2).Determination of the number of observations (12 in this case) and 3. Calculation of the standard deviation (0.099 in this example). This allows to calculate the standard error (standard deviation: (square root of n), i.e. (0.099/(square root of 12)) = 0.0286)). The z value for alpha equalling 0.05 is 1.96. Multiplying the standard error with the z-value (0.0286*1.96) would give the confidence interval (+/- 0.056). But, given the low number of observations (where n< 30), the use of t-statistics is indicated. In this case, the standard error must be multiplied with the appropriate t-value (2.201 in this example for 12 observations and alpha equalling 0.05 for two-sided t-statistics as can be found in t-value statistics). The result is a confidence interval of +/- 0.0629 (=0.0286 * 2.201). Several spreadsheet programs provide such statistics automatically. In Excel, for instance, the 'descriptive statistics' in tool menu under 'data analysis' calculates the confidence interval automatically and uses the t-statistics, wherever appropriate. Applying the +/-0.063 confidence interval to the average ratio calculated above to the mean ratio of 0.347 gives a range of ratios of 0.282 to 0.41. Using the two ratios one arrives at a minimum estimate of the annual prevalence rate of 0.56% (2% * 0.282) and a maximum estimate of the annual prevalence rate of 0.82% (2% * 0.41).

**Estimates of annual prevalence of cannabis use among the general population in new EU member countries**

| | Age group | Life-time prevalence | Annual prevalence | Range (95% confidence interval) | Ratio | Population |
|---|---|---|---|---|---|---|
| Czech Republic | 15-65 | 21.1 | 10.9 | | 0.52 | |
| Slovakia | 15-64 | 14.6 | 3.6 | | 0.25 | |
| Poland | 16+ | 6.5 | 2.4 | | 0.37 | |
| Estonia | 18-70 | 5.0 | 2.0 | | 0.40 | |
| Average ratio | | | | | 0.38 | |
| | | | | | | |
| | | | Estimates of annual prevalence | | | |
| Hungary | 18-65 | 5.7 | 2.2 (5.7*0.38) | 1.2 – 3.2 | | |
| | | | | | | |
| Slovenia | 18+ | 8.8 | | | | 1,579,624 |
| Adjusted | 15-64 | 10.0 | | | | 1,394,414 |
| Slovenia | 15-64 | 10.0 | 3.8 (10*0.38) | 2.1 – 5.6 | | |

*Extrapolation of results from IDU related HIV cases and other indicators*

In a number of cases, countries have supplied UNODC with information that is not directly comparable with information from other countries. In such cases reported data as well as all available estimates based on extrapolation from other sources have been used to arrive at an 'UNODC estimate'.

The problem can be demonstrated using the example of the Ukraine. Official data, submitted to UNODC, showed a prevalence rate of opiate abuse of 0.16%. Using such data would have implied that the country – in comparative terms – would have had one of the lowest levels of opiate abuse in Europe. Other available (mainly qualitative) information suggested, however, that this was not likely to be the case. Indeed, the data provided only covered the number of registered opiate users, and thus represented the lowest possible estimate of opiate abuse in the country. Based on the country's participation in the ESPAD school surveys, a regression analysis[g] with data from other countries in the region suggested that a prevalence rate of around 0.9% could be expected. Based on the number of newly registered HIV cases in this country in 2002, related to injecting drug use (and thus to injecting of opiates), a linear regression analysis with opiate abuse in other countries of the region suggested that a prevalence rate of 1.2% of the population age 15-64 could be possible. However, it must be taken into account that the correlation of opiate use and school survey results is not very strong and that the correlation between opiate abuse and IDU-related HIV is very weak, as shown by available data from both Eastern Europe and Western Europe. The actual spread of the HIV virus among IDUs and differences in drug policies (such as needle exchange programmes) seem to account for this. It is thus not possible to rely merely on school survey data or HIV data for extrapolation purposes. It is nonetheless likely that the actual prevalence rate falls within the range of 0.2% to 1.2%. Given the lack of any clear indication of the superiority of one method over another, the average of all three estimates was calculated and is used, for the moment, as the UNODC estimate for the country. The resulting estimate (0.8%) is about 4 times the number of registered opiate users in the country. This is not uncommon, as similar ratios between total use and registered use have also been found in a number of other countries.

---

[g] The linear regression was calculated by using the 'forecast' function in an Excel spreadsheet. The equation for FORECAST is a+bx, where:

$$a = \overline{Y} - b\overline{X}$$

and:

$$b = \frac{n\Sigma xy - (\Sigma x)(\Sigma y)}{n\Sigma x^2 - (\Sigma x)^2}$$

**Estimate for opiate abuse based on IDU-related HIV data and other indicators**

| | Opiate abuse in % of population age 15-64 | Source | ESPAD 1999 in % of 15-16 year olds | IDU related HIV cases per million inhabitants in 2002 based on Euro HIV |
|---|---|---|---|---|
| Estonia | 1.20 | EMCDDA (problem drug use) | 2 | 516 |
| Latvia | 1.72 | EMCDDA (problem drug use) | 4 | 164 |
| Poland | 0.24 | EMCDDA (problem drug use) | 2 | 5 |
| Russia | 2.10 | Russian authorities | 2 | 125 |
| | Estimates of opiate abuse (for population age 15-64) | Source / method | | |
| Ukraine | 0.16 | ARQ, registered users, | 1 | 94 |
| Ukraine | 0.9 | ESPAD, using a regression analysis | | |
| Ukraine | 1.2 | HIV, using a regression analysis | | |
| Ukraine | **0.8** | Average ('UNODC estimate') | | |

*Extrapolations based on school surveys*

Analysis of countries which have conducted both school surveys and national household surveys shows that there is, in general, a positive correlation between the two variables, particularly for cannabis, ATS and cocaine. The correlation, however, is weaker than that of lifetime and annual prevalence or current use and annual prevalence among the general population but stronger than the correlation between opiate use and IDU-related HIV cases.

The following example shows the extrapolation of school survey results for cocaine abuse in the Americas. Overall 10 countries in the region provided estimates for both annual prevalence from household surveys and estimates from student surveys. The correlation between results of annual prevalence in household surveys is clearly positive, though not very strong (R = 0.67), leading to rather large confidence intervals.

In Colombia, for instance, a youth survey, conducted in 2001, revealed a lifetime prevalence of cocaine abuse of 4.5 % among those age 10-24 and - within this group - a lifetime prevalence of 4.2% among secondary school students. Based on the average ratio between annual prevalence in household surveys and lifetime prevalence among secondary school students, an annual prevalence of 2.3% could be estimated. Using a linear regression analysis[h], based on the results of other countries in the Americas, an annual prevalence of cocaine use of 1.6% can be expected. For calculation of the global cocaine estimates, the estimates resulting from the linear regression were used. However, the range of the estimates is rather large. With 95% confidence the true results for Colombia should fall within a range of 0.8% to 2.4%.[i]

---

[h] The regression analysis was done using the 'Forecast' function in Excel.

[i] Calculations of the confidence interval based on a regression analysis are too detailed to provide here, but can be documented if necessary.

**Estimates of annual prevalence of cocaine use in the Americas based on school survey data**

| | Year | Age group | Annual prevalence based on household survey | | School survey | life-time | Source | Ratio |
|---|---|---|---|---|---|---|---|---|
| USA | 2002 | 15-64 | **3.1** | | 13 to 18 | 5.8 | UNODC | 0.53 |
| Argentina | 1999 | 16-64 | 1.9 | | 12 to 18 | 1.3 | UNODC | 1.47 |
| Chile | 2002 | 15-64 | 1.6 | | 13 to 18 | 5.1 | UNODC | 0.31 |
| Ontario (Canada) | 2000 | 15-64 | **1.4** | | 11 to 19 | 5.2 | Govt. | 0.27 |
| Bolivia | 2000 | 12+ | 1.1 | | 12 to 19 | 1.7 | UNODC | 0.66 |
| Ecuador | 1995 | 15-64 | 0.9 | | 13 to 18 | 2.4 | UNODC | 0.38 |
| Peru | 2002 | 12-64 | 0.7 | | 12 to 17 | 1.6 | UNODC | 0.43 |
| Brazil | 2001 | 15-64 | **0.5** | | 10 to 19 | 2.0 | UNODC | 0.25 |
| Costa Rica | 2000 | 12-70 | 0.4 | | 13 to 18 | 0.4 | UNODC | 1.00 |
| Uruguay | 2001 | 12-65 | 0.3 | | 13 to 17 | 2.4 | UNODC | 0.13 |
| Average | | | | | | | | 0.54 |
| **Estimates of annual prevalence School surveys data** | | | | | | | | |
| | Year | Age group | Based on regression analysis | Based on average ratio | Age group | Life-time | Source: | |
| Colombia | 2001 | 15-65 | *1.6* | 2.3 | 10 to 18 | 4.2 | UNODC | |
| Guatemala | 2001 | 15-65 | *1.0* | 1.2 | 12 to 19 | 2.2 | CICAD | |
| Nicaragua | 2001 | 15-65 | *1.0* | 1.1 | 12 to 19 | 2.1 | CICAD | |
| St. Lucia | 2002 | 15-65 | *1.0* | 1.1 | 12 to 19 | 2.1 | GAP | |
| Barbados | 2002 | 15-65 | *0.9* | 1.1 | 12 to 19 | 2.0 | UNODC | |
| Nicaragua | 2002 | 15-65 | *0.9* | 1.1 | 12 to 19 | 2.0 | UNODC | |
| Jamaica | 2001 | 15-65 | *0.9* | 1.0 | 12 to 16 | 1.9 | GAP | |
| Guatemala | 2002 | 15-65 | *0.9* | 1.0 | 12 to 19 | 1.8 | UNODC | |
| El Salvador | 2002 | 15-65 | *0.8* | 0.8 | 12 to 19 | 1.5 | UNODC | |
| Bahamas | 2001 | 15-65 | *0.8* | 0.8 | 12 to 19 | 1.5 | UNODC | |
| Honduras | 2002 | 15-65 | *0.8* | 0.8 | 12 to 19 | 1.5 | UNODC | |
| Bahamas | 2002 | 15-65 | *0.7* | 0.6 | 12 to 19 | 1.1 | GAP | |
| St. Vincent & Grenadines | 2002 | 15-65 | *0.7* | 0.6 | 12 to 19 | 1.1 | GAP | |
| Paraguay | 2001 | 15-65 | *0.6* | 0.5 | 12 to 19 | 1.0 | CICAD | |
| Suriname | 2002 | 15-65 | *0.5* | 0.4 | 12 to 19 | 0.7 | UNODC | |
| Belize | 1998 | 15-65 | *0.6* | 0.4 | 12 to 19 | 0.7 | UNODC | |

Note: **bold** indicates that data were adjusted for differences in age groups; *italic* indicates UNODC estimates, which were also applied for subsequent calculation purposes to estimate the global extent of cocaine abuse.

*Extrapolation to regional and global level*

The next step, after having filled, as far as possible, the data gaps, was to calculate the average prevalence for each sub-region. This is shown below in the example of opiate abuse in the Central and East European countries. For this purpose country specific prevalence rates were applied to the population age 15-64, as provided by the United Nations Population Division for the year 2002. The calculations showed an average prevalence rate of 1.2% for the sub-region. For the remaining countries in each sub-region the average prevalence rate was usually applied, unless some additional information suggested that the sub-regional average would be too high or too low for the countries concerned. For instance, all available information (mostly qualitative) suggests that opiate abuse is a problem in Serbia & Montenegro and in Bosnia Herzegovina and that it is higher there than in several other European countries; but there are no indications that opiate abuse would be substantially higher than in neighbouring countries. Using the sub-regional average would have meant estimating abuse in these two countries as higher than in neighbouring countries. However, there are also indications that due to the war-related isolation and lack of financial means of large sections of the population, prevalence of opiate abuse (though growing) could be well lower than in the neighbouring countries. Against this background, an alternative way of estimating the prevalence rate was used: the prevalence rate was estimated by taking the average prevalence rate of other countries in the immediate neighbourhood (Bulgaria, Croatia and Slovenia); in addition, the rates were adjusted downwards. A similar method was also applied to other regions whenever existing quantitative or qualitative information indicated good reasons not to apply the sub-regional average. In general, all of these 'adjustments' affected the overall sub-regional estimate only slightly. If the sub-regional average had been applied for the two countries, the overall estimate for Central and Eastern Europe would have amounted to 2.8 million instead of 2.7 million people.

Following the detailed calculation of all of the sub-regional estimates as outlined above, the individual sub-regional estimates ('number of drug users') were aggregated to form a regional estimate, and the regional estimates were then aggregated to arrive at the global estimates.

**Estimate of opiate abuse use in the countries of Central and Eastern Europe**

| | Population age 15-64 in million | Estimated number of opiate abusers in thousand | Prevalence rate in % |
|---|---|---|---|
| Belarus | 6.83 | 6.2 | 0.09 |
| Albania | 2.05 | 10.3 | 0.50 |
| Bulgaria | 5.48 | 27.4 | 0.50 |
| Croatia | 2.97 | 20.8 | 0.70 |
| Czech Republic | 7.21 | 37.5 | 0.52 |
| Estonia | 0.90 | 10.9 | 1.20 |
| Hungary | 6.82 | 28.5 | 0.42 |
| Latvia | 1.58 | 27.1 | 1.72 |
| Lithuania | 2.30 | 12.7 | 0.55 |
| TFYR Macedonia | 1.38 | 5.5 | 0.40 |
| Republic of Moldova | 2.95 | 2.2 | 0.07 |
| Poland | 26.86 | 64.5 | 0.24 |
| Romania | 15.44 | 46.3 | 0.30 |
| Russian Federation | 101.36 | 2,128.6 | 2.10 |
| Slovakia | 3.78 | 11.4 | 0.30 |
| Slovenia | 1.40 | 7.7 | 0.55 |
| Ukraine | 33.68 | 269.4 | 0.80 |
| | | | |
| **Subtotal I** | 223.0 | 2,716.9 | 1.22 |
| *Countries for which no estimates exist:* | | | |
| Bosnia Herzegovina | 2.96 | | |
| Serbia & Montenegro | 7.07 | | |
| **Subtotal II** | 10.0 | 46.9 | 0.44* |
| | | | |
| **Central and Eastern Europe** | 233.0 | 2,763.8 | 1.19 |
| * Average rate of Croatia, Bulgaria, Slovenia; adjusted (75%). | | | |

### d. Concluding remarks

This process of estimation and the methods used for extrapolating the estimates are not free from risk. All of the extrapolations can potentially lead to substantial over-estimation or an under-estimation. While this is definitely true for individual countries, it can be expected that over-estimates and under-estimates partly offset each other at the global level. Moreover, in order to reduce the risk of any systematic bias, estimations were based, as far as possible, on the data from a series of neighbouring countries in the region. It is, however, recognized that the currently provided estimations can change considerably once actual survey data becomes available. This makes it difficult, if not impossible, to derive trends in drug consumption from these consumption estimates. Indeed, as previous 'guesstimates' were replaced with 'estimates' derived from household surveys (or from student surveys), some of the totals (notably for cannabis and, to a lesser extent for amphetamines and cocaine) declined as compared to UNODC's last estimate presented in the *Global Illicit Drug Trends 2003* publication, though other indicators suggested that drug abuse, notably for cannabis and, to a lesser extent for amphetamines, continued to increase. UNODC's methodology to arrive at global estimates by extrapolating results from a sample of countries (for which data is available) to a sub-region, also meant that such methodological changes had a significant impact on the final estimates.

The global estimates presented in this report must therefore be treated with a high degree of caution. They provide likely orders of magnitude, as opposed to precise statistics on the prevalence and evolution of global drug abuse. Further changes can be still expected as countries provide more robust estimates based on rigorous scientific methods. Nonetheless, in the absence of global studies on drug abuse, the estimations and the estimation procedures provided in this report guarantee the best picture that is currently obtainable.

### Trends in drug abuse

#### a. Overview

Ideally, global trends in drug abuse should be monitored by comparing estimates of drug abuse in one year with those found in a subsequent year. In practice, however, this approach does not work – at least not for the time being - as a number of changes in the global estimates are due to methodological improvements and not due to underlying changes in drug abuse. Moreover, general population surveys are very expensive to conduct and only a few countries have an ongoing monitoring system based on these instruments.

What many countries do collect, however, is routine data such as number of persons arrested for drug abuse, urine testing of arrestees, number of persons undergoing drug treatment, or they monitor drug abuse based on school surveys. In addition, drug experts dealing on a regular basis with drug issues – even without having precise data at hand – often have a good feeling about whether abuse of certain drugs is increasing, stabilizing or declining in their constituency.

This knowledge base is regularly tapped by UNODC. Member States usually pass the Annual Reports Questionnaire to drug experts in the country (often in the ministry of health) who provide UNODC with their perception, on a five-point scale, of whether there has been a 'large increase', ' some increase', ' no great change', some decrease' or a 'large decrease' in the abuse of the various drugs over the past year. The perceptions may be influenced by a number of factors and partial information, including police reports on seizures and arrests, reports from drug treatment centres, reports from social workers, press reports, personal impressions, etc. Any of these influencing factors could contain a reporting bias which has the potential to skew the data towards a misleading increase or decrease. Prioritization of the drug issue is another factor which influences reporting. It can probably be assumed that the countries which reply regularly to the ARQ are those which take the drug problem more seriously. In a number of cases this is a consequence of rising levels of drug abuse and thus increased public awareness of the problem. All of this suggests that the sample of countries replying to the ARQs may be slightly biased towards countries faced with a deteriorating drug problem. Results must thus be treated with some caution and should not be over-interpreted.

Despite these caveats, trend data provide interesting insights into the growth patterns of individual drugs as well as into regional and global growth patterns. They represent the most comprehensive data set of expert opinion available on the development of the drug abuse problem at the global level, provided in a consistent manner over more than a decade.

### Number of countries & territories reporting drug abuse trends to UNODC

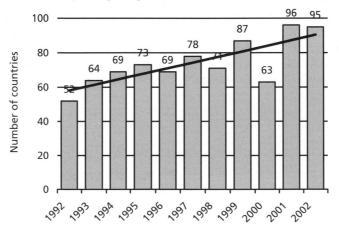

Source: UNODC, Annual Reports Questionnaire Data

Replies to the Annual Report Questionnaire (ARQ) on trends in drug abuse are more comprehensive than on estimating the numbers of drug abusers. About 90% of all countries and territories which returned Part II of the ARQ for the year 2002, in compliance with their obligations under the international drug control treaties (n = 106), provided information on drug abuse trends (n = 95). (The ARQ was distributed to 194 countries and territories; the overall response rate of the questionnaire for the year 2002 was thus 55%, in line with annual response rates varying between 40 and 60% over the last five years)[j]. The analysis on drug abuse trends for the year 2002 was based on the replies of 95 countries and territories, about the same number as a year earlier, up from 52 countries and territories a decade earlier. Overall 151 countries and territories reported drug abuse trends to UNODC over the last decade. The distribution of countries reporting in 2002 was roughly the same as a year earlier and provides a reasonably good coverage across all regions.

**Regional distribution of reports received on drug abuse trends for the years 2001 and 2002**

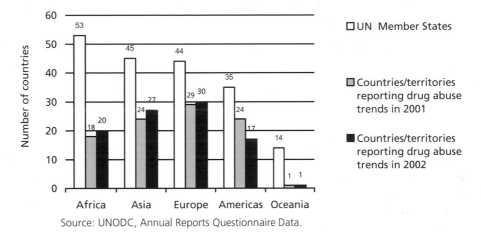

Source: UNODC, Annual Reports Questionnaire Data.

### b. Aggregating trend data

Various methods have been developed and have been used in this report for the trend aggregation.

The 'traditional' method consisted of simply counting the number of countries reporting increasing, stable and declining levels of drug abuse. This is in line with business cycle trend analysis where enterprises are asked on a routine basis about their perceptions of whether production is expected to increase, remain stable, or fall over the new few months. Changes in the 'net results', i.e. number of respondents reporting increases less those reporting declines, have proven to be a good and useful indicator for showing overall changes in the trend. For the purpose of calculating this indicator, the categories 'strong increase' and 'some increase' were combined into a new category 'increase'. Similarly, the categories 'strong decline' and 'some decline' were combined into a new category 'decline'.

The advantage of using this method for describing drug trends at the global level is that a large number of actors, independent of each other, express their views on the trend in their countries. Though some experts may well report wrong trend data, it is unlikely that mistakes all go in the same direction. Thus, trend data for 2002, for instance, showed that there were more countries reporting increases in drug abuse than those reporting declines. However, the rate of increase declined in 2002 as compared to 2001, including for opiates, cocaine-type substances and ATS. The only exceptions to this 'downward trend' in 'the rate of increase' were cannabis and benzodiazepines.

---

[j] The response rate was 54 per cent (103 replies submitted) for the reporting year 2001, 41 per cent (80 replies submitted) for 2000, 49 per cent (94 replies submitted) for 1999 and 58 per cent (112 replies submitted) for 1998.

**Drug abuse trends in 2001 and 2002: Number of countries reporting increases less number of countries reporting declines**

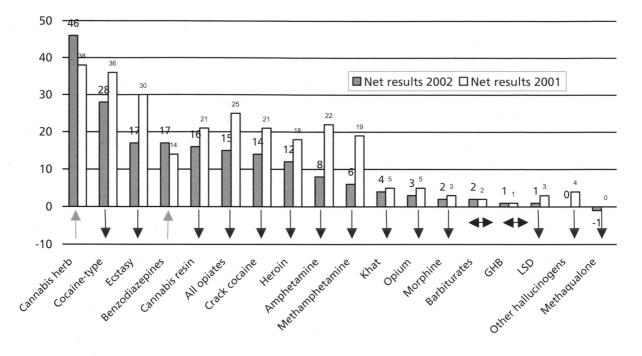

A variation of this method was used as well. Instead of showing the number of countries reporting increases less those reporting declines, an alternative approach was to calculate the number of countries reporting increases less those reporting stable or declining levels of abuse. The reasons for this was that authorities in a number of countries are apparently reluctant to report declining levels of abuse and, in order to be 'on the safe side', prefer to report a 'stable' trend instead. In the case of heroin, for instance, this approach shows a strong increase of heroin abuse at the global level until the late 1990s and a stabilization/decline until 2002. Detailed data from a number of countries with functioning monitoring systems in place have shown a similar trend pattern.

**Heroin abuse trend: Number of countries reporting increases less number of countries reporting stable/declining levels of abuse**

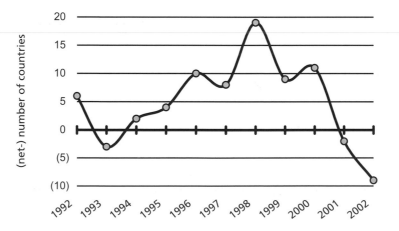

*c. Weighted Analysis on Drug Abuse Trends ("Drug Abuse Trend Index")*

A new analytical tool, called the *Weighted Analysis on Drug Abuse Trends* (WADAT), referred to in this report as *Drug Abuse Trend Index,* was designed by UNODC to allow for a better estimation of regional trends in drug abuse, taking into consideration the different population size of the countries within the regions.

For this purpose, each degree of trend estimation was given a numerical value ranging from −2 to +2 (−2 representing a 'large decrease'; −1, 'some decrease'; 0, 'no great change'; +1, 'some increase'; and +2, 'a large increase'). Estimates for each drug type were then multiplied by the proportion of the population of the country in relation to the total population of the region. The national estimates were added to represent annual regional trend estimate for each drug type and a cumulative trend for each region was calculated.

Ideally, the weighting should be based on the size of the drug abusing population under consideration. However, estimates are not available for all countries. This would have meant that trends reported for a number of countries would have to be ignored. Thus the size of the population was chosen as a more objective measure to calculate the relative importance of a trend reported by a country. Another question to solve was whether to use the population of the countries reporting or the total population of a region. It was decided to use the latter for this index. This allows, to some extent, better comparisons with other regions. There are, for instance, only a few countries in Africa reporting trends in ecstasy consumption. These few countries report, however, an increase. If the index were construed to take only the countries reporting into account, the result would have been a massive increase of ecstasy use across Africa, which has not been the case in Africa. Using the total population of Africa to calculate the countries' proportions, the Drug Abuse Trend Index shows only some minor increases of ecstasy use in Africa, which is more realistic.

The following table shows in some detail how the results in Africa were obtained for cannabis, the most widely consumed illegal substance in the region. If one takes South Africa for example, one can see that the country accounts for 6.2% of Africa's total population (age 15-64). South Africa reported a stable trend of cannabis use in 2001 and an increase in 2002; while cannabis herb was reported to have increased (1), cannabis resin was reported to have remained stable (0) in 2002. In such cases, the average was calculated (0.5). Applying South Africa's proportion in Africa's total population, the weighted trend for South Africa showed a value of 0.031. In the same way, the weighted trend data for all of other African countries were calculated. The sum amounted to +0.41, suggesting that there was a significant net increase in cannabis consumption in Africa in 2002. (If all countries in Africa had reported an increase, the rise in the index would have amounted to 1). The cumulative trend index, shown in this report, started with the year 1991 = 1. In 2001 it amounted to 3.39. For 2002 the new figure (0.41) was added, resulting in a total figure of 3.80 for Africa as a whole. Compared to other regions (and compared to other drugs) the increase of cannabis use in Africa was thus rather strong. The calculations show clearly that Africa – based on expert opinion - experienced an ongoing increase of cannabis use over the last decade.

**Cannabis consumption trend in Africa: based on national experts' perceptions**

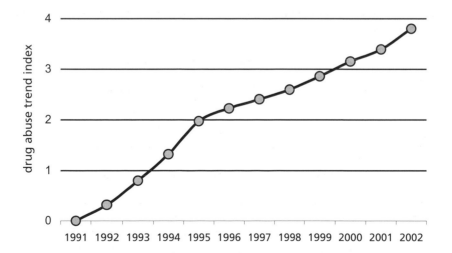

425

## Cannabis consumption trend Index for Africa

| | Population age 15-64 in thousand | Proportion in total African population | Trends reported 2001 | Trends reported 2002 | | Weighted trends 2001 | Weighted trends 2002 |
|---|---|---|---|---|---|---|---|
| Benin | 3393.7 | 0.75% | 1.0 | | | 0.0075 | |
| Burkina Faso | 6115.6 | 1.35% | 1.5 | | | 0.0202 | |
| Burundi | 3318.6 | 0.73% | 0.0 | | | 0.0000 | |
| Cameroon | 8478.5 | 1.87% | 1.0 | 1.0 | | 0.0187 | 0.0187 |
| Comoros | 410.9 | 0.09% | -1.0 | | | -0.0009 | |
| Côte d'Ivoire | 9005.4 | 1.99% | | 2.0 | | | 0.0397 |
| Egypt | 42470.9 | 9.37% | | | | | |
| Ethiopia | 35457.9 | 7.82% | 1.0 | 1.0 | | 0.0782 | 0.0782 |
| Gambia | 771.7 | 0.17% | 1.5 | | | 0.0026 | |
| Ghana | 11576.5 | 2.55% | 1.0 | 1.0 | | 0.0255 | 0.0255 |
| Kenya | 17359.1 | 3.83% | | 0.5 | | | 0.0191 |
| Madagascar | 8858.9 | 1.95% | 1.0 | 0.0 | | 0.0195 | 0.0000 |
| Malawi | 5974.3 | 1.32% | | 2.0 | | | 0.0264 |
| Mauritius | 828.5 | 0.18% | 0.5 | 0.5 | | 0.0009 | 0.0009 |
| Morocco | 19195.2 | 4.23% | | 2.0 | | | 0.0847 |
| Namibia | 1040.9 | 0.23% | 1.0 | 1.0 | | 0.0023 | 0.0023 |
| Rwanda | 4322.8 | 0.95% | | 0.0 | | | 0.0000 |
| Sao Tome and Principe | 85.6 | 0.02% | -1.0 | | | -0.0002 | |
| Seychelles | 41.8 | 0.01% | 1.0 | 1.0 | | 0.0001 | 0.0001 |
| Somalia | 4709.4 | 1.04% | | 2.0 | | | 0.0208 |
| South Africa | 28140.0 | 6.21% | 0 | 0.5 | | 0.0000 | 0.0310 |
| Togo | 2542.1 | 0.56% | 2 | 1 | | 0.0112 | 0.0056 |
| Tunisia | 6383.5 | 1.41% | 0 | -1 | | 0.0000 | -0.0141 |
| Uganda | 11841.6 | 2.61% | 1.5 | | | 0.0392 | |
| United Republic of Tanzania | 18983.3 | 4.19% | | 1 | | | 0.0419 |
| Zambia | 5400.8 | 1.19% | | 1 | | | 0.0119 |
| Zimbabwe | 6858.1 | 1.51% | 1 | 1 | | 0.0151 | 0.0151 |
| | | | | | | | |
| Total population in Africa | 453281.452 | 100.0% | | | | | |
| **Sum** | | | | | | **0.2400** | **0.4080** |
| | | | | | | | |
| | | | | | | | |
| Index | | | | | | | |
| Years | 1991 | | 1998 | 1999 | 2000 | 2001 | 2002 |
| Yearly results | | | 0.19 | 0.26 | 0.30 | 0.24 | 0.41 |
| **Cumulative trend index** | **1.0** | .. | **2.60** | **2.86** | **3.15** | **3.39** | **3.80** |

One advantage of such an analysis is that it takes the size of countries into account. In other words, the index gives more weight to the results reported from larger countries which – in absolute terms – are likely to have a higher addict population than smaller countries. This is in line with the observation that the overall impact of a rise of drug abuse in a larger country tends to have a far greater impact on global drug abuse than the rise in a smaller country. Another advantage is that the index takes into account the degree of change in drug abuse levels, thus making better use of all available information.

The Drug Abuse Trend Index is likely to show good results whenever levels of drug abuse are similar which is, in general, the case at the regional level. (Cocaine abuse is high in countries in the Americas; opiate abuse is high in countries in Asia, ecstasy use is high in countries of Western Europe etc.). It can, however, create problems if the index is used at the global level, without any further adjustments, in cases the distribution of drug abuse is very skewed. Calculating a Drug Abuse Trend Index for cocaine at the global level for instance, shows a distorted pattern as India, the world's second largest country in terms of population, recently started to report increases in cocaine use. Cocaine abuse, though rising in India, is still at very low levels in the country. But the weight of this country in terms of population meant that the index would show a sharp rise - which was not in line with actual cocaine consumption trends at the global level. Against this background, it was decided not to use the index, as it is, for the global analysis of trends for the cocaine market or the opiate market. In contrast, for cannabis or ATS which are found in all continents, the Drug Abuse Trend Index data were calculated and presented in this report.

There are also other limitations that need to be taken into account when interpreting the results. The information provided remains – in most cases – an expert opinion and is not necessarily based on hard scientific evidence. A mistake made by one expert in a country with a large population can seriously distort the global trend estimates. Moreover, it cannot be assumed that the difference between various degrees of drug abuse trends (for example, between "some decrease" and "large decrease") are interpreted in the same way in different countries (a large increase in a country with low prevalence may not have the same impact on regional trends as some increase in a country with high prevalence) or even in the same country in different reporting years, as the ARQs are often filled in by different persons. Reporting trends in the abuse of a drug type, such as cannabis, may be biased by differing trends in the abuse of substances in the same drug category (for example, the trend in the use of cannabis herb may be increasing while the trend in the use of cannabis resin is decreasing). For the purposes of this report each individual drug category was taken and an unweighted average was calculated. Of course, this is not without problems. In the example of South Africa, as shown above, it is known that cannabis resin does not play a role while cannabis herb is of major importance. The use of a simple average thus under-estimates the actual increase of cannabis in this country. While for some countries, the detailed profile of substance abuse is well known, this would not be the case for others. Thus the general rule of averaging all drugs within one category was applied, though it is not without problems.

It should be also be noted that the Drug Abuse Trend Index is limited in that it only provides general directions with regard to the main drug types reported by Member States, inevitably leading to very broad generalization. Thus, there is, in addition, a need for more drug-specific trend analysis to support its conclusions.

Irrespective of these caveats, the overall results derived from the Drug Abuse Trend Index were found to be basically in line with other indicators at the regional level – wherever comparisons could be made - thus suggesting that the Index is a valuable tool for the analysis of drug abuse trends at the regional level, and, for cannabis and ATS, at the global level as well.